# INTEGRATED HEALTH CARE DELIVERY
## Theory, Practice, Evaluation, and Prognosis

Edited by

**Montague Brown, MBA, DrPH, JD**
Editor, *Health Care Management Review*
and
Chairman
Strategic Management Services, Inc.
Tucson, Arizona

## HEALTH CARE MANAGEMENT REVIEW

AN ASPEN PUBLICATION®
Aspen Publishers, Inc.
Gaithersburg, Maryland
1996

Library of Congress Cataloging-in-Publication Data

Brown, Montague.
Integrated health care delivery : theory, practice, evaluation,
and prognosis / Montague Brown.
p.  cm.—(Health care management review series)
Includes bibliographical references and index.
ISBN 0-8342-0814-8
1. Health services administration.  2. Vertical integration.
I. Title.  II. Series.
RA413.B755  1996
362.1'068—dc20
95-52251
CIP

Editorial Services: David A. Uffelman

Library of Congress Catalog Card Number: 95-52251
ISBN: 0-8342-0814-8
Series: 0-8342-0337-5

*Printed in the United States of America*

1  2  3  4  5

# Contents

## II State of Knowledge: Success and Failure of Integration

## III Making Alliances Work

Organized vertically integrated health systems are in a key position to play a major role in present health care reform efforts. To demonstrate a competitive advantage in the new health care environment, however, integration efforts must be successful. Based on a national study of nine organized delivery systems, this article develops measures of three types of integration that occur in vertically integrated health systems—functional, physician-system, and clinical. These measures can be used as a "scorecard" to assess progress toward achieving integration objectives.

Because of the wide diversity among health care organizations, interorganizational relationships (IORs) among them are difficult to manage. This article describes three case studies that, taken together, suggest that IOR performance is related to IOR development processes. Specifically, IOR performance is related to the way managers process information to manage uncertainty and ambiguity.

American health care, both nationally and locally, has entered a time of uncertainty, yet with the certainty of change. In this article, the authors take a fresh look at patient/community needs and propose a new level of integration of administration/management, clinical services, education, and public health in the health care organization of the future.

Health systems will profit most under capitation if their vertical integration strategy provides operational stability, a strong primary care physician base, efficient delivery of medical services, and geographic access to physicians. Staff- and equity-based systems best meet these characteristics for success because they have one governance structure and a defined mission statement. Moreover, physician bonds are strong because these systems maximize physicians' income potential and control the revenue stream.

The erosion of the traditional market is forcing hospitals and physicians to reevaluate their historical relationships. One method for addressing the potential conflicts created by current pressures is the formation of physician–hospital networks. These entities are formed and function on the basis of mutual interests and responsiveness to change.

# Preface

This volume of the *Health Care Management Review (HCMR)* book series contains articles dealing with the transformation of the health care system. Managed care, vertical integration, networking, collaboration, and sharing are examined from a variety of system perspectives.

Voluntary and public hospitals continue to respond to the competitive movements of investor-owned hospitals. Managed care has been a driving force in mergers, vertical integration, and network building since at least the late 1970s and is a pervasive influence today. In the 1970s one could easily wonder if hospitals would ever get together into more rational regional configurations so that economies of scale for major clinical programs could be achieved. Today, institutions are quickly merging, selling, joint venturing, and networking to try to get the opportunity for such savings. However, it remains a judgment call as to whether or not having gotten together into tight economic alliances the new institutions will actually lead to more rational allocation of programs across the system. There is more than a mere possibility that once integration and consolidation occur, the new institutions will use their power to keep prices up and to maintain the status quo. When buyers have no choices, sellers set the prices.

Some authors make a strong case for merging hospitals and insurers across regions. There are millions in administrative expenses tied up in the armies of accountants and data people who do constant battle between managed care and providers. Creating an integrated firm would free these resources for price cuts or alternative investments to improve the system. Others point out that there is a rapidly developing market for efficient care, a notion widely considered by others but not often so sharply focused as it is here. At the same time, other authors note that many of the integrative efforts to data have not achieved significant results for the public and that other methods should be tried in the future.

Entrepreneurs, capitalists, farsighted health care executives, and a variety of other interested parties are transforming the face of health care. While some focus on building integrated systems including physician integration, others point to the evidence to date and argue that the right direction is not full integration but contractual networks. Noted in many of these articles but not yet fully analyzed is the movement to organize physicians into larger economic entities utilizing equity market capital. By the end of the decade, this story will overshadow the hospital and insurance changes now dominating the news.

Many authors show how to build and evaluate systems. A number of authors highlight the many differences small rural hospitals face and what they can do to benefit from these larger trends impacting urban markets.

Several articles deal with issues of governance in systems, a subject of growing importance during a time of major change in ownership and control of institutions. With a shift from charity to full bore economic entities, those whose investments and livelihoods are tied up in the integrated enterprise naturally want a larger role in governance and management. In fact since governance and steering and managing the enterprise requires critical knowledge of production control systems, it is impossible to imagine a medically integrated enterprise without substantial physician input. The authors of the articles on this subject have widely varying views about what is important and what should go into redesigning the governance system.

As integration occurs issues of economies to be achieved begin to fade as do issues of whether or not the power derived from more control of market variables will be used for consumer benefit or for private benefit. Antitrust vigilance becomes more important than ever as hospitals acquire physician practices, build their own managed care capability, and merge with other hospitals to function as a market-dominant entity with little or minor competition.

This volume contains a critical assessment of the vertical integration movement and points the way toward questions that need to be more fully addressed. As the industry has shifted from a fairly open and sharing environment to one of intense and growing competition, professionals are sharing their ideas for publication less and less. Some of the issues raised here cut across professional interest in particular organizational roles and will no doubt raise concerns among the readers. That is the purpose of this series and *HCMR*, to hit the issues and let the readers ultimately determine the usefulness of the material presented. Some of the articles originally were published in a point–counterpoint format in order to bring the issues into better focus for the reader. Hopefully the disparate views presented here will serve a similar purpose.

—*Montague Brown*
*Editor*

PART I

# TRENDS AND CHANGES

# Mergers, networking, and vertical integration: Managed care and investor-owned hospitals

Montague Brown

*This article links the forces of managed care and investor-owned firms as major factors driving the industry toward consolidation into vertically integrated, merged firms, often financed with investor capital. This relentless pressure to build regional systems of health services has transformed the industry from a charitable, community orientation to one of business, market shares, and profits.*

**Hospitals, physicians, insurers**, and managed care firms are networking, merging, and forming horizontally and vertically integrated organizations to finance and deliver health care. Organizations, investors, health professionals, governments, and others are positioning themselves to gain or preserve market share, income, revenue, and power in a radically agitated marketplace. Power and control of the health care enterprise is shifting, threatening to topple traditional institutions even as traditional institutions try to reinvent themselves into what the leaders of those institutions think will be the most logical inheritor of power in the future. (Power is used here to mean control, authority, and ability to make things happen in the way those in control of the organization want these things to happen. Physicians, hospitals, managed care firms, traditional insurers, and those controlling such organizations are pursuing strategies they each hope will position them to have substantial power. That not all can occupy the same space simultaneously accounts for much of the attempts to establish networks and other loose forms of affiliation.)

Where is the field going and what does all of this shifting herald? Are we seeing the elaboration of the next generation of organizations, which are going to solve the riddle of affordable, accessible, quality health services for all Americans? Or are we in the middle of a transition that holds yet other surprises just up the road? What ideas are driving the field toward integration and consolidation?

A central thesis of this article is that ideas have power. People who lead institutions are doing things that they think will position themselves for success in a changed world of health care. What they think are the major changes necessary to make health care more affordable is what will drive them to reposition their organizations. Much of the change of the past 30 years has been driven in large part by expectations of how managed care will evolve and how competing provider institutions will compete. Ideas help to explain why people pursue networks and alliance building. For many volunteer hospitals the ideas of networking, alliance building, mergers, and vertical integration are further conditioned by expectations of what investor-owned institutions can and will do with their access to equity market capital. (Over the years the au-

*Montague Brown*, M.B.A., Dr. P.H., J.D., *is Editor of* Health Care Management Review, *and Chairman, Strategic Management Services, Inc., Tucson, Arizona.*

*Health Care Manage Rev*, 1996, 21(1), 29–37
© 1996 Aspen Publishers, Inc.

thor has noted that investor-owned institutions have done many things well but they come only recently to regional integration of their units. But now that they have moved in this direction, they are moving aggressively, with Columbia/HCA going for tertiary referral hospitals to complement its networks in all regions in which it aspires to have a major presence.)

Managed care and investor-owned institutions with presumed unlimited access to new equity capital have been powerful motivators for voluntary and many governmental hospitals to find competitive strategies for coping. Those strategies have ranged from loose affiliation to total consolidation under single ownership. The most recent strategy has involved the merging of physicians with the hospital. Ultimate ideas include putting managed care, hospitals, and physicians under one corporate control. Naturally, each competitor envisions its group leading this new integrated entity. This struggle for power and control accounts for many of the failures to create successful alliances, networks, and mergers.

In summary, this review of trends, prognostications, and recent writings on the subject is approached from the perspective of how the ideas of managed care and competition with investor-owned operation of hospitals and other elements of health care delivery have impacted the trends and events noted so well in the many reviews of the subject presented in *Health Care Management Review*. (A collection of earlier papers on this subject is contained in *Strategy and Structures in Health Care Management*, a best-of-HCMR publication, Aspen Publishers, Inc., 1992, Montague Brown, Editor.)

## BACKGROUND

As Medicare and Medicaid passed in the mid-1960s, the health care industry geared up for heady growth. For many, this heralded the promise of health care as a right, with the government picking up the tab for the elderly and poor. New York and California each exceeded the Johnson administration's estimates for the nation. The new plans with their mandate to continue fee-for-service payment to physicians and cost plus for hospitals looked like a steady increase in money and a practical federal guarantee for whatever it would take to make an investment in health services pay off.

As this promise for cost plus reimbursement for hospitals and universal coverage came into play, entrepreneurial physicians and others were able to con-

vince equity market players that the industry would be a gold mine for investor capital. Medicare standards required many hospitals to be rebuilt, making it attractive for individual physician-owned institutions to join this new use of equity market financed modern corporations, the investor-owned hospital chain. The South, Southeast and West, where for-profit hospitals already existed in fair numbers, soon became the regions with greatest chain growth. Many small hospitals built with federal funds sold out to the new chains, which then scrapped obsolete plants and built modern hospitals in small towns and second or third hospitals in many larger cities. Many large, well-established not-for-profit hospitals began to find these firms coming to town, taking over marginal hospitals, replacing them with first class facilities, and trying to recruit some of their physicians.

By the early 1970s the need for cost containment was becoming screamingly evident, putting pressure on providers to find ways to contain cost. Shared services, especially purchasing programs, became popular mechanisms to deflect criticism from rising cost. Health planning attempted to curtail duplication of costly technologies. With new capital flooding into the market and competition growing, solutions were being sought but nothing seemed to be working well. It was during this period that the idea of using health maintenance organizations (HMOs) to contain cost evolved. Modeled basically on an older idea of prepaid group practice, adoption was slow but many agreed that it would take something like this with strong economic incentives for physicians to keep cost down and for patients to accept the discipline of such regimes. By the 1980s both managed care and investor-owned hospitals appeared, with their built-in scale advantages for national purchasing and the use of standardized approaches to building and operating hospitals. (By talking here about their purported advantages of scale for purchasing, the author does not believe that the chains actually benefited from trying to use this power until nearer the mid-1980s. Many authors have noted that these chains benefited greatly from their ability, like all hospitals, to price their product to produce the profits they required for their business. This is changing now but provided a solid basis for growth throughout the 1970s and 1980s.)

In the 1970s, the nation tried price controls, voluntary efforts, and other slogans to contain cost. (Any starting point for consideration of a subject as broad as networking and alliances is somewhat arbitrary. Hospital associations grew after the first world war and got another big boost during the days of Hill–Burton facilities financing. Many of these associations built additional shared services. The rationale for cutting the time reviewed around early 1970 is that the big national alliances getting so much attention today were built to give one group of hospitals a competitive advantage vis a vis their neighboring hospitals. Earlier and most current hospital association efforts included all hospitals. These were called shared service programs. All could benefit. Today's alliances, for the most part, consider competitive advantage as a major deciding factor in admitting members and designing programs.) Shared purchasing grew from hospital association efforts to construct national alliances built outside the political structure of hospital associations. A number of these national alliances merged; indeed the merger of these giant purchasing organizations continues today. (In this merger of buying organizations, American Healthcare System's 500 million annual purchases from Johnson and Johnson make them J&J's biggest customer. Look out little niche companies, when elephants dance they can be dangerous.[1]) A comprehensive assessment of alliances is presented by Zuckerman, Kaluzny, and Ricketts.[2]

Hospital mergers and consolidations held out the promise that if the number of owners were reduced, then hospitals could plan more rationally and reduce the duplication of high cost technologies in individual markets. This was the promise. Shortell has studied many of the systems that built upon mergers and concluded that many of the promises of such systems have not been realized.[3] The potential exists but has not been realized.

Many reasons for these unrealized aspirations have been asserted and speculated upon. Getting a larger market share in adjacent markets locks in sufficient scale to justify the more complex procedures that require access to large population bases and it provides primary care sites to attract managed care. If the market does not have strong competitors, which leads to price and cost reductions, it would seem that many systems have gained major advantages from mergers and system building without having to go through the harder job of rationing programs and services among several owned hospitals.

Before the nation's antitrust laws were applied, hospitals planned "voluntarily" and each hospital sorted out what it would do and what others would do. Much of this behavior was encouraged by health planning agencies, based on a long history of voluntary planning. During this era, collaboration, sharing, and other adjectives aptly described much hospital behavior vis a vis neighboring hospitals. Everyone got the programs they wanted so voluntary collaboration worked fairly well. Even when not everyone got everything they wanted, there was usually an explicit or implicit quid pro quo for the "losing" organizations.

Dividing markets through agreement became a verboten topic once the antitrust laws were applied directly to medicine.[4] Since agreements to fix price or divide markets[5] became illegal, it became necessary to look at whether or not more total integration might be necessary to achieve collective, regional action. (The author would not, of course, argue that everyone was satisfied with voluntary dividing up of markets. Those who got the heart programs from such past divisions have done very well, much to the chagrin of those who got behavioral units.) While multihospital systems grew during the 1970s[6], after the antitrust moves dampened the ability of hospitals to voluntarily assign markets and roles, local and regional mergers grew.

---

*The growth of managed care during the 1980s and its further acceleration in the 1990s became driving forces behind physician alliances, hospital mergers, and national and regional hospital alliances.*

---

The growth of managed care during the 1980s and its further acceleration in the 1990s became driving forces behind physician alliances, hospital mergers, and national and regional hospital alliances. The idea driving providers was the thought that managed care firms would eventually narrow their provider list to those most efficient in their delivery of a comprehensive range of services. That the reality might not have caught up with the theory did little to stop attempts by providers to form their own networks so that they could collectively bargain with insurers. From the beginning of the formation of the large voluntary hospital alliances, competitive advantage in local competing networks was a prime factor in building these alliances. (Having studied one of the early multihospital systems in the late 1960s and early 1970s for my doctoral work in public health, I personally met with and had discussions regarding such matters with many of the chief executive officers [CEOs] running such systems. Later I served as consultant and conceptualizer for the CEOs who started many of the national alliances. So much of this history reflects personal involvement as well as following and contributing to the literature of the period.) Even in the 1970s there was an expectation of managed care networks that would be exclusive to selected groups of providers, and providers have been positioning for this eventuality. Ideas have power. Ideas can drive the field even when marketplace realities have not caught up.

Of course, managed care firms have the theoretical possibility of signing up just the best providers and leaving the rest off their preferred list. While the idea of managed care was popular and anticipated, many physicians and hospitals dreaded its introduction to the market. Many of the concepts of networking, mergers, alliances, and the like, often touted for their likelihood of bringing economic and other advantages, often obscured the underlying fact that such linkages also made it more difficult for managed care to emerge or if it did emerge, such networks had some inherent advantages because of their geographic dispersion of members and the comprehensives of their services.

Managed care firms only recently have gained sufficient expertise and market penetration to begin to put the kind of pressure on providers for more efficient care that was anticipated by the pioneers in networks, alliances, and regional hospital systems. Those who prepared early and moved expeditiously are in a position today to benefit from their early efforts to build regional systems. Many single hospitals that ignored these trends often have found themselves closed out or severely handicapped in their marketplace.

## ALLIANCES

Earlier efforts to develop joint purchasing programs, training, and industrial engineering were carried out by trade associations and catered to all hospitals, not some subset. When asked for public evidence of what was being done to contain the rising cost of health care, these programs were trotted out and displayed for all to see. The industry was responding to cost through collective programs to contain the cost of purchases and improve the efficiency of individual operations. (There are many other activities of the major alliances, but their central dollar impact and the source of funding for such alliances comes in large part from imposed group purchasing activities.) By

the late 1970s hospitals were organizing national cooperative enterprises like the Voluntary Hospitals of America, SunHealth, Premier Alliance, and American Healthcare Systems to carry out collective enterprises, most notably purchasing. The major national alliances strategies were begun after HMOs were identified more clearly as a likely winning strategic concept and the investor-owned hospital groups had gained substantial stature in the marketplace.

Were these purchasing efforts successful? All claim great advantages from such buying cooperatives. If one assumes that such programs impact 10 percent or so of hospital budgets and that group buying gets a 10 percent or more better price, this would moderate hospital costs only 1 percent. While not yielding much on a yearly basis, compounding such savings would show a sizable amount of money ultimately saved.

However, it is difficult to assess the overall impact of such buying practices. As the hospitals developed oligopolistic buying behavior, the companies able to respond grew increasingly few and more powerful. Since there is no discernible lowering of the growth in health care cost during the period, it is not easy to point to any discernible consumer benefit coming from this new level of aggregation in the industry. Rebates and price discounts make good public relations copy, however, and thus one hears little or no complaints about the efficacy of these programs. At a minimum, hospitals probably gained some clout vis a vis powerful national suppliers and moderated their pricing policies. It would seem that these programs represent a modest success in dealing with a modest share of the hospital budget.

Suppliers may have lost a bit of margin in their dealings early on but probably recouped those losses later as smaller competitors found it difficult to compete with the integrated buyer alliances doing business with the integrated supplier firm. Also, with more comprehensive, committed volume contracts, economic savings can be achieved and are probably shared between buyer and seller. Savings of this sort make good economic sense. Will these advantages offset the squeeze on the small supplier, the entrepreneur with a better idea but no access to the large, overarching contracts? The studies of this aspect of alliances are yet to be told.

The trading of profits and business volumes among firms within the industry has little positive meaning ultimately for the consumer. Providers do not necessarily pass on purchasing savings to consumers. Some of the savings are retained in the alliance organizations while much are used for ancillary needs of the members and the alliance. For the buyer of health services it makes little difference who profits from the vast purchasing power unless the benefits are passed on to consumers. Of course with savings there is a potential for consumer benefit, but one would expect that benefit to be conferred only after buyers for health care services make price demands on competing provider groups. With substantial aggregation occurring on the provider side and still little buyer pressure for deep price concessions, there is a possibility that by the time buyers get well organized to purchase, sellers may already have reached a critical mass, making it possible for them to exert pressure to keep prices up.

## MANAGED CARE

Being positioned for survival in a managed care marketplace was and is the crown jewel of purpose of the major national alliances. (This is not to argue that other purposes were and are not now important. Once institutions are developed, it is a well-known phenomenon that they take on a life of their own and that the "profits" from most such entities, especially those that are "not for profit," are the benefits that participants derive through participation. Although many of the not-for-profits and cooperatives have developed spin-off operations into for-profit formats, allowing executives and members to benefit personally from their success, for the most part the alliances remain a not-for-profit type of enterprise. Executives and compensation experts have long since found many ways to extend equity types of rewards to these executives so they too can be expected to operate with many of the same incentives in place that permeate big business in the nation.) Managed care makes it theoretically possible for the most efficient, highest quality places to win the competition for dedicated blocks of patients and thus become the survivors. Remember in the mid-1970s when these national alliances were being built, managed care as we know it today did not exist. In fact, managed care, as it was envisioned in those days, has yet to emerge in most markets. Every professional in the field knew that the nation had too many hospitals and too many beds. And, in a fragmented marketplace, managed care firms could induce hospitals and physicians to give discounts to get business. But if hospitals were merged or "held together" in regional networks, few buyers would be able to resist buying from such networks. Even today, tight, exclusive networks with full capitation are still a small part of managed care. Yet most of the national and regional alliances represented steps along the path toward that end when they were formed in the late 1970s.

Managed care enterprises promise to offer greater opportunity to achieve consumer benefit but they require great investment and strong discipline to make them work. They also require incentives that strike at the heart of medical decision making: the medical staff. To make such an enterprise work requires a highly disciplined medical staff and one of two other things: either a very efficient system that could offer lower prices because of its lower utilization, and/or a regional monopoly or superior concentration and range of services. In short, success requires a highly disciplined medical staff (or panel of physicians) who are committed to actually reducing the use of resources (including their own activities) to get cost down so that prices can be lowered for customers!

A number of the alliances have tried national managed care ventures with insurers. Most dropped the national efforts after years trying to get members prepared for something for which the market was not yet ready. Readiness was and is not merely one of provider nor insurer preference. It is as much or more individual consumer preference and the ability of corporations to channel their employees into a narrow set of choices. Managed care is moving slowly in this direction. Everyone has a steep learning curve ahead. Even the traditional Kaiser-Permanente staff model has problems competing for populations that want a bit more choice. Still, provider opinion and the models providers continue to build and elaborate upon anticipate this kind of change.

Alliances have worked hard to aid individual and regional collections of members to build managed care alliances. Preferred provider organizations (PPOs) abound, many regional alliances seek contracts, and a number have chosen to fund and operate regional HMOs that accept risk. Being positioned to offer a geographically dispersed, comprehensive range of service networks is probably one of the greatest positioning benefits of the major national alliances. Unlike trade association efforts at purchasing, the national alliances have pushed to segregate out hospitals into competitive clusters to prepare for a managed care world of the future, a future still on the way.

The record around the country in building managed care networks is mixed. For those regional networks built on ownership, it is relatively easy for a cluster of hospitals to deal with managed care firms. For those networks built on contracts and jointly owned organizations, it is necessary to bargain on discounts off of charges that are set independently by the separate institutions. Since most managed care organizations seek large networks and discounts off charges, this early form of network works fairly well. But when the choices need to be made about what smaller subset of physicians and hospitals get the capitation contract, such networks will likely fail from a provider perspective although insurers will find it to their benefit. (In theory one expects that the more tightly managed care under capitation will involve procedures that require using fewer physicians who themselves work more and more exclusively for patients in this type of plan. No one expects to get both the tight management and low resource use from physicians and other providers when they are moving from patients where they make more money for more work to patients where they make money by using fewer resources. Those involved in this kind of split environment report difficulty in their practice.) When such networks have a hard time getting committed volume purchasing contracts because hospitals cannot exert sufficient control over personnel and physicians to buy one brand versus others, it challenges credibility to believe that these voluntary alliances can make the hard choices of dropping some physicians and hospitals from the existing networks. Even in networks owned by one hospital system, it is nearly impossible to limit networks to select groups of physicians. (At a larger system level, legislation to allow any willing provider to participate reflects this underlying battle to be included in any networks. As this article is written, this epic battle to limit networks to allow for competition among tightly managed networks is being waged.) Much of the difficulty in building owned or contractual networks stems from the natural and pervasive desire by professionals to keep their practices intact, avoid change until it becomes essential, and modify the change if possible to accommodate their preferred form of practice. These major fault lines underlie most networks—keeping them in a fragile state—while managed care firms are relatively free to exploit this weakness in such alliances.

Pointing out this difficulty in overcoming the large odds against making tight, limited networks is no criticism toward hospitals per se since many managed care firms have failed, others have merged to survive, and many have had many owners before strong profitability emerged. Employers have difficulty getting

*Much of the difficulty in building owned or contractual networks stems from the natural and pervasive desire by professionals to keep their practices intact, avoid change until it becomes essential, and modify the change if possible to accommodate their preferred form of practice.*

employees to accept limited networks. Building managed care organizations, recruiting providers, selling to buyers, and making it work are real challenges since providers resist the constraints of managed care just as do many consumers.

Hospital organizations operating successful regional managed care organizations often find that the success of the operation actually outgrows the needs of the hospital owner. In some cases this inappropriateness has stemmed from the fact that other managed care organizations would resent and react negatively to contracting with hospitals who were in fact their competitors in providing managed care products and services. Second, hospitals often have partnered with physicians who during the process have sought opportunities to maximize the return on their investment, an expectation that requires selling out at some point. This factor makes it likely that a competitive bid would be used to make a sale, often to competing organizations that could gain market share advantages in the regional market involved. (A colleague related a story that highlights some of the difficulties with the buying and selling of physician practices and managed care firms. A local physician group built a successful HMO. The group reportedly saw themselves as offering a community benefit. They made many contributions to the community. Then they sold the firm and rapidly found that by getting a generous price for the firm the new owner was mostly interested in keeping cost down and prices up.) Third, other successful ventures simply have outrun their usefulness and appropriateness for a local hospital. These organizations simply needed new capital and a much broader scope to best use their talents and organizational infrastructure. Fourth, still other successful organizations have been merged into other managed care operations in the region, leading to dilution and broadening of ownership and operation of the managed care operation. So, even with success, the size, scope, and nature of the managed care operation often does not fit with the owners' capability of using, supporting, or growing it.

Walston, et al. (see "Owned vertical integration and health care," pages 72–81) raise serious questions as to whether hospitals use ownership as the better mode of relating; instead, they recommend contracting. The requirements for making an integrated network ultimately will be manifested when the incentives of the various parties are aligned and owning does not overcome the ability of persons and organizations that are part of the owned network from resisting or keeping the organization from functioning smoothly.

Overall, single hospitals and regional hospital systems with the greatest success with managed care have been those organizations that had a strong share in their market, making it possible for them to compete with other managed care organizations without at the same time losing their business. This ability normally requires substantial market share and a reputation among consumers that make it necessary for all or most managed care organizations to contract with them in order for them to attract major business clients for their products.

National chain organizations had a different kind of experience with managed care. Hospital Corporation of America (HCA) was engaged in a major joint venture with a major insurance company. That venture failed to become a major force in the field. HCA hospitals were unable to give the joint venture any major advantage in markets where the hospitals themselves were less than market leaders. Humana (then a hospital company) started its own managed care firm but encountered major resistance to their insurance products from physicians and hospital administrators who saw their profitability drained away to promote the managed care product. These kinds of difficulties ultimately led Humana to split off the insurance firm from the hospital company; later, they sold the hospital company to another firm, Columbia, which still later merged further with HCA and Health Trust. By 1995 none of the major hospital chains had a significant interest in managed care firms. Their current strategy seems to be to gain sufficient market share in each regional market and sufficient cost effectiveness to become the provider of choice for managed care firms. It is important to note that announced strategies, while true, can also mask fall-back strategies, which are also true. Provider groups that cannot be ignored by managed care firms because of substantial market presence (size, geographic dispersion,

comprehensiveness) can, when the market is ready, sell direct to employers.

## FUTURE TRENDS

Given the forces driving the current waves of integration, what seems likely in the next 5 or so years?

### Physicians

The question of how physicians will fit into the overall scenarios envisioned by hospitals and many managed care firms remains open. Physicians see the trends and expectations as well as anyone else. Managed care and investor-owned health services are somewhat less frightening to physicians than executives of not-for-profit hospitals. But they too see the consolidation trend and are finding ways to join the trend and to resist it.

Several trends seem likely to continue. Physicians will continue to form networks for managed care. Many of these will be in conjunction with hospitals. However, these forms of affiliation are relatively weak, with each party continuing to protect individual interests. More group practices will form. Groups represent a more firm commitment among physicians as to how they will govern and how revenue will be split. Groups also have a hefty advantage over alliances and networks. They are one economic unit, sharing risk, and can deal with the whole world as a unit without the antitrust strictures that are applied to independent economic units acting collectively.

As physicians seek capital to expand and managerial expertise they will increasingly turn to firms like Caremark, InPhyNet, PhyCor, and Coastal Physician Group, which bring capital and management expertise to the table.[7] The appeal of these groups is that neither *at this point* represents hospitals and managed care. Physicians retain more input into decisions and operate as free agents and/or corporate partners when dealing with hospitals and managed care firms.

### Insurers

Some of the most dramatic changes in health care have come in the insurance side of the business. Major insurers have been in and out of managed care, with many venerable insurers ultimately getting out of managed care and leaving it more to the firms dealing with it exclusively. The Blue Cross and Blue Shield firms have made the most impressive turnaround, converting their business from service and indemnity contracts to managed care. The Blues have been going through a consolidation phase and now appear fully poised to become equity market firms, which frees them to merge with many others as well as to tap Wall Street for more equity. The Blues are experimenting with all kinds of integrative moves.

---

*The Blue Cross and Blue Shield firms have made the most impressive turnaround, converting their business from service and indemnity contracts to managed care.*

---

Insurers must build a niche for themselves that fends off or negates the effort by providers to gain sufficient market clout to deal directly with buyers. One way to do that will be for the insurers to merge with or buy out the providers. (For a more detailed examination of some of the issues involved here, see, "Getting To Go in Managed Care" by Wolford, Brown, and McCool, pages 12–24.) A key issue when speculating about the concept of full merger is the question of whether or not it is driven by a vision of market protection or a brave new age of efficient care. As with any of these massively integrated firms, the cost of internal transactions can go down, but human frailty and the tendency to build fiefdoms when the market allows it can frustrate such hopes and actually lead to higher cost. Furthermore, there is the question of competition and monopoly behavior. With fewer entities in the market, there will be a great danger that provider–insurer entities will use their power to benefit the sellers and rip off consumers. Getting providers and insurers to be more efficient and price competitive has been a tough job for buyers even when the field was relatively fragmented. Will it get better with consolidation or worse? (For a more complete discussion of some of these issues see "Hospital Markets and Competition: Implications for Antitrust Policy" by Nguyen and Derrick, pages 212–221.) For a candid description of how price fixing and market allocation works, see "My Life as a Corporate Mole for the FBI," in *Fortune* (4 September 1995):52–62. In this view, sellers agree on market share and price and then move to bid work in order to achieve these goals. Customers are described as enemies who must be made to pay to keep up prices and profits to sellers.) As providers seek legislative approval for market consolidations

that go beyond current antitrust guidelines, providers are seeking approval to be the communities' guardians of supply and price. If they had done a better job of reforming in the past, then giving them such powers would be less risky than it is when we know from recent history that the industry resists mightily any attempts to change its ways. Most likely this type of move will be resisted by managed care firms and insurers . . . unless they are part of the deal in some assured manner.

### Academic medical centers

Academic medical centers have been the last to join the parade. Now we see many investor-owned chains looking for economic ties to such centers of excellence. If one seeks to play the regional provider of choice card and go for a major portion of any market, then these institutions need to be part of the package. The Mayo Clinic recognized this necessity early on and moved to develop national and regional satellites. Nationally, teaching centers are reaching out in ways unheard of 5 years ago. Some are joining Columbia/HCA in markets where the academic medical center completes a regional, full-service package of services. In the future we can expect more of these alliances. And, we can expect the not-for-profit hospital systems to seek to link up as a competitive response to a real threat of investor-owned market dominance.

### Community hospitals

Community hospitals will continue to merge with regional players including selling out to investor-owned chains. No hospital will believe that it can remain outside and independent when the dominant belief is that buyers will choose networks. And, network hospitals will choose to send business to owned hospitals over affiliated hospitals. A very sophisticated buyer group might select such hospitals if they were the most efficient but providers have 10 years of system building under their belt and buyers are just beginning to consider major buying coalitions. Sellers of service are bundling product while buyers, including managed care firms, will seek to unbundle. That tug of war will continue for the near term.

### Regional multihospital health systems

Regional multihospital health systems are the best positioned organizations to become the providers of choice for managed care or direct contracting. They will continue their push to bring more and more physicians, especially in primary care, into the fold through a variety of devices. The most extensive elaboration of this model is playing out in Minneapolis and environs where three or four systems are integrated with physicians and managed care. One might also examine this area for issues raised regarding concentration and pricing. Employers in that region seem to be concerned with how to break through this control by provider–insurer conglomerate to get even greater efficiencies than currently are available.

In Missouri the regional hospital system to watch is BJC, an entity formed from Barnes, Jewish, Christian, Baptist and a variety of other hospitals in the region.

Unfortunately many of these systems have managed to get ownership consolidated but have themselves become captive to the status quo and have not achieved anywhere near the economies anticipated by the theorists. Many have troubles incorporating different cultures. And, no doubt, some merged to reduce consumer choice, which might have forced their independent units to compete and change.

In the near term we can anticipate that more single hospitals will merge with systems, systems will merge, and a growing number will forge strong bonds—even merge or sell—to insurers. However, we can also expect insurers to continue their use of contracts to build virtual networks and avoid asset acquisition until the price for such operations comes down. And the price will come down as hospitals are forced to compete. The mergers being sought by hospitals in smaller markets do promise to lower some hospital costs for technology and overhead but they simultaneously promise to eliminate price competition.

## OVERALL PROGNOSIS

The health care field's anticipation of managed care and fear of investor-owned hospital chains continue to drive the consolidation effort. This will continue into the indefinite future. Physicians will join the trend. Before physicians become fully integrated they will go through some intermediary forms including group practice, becoming units of national firms, employees of managed care firms, and employees of hospitals. By going through the intermediary forms of ownership it will be possible for physicians to raise the value of their business. Why? A well-oiled group with a good balance of primary and specialty is worth more than a herd of cats!

As components of the field consolidate, future consolidations will be even more complex. Like the Disney–NBC consolidation, we will see some even bigger and more complex deals ahead in health care. There is a real possibility that a handful of national firms will dominate health care but the route to that end is two steps forward, three back, and forward again. The dance goes on.

## REFERENCES

1. "AmHS, Premier Alliances to Merge." *Modern Healthcare* 2–3 (7 August 1995): 2–3.
2. Zuckerman, H., Kaluzny, A.D., and Ricketts, T.C. "Alliances in Health Care: What We Know, What We Think We Know, and What We Should Know." *Health Care Management Review* 20, no. 1 (1995): 54–64.
3. Shortell, S.M. "The Evolution of Hospital Systems: Unfulfilled Promises and Self-Fulfilling Prophesies." *Medical Care Review* 45, no. 2 (1988): 177–214.
4. Brown, M., and Nichelos, P. "Court Shoots Down Antitrust Immunity." *Modern Healthcare* 12 (August 1982):164–68.
5. Brown, M., and Nichelos, P. " Analysis Probes Risk of Antitrust Suit." *Modern Healthcare* (December 1982): 104–09.
6. Brown, M., Warner, M., and Steinberg, J. "Trends in Multihospital Systems: A Multiyear Comparison." *Health Care Management Review* 5, no. 4 (1980).
7. "Doc Practice Management Set to Explode." *Modern Healthcare* 25 (14 August 1995): 26–31.

# Getting to go in managed care

G. Rodney Wolford,
Montague Brown,
and
Barbara P. McCool

*Managed care has clearly pointed the way to bringing health care costs under control. But the providers themselves, right now, must either take on the responsibility of more directly managing care, bringing utilization down, and sharing in the rewards, or they could find themselves asked to sacrifice while intermediaries prosper.*

**The American** health care system operates on a commodity and commerce basis in a marketplace that does not respond to classic market principles of supply, demand, price, or quality. The system is bloated with unaffordable insurance packages and services. It is also heavily burdened with good intentions, overindulgence, and self-interest, all serving to increase societal cost for care that is considered a right by many and directly paid for by few. While new technologies flood the market, less incremental improvements occur in our overall health status. The fix, because of lack of national direction, could be long and painful, but there will be a sigh of relief when it is over.

The panacea emerging as the most touted for our salvation is managed competition, which, in essence, is a comprehensive use of managed care organizations in the marketplace. Managed care in its existing and likely emulated formats means many things including the micromanaging of consumer choice, consumer selection of providers, providers' use of procedures, diagnosis, and treatment. Coupled with this new set of micromanagement tools are myriad financial incentives presumed to alter the behavior of physicians, hospitals, and other providers.

Will managed care in the form that has emerged be capable of delivering a more efficient, competitively managed health care system? Have we lost a sense of

*G. Rodney Wolford*, C.P.A., M.B.A., is President/CEO of Alliant Health System in Louisville, Kentucky.

*Montague Brown*, M.B.A., Dr.P.H., J.D., consults on health care strategy and structure and is Editor of Health Care Management Review.

*Barbara P. McCool*, R.N., M.H.A., Ph.D., consults on health care strategy and structure and is Associated Editor of Health Care Management Review.

This article was initially written for a speech made before the Health Systems Section of the American Hospital Association. Many of the thoughts expressed here were developed and tested during several years of work by the authors in attempting to put together more integrated systems of services that go beyond the traditional separation of managed care from provider networks. This work continues and has included attempts to merge and joint venture with insurers, development of networks of providers who own and operate full-fledged managed care operations, and other related strategies designed to reduce the layering between consumers and providers and to build organizations more attuned to long-term community interest.

In the process of development, this article has been reviewed and critiqued by dozens of reviewers. It is also the product of many years of building vertically integrated systems, both by the authors and their many colleagues too numerous to name, who refuse to accept the system as given and strive to wrest change from it.

Of course the faults remain with the authors. We readily admit to wanting far more from the field than we can expect any time soon. Still we remain optimistic and intend to work with any and all who aspire to do better for the community than we have accomplished so far.

*Health Care Manage Rev*, 1993, 18(1), 7–19
© 1993 Aspen Publishers, Inc.

community sharing in the risk of health care with the growth of our current system of managed care? Can insurers and providers come together to form organizations focused on community health? Are there structural barriers that virtually prohibit us from making those positive changes? This article explores these and other issues.

## HISTORICAL PERSPECTIVE

Our traditional financing methods gave us nearly unlimited license to overspend. Third party financing and marketing of health insurance and financing created third parties to collect and dispense monies to purchase health care as needed. For many years this worked well; growing risk pools making it possible to meet the big needs of the few from the small payments of the many. But contained within the payment system were the seeds of its destruction. Costs plus for hospitals, fee-for-service for physicians, and other incentives to use resources provided the impetus to spend, but not to be efficient. Neither providers nor insurers had strong incentives to meet health care needs within a budget.

Medicare adopted this spendthrift approach to financing against the advice of some, but with the approval of many who feared fixed budgets or prices. Faced with unlimited demand, the prospect of unlimited payment for the likely sickest of our population, the race was on. The commercialization of the field began in earnest.

Little time elapsed before growing health care cost burdens caused employers and governments to demand change. The first major round of attempts to control came shortly after Medicare and Medicaid passed. The nation turned to centralized planning to allocate capital resources. This strategy failed in the face of demand increases fueled by a flawed payment system that kept usual and customary treatment patterns that rewarded health professionals handsomely.

While the national health planning strategies were failing, the concept of managed care began to develop through the creation of health maintenance organizations (HMOs), preferred provider organizations (PPOs), and through health insurers who began to manage more closely their payments for health services. The early round of HMOs, financed largely with federal grants, were later converted to public market–financed commercial entities, pushing to expand and produce profits. In markets where indemnity payment had heavily bloated the system, these new managed care insurance entities could produce profits with even the most minor

changes in benefit structures and with price discounts from providers who could easily pass on the cost of discounts to others less able to get discounts.

The emergence of HMOs came at a time when health insurance companies were moving away from community-rated insurance to corporate or group-rated insurance. The sense of community sharing of health care risk was being lost as corporations and other groups chose to reduce their health care cost by extracting themselves from the community pool. The focused marketing of HMOs toward young, healthy groups exacerbated the flight from the concept of community health. The results are massive cost shifting among buyers of health services and massive displacement of potential buyers of health insurance who are either deemed an unhealthy risk or insufficient in group size to be offered affordable health care rates. Selective underwriting has left millions of Americans uninsured.

Providers of care responded well to a growing but false sense of price competition. Huge discounts were offered to the HMOs, insurers, or employers who had large numbers of purchasers. As a result, the displacement of the uninsured or underinsured became even more severe. Providers had slipped unwittingly into the mode of discriminatory pricing. Those individuals who were good insurance risks or employed by the wealthiest corporations now paid less for the same health care service than those who were uninsured, underinsured, or employed by smaller, less wealthy corporations.

Without major structural changes, will this evolution of insurance markets, preferential risks, and discriminatory pricing continue? With these structural and behavioral flaws, will managed competition with more extensive use of managed care work, or are we just laying down another facade of bandages?

For those who count on making the market system work more effectively some cautions are in order. If we could go to a system where the user paid everything out of pocket, then providers could offer anything anyone wanted to buy. But when average major encounters with the medical care system can run around $20,000, who can pay?

---

*Reform proposals in the Clinton era will most likely call for national and state boards, managed care networks, more protocols, and greater discipline on the part of customers.*

---

If we use collective buying and government payments, can we leave the ultimate choices to patients? When the payment comes from the collective pocket, the product must meet community or societal standards of efficient, good and needed value criterion. Unbridled use of health services paid for by collective means cannot stand.

Reform proposals likely to pass muster in the Clinton era will most likely call for national and state boards, managed care networks, more protocols, and greater discipline on the part of customers who must, early in seeking health care, make broad choices that link them into a more narrow range of choices, if and when they might actually need medical care.

Health care providers must be restructured and managed in a manner that recognizes provider accountability and reward efficiency, quality, and value. If this restructuring is to happen, the distance between buyers and providers must be shortened to make the providers more direct sellers with nothing between them and the buyer to alter incentives for efficiency or the certainty that success or failure is felt directly by providers. An extra layering of micromanagement of care systems adds cost and helps providers avoid the necessity for taking on the responsibility for their own management systems.

Current reform proposals fail to recognize this fundamental issue. If we go with the emerging managed care companies and place other layers of control systems on top, we can look forward to the world's most expensive and micromanaged health care system with an increasing share of cost going into the battles between the experts and accountants.

## PROVIDER ACCOUNTABILITY

It is time for real reform that puts resources and accountability directly with provider organizations. Make them responsible and accountable through their own management skills and recognition of value and quality. The worst possible approach to ultimately mastering cost-effective care would entail reliance on outside control, second guessing, and micromanaging of essentially professional tasks and duties by outsiders.

On the other hand, none of us is naive enough to believe that providers would have realized the need for or been willing to make the necessary changes without outsider intervention. Purchasers and insurers have done us a favor, but now we need to move to ensure that the job is done properly. Having recognized the need, do we need to continue to support an army of micromanagers in order to get the job done?

Everyone must change. Our communities have suffered from this dysfunctional system and the powerful efforts put forth to ensure the survival of providers in their current organizational forms, along with their management and boards of directors. Today we need leadership for radical reform, but the radical reform we need originates at home, not in Washington, in big towns, small towns, medical practices, hospitals, and especially in regional systems of care.

In recent months, proposals have been stacking up in Congress to reform the health care system. With Clinton's election, interest groups are in high gear producing these proposals. Moreover, major newspapers are calling for quick action. There are so many patchwork proposals that government is paralyzed and likely little or nothing will be done except for minor adjustments to a flawed delivery model.

It will take more than "simple tweaks" to the system to modify the culture and the behaviors of the current players. To achieve the level of services and value our society needs and to remain competitive in a worldwide economy, more dramatic action is needed.

Signals from Clinton suggest new, more powerful, "managed competition" models that will take the best of competition and of regulation. These models, however, keep the separation between insurer and network micromanagement and provider systems of care. Maintaining this separation will further postpone necessary reform.

The challenge for physicians, hospitals, and insurers—the power brokers of the health care system—is to radically rethink our organizations and construct delivery models. Can there be any doubt that this is true?

Currently our health care system reels from chronic schizophrenia. When we ask, "Does everyone have the right to basic health care?" we respond by saying "Yes," but our system fails to deliver to millions of Americans who are simply priced out of the market. When asked if the health care dollar is a limited scarce resource, most in society say "Yes," but we practice "No" by making few "value judgments" as to the right level of health services.

Far too many businesses have opted out of the community solution to health care financing. Larger businesses, including most of America's hospitals, now self-insure and thus take themselves out of the community health risk pool, which only adds to the difficulty of smaller firms and individuals who need insurance and access to health care.

Competition is not working either. When we encourage a good dose of adversarial competition as a solution, we find that basic self-balancing economic fundamentals are not present, and the costs continue to spiral upward. Competition merely makes it easier for larger businesses and governments to shift further cost to the smaller businesses and individuals with no power to obtain discounts. Self-insurance and insurance company competition on rates to employers was first in line to destroy the community rating risk pool. Today, managed care, HMOs, PPOs, and other methods of getting price breaks for a select few further burdens the uninsured, the small businesses, and the individuals who must self-pay. And, in the process, a mountain of administrative cost overburdens the care that is given.

This flight from responsibility must stop. We would do well to heed Clinton's call for us to be Americans again, recognizing that we are all in this together and need to pull ourselves through it together. Health system leaders can do something to turn this shameful tide of irresponsibility. But we cannot get anyone, except perhaps ourselves, to rejoin the community unless we move aggressively on utilization and cost. We must master efficient care. We must organize to prevent unnecessary duplication. And, we must move to deal directly with our customers, at risk and with full responsibility and accountability for results.

Our goal should be to build health care financing and delivery models aimed at "community good" versus the good of individual providers, individual businesses, or individual insurance or managed care businesses. Some fear that no one will come back into the game on behalf of the greater community. We may well be pleasantly surprised when individual patients and their families understand that much of what can be done often does little good and may be counter to their supposed goals.

Do we need to just wait for the perfect model? No! The most challenging reform for each of us is to stop passing the buck for what happens. We must take a stand and lead our own organizations step by step to reform at the local level. If the ideal of community is ever to mean anything in this country, then community institutions need to stop whining and get on with leading the grass roots revolt for change.

One place to start this revolt is with managed care. The concept of managed care in the hands of fiscal intermediaries falls far short of the capabilities of the fully integrated organizations such as Kaiser, Group Health of Puget Sound, and others. Something can be learned from the vast differences between the success of one form, and the failure of the other. One uses an external agent or fiscal intermediary third party to micromanage; the other form accepts risk from the buyer. One works, the other does not. We must learn what is critical to this success and failure.

Why must we learn? Because most professional policymakers and certainly every "get on the wagon" policymaker are offering managed care as a solution without making the critical distinction made here. We are about to embrace the wrong kind of managed care.

For those who believe that only an integrated form of managed care will ever work well, the challenge is "getting to go" in managed care.

## MANAGED CARE: HAS IT WORKED?

In the early 1970s, the concept of managed care was introduced as the magic pill to cure the growing health care cost problem. While Kaiser and Group Health of Puget Sound provided an integrated type of managed care, the concept was not given much attention until Paul Ellwood with the Interstudy think tank group championed it as a solution for the future. Dubbed health maintenance organizations, few have become the solid foundation of economically based health care of the early models and have successfully adopted a solid approach to wellness and health maintenance.

*Health maintenance organizations and their modern day clones—managed care businesses—have rarely come close to the concept from which they sprang.*

Since the launching of HMOs in a blizzard of promotion, health maintenance organizations and their modern day clones—managed care businesses—have rarely come close to the totally dedicated, vertically integrated concept from which they sprang. Most of the managed care movement is in fact aimed at making sure that vertical integration and whole organizations at risk never happen.

The concept of organizing hospitals, physicians, and other services to provide health care for a given population for a fixed price seems simple, but it has not happened. Insurers going into the business act more as brokers, not integrated organizations. Providers shy away from what they view as strange territory of insuring and processing claims. Insurers are comfortable with contracts, pricing, and processing, but not with delivering care. Therefore they stay away from the responsibilities of giving care. As a result, professional autonomy, financial independence, and fee-for-service flourish under the guise of concepts of managed care.

Thus we have insurers attempting remote-controlled micromanagement of providers, risks underwriting, and a national call for "managed care" without an effective model to do the job. Providers must ultimately do the job, but are we prepared to move aggressively in that direction? Are we instead preparing for another round of policy being implemented with failures likely to cost more and destroy what is left of the strong organizations that might build vertically integrated systems of service?

Is there room for pessimism? If what is today called managed care has the flaws noted here, can we survive a decade of more of the same or a more modern version with the added regulatory features called for in "managed competition"? Managed competition proposals, fragmentary as they are and probably must be at this stage, call for roles for all the old players and the same distancing between controller managers and provider systems of the earlier varieties.

Have the existing managed care approaches solved our most pressing problems? Hardly. Managed care and indemnity underwriters have pursued aggressive underwriting techniques leading to groups and individuals at the highest risk of needing health services being left uncovered by insurance. Groups lose their insurance, people with chronic health problems cause their group to lose their insurance, or people are locked into their job because of insurance. In short, insurance for those in need only goes to those in very large organizations who can spread the risk internally within the group. Organizations with aging work forces who sought escape from community rating, now find their own groups caught in the squeeze. They want back in now that they too need subsidy and support from a still larger and younger group. In short, nearly everyone wants change. How does managed care differ from the more traditional insurance? It is sharper and more determined to profit from the many ways one can use to avoid people who may need large amounts of care and keep down the amount given to those who get into their plans. Is this an exaggeration? A bit perhaps, but who really doubts the larger truth of it? We do not get many chances for major reform. And, major attempts have been made to secure health care for all in America. If we are to do it with any hope of not bankrupting the country, we need to get it right on this go around.

Uwe Reinhart of Princeton University, an active policy critic and frequent "talking head," says managed care is simply a new snake oil that has come down the pike that has done nothing so far and has just a few local victories. Mainly it has shifted cost. If we expect managed care to be the savior of the health care delivery system, the start has not been good. If there are local victories, these organizations should show the way. Vertically integrated organizations delivering managed care do an outstanding job. Can we emulate the best and abandon the worst of managed care?

## MANAGED CARE EVOLUTION

What does our present system of managed care look like? How has it evolved from traditions of the past and, more specifically, where must it go in the future if we are to "get to go"? Figure 1 outlines the progression from the past through the future. The past and the present generally describe the system as it has progressed. Obviously exceptions can be made to any of these specifications. The future outlines the conceptual elements necessary to "get to go."

### Past (traditional)

In the traditional health care model, government provided capital and generous payments to allow ample profits to fuel access and provider growth. Purchasers hired insurers from a relatively homogeneous market to insure, process, and pay their bills. Physicians and hospitals provided services and collected a charge. The employer gave little, if any, choice of insurer, and the patient had little knowledge of health care treatment options and regarded his or her hospital and physicians with great sanctity. Traditional patterns of care prevailed. These times were great. Everyone seemed to be happy, but the components of the system were increasing their capability to consume more dollars. A form of fiscal hypertension was developing.

### Present (traditional and managed care)

Elements of the past still exist, but many varieties of managed care have taken root in the market. Government no longer provides capital and certainly does not provide profits through Medicare and Medicaid rates. The purchaser (employer and government) functions, with a great deal of self-interest, wishing to pay only cost (less if possible), for only the people for which they are directly responsible. Pure self-interest by the powerful has placed greater financial burden on the private pay, uninsured, and underinsured. Many small employers are out of the insurance market; one big claim ends their prospects for insurance.

Insurers have moved from merely processing and paying bills to seeking ways of using market power

## FIGURE 1

## MANAGED CARE EVOLUTION

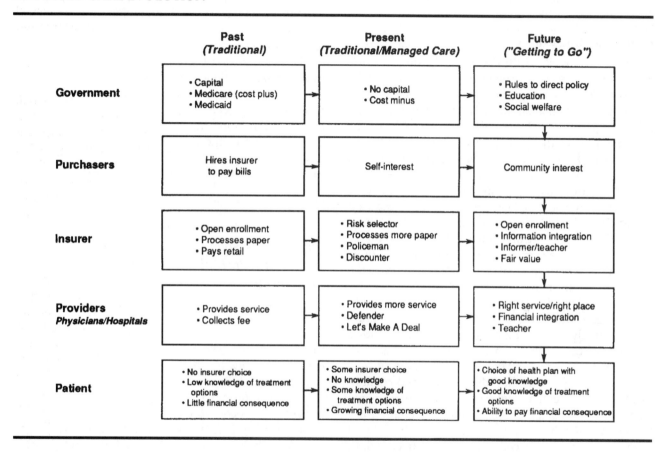

| | Past (Traditional) | Present (Traditional/Managed Care) | Future ("Getting to Go") |
|---|---|---|---|
| **Government** | • Capital<br>• Medicare (cost plus)<br>• Medicaid | • No capital<br>• Cost minus | • Rules to direct policy<br>• Education<br>• Social welfare |
| **Purchasers** | Hires insurer to pay bills | Self-interest | Community interest |
| **Insurer** | • Open enrollment<br>• Processes paper<br>• Pays retail | • Risk selector<br>• Processes more paper<br>• Policeman<br>• Discounter | • Open enrollment<br>• Information integration<br>• Informer/teacher<br>• Fair value |
| **Providers**<br>*Physicians/Hospitals* | • Provides service<br>• Collects fee | • Provides more service<br>• Defender<br>• Let's Make A Deal | • Right service/right place<br>• Financial integration<br>• Teacher |
| **Patient** | • No insurer choice<br>• Low knowledge of treatment options<br>• Little financial consequence | • Some insurer choice<br>• No knowledge<br>• Some knowledge of treatment options<br>• Growing financial consequence | • Choice of health plan with good knowledge<br>• Good knowledge of treatment options<br>• Ability to pay financial consequence |

and provider competitive fear in order to become a super discount payor of services. The cost shift problem has been exacerbated.

Providers have accepted this change by assuming this is real and productive competition and pursue a "Let's make a deal" mentality. The high level of payor inspection of ordered services has caused providers to spend enormous resources defending their actions. The past had no controls to moderate increases in cost. The present has seen insurers with managed care leading the way to cultivate onerous inspection controls that have not proven to be effective in moderating cost, while causing administrative cost to explode in growth. Estimates for administrative costs built into our health care system now range up to 25 percent and is climbing. And no doubt this cost represents thousands of jobs, a powerful lever when it comes to political maneuvering to give everyone a role in the changed system. Whatever savings might have come

from managed care have easily been consumed by the heavy administrative load of managed care businesses and related expenses by providers.

The endpoint consumer (predominantly employees) is now given some choice of insurers, but with relatively no knowledge as to the quality of the options. Frankly, most people do not have the energy to consider complex networks, much less the qualifications of the hundreds of physicians and hospitals on such a list. Given the variety of possible medical needs, it is totally unrealistic for anyone to expect that individual consumers can make such decisions rationally, especially when the many needs that might have to be faced in a lifetime do in fact only occur once or twice in a lifetime. Choose a network to meet such possible needs whose probabilities would require cosmic numbers to express? Just who is kidding whom about making real choices of networks? Through enhanced media attention, and growing individual awareness of health needs, consumers seem to be gaining knowledge of treatment options, but most are certainly not informed enough or sufficiently sensitized economically to make rational cost and quality decisions of selected insurers or providers.

## Future ("getting to go")

Neither the past traditional health system nor the present attempts at managed care appear to be viable. Let us assume, however, that some form of managed care is a solution that should be pursued. In fact, some fully integrated models do work. If we are to direct our attention toward this goal, then we must begin to create a vision of a managed care delivery system that can work.

First, the ideal managed care delivery system will be an organized body of health services and financial mechanisms. It will operate in an integrated and systematic fashion to manage and provide the right wellness, medical, and related services at the right place and time. The system's organizational goal will be to improve the long-term health status of the community.

Moreover, the ideal organization will be designed to function as a seamless system of services. Information will flow freely between the organized parts to provide a basis for customer convenience, provider and consumer learning, continuous improvement in delivery processes, avoidance of medical duplication, and containment of costs. Incentives will exist to focus the organized parts on the long-term improvement of community health status. The organized parts will be related through ownership and collaborative incentives to optimize the system versus optimizing the individual parts. Furthermore, mechanisms will be in place to assure community accountability and responsibility.

Step back and compare this vision with the present health care system, and you will find that most of the key elements do not exist. There are pieces that may be found randomly in various geographic areas, but no system embodies all of the elements.

The goal of long-term improvement in community health status is the most noble element. One might even argue that it is elusive, even unattainable. While most health professionals hold this goal as an ideal, there is growing concern that the present system is incapable of being modified to accomplish this goal. Such a goal is almost totally absent in our independent organizational and individual goals. We lack systems. We lack a wellness focus. We lack incentives for resource conservation or prudence in resource use. We profit most from waste. Our paradigms, regulations,

incentives, and adversarial competition combine to form high-growth, self-optimizing units of health delivery and financing. Reverse synergism occurs resulting in costs that are out of control. How many organizations, managed care companies, insurers, providers, or others in the overall business have an ongoing, long-term interest in just one major community?

The key question becomes, Can we create an organized system that has the goal of improving the health status of the community and encouraging prudence in resource use? Given our inherent lack of trust for government, the more important question is, Can we accomplish this in the private sector? The authors believe we can if government pursues it as a policy, and providers constructively embrace the goal.

---

*The key question becomes, Can we create an organized system that has the goal of improving the health status of the community and encouraging prudence in resource use?*

---

The American Hospital Association (AHA), in its most recent reform scenarios, proposes the formation of community networks that integrate health care services with accountability and responsibility to the community. The community network proposal is just beginning to evolve in its conceptual state at the AHA. While the many conflicting interests in the association will batter and mold the concept, what is most important is that it represents the potential for a radical departure from the past and a brave proposal for the future.

By comparison, the managed competition approach apparently assumes at least two systems per community. Many communities simply are too small to afford more than one full-fledged system of services. This issue of size is especially a factor if one assumes that tertiary and referral services are to be contained within the overall system.

If the AHA community networks and managed competition models are to have some hope of working out, then one may well need to carve out some level of referral services and have those designated nationally or at the state level and not allow them to be duplicated. In this fashion, community care networks and managed competition will be left to provide more primary, preventive, and long-term services. Any attempt to have truly comprehensive networks and competition will create tremendous pressures to differentiate networks by more and more esoteric service offerings. This differentiation means costly duplication.

Underlying our ability to achieve this future is the notion that our behaviors, rules, and incentives as purchasers and consumers must change if we are to develop the ideal health care system. Without being encumbered by these learned or regulated behaviors, the future portrayed in Figure 1 outlines the attributes of our system described in the vision that could "get us to go."

The delivery model that would "get us to go" will have citizens, including professionals, ready to demand that government tackle existing laws, regulations, and policies to pave the way for productive change. Provisions such as malpractice, antitrust laws, and guild restrictions are all well entrenched, leaving the health system with great inflexibility for change. A government wishing to promote positive change must modify or remove existing regulations and establish new rules to achieve the desired policy. Furthermore, the government must play a very significant role in changing attitudes and promoting actions necessary for health prevention using educational devices and incentives. Finally, the government must provide for the social welfare of the overall population through appropriate financing for that part of the population that is unable to obtain health care services through their own financial means.

Health insurance purchasers must change their purchasing philosophy. Through an intensely individualistic and competitive system, we have conditioned ourselves and corporate America to put self-interest first. Health insurance purchasers of the future must place the needs of the community first. Only then can they ensure their own long-term survival.

To insure against routine and catastrophic health care costs, we must all recognize that we live in the same life boat. However, the costs that go into this pool must be truly affordable and insurable. Optional, opulent, discretionary, and wasteful practices and procedures cannot be allowed in the pool. To work, careful attention to ethics and need must be incorporated into designing the basic coverage plan.

The insurer must become a part of the system, but as a function, and not as a totally discrete entity. Joint ventures might work, but over the long term the separate goals of brokers and suppliers must mesh.

The insurer function must experience a transformation from a paper-bound, health policeman seeking to pay discount fees for selected risks to a more community-oriented organization known as a "health plan." The health plan must make open enrollment available to all businesses and individuals at community rates. The only allowed price adjustment would be to adjust for company or employee actions to learn and practice healthy life styles. Use of data systems must eliminate most paper transfer, while assembling an electronic medical record that will follow the patient throughout the system.

The information collected on treatment and outcome must be assembled to inform and teach the public of the most efficient and appropriate use of resources. It must also provide data tools for the providers to foster continuous improvement in quality and value, with little or no inspection required by the health plan. Finally, the health plan must seek to optimize the system of quality providers through integration of finances and incentives, where possible, and by establishing fair values for the services provided by those not consolidated into the system.

Ultimately the insurer role must merge with the provider role. Where Blue Cross and Blue Shield plans still have a strong community service ethic, mergers or amalgamations of these units with providers may well occur. In states with multiple regions, farsighted plans may well find ways to merge by region, perhaps keeping some of the technical support services needed by the regions in cooperatives as service bureaus. We need innovation in this arena. As long as Blue Cross and Blue Shield plans adhere to their policeman role and do not see themselves as part and parcel of the delivery system such change will not occur. Over the short term, providers must integrate further. Some may well build their own managed care machinery in order to go direct to customers and bypass the third parties.

The providers—physicians, hospitals, and others—must collaborate and integrate to develop a system that delivers the right service at the right place for the right value. Guild restrictions must be modified to allow manpower capabilities to be fully utilized. Multidisciplinary group practices integrated with a health plan must be the dominant form of physician organization. Financial integration must provide incentives for each provider to be sensitized to overpriced, inappropriate, or poor quality care. Finally, the provider must be armed with information and have the incentive to teach the patient of appropriate treatments and preventive care.

The patient must be a knowledgeable consumer, possessing information gained through lifelong learning. Adequate information must be available to the consumer enabling quality and value judgments regarding the selection of health plan (insurer) and providers. Choice of health plans must be limited to two or three in major metropolitan areas. In rural and smaller communities, it may only be a single choice. Furthermore, the knowledge consumers gain must give them the ability to make choices relative to needed treatment, taking into account both cost and quality-of-life considerations. Finally, the consumer must have financial obligations for the health services received, based on the individual's ability to pay. Discretionary use, overuse, and misuse must have individual financial consequences. The common pool cannot be wasted and still retain the confidence of the broader community.

The vision therefore comprises a system of parts working together, each having an interest in the success and outcome of the other's action. The provider and insurer component under ideal circumstances would be a single integrated unit that is directed at creating a healthier community instead of a fragmented, suboptimized system of multiple providers and insurers that strive for their own individual success.

## CHANGES REQUIRED

"Getting to go" will require significant changes in the financing and organization of health services. This level of change can only be achieved through leadership that is willing and able to do what is necessary to achieve the vision. Figure 2 outlines the transition in leadership, financing, and organization required to "get to go." A snapshot of our present behaviors and structures would place us between the "old way" and "getting there." Thus, many leadership challenges remain ahead.

### Leadership

The speed of change and the ultimate ability to achieve our vision are in the hands of leadership. Years and years of the American management paradigm has left us with learned and comfortable habits to lead with command-and-control techniques with a self-interest focus for the short-term financial success of the organization and the leadership itself. A management leadership revolution is beginning to occur in America's battered, intensely competitive industries that compete in world markets. There are lessons to be learned from their experiences.

Deming and Juran, who brought great change to postwar Japan, are being heard by American industry. Their philosophies of organizational design to optimize the system and managed and collaborative com-

---

**FIGURE 2**

CHANGES REQUIRED TO "GET TO GO"

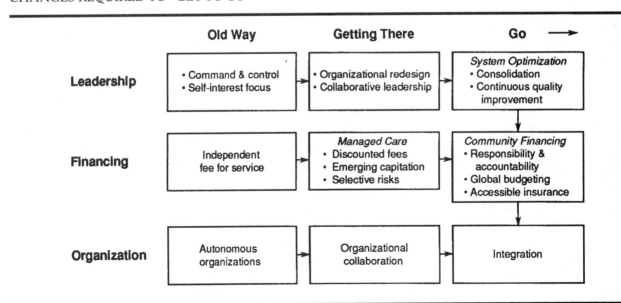

*Refocusing from institutional loyalty to community loyalty is a lofty demand of the vision, but essential and certainly not impossible.*

petition have great applicability to the American health system. Many health care organizations have adopted quality initiatives that are leading to organizational redesign, increased value, and a recognition that cooperative collaboration is required if the community (system) is to be well served.

Management, however, is not the only component of leadership that must play a part in this chain. Boards of directors, volunteers, staffs, and concerned members in the communities are the best links with the needs of the community. They must be informed and lead in their own external circles. More important, they must ultimately inform management and other professionals of what the consumer, the patient, and the community want from health care leaders.

External leaders have not been given an appropriate role in helping us change the system. We must be accountable to our community links. While we must provide them with professional advice, education, and guidance, these external leaders must ultimately be the masters of a change paradigm requiring vast changes in organizational and political circles far beyond our own narrow professional domains.

Leadership, both internal and external, will arrive at "getting to go" when we all speak passionately for achieving maximum value for the community, not for the individual organizations. Most professionals demand institutional loyalty from trustees, not community loyalty. To progress, we must refocus this loyalty. Refocusing is a lofty demand of the vision, but essential and certainly not impossible.

### Financing

The adage that where the dollars go, so goes the mind applies to health care. Consequently the financing system must change if we are to "get to go." The struggle between independent fee-for-service payments and discounted fees and capitation used in managed care has been long and miserable. Adversarial relationships and loss of trust between provider and payor have prospered and the likelihood of correcting this conflict seems remote. Again, suboptimization of the system occurs through self-interest in-

centives provided to each of the parts. "Getting to go" will ultimately require merging of the finance and delivery mechanisms.

"Getting to go" will require a broader community perspective with both provider and financing systems having some community responsibility and accountability. Global budgeting for defined populations has been suggested as a means to assure that health expenditures stay within some reasonable value limits for the community. A major departure from our present system, global budgeting conjures up images of onerous government control. Examples of successful structures such as state or community utility commissions may provide some direction or examples of the solutions, but we must recognize that they are diametrically opposed to the prevailing paradigm.

Furthermore, some portion of the health care dollar must begin to be invested for future improvements. Wellness prevention, community education, research on best demonstrated clinical processes and outcomes must receive an appropriate and ongoing investment. In a system with heavy constraints on costs, it would be easy to avoid investing in the future. We must not repeat the mistake of only investing in technology.

### Organization

Finally, the organization of the health care system must change to "get to go." Our health care system at a community level predominantly consists of autonomous organizations conditioned to compete for resources, survival, and growth. Some examples of provider collaboration have emerged but only after purchasers have proposed a system and community philosophy and exerted the necessary economic pressure to force collaboration.

Financial integration is integral to functioning as a system. Financial integration requires all of the provider and insurer parts to focus on delivering services within the financial constraint of the overall price paid by the purchasers in the form of insurance. Fee-for-service (piecework payment) is the antithesis of this concept. The natural tendency embedded in any piecework payment system is to revert to optimizing the parts, as measured by individual or organizational income, as opposed to optimizing the system. Kaiser and other well-developed, closed panel, staff model HMOs serve as examples of the "systemness" created when piecework payment is removed.

With calls for consolidation, the first question that arises is "Who owns the system?" In the existing "system," many owners exist. Few, however, have the range of resources needed to take on the comprehensive job suggested by the vision proposed here. Only the major metropolitan areas possess a population base sufficient to have more than two or three competing systems.

In a pluralistic economy, there will not be one right answer. Not-for-profit and for-profit, investor-owned organizations may emerge. As our analysis here indicates, America pays a high price for its pluralistic amalgam of providers, insurers, and consumer methods. Perhaps we must think more boldly and take none of the current modes of insuring and caring as the starting point for reform. Whatever form of ownership and control that is chosen, it must be yoked to strong incentives that give the entity a long-term incentive to pay attention to wellness and community health status.

If a sense of community is to be achieved, the concept of consumer cooperatives should be considered as a method of bringing the community into the role of defining, using, and building the policies and programs that will help them to help themselves. Managed competition calls for consumer cooperatives, but it makes them mere intermediaries between consumers and the more traditional insurers and providers. In our version of the cooperative, it might be desirable to convert existing Blue Cross plans, voluntary hospitals, and other community health resources into property of the consumer cooperative. Put people back in the loop through ownership via the consumer cooperative! The separation of people from the institutions is undoubtedly one of the core problems. It might be reversed, in part, through consumer cooperatives.

## STRUCTURAL IMPEDIMENTS

Even with national policy consensus it will be difficult to "get to go" swiftly or efficiently. Our health care system is constructed around structures created or protected by incentives, laws, and behaviors learned and established over many years. These structures and incentives will act as impediments to a positive evolutionary change unless they are identified and changed or removed. The following sections discuss some significant impediments that should be evaluated.

### Consumer information

The best way to create positive change in the health system is to develop knowledgeable consumers. The more consumers know about price, quality, and medi-

cal alternatives, the more effective the private competitive market will be in delivering a continuously improving, high-value product. Consumers are generally confused and unknowledgeable relative to health care prices and quality. Providers have resisted dispensing information based on claims of professionalism, patient confidentiality, or a variety of other excuses. Consumer information and action are keys to positive change.

*Solution:* Information should be collected and disseminated by the government if not voluntarily and systematically done by providers and insurers. User groups, self-help groups, and other modes of consumer involvement should be fully exploited in this process.

### Community philosophy

The current health system is not geared toward health care as a social responsibility of the community. Insurers have turned to aggressive selection of the best risks in the market, and business purchasers of health insurance want no part of community responsibility. The result has been low rates for some and unaffordable rates or unavailability for others. A return to the traditional community rating with open enrollment would be far superior to the current practice.

*Solution:* License only those insurers who agree to provide open enrollment with community rating to businesses and individuals in specified geographical regions. No licensed insurer may turn away any person or group for a pre-existing condition or risk factor. Insurers, however, can obtain reinsurance for extraordinarily high individual health care costs through a state or national pool funded by a revenue tax on all health insurers.

Second, providers have created an insidious form of discrimination through pricing systems. Discounts given to insurers who market to large business and good risks are balanced by charging extraordinarily high retail prices to those who cannot obtain insurance through mainstream insurers or who cannot afford insurance. This "reverse Robin Hood" principle is working to exacerbate the growing problem of access to health care.

*Solution:* Prohibit excessive or discriminatory price discounting.

### Guild laws

Over the years, the health professions have crafted laws with the purported purpose of protecting consumers seeking their services. A second, and many times more powerful motivation, is the protection of the professional status, supply of manpower, and income of the profession. Many states protect the independence of the physician through corporate practice of medicine laws. These laws, plus inappropriate Medicare fraud and abuse regulations, limit the ways physicians, hospitals, and other providers can band together as a group or system. If we are to achieve systemness, such artificial constraints must be removed.

Also, physicians and other health professionals have created restrictions as to who may provide certain services. These restrictions sometimes serve as barriers to more efficient, alternative practices. Removing these restrictions would allow quality alternatives to be explored thereby increasing value and accessibility.

*Solution I:* Repeal laws that inappropriately protect physicians or other health care providers.

*Solution II:* Repeal laws or regulations that deter financial relationships between physicians and other providers.

*Solution III:* Repeal or amend professional work protections not necessary to protect the consumer.

*Solution IV:* Establish a national program of research, experimentation, and demonstration to work toward more efficient ways to use medical manpower to deliver health care. Provide federal exemptions for such projects. When amply demonstrated, disallow federal funds to any state that bars the use of the procedures demonstrated to be more efficacious.

### Fee-for-service

Piecework payment is an insidious deterrent to achieving an optimized system. It represents an incentive to provide (consume) more. Much of the micromanagement and utilization review that exist today are an outgrowth of piecework payment.

*Solution:* Systematically move away from fee-for-service payment structures. A powerful first step toward this objective would be modifying Medicare and Medicaid payment policies to adopt capitated or global payments.

### Ownership

For years the voluntary not-for-profit hospital has been the backbone of hospital services. The remaining providers in the system have been proprietary tax-paying organizations and individuals. The sanctity of the tax-exempt community ownership acts as a barrier to uniting tax-exempt and for-profit, proprietary interest—an essential element of creating systems. Further-more, tax exemption has many times shielded economic decisions that would have been made differently if proprietary ownership interests were involved. Tax exemption has served a very valuable part in building our system, but it should not be allowed to serve as a deterrent for change in the system.

*Solution:* Careful and rational examination of not-for-profit laws and modifying them to achieve desired public policy purpose.

---

*Much of the micromanagement and utilization review that exist today are an outgrowth of the piecework payment inherent in fee-for-service structures.*

---

There may be many possible ownership combinations for promoting community interest in a health care system. Neither not-for-profits nor for-profits should be excluded from the opportunity. In some areas of the country public hospital systems have worked exceptionally well. Many of the public authorities in California, the Broward Hospital District in Ft. Lauderdale, the Greenville Hospital System in South Carolina, and others are outstanding systems. Public ownership may be distasteful to many due to the widely held belief that the government should only do what the private sector cannot do for itself. Many models work well making one model for all an unlikely option for provider systems. Therefore, new models must be developed to bridge the concerns.

The creation of community health cooperatives could bring a broad section of the community into play with providers, workers, and industry participating in a community-type ownership. Existing not-for-profit and public models along with Blue Cross plans could be integrated under a cooperative model. And, for community responsiveness, an ownership model that vested control in the people of the community could be a powerful incentive to put prevention first, a goal worth trying.

*Solution:* Examine and change regulations to ease the formation of community health cooperatives and encourage and allow not-for-profit providers and mutual insurers to contribute their assets to these cooperatives.

### Antitrust laws

The antitrust laws, now used so much in health care, were written in a different time for a different purpose.

The desires of the communities and policymakers seem to differ from the application of these laws. The laws perpetuate a fractionated system that avoids integrating, while fearing expensive scrutiny or prosecution from a schizophrenic government policy.

A counter to this argument is that until the health care industry finds methods of truly putting the community and consumers into effective power positions so that accountability is restored, it will remain difficult to abolish or significantly change antitrust laws that are designed to punish anticonsumer behavior. To the extent that we keep professional control of health care, we are more likely to have antitrust laws to regulate our behavior. If we want change in antitrust laws, we must accept much more public accountability as the price for that change.

*Solution:* Revise antitrust laws and their application to health care but provide specific exemptions for monopoly-like consolidations when public accountability is assured by its structure and appropriate governmental oversight.

### Opportunities

Whether the solution is public or private, massive consolidation needs to take place in the health system to create integrated health systems combining provider services and financing mechanisms.

If one concurs with the vision, and the structural impediments begin to fall, what are some of the practical opportunities available?

*Opportunity 1: Voluntary consolidation.* With some change in the antitrust laws and a newfound community purpose of health provider leadership (managers and board), renewed efforts could be made to create managed care corporations that overarch the various provider and insurance parts. Authorization to create such entities would only be granted after assurances of public accountability have been made through a formal contract with the community.

*Opportunity 2: Consumer cooperatives.* New organizations such as the consumer cooperative, Puget Sound, could be promoted and formed. Proper clearances and existing laws would be required to allow not-for-profit assets to be contributed to these consumer cooperatives and to Blue Cross mutual insurance organizations that may be converted to consumer cooperatives.

*Opportunity 3: Utility commissions.* Communities could take charge of health care financing and operate in a utility commission fashion, establishing rates and demanding service integration. Demands made by the utility commission would encourage a natural consolidation among providers to protect their solvency and ownership interests. As in existing utilities, these organizations could be investor owned or not-for-profit (community owned).

*Opportunity 4: Give your assets to those most likely to use them to promote the goals enunciated here.* Not-for-profits who simply do not want to struggle with changes coming about in health care could give their assets to another not-for-profit organization on the condition that these assets be used to build a new vision of managed care in a community health system.

*Opportunity 5: Declare defeat and nationalize the system.* The system could be financed on a budgetary basis, forcing everyone into some national bargaining over roles, allocations, and the like. Having no enthusiasm for this opportunity, we offer no further details.

•   •   •

The challenge for leadership and the required changes are great. Our personal limitations include a limited view of the world and the threat of an overwhelming risk if one gets too far out on the limb. "Getting to go" will open up new and strange territories that will provide opportunity and failure for leaders. Capable leaders will pursue the opportunity. Threatened leaders will resist the change.

For those leaders who feel that the managed care existing today provides the most cost-effective, quality outcome for the individual, his or her sponsor in the community, they will go no further. Unfortunately for many of us, managed care means a third party trying to micromanage patients (deductions, authorizations, and so on), employers (claims, incentives, and so forth), and providers (approvals, forums, payment, tricks, and the like). Providers need to go ahead and master efficient care. We owe that to the community and the third party nightmare of administrative overkill must be laid to rest.

For those healthcare leaders who believe that managed care as a system focused on improving the health status of our communities is superior to our existing system, their individual goals and leadership focus must be changed accordingly. We cannot sit by idly and wait for the system to change us. Instead our obligation is to lead our organizations toward a new era in health care.

# New directions for hospital strategic management: The market for efficient care

## Jon A. Chilingerian

*An analysis of current trends in the health care industry points to buyers seeking high quality, yet efficient, care as an emerging market segment. To target this market segment, hospitals must be prepared to market the efficient physicians. In the coming years, hospitals that can identify and market their best practicing providers will achieve a competitive advantage.*

**How will acute care** hospitals define the marketplace in the 1990s? Which emerging market segments will offer hospitals the greatest growth opportunity? Developing strategic marketing plans to answer these questions will not be easy, but such plans will become increasingly important in an era of budget ceilings, prospective payment, declining admissions, and shorter lengths of stay.

In the 1980s, hospital chief executive officers (CEOs) became aware of the need for strategic marketing plans.[1] Although dozens of new markets have been targeted and sought after, there is one group of customers that has not effectively been singled out: the customer market for efficient care. This customer market wants not only high quality hospital care, but also physicians who can provide the quick route to health. That is, physicians whose clinical experience and judgment reduce the amount of unnecessary tests, drugs, and days in the hospital. The market for efficient care is a segment that may offer hospitals the greatest single opportunity for differentiation in the future.

In the coming years, hospitals that can identify and market their best practicing providers will achieve a competitive advantage. There are four reasons why evaluating best practices is an exciting opportunity for hospitals. First, there is absolutely no better place than the hospital to understand variations in physician practice style. Second, hospital medical records contain much better information about physician practices than do insurance claims files. Third, many hospital information systems can combine case mix and financial information by physician. Finally, hospitals are often socially (and politically) closer to the physician providers than anyone else.

This is the first of two articles on how hospitals might target this market in the future. In this article, the market for efficient care is identified as an emerging segment that could be targeted with profit. The second article will introduce a new marketing evalua-

*Jon A. Chilingerian, Ph.D., is Assistant Professor of Management at the Heller School at Brandeis University. Professor Chilingerian's current work has focused on measuring and managing physician efficiency and effectiveness. For his work on measuring physician efficiency, he recently received the "Best Paper Award" from the Health Care Division of the Academy of Management. He received his doctorate in management from MIT's Sloan School of Management.*

The helpful comments of Stuart Altman, Barbara Bigelow, Dianne Chilingerian, Gene Guselli, David Rosenbloom, and Stanley Wallack are gratefully acknowledged.

tion technique that identifies efficient physicians and will illustrate how this technique could be used as an integrative element of a strategic market plan.

## HOSPITAL MARKET SEGMENTATION: THEORY AND PRACTICE

Market segmentation (i.e., disaggregating consumers into discrete subunits or segments) is the managerial concept used to identify consumers or firms likely to use or buy services. Defining a market segment requires identifying which customers to target and defining what service elements they desire.[2] Table 1 selects some typical criteria used by hospitals to define market segments in terms of generic service elements and customer targets. These market dimensions are not mutually exclusive. Hospitals typically combine several of these dimensions to pursue various product line strategies. For example, some plausible dimensions used to segment the market for hospital services include the admitting decision maker, the clinical specialties, and the usual demographic and socioeconomic attributes (e.g., age, sex, and income).[3]

Many hospitals define markets in terms of clinical specialties. They determine geographic market share by clinical specialty (e.g., cardiology; general surgery; oncology; orthopedics; and ear, nose, and throat disorders) and predict future trends. For example, the cardiology market needs electrocardiograms, stress tests, cardiac catheterization laboratories, cardiac surgery, cardiac rehabilitation, and so on. The service concept is defined as offering centers of excellence to specific populations, such as cardiology patients and cardiologists.

## TABLE 1

### OPERATIONALIZING HOSPITAL MARKETING STRATEGIES

| Marketing dimension | Customer segment | Service concept |
| --- | --- | --- |
| Clinical specialty | Cardiology patients and cardiologists, oncology patients and oncologists, etc. | Centers of excellence<br>• Cardiology program<br>• Radiation program<br>• Oncology program<br>• Amnio program |
| Human activities and life styles by age/sex | Corporate executives, women, substance abusers, elderly persons, people who have had heart attacks | Special needs programs<br>• Sports medicine<br>• Screening programs<br>• Wellness programs<br>• Women's health |
| Price-sensitive or quality-sensitive buyers (or both) | Fortune 500 and top 250 nonindustrials, smaller employers, Blue Cross, HMOs, PPOs, EPOs | Efficient care<br>• Specialty groups<br>• Hernia clinics<br>• Managed care<br>• Geographical access |
| Admitting and attending physician; usage rates | Physicians, HMOs, patients | Customized access to acute care<br>• Physician recruitment program |
| Geographic service area | Urban/rural<br>Local/regional<br>National/global | Convenient access<br>• Walk-in clinics |
| Income or payor class | Patients with co-insurance, deductibles, Medicaid, Medicare, etc. | Access/amenities<br>• Free care<br>• VIP rooms with gourmet meals |
| Catastrophic illnesses | People with AIDS, stroke patients, comatose patients and their families | Psychological support<br>• AIDS/hospice programs<br>• Home health/infusion therapy |

NOTES: AIDS = acquired immune deficiency syndrome; VIP = very important person.

Narrow clinical specialty segments have been identified with the advent of diagnostic-related groups (DRGs) and other clinical classification schemes. *Segments* are defined as groups of patients with a common diagnosis or type of surgical procedure, such as patients admitted for coronary artery bypass grafts. Another example is the outpatient oncology market, which has become a small, but important, market opportunity for some acute care hospitals.[4] The oncology program is designed with oncologists and their patients in mind.

Life style is a criterion that has been used by many hospitals to define market segments whose special needs have more to do with fashion than with medical care. *Life style* here refers to an individual, group, or organization's behavior, values, or interests. Services that have a psychological appeal to individuals, like birthing rooms and sports medicine, have been offered to serve certain populations with great success. Other examples of services aimed at these life-style segments include wellness and screening programs, executive physicals, and, for corporations, emergency care for industrial accidents.

Another criterion to define customer segments is price–quality sensitivity. The price-sensitive market consists of firms looking for cost protection with quality guarantees. Some large firms are beginning to negotiate directly with physicians and hospitals for health care services. To win these customers, one successful service concept is to provide efficient care to a low-risk, large firm customer. By doing so, hospitals prove their ability to serve other large firm customers. To get this market, the service delivery system relies on specialization and high volume.

Despite the multitude of market segments, by far the most popular way to segment hospital markets is to concentrate on the admitting and attending physicians who are heavy users. In practice, virtually all managerial attention has focused on working with existing members of the medical staff and recruiting new physicians. These physician marketing programs help physicians to recruit associates, offer low-cost loans, build referral networks, and grant admitting privileges without credential hassles.

*In an era when patients have become a very "hot commodity," marketing to physicians has been beneficial for many hospitals. It has not gone without criticism, however.*

In an era when patients have become a very "hot commodity," marketing to physicians has been beneficial for many hospitals. It has not gone without criticism, however. A few hospitals have resorted to offering financial incentives (e.g., physician practice enhancements or consulting fees) for each patient admission. A few years ago, in an interview in *The Wall Street Journal*, a physician who supported these "dubious" marketing practices offered an explanation of why it happens:

> I can admit to any hospital I want to for any reason I want. I don't have to justify that to anybody. I can admit because I don't like the color of the carpet [at a competing hospital], or I don't like my parking spot.[5(p.1)]

The quote implies that a physician with admitting privileges at several hospitals has no contractual obligation to choose one hospital over another. If some physicians adopt this type of market mentality and look around for deals, then hospitals must compete for patients by offering financial (or other) incentives. Although there is no evidence that the foregoing attitude is widespread, it represents a bad tendency. Rather than putting bounties on patients, hospitals need to rethink their relationship with physicians. There is some evidence that buyers seeking efficient care may offer an interesting, new alternative for some hospitals; that is, offering large patient volumes in exchange for direct proof of efficient performance. Such an opportunity would push the hospital–physician relationship toward a more responsible alliance.

## BUYERS SEEKING EFFICIENT CARE: CURRENT TRENDS

During the past decade, a number of organizations and provider groups have become a potential force in the buyer's side of the market for efficient care. Figure 1 illustrates some of the most important customers in this market.

Two facts bring the market for efficient care into sharp relief. First, the U.S. health care system has come to cost more than $2 billion a day. Second, the federal government and corporate America have become the two most significant buyers of health care services. Staggering growth in medical costs have led Fortune 500 corporations and the top 250 nonindustrials to become more aggressive purchasers of health care. Pressure from corporate buyers seeking more efficient service delivery has led to a growth in alternative delivery systems aimed at improving health care efficiency and effectiveness.

## FIGURE 1

U.S. BUYER MARKET FOR EFFICIENT HOSPITAL CARE

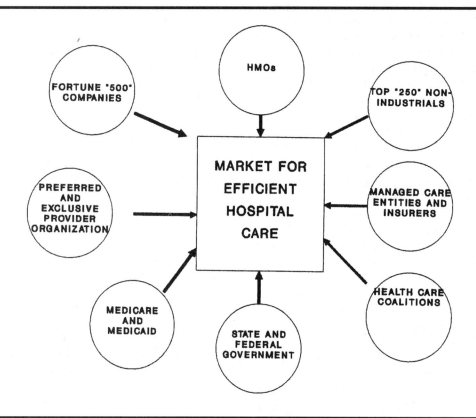

In fact, more and more of America's corporate employees are going to managed care. One prediction is that during this decade 60 percent of all employees and their dependents will be enrolled in a managed care indemnity plan.[6] As a result, health maintenance organizations (HMOs), preferred provider organizations (PPOs), exclusive provider organizations (EPOs), and other managed care plans have become the fastest growing stakeholders in this market segment.[7]

The EPOs represent an interesting example of where the efficient care segment is headed. To start an EPO, an outside organization selects efficient, high-quality providers; finds an insurance company to process the claims; and then markets the plan to employers. People enrolled in the plans are eligible to receive benefits if and only if they use the services of the contracting providers. In exchange for contracts for large numbers of patients, hospitals and physicians agree to discount their charges and offer per diem rates or capitated rates. Hence, the contract assumes that the

providers are equally efficient. If some providers are inefficient, the physicians and the hospital, not the plan, are at risk.

So far, the market for efficient care has remained a thin ecological niche, largely ignored by hospitals. Pressure, however, will be on physicians and hospitals to go after this market segment. To reach the buyer seeking more efficient care, a hospital has an incentive to reduce inefficient behavior such as unnecessary ancillary services and days of stay. Yet, few hospitals have shaped their competitive strategies and positioned their product lines to target buyers seeking efficient care. To understand why, it may be helpful to review four old trends and the gradual shift away from them.

### Selection criterion: From "all-or-none" to selective contracting

The idea of selective contracts, or selecting just the efficient physicians, has no historical precedent. Licensed physicians have never been excluded from participating in new insurance arrangements. Companies like Blue Cross and Blue Shield traditionally contracted with every hospital and every physician. That custom holds true today; physicians have been bitterly opposed to selective contracting.

Even most PPOs, which are supposed to contract selectively with the better practicing physicians, set up a table in front of the medical staff lounge and sign contracts with nearly every physician. Physician selection amounts to doing credential checks, malpractice checks, drug-dependency checks, and so on, but little progress has been made in developing a technology for selecting more efficient physicians.

Despite widespread physician resistance to selective contracts, exceptions do exist. For example, some multispecialty groups and group practice HMOs select physicians on the basis of elaborate practice criteria, such as their performance. These groups have developed selection criteria for picking "best-practicing" physicians and created corporate incentives for more efficient practice. Because there is no shortage of physicians willing to work for these strategic entities, there are at least some physicians who do not object to having their performance screened and evaluated.

The market for efficient care offers an important strategic opportunity for physician specialists. First, there is growing evidence that physicians who specialize may, indeed, be more efficient. Specialization, however, can be sustained only by large patient volumes. If physicians do not market their services, they will be doing a lot of "bread and butter" work. Because of economies of scale, hospitals are in a better position than physician practices to build referral linkages that will bring to specialists large volumes of patients from local and regional markets.

### Changing assumptions about physician practice styles: From constant to variable

The second reason that the market for efficient care has been ignored is that until the Wennberg studies, physician judgments were never questioned by the lay community.[8] Although it was known that hospital prices could vary by 100 percent in the same city, few realized that price variation might be attributed to physician practice patterns.

There is growing evidence today that physician practice patterns in hospitals do vary. Moreover, the variations that arise from an inefficient use of resources cannot be explained by the attributes of the patients or the complexity and severity of their ill-

nesses. Physicians who practice the same type of medicine on a similar case mix, in the same hospital, could be less efficient with respect to resource utilization, while obtaining equivalent outcomes. These differences have marketing implications for the efficient care segment.

### Corporate cultures: From indifference to more aggressive purchasing strategies

#### Changing attitudes

A few years ago corporate America had little interest in health costs.[9] No attitude has changed more radically, across more industries in the past decade than have corporate attitudes toward health care costs. Professor Regina E. Herzlinger of the Harvard Business School has found that, assuming nothing else changes, rising corporate expenses for health care eventually will wipe out after-tax corporate profits for the average Fortune 500 company.[10] The changing cost structure of American industry has made the cost of health care a matter of competitive strategy. Nevertheless, most of the hospital industry is unprepared for these changes and unlikely to welcome them.

#### Incipience of corporate buyer "cherry-picking"

Another piece of evidence that the market for efficient care is an emerging segment consists of statements of intention and promise from corporate executives. For instance, one Fortune 500 executive recently said, "Anybody that can prove that they have more efficient, high quality physicians will get our business" (personal communication).

The fact that hospitals have not consciously served this market segment has not stopped corporations from "picking their own cherries." Many large corporate health care purchasers have already begun to develop local purchasing strategies, which include identifying the more efficient physicians and hospitals.

Some companies have even begun programs to send employees to so-called centers of excellence across the country. Companies on the forefront of this market, like Hewlett Packard, have selected several hospitals exclusively to do transplants and other expensive procedures. Because these companies also believe in the employees' right to choose, they are creating cost-sharing incentives to encourage their employees to use the more efficient hospital.

The greatest threat to hospitals is how these companies pick the more efficient providers. Efficient providers have been selected principally by studying av-

*Efficient providers have been selected principally by studying average lengths of stay and average prices per hospital discharge, claims review studies, and modified peer review. The mistake in these techniques is oversimplification.*

erage lengths of stay and average prices per hospital discharge, claims review studies, and modified peer review. The mistake often made in these techniques is oversimplification; critical factors such as case mix complexity and severity are often ignored. Thus hospitals that adopt a more passive attitude (i.e., let the buyers pick their own cherries) run the risk of being forgotten, disregarded, or unfairly rejected.

On the other hand, hospitals that choose to go after a share in this market are not finding an easy customer. Corporations want guarantees of quality and efficiency. They also want to trade high volume (via preferred and exclusive care arrangements) for a share in the savings.[11]

The ostensible question may be, Is it worth the time and effort to identify the hospital's best practicing physicians? The real question, however, is whether hospitals will take the lead and conduct the evaluation or have someone else's evaluation forced on them. Hospitals that wait will have little choice in the matter.

### Managing physician efficiency: From cryptic surveillance to better management controls

The need to evaluate and manage physician behavior in hospitals poses the most difficult of hospital control problems. The reason for this is that the hospital service production process is a two-part process: one controlled by hospital managers and the other controlled by physicians. The outputs of the manager-controlled side of the hospital are the intermediate (not final) outputs; they become the inputs for the physician-controlled side of the hospital. The physicians in community hospitals are like general managers of small, temporary firms that produce a highly customized service package for each patient.[12]

Hospital CEOs can be accountable only for those activities under their control. They should be accountable for the average cost per unit of hospital service (cost per test, cost per hour of nursing care, cost per prescription, and so on). The quantity of those service

inputs used (lengths of stay, ancillary tests, and drug usage) or, to put it another way, the bundle of services that each patient receives is almost entirely under the discretion of the attending physician. Because each physician-run firm is given nearly an unlimited credit line to operate inside the hospital, better management controls are needed.

Although physicians play a prominent role in hospital service production, managerial attention has focused almost entirely on the efficiency of the inputs to the physician's firm (i.e., improving the labor productivity of laboratories, radiology, nurses, dietetic workers, housekeepers, and so on). They have ignored how physicians ultimately use those resource inputs to care for patients.

The reason is no mystery. First, physicians have a cooperative, rather than a hierarchical, relationship with the hospital. A cooperative relationship implies a loose or incomplete contract in which the hospital's obligations are clear, but the physician's are unclear. The hospital promises operational readiness, that is, a bed with various levels of nursing care ready and a full inventory of ancillary services. On the other hand, the physician's performance clause is not clearly spelled out.

Under retrospective reimbursement, there was no reason to evaluate physician performance, and certainly doing so was tantamount to committing managerial suicide. The hospital CEO's answer was rational: Why should I invest in planning and control systems that will alienate the people who fill the beds?

Unfortunately, as the census declines by as much as 15 percent in some places, physicians remain the "prima donnas." This incomplete relationship will continue as long as physicians can admit patients to the hospital of their choice. As Figure 2 suggests, the iron rule of hospital management is still at work.

No matter how important low unit prices may be to the hospital manager and the public interest, they are not the reason that a physician chooses to admit a patient to a hospital. Reasons such as service reliability, high quality, fit with their service delivery approach, courteousness of service providers, or reservation availability are more important to physicians. So hospitals that must compete for physician admissions will never find it easy to adopt the strategy of being a more efficient provider. Instead, these hospitals will rely on incentives that include leasing beds, offering free dinners and golf memberships, and so on.

On the other hand, under prospective payment systems, and with an emerging market for efficient care, there are clear advantages in evaluating physician per-

**FIGURE 2**

THE IRON RULE OF HOSPITAL MANAGEMENT

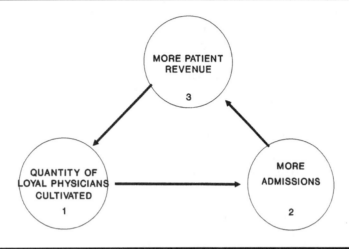

formance. Furthermore, there are new information technologies and management techniques to conduct these evaluations.

Every hospital has planning and marketing departments that can focus attention on how to market clinical outputs. Before that happens, however, management control systems are needed that can evaluate physician performance in treating patients. More importantly, strong executive leadership will be needed for this to work. Needless to say, it is still much easier for the hospital CEO to fight rate-setting boards than the medical staff.

**SERVING THE MARKET FOR EFFICIENT CARE**

There are several ways that the market for efficient care can become a legitimate target for a community hospital. The first way is if the market grows rapidly during the next decade. The evidence cited in this article suggests that this trend may already be taking place. The second way is if a hospital targets a broader geographical market (regional or even national) by offering highly specialized, efficient services. Some hospitals (including the Mayo and Cleveland Clinics and El Camino and Shouldice Hospitals) have adopted this market strategy and begun to go after national and international markets. The Mayo Clinic in Jacksonville has developed a large regional tertiary medical center,

and it has begun to do laboratory tests for physicians and hospitals across the country. Other U.S. hospitals like the Cleveland Clinic and El Camino have begun to offer their services to corporate buyers around the country.

The Shouldice Hospital in Toronto is an interesting example of how focusing on a clinical specialty enabled this hospital to target a market for efficient care. Shouldice Hospital concentrates on one illness (i.e., inguinal hernias) and attracts patients not only from Canada, but from the United States and Europe as well. Shouldice succeeds because its patients and referral customers believe that the hospital's services are not only highly efficient, but also the highest quality of care. Once the Shouldice method has been used, the hernia recurrence rates are half of 1 percent (.005), which is the lowest in the world. Some believe that it would be cheaper to send American patients to Toronto to get a hernia repair than to use the day surgery facility in most U.S. hospitals. In the coming years, highly specialized institutions like Shouldice may compete with vulnerable, local hospitals for high-volume, common surgical procedures.

•     •     •

All the trends discussed in this article point to a need to focus more managerial attention on the market for efficient care. If this market represents such a great opportunity, what is the holdup? The principal obstacle has been in finding management approaches and techniques to evaluate and manage the efficiency of service production in hospitals.

In our next article a new marketing evaluation technique called data envelopment analysis (DEA) will be introduced. It is capable of locating best practicing physicians as well as inefficient physicians who use excess resources, while explicitly considering quality of care. Finally, it will be shown that DEA can be adapted to the strategic planning process. These ideas, however, must await a future edition.

## REFERENCES

1. Kotler, P., and Andreasen, A.R. *Strategic Marketing for Nonprofit Organizations.* 3d ed. Englewood Cliffs, N.J.: Prentice Hall, 1987.
2. Heskett, J.L. *Managing in the Service Economy.* Boston, Mass.: Harvard Business School Press, 1986.
3. Louden, T. "Entry Strategies in Emerging Markets." In *The Strategic Planning Management Reader*, edited by L. Fahey. Englewood Cliffs, N.J.: Prentice Hall, 1989.
4. *Health Care Strategic Management*, February 1989, 18–20.
5. "Hospitals that Need Patients Pay Bounties for Doctors' Referrals." *The Wall Street Journal*, February 27, 1989, 1.
6. Coddington, D.C., and Moore, K.D. *Market Driven Strategies in Health Care.* San Francisco, Calif.: Jossey-Bass, 1987.
7. Coddington, D.C., et al. *The Crisis in Health Care: Costs, Choices, and Strategies.* San Francisco, Calif.: Jossey-Bass, 1987.
8. Wennberg, J. "Unnecessary Surgery." Testimony presented at the hearings before the Subcommittee on Oversight and Investigations of the Committee on Interstate and Foreign Commerce, 94th Congress, July 15, 1975.
9. Sapolsky, H.M., Altman, D., and Moore, J.D. "Corporate Attitudes Toward Health Care Costs." *Milbank Memorial Fund Quarterly/Health and Society* 59, no. 4 (1981): 561–85.
10. Herzlinger, R. "How Companies Tackle Health Care Costs." *Harvard Business Review*, July–August, 1985, 69–81.
11. Pope, T. "On Sale Now: Hospital Services." *Business and Health*, December 1991, 72.
12. Chilingerian, J., and Sherman, H.D. "Managing Physician Efficiency and Effectiveness in Providing Hospital Services." *Health Services Management Research* 3, no. 1 (March 1990): 3–15.

# The movement toward vertically integrated regional health systems

## F. Kenneth Ackerman, III

*Due to existing internal forces, a movement toward vertically integrated regional health systems is imperative in order to ensure the future viability of our health care system. However, in order for these systems to be successful, they must first overcome several imposing barriers.*

The question of what current forms of systems, if any, will ultimately lead health care in the direction of a high-quality, comprehensive, efficient, and more caring system of services for the American people is the predominant question in the health care industry and is one not easily answered. There is currently no national consensus on what the ideal health care delivery and financing system will be; however, there is evidence that vertically integrated regional health systems might prove to be the model of the future.

## MOVEMENT TOWARD VERTICALLY INTEGRATED REGIONAL HEALTH SYSTEMS

Several significant indicators have been prevalent during the past 20 years signifying the fact that a movement toward regional health systems was imminent. One notable early indicator was the Perloff Report.[1] The Perloff Report was established in 1970 as a report of The Special Committee on the Provision of Health Services of the American Hospital Association. This report identified the community-based health care organization as the hub of the health care system. This community-based health care organization was to be regional in scope, serving a geographically defined population. It was intended that such organizations would attempt to ensure that access to health care was attainable by all people. In addition, a comprehensive continuum of care was to be offered through this health care system. Quality and effectiveness were key characteristics in this report as well. Furthermore, the report stated that it was the responsibility of the health care system to recognize the need to control the utilization of facilities and services. Finally, the report held the system responsible for the appropriate and economical use of health care resources. It was suggested through the report that unnecessary duplication of facilities and services should be avoided. Thus, controlled growth was encouraged. As Warden states, "The report seemed significant at the time, but received much less attention than was expected. Twenty years later we recognize that in many respects it described the regional health care system of the future."[2(p6)]

*F. Kenneth Ackerman, III*, M.H.A., *is currently an Administrative Fellow at Thomas Jefferson University Hospital, Philadelphia, Pa.*

The author thanks J. Alexander McMahon, J.D., Chairman of the Department of Health Administration, Duke University; B. Jon Jaeger, M.H.A., Ph.D., Professor in the Department of Health Administration, Duke University; and F. Kenneth Ackerman, Jr., President of Geisinger Medical Center, Danville, Pa, for their helpful suggestions and advice during the writing of this article.

Another significant indicator to appear was horizontal integration. According to Toomey, horizontal integration is simply reflected through a "chain of institutions that provide essentially the same kind of clinical services to residents of geographic communities physically distant from one another (i.e., chains of acute care hospitals)."[3(p6)] Institutions increasingly began to engage in horizontal integration as a way of controlling the geographic distribution of health care services. Also, most health care systems aimed to build organizations devoted to becoming comprehensive, accessible, affordable, and integrated systems of service for their communities. These chains should be assessed by how well they meet the community's needs in each market, rather than how they relate nationally in order to determine their effectiveness.[4]

Finally, vertical integration in health care emerged as an ongoing effort to establish continuity of care for the patient. According to Shortell et al., "These largely local delivery systems involve prehospital primary care, hospital care, and posthospital care."[5] This continuity of care, provided by an organization, would assist the patient in health, in sickness, and even at death. This system is patient focused. Thus, the patient benefits greatly in such a system. Nevertheless, vertically integrated systems should continue to be assessed market-by-market. More importantly, a major determination of how well vertical integration works in the future should be determined, in large part, by the buyers in those particular markets. The question that needs to be answered here is "Will the vertically integrated systems (i.e., The Greenville Hospital System, Greenville, S.C.) be able to successfully compete on a quality and cost basis with other units that are part of horizontally integrated systems?"

## DRIVING FORCES BEHIND THE MOVEMENT TOWARD VERTICALLY INTEGRATED REGIONAL HEALTH SYSTEMS

In addition to the indicators mentioned that signified this movement toward vertically integrated regional systems of health care, there are currently four driving forces that continue to shape today's health care environment. Such forces will ultimately lead to the development of regional systems of health care.

### Health care costs

The spiraling cost of health care is a critical concern among most of the players in health care today: government (federal as well as state), insurance companies, employers, consumers, health care administrators, and physicians. Therefore, it is the chief driving force toward the reshaping of the health care system as it now stands.

Currently, more than $745 billion are spent on health care in the United States—approximately 12.4 percent of the gross national product. To put things in more perspective, the United States spends approximately an average of $2,500 per person per year. By the year 2000, this level is expected to be around $5,500 per person per year.[6] In the words of Dr. Louis Sullivan, Secretary of Health and Human Services, "The data are not cause for celebration!"

*The vertically integrated regional health system would be a more cost-effective delivery system than the more disparately organized.*

Financing health care in the United States will continue to have a tremendous impact on the field. For example, the federal government will continue to collapse more things into some sort of prospective payment [i.e., diagnosis related groups (DRGs)]. The next possible step would be the implementation of a prospective payment system for outpatient procedures. Also, through the influence of managed care companies, insurance companies, and employers, there will be an increase in "patient prodding," channeling the patients to the most cost-effective providers.[6] These are just a couple of ways the health care system will react to the ever-increasing cost pressures. Therefore, the rising cost of health care will continue to burden individuals, businesses, and the government, thus forcing these players to consider alternative ways of buying care. The vertically integrated regional health system would be a more cost-effective delivery system than the more disparately organized.

### Demographics

It is a well-known fact that our society is aging. The largest volume increase can be seen in the 45 to 54 age group. It is believed that, in the year 2000, this age group will have increased by 12 million people. This will present a major challenge for the current health care system because as people age, they become more and more dependent upon health care services. For example, 90 percent of the people over 65 years of age see a physician at least once a year. In addition, the elderly are hospitalized two-and-a-half times that of the rest of the population.[6]

It should be mentioned that there are distinctive differences in the service needs of the middle aged (45 to 54 years of age) and the elderly, as well as the way these groups want their care to be delivered. For instance, because the needs of those between the ages of 45 and 54 tend to be more along the lines of body repair, these people desire health care that is convenient, cost effective, and customer oriented. On the other hand, the elderly's needs are more chronic and complex in nature. Therefore, these people simply desire "good health care" that is comprehensive and, more importantly, comfortable.[6] This vast demographic shift will thus require our health care system to be extremely flexible.

Therefore, the aging society will force a move toward the vertically integrated regional health system. Clearly, hospitals will treat more elderly people with chronic diseases in years to come, thus making the government an even more integral player in the health care field. The government is the big buyer in care for the elderly. Also, it is highly likely that the government will continue to search for *one* seller of services for a whole bundle of things. Therefore, because of the diversity and flexibility of these vertically integrated regional health systems, these systems will prevail.

### Technology

Technology has had a substantial impact on the health care system in recent years—and it is believed that this trend will continue. For example, the way things are done is constantly changing in order to provide the highest quality care possible. In recent years, there has been a significant decrease in the average length-of-stay in American hospitals due to the movement toward the most cost-effective outpatient procedures. In addition, the ability to do things on an ambulatory basis will provide an incentive for hospitals, who are losing inpatient business, to expand into ambulatory care, therefore becoming more vertically integrated.

These rapid advancements in technology have led to two significant trends, however. One noticeable trend, due to advancements in technology, is the fact that people are living longer. While many believe that there is ultimately a fixed life span (approximately 100 years of age), the challenge of the health care system is not to simply keep people alive longer, but to allow these people to remain productive longer.

The second significant trend that can be seen as a result of the technology advancements is the fact that patients entering the hospital today tend to be older, sicker, and, thus, need more specialized resources. It is

imperative that the health care system have the reserves to care for this more costly patient. Furthermore, because of the costs, the number of places that perform high-tech procedures and certain expensive diagnostics must be limited. Thus, because systems can more effectively cut down on this duplication, technology is also forcing a movement toward vertically integrated regional health systems.

### Human resources

Human resources will become increasingly vital to ensuring the future viability of health care organizations. For example, research shows that there has been a significant shift in the type of worker desired by health care organizations. One example is the demand for more registered nurses and, therefore, fewer aides. However, demographics reveal the fact that there is currently no growth in the 0 to 24 age group. Therefore, although the demand may be greater, the supply may not be there. As a result, recruiting efforts by health care organizations will become increasingly competitive. In addition, health care organizations may also find it necessary to train older workers, thereby encouraging independence among the older population. Therefore, health care organizations must meet the challenge of manpower self-sufficiency in order to ensure future success.[6]

Furthermore, people within the vertically integrated system have substantial career mobility within the system. For example, larger system organizations can often contain sufficient opportunities internally for those who prefer to enhance their skills and productivity without moving away from the geographic region. People in disparate organizations, on the other hand, have to move from organization to organization in different places around the country. This can ultimately limit the mobility and the motivation of those who do not want to move geographically in order to become more highly skilled and more productive.

The four key factors mentioned above—(1) health care costs, (2) demographics, (3) technology, and (4) human resources—are forcing the U.S. health care system down a one-way street that demands a movement toward a better, more comprehensive, more affordable system of delivering health care. To continue to operate as the U.S. health care system currently operates will simply prove to be too costly.

Although horizontal and vertical integration have taken place and can be seen in the health care environment, it is believed that horizontal integration has subsided and most likely very little of it will be seen in years to come. This is primarily due to the fact that opportunities for profits from a patient base increasingly constrained by DRGs, managed care, Health Care Financing Administration regulations regarding capital, and so forth, are declining. In other words, currently there is an oversupply in health care. Thus, as the buyers strive for bargains, natural buyer-seller behavior results. This ultimately causes the price to drop, therefore, negatively impacting the return on investment.

It is evident, however, that Humana is still expanding as a chain. It is important to mention here that they are doing so primarily by way of diversification. For example, they have gone into the managed care business as well. This allows one business to feed the other, thus enabling them to leverage off each of these resources internally. It is important to mention that, according to Brown and McCool, "from the standpoint of regional, vertically integrated care, larger horizontally related chain organizations need to be assessed by how well they work in each market rather than how they relate nationally."[4(p88,89)] Thus the goal for chains such as Humana should be to establish and maintain outstanding examples of vertically integrated regional systems within their overall organizations.

Finally, it has been observed by some that health care institutions left isolated in a region, including those now owned by national chains, will probably fail. According to Brown and McCool, "the ultimate test of effectiveness for the larger horizontally related chains will be how well they perform in building regional system linkages in and around their initial holdings in a particular market."[4(p88,89)] Thus, no strategic direction is more vitally important than the building of market share in multiple locations within a geographic region.

Currently, the situation exists in many cities where there are three, four, and even five hospitals that are similar in nature operating within a five-mile radius. Something needs to change or there will continue to be excess bed capacity, hospitals struggling to achieve positive operating margins, and wasted scarce resources.

Vertically integrated regional systems of health care will enable hospitals to achieve economies of scale through the reduction or elimination of duplication of services—except for certain high-volume, low-cost services. It is a move from the "medical disease treatment model to a comprehensive health care continuum that incorporates activity from prevention to follow-up care."[7(p32)]

Also important to mention is the actual savings that can be achieved in the vertically integrated regional health systems through the channeling of patients to fewer service sites. This is most directly applicable to tertiary-level services and high-cost diagnostics. This movement is imperative for the future viability of our health care system.

## FACTORS INHIBITING THE MOVEMENT TOWARD VERTICALLY INTEGRATED REGIONAL HEALTH SYSTEMS

While it appears inevitable that there will indeed be a movement toward vertically integrated regional health systems, thus far we have yet to really see this movement make great strides nationwide. The reason for this is simple. Currently, there are five, seemingly insurmountable, barriers that must be overcome in order for these systems to flourish.

### The Federal Trade Commission

The primary objective of antitrust laws is the promotion of free competition in the marketplace. Therefore, any attempts that are perceived to reduce this free competition are highly likely to be scrutinized by the Federal Trade Commission (FTC) and laws regarding antitrust. Specifically, the FTC is primarily concerned with the violation of both Section 7 of the Clayton Act, which prohibits anticompetitive acquisitions, and Section 2 of the Sherman Act, which prohibits monopolization. Multihospital arrangements of all types have been challenged by the FTC—most recently, hospital mergers.

Quality has become an issue of paramount importance in the health care field today. A major concern with the establishment of vertically integrated regional health systems is that they may create a monopoly situation that, in turn, may tend to promote laxness, if one accepts the theoretical benefits of competition.

It is apparent that the FTC views cooperation and coordination as antonyms for competition. As a result, laws geared to preserving competition in health care will continue to hinder the establishment of vertically integrated regional health systems.[8]

### Hospital autonomy

In order for vertically integrated regional health systems to achieve true economies of scale, it is imperative for the hospitals within this system to cooperate and act in good faith for the better of the system as a whole. The players in the system must think in terms of the "team," instead of individually. Because of the natural independence of health care providers, this line of thinking can prove to be quite uncomfortable.

According to Kinzer's *Twelve Laws of Hospital Interaction*, three laws, in particular, have played major roles in preventing the formation of a successful system.[9] For example, Kinzer states in his "Law of Proximate Polarity" that the "closer hospitals are geographically, the more likely that the main themes of their relationships will be mutual distrust, secretiveness, and competitiveness."[9(p17)] Thus, hospitals are more likely to cooperate and trust in each other only when they are miles apart.

Kinzer's "Law of Mutual Noncooperation" states that when "hospitals and other provider organizations are equals, or when their administrators think of their organizations as equals, their first instinct is to compete, not to share."[9(p18)] This contradicts that of the previously mentioned "team" line of thinking. Instead, with this way of thinking, as revenues and market share begin to be depleted while costs continually grow, the natural instinct is to intensify competition, share less information, and cooperate less.

Finally, Kinzer's "Law of Relative Inequality" states that "while there can be few systems consolidations of true equals, there are also serious hangups when you try to bring together unequals."[9(p18)] For instance, the larger hospitals within these systems may encounter opposition or competition from the other smaller health care organizations in the system, especially if these smaller entities perceive themselves as being treated unfairly or like a second-class citizen.

These laws reveal the fact that hospitals are naturally competitive and, thus, greatly value their autonomy. Unfortunately, vertically integrated regional health systems require a certain amount of interdependence among their members and will not succeed until this individualistic line of thinking can be overcome.

### Physician autonomy

Physicians, like hospitals, greatly value their autonomy. Physicians have always been aware of the power and influence of the hospital—particularly the financially strong, healthy hospital. Therefore, in order to offset this power and influence, physicians have, for the most part, been able to keep a strong hold on patient referrals and hospital-use patterns.

One of the major concerns of the movement toward vertically integrated regional health systems, however, is that this movement could enable institutions to "gain control of physicians through their ability to shift referrals among competing physician specialists and among competing hospitals."[10(p9)] Therefore, if only one vertically integrated set of services existed within a region, the physicians' leverage over hospitals would be greatly diminished, or even lost.

### Impact of the resource-based relative value scale

The resource-based relative value scale (RBRVS) was designed out of Congress's creation of the Physician Payment Review Commission (PPRC) as a means for physician payment reform. The PPRC, in a 1988 report to Congress, recommended that the usual/customary/reasonable system of physician payment be abolished in favor of a system that would "reward physicians for the resource costs, including time spent with patients, that physicians used in their practices."[11(p24)] Therefore, the main objective of this system is to increase reimbursement for primary care physicians (i.e., family practitioners and internists) at the expense of the specialist physicians (i.e., thoracic surgeons, radiologists, and pathologists).

This reform could have major implications on the movement toward vertically integrated regional health systems. For example, even before RBRVS came on-line, in January of 1992, physicians began moving services out of the hospital in order to offset anticipated income losses. As a result, hospitals not only face lower revenues, but it is quite possible that this could spark tension as they compete for services with their medical staffs. In addition, it has been suggested that RBRVS will also most likely affect the relationship between the primary care physicians and the specialists. According to many experts, the result will be an "intense scramble for a portion of the decreased Medicare pie."[12(p60)] Without complete cooperation between hospitals and physicians, and just as importantly, primary care physicians and specialists, the formation of a successful vertically integrated regional health system does not stand a chance.

### The patient

Because McMahon's saying, "Those who pay do not benefit, and those who benefit, do not pay (for health care)" is still primarily the truth, the patient is not typically an educated consumer of health services. Nevertheless, it is still important for health care organizations to gauge the quality of their services by the ultimate satisfaction of the patients they serve.

Therefore, the patient, too, may well be a barrier to the movement toward vertically integrated regional health systems. For example, one of the main disadvantages within these systems is that they require high mobility of a sick population. It is expected that patients will move through the system that provides a continuity of care. One of the requirements of a successful system is that the referral lines remain clear. Because it is highly unlikely that the members of the system will be located on one campus, this could cause a great inconvenience to the patients within the system. Therefore, it will remain a tremendous challenge for these systems to gain the support of an extremely integral part of the health care field—the patient.

An appropriate way of summing up the various obstacles that currently stand in the way of the movement toward vertically integrated regional health systems can be seen in Kinzer's "Law of Diffused Motivation." This law states that

> One problem frequently encountered in the hospital world is that, even when consultants report that consolidation is desirable or even a condition for survival and the report is supported by the hospital board, it should not be assumed that the proposal can be made acceptable to all of the vested interests involved. You start with institutional management that is nearly always threatened by consolidation. Then you get the lawyers into the act, bringing with them the specter of antitrust. Then there are the medical staff pecking orders and the subsurface rivalries of the physicians in the hospitals being consolidated. Similar concerns affect department heads and other employees. Beyond that, there are the auxiliaries and other volunteer groups that sometimes behave like social clubs, and you may have a situation where one hospital is unionized and the other is not, or they have contracts with different unions. It goes on from there.[9(p18)]

Therefore, while the movement toward vertically integrated regional health systems is imperative for the future viability of the health care system, until the previously mentioned barriers can be hurdled, the successes of these systems will never be realized.

## STRATEGIC CHARACTERISTICS OF THE VERTICALLY INTEGRATED REGIONAL HEALTH SYSTEM

In order for vertically integrated regional health care systems to become the model of the future, they must maintain a number of strategic characteristics. These strategic characteristics include the following:

*Accompanying the collapsing of management levels and combining of departments will come a streamlining of decision making.*

### Achieve economies of scale

Some believe that "no economies have ever been achieved in any of the major systems" and that the "cost of the system has always been greater than the sum of its parts." In the future, this must no longer be the case.[6] Thus, systems will move toward consolidation of management layers. One example of this might be through the combination of corporate functions (i.e., marketing and planning). Accompanying the collapsing of management levels and combining of departments will come a streamlining of decision making. It is important that decision making become more value added, or exhibit "greater perceived quality and improvement in health status for a given cost or lower cost for a given level of perceived quality and improvement in health status."[5]

### Physicians must be closely linked to the system

The physicians are the key link in all health care institutions—they control the use of most health care services. It is believed that multispecialty group practices will continue to be established within systems, as more physicians continue to align themselves with the institution in which they practice.[2] Several of these models, which are currently in place, illustrate this movement: Cleveland Clinic (Cleveland, Ohio), Geisinger Foundation (Danville, Pa.), Henry Ford Health System (Detroit, Mich.), Mayo Foundation (Rochester, Minn.), and Ochsner Foundation (New Orleans, La.). In addition, it will be important for these vertically integrated regional health systems to maintain one single organized medical staff throughout. This will aid in the promotion of a common culture and shared values among all components of the system.[13]

### Appropriate access to care must be achieved

A discrete geographically defined service area must be identified by the vertically integrated regional health system. It is imperative that the system "serve a large enough population to support the provision of the full scope of services and delivery settings in a manner allowing the system to operate cost effectively. On the other hand, the system should not serve populations so large as to make the system unmanageable."[13(p9)] It is also important that vertically integrated regional health systems continue to push out away from simply merging on one centralized campus, while at the same time, maintaining primary care feeder systems that link to the physicians. Physicians must understand the role of primary care versus specialty care. This will prove to be important in screening unnecessary referrals. Thus, these systems must have in place successful methods of providing timely access for patients with physician availability sufficient to avoid external referrals or the unnecessary use of emergency services.[2]

### Quality process management must emerge

Protocols and methodologies are already beginning to undergo rigorous testing in order to determine the most cost-efficient, effective ways of rendering care. Well-defined, standardized care protocols and clinical indicators may begin to be developed for systemwide use. Thus, physicians will be better equipped to monitor the performance of their peers and, as a result, take corrective action when necessary.[4] This will undoubtedly result in real economies of scale. In addition, it may prove to be even more beneficial if the system owns its own managed care program, which enables it to do its own quality review, its own utilization review, and ultimately develop its own protocols.

### Capitation as a method of financing health care

While capitation has traditionally been utilized as a cost-containment method or an alternative method of utilization management, capitation will become increasingly important due to the predictability of revenue. Therefore, physicians will be expected to know and understand managed care, or employ people who do.[2] Capitation for the total care makes a lot of sense. Ties between the physician capitation and the hospital capitation cross-guarantees efforts to work together. The hospital–physician relationship, as mentioned, is integral to the success of the vertically integrated regional health system.

### Focus on epidemiology must broaden

There is currently a recognized need to understand the characteristics of a given population (i.e., age, sex) and what effects these characteristics may create (i.e., morbidity, mortality). With knowledge of these characteristics, the organization can better anticipate patient mix, volume, and so forth. While it will continue to be important to remain informed about the patient mix in the particular service market, it will be necessary for leadership in regional systems to also become sensitive to the insurance market, outside regulation, and the attitudes of the employers in the region. Thus, most likely, more contractual relationships will emerge with these employers.[2]

### Recognition of the importance of manpower self-sufficiency

Recruitment among health care organizations is beginning to take place on a worldwide basis. In addition, because of the age composition, an increased emphasis will be placed on independence among the elderly. This will be reflected through the training of older workers by many health care organizations. Vertically integrated regional health systems must have the ability to utilize these people who are not ready to retire just because they have reached the age of 65. In addition, the aging of the population will most likely cause an increase in the desire of regional health systems to affiliate with colleges and universities in order to ensure the availability to health manpower.[6] For example, "the ability to maintain strong graduate medical education programs contributes significantly toward the system's continued ability over time to bring physicians into the system to meet physician personnel needs."[13(p13)]

### More emphasis placed on the customer

Regional health systems need to realize and understand and be able to successfully focus on the needs of their service community. With the understanding that, while the physician drives the system, it is the patient or customer who drives the physician, marketing departments within these systems will begin to focus more on the customer. Because of the close ties between the physician and the system, a customer-focused environment can be realized. Thus, customer relations shall be enhanced as the entire system becomes service oriented.[6]

### Diversification must be emphasized

Finally, diversification of services within the health system will be a key factor in the development of the whole continuum of care. This continuum is important in aiding the patient during health, sickness, and even when death is evident. The vertically integrated regional health system that can effectively diversify its services in order to meet a broader, yet still manageable, range of patients, will be most successful.

● ● ●

The movement in health care is clearly toward vertically integrated regional health systems. These regional health systems will emerge as the big winners in the health care industry. As a matter of fact, some believe that competition will be defined in the future by competition among major regional systems—not between individual institutions (i.e., hospitals).[4] Therefore, individual institutions will begin attempting to merge to become part of larger regional systems of health care in order to better compete, if not survive. Fortunately, the American people will reap the benefits of this more effective system of health care that concentrates on access, effectiveness, efficiency, appropriateness, quality, and service.

## REFERENCES

1.  American Hospital Association. Special Committee on the Provision of Health Services. "The Perloff Report." *Hospitals* 44(1970): 43–47.

2.  Warden, G. "The Evolution of Regional Health Systems and Their Role in the 1990s." Duke University, Durham, NC, August 1989.

3.  Toomey, R.E. "Colloquium on Hospital System Organizational Structure." Duke University, Durham, NC, August 1989.

4.  Brown, M., and McCool, B.P. "Health Care Systems: Predictions for the Future." *Health Care Management Review* 15, no. 3 (1990): 87–94.

5.  Shortell, S.M., Morrison, E.M., and Friedman, B. "Key Requirements for Success in a Changing Health Care Environment." *Strategic Choices for America's Hospitals.* San Francisco, Calif.: Jossey-Bass, 1990.

6.  Goldman, E. "Vision 2000: A View of the Emerging Delivery System." American College of Healthcare Executives: 34th Congress on Administration, Chicago, Ill., February 11–15, 1991.

7.  Philbin, P.W. "How to Replace a Health System." *Modern Healthcare* (June 1991): 32.

8.  MacStravic, R.E. "Many Benefits Possible with Vertical Integration." *Hospitals* (December 1979): 67–70.

9.  Kinzer, D.M. "Twelve Laws of Hospital Interaction." *Health Care Management Review* 15, no. 2 (1990): 15–19.

10. Brown, M., and McCool, B.P. "Vertical Integration: Exploration of a Popular Strategic Concept." *Health Care Management Review* 11, no. 4 (1986): 7–19.

11. Hagland, M.M. "The RBRVS and Hospitals: The Physician Payment Revolution on Our Doorstep." *Hospitals* (February 1991): 24–27.

12. Johnsson, J. "RBRVS: Execs Defuse Touchy Med Staff Issues." *Hospitals* (April 1991): 60.

13. Gottlieb, S.R. *Restructuring the Health Care Delivery System: Integrated Regional Health Care Systems.* Detroit, Mich.: Greater Detroit Area Health Council, 1989.

# HCMR perspective: The Economic Era of health care

Richard L. Johnson

The current deep public interest in reforming the nation's health care system has its roots going back to the turn of the 20th century. Over the course of decades, health care has gone from a hospital setting of caring for the sick and dying to a loosely coordinated system of ambulatory and hospital services. This is a valued activity regarded as so important that it is now a necessity and must be available to all individuals. The unquestioned desirability of having immediate access to health care stands as a testament to both physicians and hospitals. The nonavailability of health care services is no longer acceptable to the public.

An avalanche of health care proposals has been unleashed on the public, not only at the federal level but also by state governments as well. In addition, purchasers of health care have formed coalitions at the local level, companies have become self-funded for health care, and third-party carriers have developed new and innovative financial arrangements for contracting for health care. Clearly, a new era in health care is underway that is evolutionary and builds on the shoulders of the two previous eras.

## THE CHARITABLE ERA

Over the past century, acute hospitals have gone through two evolutionary phases and currently are in the early stages of a third phase. The first phase began at the turn of the 20th century, and can be labeled the "Charitable Era." It lasted for approximately 50 years, ending shortly after World War II. During that period, hospitals became recognized by the public as institutions that could provide care, alleviating some illnesses, and were needed as a community resource. In turn, various religious groups recognized that owning and operating hospitals was in keeping with the Ministry of Healing. Even hospitals that were nonreligious recognized a community responsibility to provide care and were organized as nonprofit entities. It was believed that a hospital had a responsibility to care for all who needed hospitalization. The theme of charitable services dominated the development of nonprofit hospitals. Because of the economic depression of the 1930s, the need for providing charity care by hospitals was reinforced, and fund-raising drives by hospitals emphasized the role of charity. If deficits

*Richard L. Johnson*, M.B.A., is President, TriBrook Group, Westmont, Illinois.

occurred, board members were expected to make up the difference.

## THE TECHNOLOGICAL ERA

Following World War II, advances in medical technology began to make themselves felt in hospitals. Specialization in clinical fields led an increasing number of medical school graduates to seek additional training in residency programs, which accelerated the transformation of the nonprofit hospital from a charitable institution into a technological enterprise. Accompanying these clinical developments was the rapid introduction of management systems into hospitals, as the result of graduate-level education in health care organization and management. As more and more professional health care executives joined the ranks of hospital management, financial operations were tightened and budgets were put in place. Governing boards no longer relied on donations and fund-raising drives. At the same time, the amount of charity became more tightly controlled as management was faced with larger and larger capital expenditures in order to keep up with the growing sophistication of technology. By the end of the 1980s, the transformation had taken place—hospitals had become technological enterprises, still nonprofit, but organizationally behaving as any large corporate entity.

During the evolutionary stage of technological development, charity care was replaced substantially with two federal programs (Medicare and Medicaid) designed to pay for hospital care on behalf of the elderly, as well as those who were poor and needy. Because these two programs do not now pay the full cost of care to hospitals, these patients are subsidized by charging higher than cost to patients who are either self-pay or covered by commercial insurance. In a very real sense, charity care was replaced by cost shifting in hospitals. Knowing their costs and revenues in a detailed manner, hospitals were able to keep up with the required capital expenditures through larger and larger bottom lines.

By the time 1990 rolled around, the second evolutionary phase was winding down. Hospitals had become technological enterprises funding capital expansion through the debt market. Public fund-raising drives were no longer a significant source of capital. Capital needs and balanced budgets had become the driving force. Management had responded with larger and larger bottom lines and larger and larger cash reserves that made the bond market comfortable

in making loans for ever-increasing amounts to nonprofit hospitals.

There were telltale signs that had begun to develop. Signs of things to come had really begun in the 1980s. Ten percent of the acute beds were owned and operated by for-profit health care companies. By 1990, these companies used not only debt for expansion but also relied heavily on equity markets. In addition, managed care was becoming a household concept as more and more companies turned away from commercial insurance and traditional Blue Cross plans. As this trend continued, physicians began forming independent practice associations (IPAs) and preferred provider organizations (PPOs), where groups of physicians would offer discounted rates to large bloc purchasers of health care. As the hew and cry from corporations, individuals, and government grew louder about the ever-increasing cost of health care premiums, organized efforts developed among payors concerned with limiting the annual price rises they were experiencing.

## THE ECONOMIC ERA OF COMPETITION

By 1990, the third era had developed enough steam so that it could be identified as "Consolidation and Competition." This era is now in its early stages. Its hallmark will be economic enterprises built on top of the foundation of medical care that, in turn, developed out of charitable concerns. The day of the freestanding hospital and the solo practitioner is now being replaced with systems of hospitals and group practices of physicians as they aggregate their services. The "Mom and Pop" era of health care is rapidly drawing to a close. As might be expected at this stage of development, a variety of approaches is being taken that will likely end up with the same outcome. Down the road, 15 to 20 years from now, it can be anticipated the end result will be a for-profit organized delivery system (ODS). It will be composed of hospitals, primary care physicians, specialists, and a prepayment plan. Since physicians' practices are for-profit, the emerging ODSs will adopt this form of corporate organization because of the central role of physicians. While such a system will be focused at a local level, it may have an overreaching prepayment arm that encompasses a number of local organized delivery systems as part of the same corporation. Since large multibillion dollar health care corporations lie years ahead for many communities, the intervening years will be filled with an array of differing organizational attempts to become larger and more encompassing.

## THE DRIVING FORCE

The driving force in health care is competition brought about by the underlying economics, not by inadequacies in the ability to provide satisfactory medical diagnosis and treatment. In this new era, those paying for health care have a major interest in limiting expenditures. Those providing health care services have a desire to retain existing profit margins but the initiative has, for the moment, been taken by those paying for care. Business corporations have concluded that their best method for limiting premium expenditures is to offer large blocs of care for bidding on a competitive basis. As a result, corporations have a preference for signing health care contracts with prepayment organizations, which offer managed care options utilizing primary care physicians as gatekeepers. Having determined that this approach has economic advantages to the buyer, corporate purchasers have recently begun to express interest in having providers bid for contracts that combine both professional services and hospital care into one price for an episode of illness. This is now leading payors to push for paying a monthly amount per subscriber to providers. By capitating providers, the economic risk is borne by those providing health care service; the payors' own economic exposure is limited. The desired end result by the payor is to be able to control all elements of the payment for health care service. For this to be successful requires hospitals and physicians to ultimately become a closed staff model.

Bypassed in the race to develop widespread capitation plans is the concept of rehooking the episode of illness with some degree of patient economic responsibility for the care that is sought. Instead, the providers are collectively made financially responsible for the services provided, and the patient has none as long as the monthly subscriber rate is paid. The theory for this approach is that providers will be forced to reduce costs because they are at economic risk. Also implied is that the quality of care and its availability will remain, at least, at existing levels. Whether this occurs or not is an open question.

Developing a series of events culminating at a closed system end point is unlikely in most communities. It will take place in major cities where giant prepayment organizations will do battle with each other for market share. Hospitals and physician groups will be pawns in a high-stakes prepayment game. Even if in the next few years hospitals link together in affiliated groups and physicians form large multispecialty groups, they will be no economic match for prepayment organizations controlling hundreds of millions of premium dollars annually.

In smaller cities the pattern is likely to be less structured and will never reach the end stage found in major metropolitan centers. As physicians recognize that managed care is on their doorstep, events can be expected to transpire rapidly in even small towns and cities, but in varying organizational relationships. Competition between managed care plans is apt to be missing because of insufficient volume, leaving the playing field up to competing physician groups or competing hospitals.

## THE NEW BUZZ WORDS

At present, the buzz words in popular usage are "managed competition" and "collaboration." The belief among those paying for health care services is that managed competition offers the best solution for effectively blunting annual premium increases in health care coverage. Recognizing the overwhelming interest in this subject, health care providers are busily developing collaborative arrangements so as to be able to provide "seamless" care when bidding on managed care contracts. The need to develop solid working relationships between hospitals and physicians is being defined as a collaborative process, one in which both parties recognize a mutual dependence on each other. This movement into a PHO, or into a variation of it as an ODS, illustrates where hospitals and physicians are joining together because they both see the need for doing so for economic survival. Among many hospitals and medical staffs this is a voluntary arrangement in response to the marketplace. To date, sufficient thought has not been given as to how to hold these parties together when bidding conditions become difficult and revenues more scarce. In the

*The need to develop solid working relationships between hospitals and physicians is being defined as a collaborative process, one in which both parties recognize a mutual dependence on each other.*

rough and tumble of a competitive environment where economic stakes become higher and higher, the need quickly will surface for binding contractual relationships between the parties to the PHO or ODS. Penalty clauses will become part and parcel of these structures so as to assure a continuation of the ability to service the contracts obtained from prepayment organizations or self-insured corporations.

In the decades since World War II, the health field has not experienced widespread conditions where there are winners and losers. Physicians and hospitals have long been accustomed to being winners with no losers, which makes learning to live in a competitive environment a difficult lesson since hospitals and physicians have lived in a risk-free environment. The major determinants have been only with whether they were big winners or little winners. In the unfolding health care environment there is expected to be a surplus of both specialist physicians and hospital beds, leaving a considerable imbalance between supply and demand among these providers. This disparity gives purchasers a golden opportunity to exploit this imbalance for their own economic interests. It can be anticipated that a "shake-out" among providers will occur, causing many internal tensions and disputes between the partners in a PHO or ODS.

In a truly competitive environment, the purchaser is unconcerned with the fallout of providers. As long as there remains a sufficient number of hospitals and physicians to provide acceptable levels of service, the focus will remain economic. As a result, alliances and affiliations, which are weak organizational structures, will break apart as each member strives to develop its own marketing strategy in order to survive. Penalties for breaking away from an alliance or an affiliation will be insignificant in comparison to the potential loss of revenues and the consequences that result.

## MARKET CAPACITY

In a marketplace with excess capacity, the aggregation of providers into large economic units is an important strategy because size increases clout. By itself, it is not enough. Within a provider organizational structure, the ties binding the various parts together must be strong, so as to withstand the internal tensions that inevitably will arise as a result of having far more suppliers of services in the marketplace than demand for services.

When in responding to a request for a proposal from a managed care organization or a self-funded

plan it is evident that a successful bid must be below current cost of operations; it should be anticipated that physician providers will expect the hospital to take the necessary hit. Likewise, the hospital may expect its partner, the physicians, to be the losers. This type of internal tension, if it is to be dealt with successfully, requires not only strong leadership, but also requires having in place known and significant economic penalties. All of the provider participants must understand the price to be paid if they fail to accommodate to the realities of the marketplace.

While it is important at this stage of consolidated competition to form these collaborative provider organizations, reliance cannot be based on the goodwill of the parties. Goodwill merely opens the door to the formation of the PHO or ODS. Once a PHO enters the competitive marketplace, the leadership needs to have the authority to commit the organization, even in circumstances that may not be desirable. To have to continue to rely on the goodwill of participants as the only organizational mechanism for securing acceptance of necessary negotiating decisions in a tough marketplace likely will result in a breaking apart of the provider organization.

## THE BEST ROUTE

Fundamental to much of the thinking going on about health care is the widespread belief that managed competition offers the best route, which has led to a rush among providers who fear they may be left out when the new health care system falls into place. The providers, physicians and hospitals, are assuming the marketplace will be the balancing mechanism between the available supply of physicians, hospital beds, and the demand for these services. However, the putting together of the provider pieces has many variations based on economic perceptions. Quite often, physicians do not view the hospital as a partner of choice, preferring to deal only with physicians. Specialists, when confronted with managed care, quickly appreciate that primary care physicians control the flow of patients and become anxious about assuring a continuation of referrals from their primary care sources. This may lead to an attempt to form multispecialty groups, locking up primary care physicians as part of the same physician organizations. Putting existing practices into one physician corporation requires considerable capital funds that go beyond the financial capabilities of many specialist organizers and, therefore, may reluctantly lead them back to the inclusion of the hospital into the same corporation.

In some communities, primary care physicians may elect to form their own corporation and take capitation, but exclude specialists from joining the group. By having control of capitation, primary care physicians are in a position to dictate the terms under which they will use selected specialists. This may take the form of asking specialists to bid for contracts and keeping them at arm's length. In addition, a group of primary care physicians, or a combination of primary care and specialist physicians acting as a PPO, might elect to seek competitive bids from hospitals and then contract with the lowest bidder. To do so would put the PPO into the position of taking the risk not just for physician services but for hospitals as well—a difficult position in the event that hospitals successfully refuse capitation and opt for a per diem or a per case method of payment.

At the present stage of development, the efforts of hospitals and physicians are being directed toward finding partners and developing arrangements that will enable providers to bid on managed care contracts, either from a federally sponsored program, a state initiative, a local business coalition, or an existing carrier offering a managed care option. Putting together provider health care conglomerates is the immediate focus of attention and will continue for the next few years.

At the moment, there is much jockeying for the best position among the providers. Specialists are trying to capture primary care physicians so as to protect their referral patterns; primary care physicians are just recognizing their pivotal role and are attempting to avoid capture by the other providers while, at the same time, maximizing their new-found economic value. Hospitals are seeking to use their economic strength to build systems that will enable them to grow and prosper. Underneath all of these efforts by providers is a recognition, shared by the payors for health care services, that fundamental changes are needed. While there may be serious differences of opinion about how best to achieve the needed changes, there is agreement that matters need changing.

## NEEDED CHANGES

Providers and payors generally agree on the following:
- guaranteed access for all persons;
- minimum standard of benefits for all;
- need for a standard reporting form;
- choice of physician and hospital, but perhaps limited by choice of plan;
- preexisting conditions not leading to denial of coverage;
- need to protect existing standards of quality of care and, to the extent possible, to improve them; and
- desirability of rehooking an episode of illness with a degree of economic consequences, but using capitation as a substitute method for achieving this result.

The root of the problem is not with the quality of care, but rather with paying for and financing health care. The issue is economic—the provider wants to protect income, the payor wants to limit expenditures. In addition, providers have an additional set of problems as they view the growth of managed care. Hospitals appreciate that managed care plans reduce patient days per thousand population, which leads to a need for fewer and fewer inpatient beds and a reduction, ultimately, in the number of hospitals. Specialists, 70 percent of all practicing physicians, are well aware that managed care uses substantially fewer specialists, and there will be an overabundance in specialty fields. On the other hand, primary care physicians recognize that they are increasingly in short supply and stand to gain economically under managed care. Even though the issues center on economics, the providers have a legitimate concern about how economics may impact their ability to provide care.

## CONSEQUENCES OF ILL–FOUNDED ECONOMICS

A prevailing concept among payors of health care is that annual increases have to be reined in for the cost of coverage. Unspoken is the belief that this can be accomplished without a lowering of quality of care or less access to medical care. A belief that quality and access are not affected by restricting payments to providers is akin to believing in the tooth fairy.

In bringing economics to the forefront in health care, both government and third-party payors are focusing their interest on restricting payments to providers, with a variety of approaches being tried. At the federal level, payments to hospitals have, over time, shifted from cost reimbursement to per diems to per case payments. The current administration is now proposing capitation with overall control of expenditures at the national level through caps on monthly premiums. At the same time, managed care plans are resorting to seeking competitive bids for large blocs of patients.

With increasing frequency, the concept of "managed competition" is gaining favor. Seemingly unrecognized is that when competition is managed, it is no longer competition. Managed competition, as a concept, implies controls or limits. The "unseen hand of the marketplace" is no longer unseen, but rather has a defined boundary. Where the boundary is set determines the economics that apply. If the boundary is set too low and a hospital cannot stay within the limit, this leads to a disruption of market forces, which is already a problem with the Medicare and Medicaid programs where payments are substantially below the operating costs of hospitals. Even though this is true, the administration has indicated it wishes to further reduce projected spending levels in excess of $200 billion over the next few years for these two programs.

With rapid growth in managed care, the application of a boundary will drastically impact institutional decisions, which may not be in accord with public expectations. It should not be assumed by payors that existing quality of care standards will remain at present levels, nor can it be assumed that hospitals and physicians will provide unrestricted access in the event that the established boundary is below operating cost levels. Up to now, hospitals have accepted Medicare and Medicaid below operating cost levels because they could cost shift to other payors. However, as the percentage of patients grows under managed care, hospitals will have less and less opportunity to use this method and the need to make tough decisions will have arrived. Likewise, physicians will be making equally tough decisions.

## CAPITATION

With capitation as the likely method of payment for primary care physicians, two behavior patterns may emerge. Since capitation pays a primary care physician a fixed monthly amount per subscriber, whether or not a medical service is provided, a physician will be inclined to work only a set number of hours per day per week, since the amount of money received is the same whether the physician works 40 hours per week or 60 hours per week. With primary care physicians now in short supply and the shortage continu-

*Under capitation, the physician enjoys no economic reward for working 12 to 14 hours per day, or 6 to 7 days per week.*

ing indefinitely, the end result will be longer and longer queue lines for patient appointments. Unless a patient is truly an emergency the primary care physician probably is going to develop 9 to 5 practice hours. Under capitation, the physician enjoys no economic reward for working 12 or 14 hours per day, or 6 or 7 days per week.

The other behavior pattern occurs when the capitation payment to a primary care physician is less than what may be paid from another source, such as self-pay or a more liberal health insurance payment policy. The capitated patients will have longer waiting times. Patients covered by the more liberal payment plans will be given preference and their waiting times will be less than those covered by capitation. Should the physician employ a nurse practitioner, capitated patients may have to clear that hurdle before being seen by the physician, while those with preferred payment sources may not have to see the nurse practitioner. Removing the economic incentive that is a built-in part of fee-for-service medicine takes away the economic reason for working 60 or 70 hours per week. Since the mean number of hours worked per week by a family practitioner has been 58.5 hours and for general medicine 62.2 hours per week,[1] a decision to reduce work hours to 40 hours per week would require an additional one-third to the supply of primary care physicians.

Capitation has a downside for hospitals. In a competitive marketplace where capitation dominates, conventional wisdom is that putting hospitals at risk for their services economically benefits the public. While this is true, it is true only to the extent that the economics of "going at risk" are stable, over a period of several years. Where capitation has been successful and hospital utilization has fallen dramatically from one year to the next, the hospital is unlikely to retain the same capitation rate from one year to the next. It is safe to assume that if a hospital is under contract with a managed care organization and has provided less services or cared for fewer patients in a given year the managed care plan will, at the end of the contract period, adjust the capitation rate downward.

## CAPITATION THROUGH CONTRACTS

The ideal model for capitation is usually envisioned as a managed care plan, hospital services, specialists, and primary care physicians all in one economic unit. However, when all of these components are contract services with the managed care plan the economics are not the same. With separate contracts, the hospital is in no position to affect the use of its facilities since the volume is controlled by physicians whose economic interests are not the same as the hospital's.

When capitation is the basis of payment to providers, the payor can ignore the volume of services provided and their cost. The responsibility for determining volume of activities is divided among the various providers. Implicit in capitation is the assumption that enough dollars are being paid to the providers so that they can render adequate care if they judiciously use health care resources. This is a more workable plan when the component parts—hospital, primary care physicians, specialists, and prepayment plans—are all in the same corporation. As an integrated entity, whatever is financially adverse for one of the components carries over to the corporate whole as well. But where the linkages between the components are by contract, the economies are markedly different. As long as a hospital could engage in cost shifting, the problem of inadequate payment was ameliorated, but when the point is reached that average cost, instead of marginal cost, must be applied, reality has to be faced.

## RISK SHIFTING

When a managed care plan contracts for hospitals, primary care physicians, and specialists, the risk is totally shifted away and becomes a responsibility of the providers. The only risks to the managed care plan are complaints about provider services. If enough complaints are made by enrollees about the ways in which they are treated, the managed care plan may have to consider contracting with other providers at contract renewal time. If only the same restricted choices are open to the managed care plan, they may be forced to increase their capitated rates in order to re-attract providers. However, when an offered capitated rate is below the average cost for providing service, it can be anticipated that providers will bid in anticipation of providing only minimum services. Where the managed care plan offers contracts with stipulated outside maximum limits, those bidding will first ascertain if the boundary permits a reasonable rate of return. If

not, the responses to the bid will treat the maximum limit as a minimum, and all bids received will be at the outside limit, if bid at all.

To the extent that providers are paid for services through controlled fees by the federal government, past experience with Medicare and Medicaid programs indicates that the managed competition limits will be set by federally driven budgets and not by quality of care concerns. It is likely that federally set boundaries will lead the way for nongovernmental payors as well. Under such circumstances, hospitals would be forced into taking a number of steps that may include

- drawing down cash reserves,
- deferring capital expenditures,
- using nonoperating revenues to meet operating expenses,
- reducing the number of personnel,
- reducing fringe benefits of employees, and
- improving control of nonpersonnel operating expenses.

These steps present both opportunities and difficulties. Where hospitals can improve on efficiencies, the payment system will be used as the justification for doing so. On the other hand, difficulties will occur in those hospitals where the intensity of illness has steadily risen over several years. Intensity factors primarily affect nursing service so that significant increases in intensity should be reflected in growth in the number of nursing hours per patient day, with a commensurate increase in nursing salary costs. However, when revenues have bumped up against a ceiling and no further revenues are in sight, the only choice open is to hold the line on costs and let the quality of care slip.

Under capitation, the intensity of illness factor is likely to escalate at an even more rapid rate than it has over the past few years because inpatients are likely to be more ill than at present, due to the effort of keeping patients out of the hands of specialists and hospitals. When admitted, patients will *really* be ill and require more services, not less. Since nursing is a hands-on activity, it will lead to serious consequences as physicians express concern about the safety of their patients.

## THE TIES THAT BIND

Where the ties that bind primary care physicians, specialists, and hospitals to a managed care plan are separate capitation contracts, the ability to cope with risk is seriously flawed. At its heart, the use of capitation assumes the volume of services provided can be standardized and controlled to predictable levels. A corollary assumption is that by the use of economic penalties any deviations beyond the established boundaries will result in corrections to bring unanticipated surges in volume back to established norms. The benchmarks typically being used are those of managed care plans that have used capitation for many years, such as Kaiser-Permanente. In attempting to achieve similar results it needs to be remembered that not only is Kaiser-Permanente a single economic unit but it has a common culture about medical care that has evolved over decades.

In the development stages of a PHO or ODS, no such culture exists. Physicians in solo practice, small single specialty groups, or small multispecialty groups lack familiarity with budgeted volumes of activities and will expect the management of the hospital to deal with the financial aspects of overages. As all providers have separate contracts with the managed care plan, no one contractual party feels fiscal responsibility for the other contractual parties if they encounter economic problems with their capitated rates. The unaffected may be, and probably will be, sympathetic to the beleaguered partner and may take what steps they believe are reasonable, but without seriously affecting their own financial status. In this type of situation, it is not the responsibility of the contractual partners to bail out the one that may be in financial trouble.

## CONCLUSIONS

Now that the health field has commenced its journey into the "Economic Era," the question is whether or not concerns about cost and access will replace the long-standing goals of quality, comprehensiveness, and availability of medical care. If cost and access become paramount, will the present standards of care be maintained? To date, there appears to be a general belief that if all of the health care eggs are put in the capitation basket the problem of escalating costs will be contained while maintaining adequate access and quality of care. This belief is fostered by the history of the last 100 years, from the Charitable Era, through the Technological Era, to the present early stages of the Economic Era. It is an unparalleled success story that is expected to continue. Physicians have been the driving force who have, for decades, consistently placed the obtaining of solid clinical results ahead of

cost. For generations physicians have been taught, and have put into practice, placing the patient's well-being first and leaving the financial aspects of care to be handled at the end of the episode of illness.

Recognized or not, that premise is under challenge. Capitation requires the physician to balance clinical judgments with economic realities. In effect, capitation states, "Doctor, do whatever you believe is clinically necessary but, understand, the costs incurred are not the responsibility of the patient or the managed care plan. It is your responsibility because you have accepted a fixed amount of money each month in return for care, whenever needed, and in whatever amount is required."

In this relationship, the providers bear all of the risk and the prepayment organization is primarily a conduit for funds. Over time, this will turn out to be an unsatisfactory relationship because the risk is too one-sided. When the one-sided relationship becomes widely recognized among providers, they are likely to terminate their relationship with the managed care plan and form their own plan, or they may be bought up by the managed care plan and form one economic unit. In either approach, the cost of forming the new organizational relationship will require a major commitment of capital dollars in order to align the components in a way that maximizes profits for those involved in ownership, as well as creating a more efficient system.

If, in working out these arrangements, it is necessary to raise equity money (which is likely) the leverage for influencing the decisions of the newly formed organization is most likely to shift from Main Street to Wall Street. When that takes place, the emphasis will move from a concern for community good to a concern for shareholder dividends. Large amounts of money will be involved, including both assets and revenue streams that will make health care increasingly attractive to the financial world. Table 1 demonstrates why this will take place.

If 15 percent is taken off of the top for administrative costs, taxes, reserves, and profits, this will amount to $63 million per year. When for-profit organizations have a spill off of that amount of money, it will attract equity investors. Results of this magnitude will be possible on an enrolled population base between 400,000 and 500,000 persons. On a population base of 250 million, the potential for the country as a whole is 500 times greater, or approximately $2.1 trillion of revenue and a 15 percent margin of $31.5 billion.

**TABLE 1**

MANAGED CARE PLAN "X"

| Number of participants | Premium/month | Premium/year | Annual total premium |
|---|---|---|---|
| 100,000 families | $300 | $3,600 | $360M |
| 50,000 singles | $100 | $1,200 | $ 60M |
| 150,000 | | | $420M |

The conclusions are indeed obvious. Since the magnitude of potential profits is going to attract a great deal of attention, whatever organization controls the premium revenue dollars is going to control the provider resources. And if the controlling organization is for-profit and, therefore, has shareholders, community good will take a back seat to dividends. Such a thought is an anathema to many who have devoted their careers and lifetime efforts to nonprofit hospitals. However, it is a possibility that must be realistically faced.

The tide of change is sweeping the health care field into uncharted waters. If the providers find themselves excluded from the overall decisions being made by either government or the financial world and do not take the initiative to control or substantially influence what takes place, the end result will be a disillusioned public. To date, the existing health care system is one that has been shaped by the providers. Tomorrow, the health care system is most likely to be shaped by government and investors seeking dividends. Controlling cost and increasing access to health care may well be achieved but the price for achieving these results will be paid by the public. They will have to deal with a provider system that has been forced to respond to a drummer not of its choosing. Instead of patients' needs coming first, the demands of government and investors will take over and patients will come to realize the health care system as they knew it no longer exists.

Finally, the question of the inevitability of this outcome needs to be addressed. Are there alternatives that might be possible? If providers continue to put their own specialized interests first and are willing to sacrifice provider partners on the alter of economic gain to themselves, then the interests of the payors will prevail. But if providers are able to put aside their differences and develop meaningful relationships with users of health care services, they may find a way to protect the values that the public has come to appreciate. To be successful, primary care physicians, specialists, and hospitals need to put together meaningful organizations that engender employer and public support. This will be a tough task requiring more determination, greater flexibility, and a heightened awareness of the consequences if failure results.

The odds are against the providers laying aside all of their differences and developing meaningful dialogues with business coalitions, self-funded corporation plans, and other user groups. The odds favor those with large amounts of money and deep pockets that come from revenue streams of monthly premium payments by many subscribers in capitated plans.

It is too early to determine the outcome. A decade from now we will know who won and who lost.

## REFERENCE

1. "Hours in All Professional Activities Per Week" (Table 2). *Physician Marketplace Statistics, 1992.* Chicago, Ill.: American Medical Association, 1992, p. 11.

# Commentary: The Economic Era: Now to the real change

Montague Brown
Editor
*Health Care Management Review*

*Health Care Manage Rev*, 1994, 19(4), 73–81
© 1994 Aspen Publishers, Inc.

**Richard Johnson presented** three essays on his views on the changing world of health care organizations, especially as it applies to hospitals and physicians. I elected to respond to those essays with another point of view and, beginning with this second essay, asked another editorial board member to respond to both of us. With this essay and response, several reviewers have been asked to join in the discussion. With this second dialogue, we get up to the very modern world which is well into the economic transformation of American medicine. (Johnson's third essay, "Hospital Governance in a Competitive Environment," appeared in *HCMR* 20:1, Winter 1995.)

As this article is being written, the politicians seeking to pass Clinton's health care package are saying that they want everyone to have what Senator Mitchell, Ms. Clinton, and Senator Dole have: guaranteed "private" health insurance to provide access to health care. In the same breath they are saying that the President supports using private health insurance and managed care as a way to provide this kind of care. The tooth fairy is loose again. If every American had what President and Ms. Clinton have, our national health bill would double. No, Mr. and Ms. America, managed care via capitation means rationing of access. No longer will providers speak of high quality. They will speak of acceptable quality, affordability, and essential care—not care on demand. We are indeed well into this "Economic Era." We have gone far, with farther to go yet. Richard Johnson recounts how we moved here. Much of what he recounts is easy to agree with. Much more, however, needs to be explored if we are to fully grasp the meaning of this shift.

## FROM ALMS HOUSES AND TECHNOLOGICAL MARVELS TO BUSINESSES

Johnson notes the shift of medical services and hospitals moving from sick houses for the poor operated by the wealthy to technological marvels whose services are demanded by everyone and sold in the marketplace by national firms whose stock is traded daily on Wall Street. Wall Street is a rock-solid American institution whose goal is old-fashioned profits expected by every successful business. As we move down this road to rationing health care, managed care firms fueled by Wall Street equity and debt will prosper. They meet the need for business and government to offer choice while at the same time constraining resource use. Voluntary hospitals and their trustees will be ill-equipped to ration care, given their bedrock value of succoring the poor while lavishing compassionate, high-tech care on all, and all the while being reimbursed whatever it cost. Paradigms may shift but institutions rarely adapt. More than likely they will be replaced. Not many buggy companies became automobile firms. Rail firms rarely see themselves in the transportation business. Old concepts are, in reality, straitjackets.

In the course of this transition from alms houses to technological marvels and now into the economic era, health insurance shifted from a pass-through mechanism and insurance mechanism to one where utilization is aggressively managed and controlled and competitively priced in a manner that determines the providers who get to provide services to which patients. Further, the controls also determine when, where, and how patients may get services, if and when they are to be provided. In very little time, we have moved light years from patients choosing whichever doctor and hospital they desire when they so choose. Federal employees may be able to keep this benefit, but for the rest of America it will be rationing time, big time.

Johnson points out that charity care was replaced by cost shifting. This is true in the sense that the alms house was all charity. But as the poor and the paying went to the same hospital, cost shifting has always been the major mode of financing charity care. And, cost shifting continues today; governments cost shift to employers, and large employers in turn shift cost to small employers, who in turn cost shift to individual buyers. Little wonder that we have an insurance and financing crisis. Managed care, whether Clinton Regular or Clinton Lite, will leave this cost shifting in place. Economic muscle counts, and the government has the biggest clout. Maybe we would all be better off going into either Medicare or the Federal Employees Health Benefit Plan. At least our bargainer would be able to shift to those who shun good, old-fashioned government care. The woes of the postal system notwithstanding, government health care might be preferable. If we are going to have managed care either way, why not use the profits to reduce the national debt rather than have it go to Wall Street (and thus to greedy investors like us)?

Johnson points to 1990 as the time when capital needs and balanced budgets became driving forces in hospitals. I would place that date more nearly to the late-1960s and mid-1970s when Medicare and Medicaid "promised" to pay for the care of all or most of the needy. Remember that during those early days Congress acted like health care was a right, even though they never got around to funding it as such. Once debt financing was well established in the 1970s, voluntary hospitals were captive to the financial ratio analysis of bond rating agencies. If hospitals wanted access to debt capital operating and financial ratios, they had to follow a business pattern. For boards of directors of many successful hospitals, bond ratings are exceedingly important indicators of success.

Some, of course, attribute the advent of the economic era of hospitals to the development of the investor-owned chain. While this was a factor, the debt financing of not-for-profit hospitals did much to ensure this shift. Ironically, many of the innovations in financing of not-for-profit hospitals are attributable to the financial ingenuity of these investor-owned chains.

During the 1980s, a business or economic orientation became so entrenched at hospitals that, by the 1990s, few if any are left that view community good and charity as dominant driving forces. This does not mean no one talks about such concepts anymore, but it does mean that talk is, after all, merely talk and few can presently claim to "walk the talk." Even the rare trustee who votes against cost cutting, rationing of services, and the like knows that if her sisters were to vote with her it would mean losing the contracts that bring growing numbers of patients to the hospital in the first place.

Much of the battle over applying managed care to Medicaid populations is about rationing services to the poor. Medicaid recipients might not get luxury care, but Medicaid does provide a number of services and benefits not available in managed care plans.

## ECONOMIC ERA MEANS PRICE COMPETITION AND MANAGED CARE

There is no doubt that this era is presently well underway. Johnson identifies this era as being associated with consolidation and competition. Other indicators are the growing numbers of investor-owned and tax paying entities. Other indicia include economic partnerships with physicians and various organizations owning and operating physician practices, albeit under a variety of guises. In the economic era, profit means more than the capital necessary to grow, replace, and innovate. It is increasingly about profit as a personal motivator. It is about profit that results in individual riches. This is a far different set of motivators than existed in our benevolent years and, subsequently, during the technological era.

Johnson points to the desire of purchasers of insurance and benefits (i.e., businesses, governments, and, to a lesser extent, individuals) to achieving better value for their premium dollars. Or, as some might put it, "It's the cost, stupid." Yes, it is cost. Buyers are not the patients. Government is not a patient. However, they are the entities who are seeing profits eroded and their deficits soaring. They want relief from this voracious appetite. They want physician fees slashed, hospital costs capped, and all cost managed. They are the folks who are willing to pay managed care firms a good price in order to ratchet down the use of medical care resources. They demand cost containment. Managed care is the seeming salvation of the private sector and, by all accounts, is one of the primary goals of the Clinton administration. Ration access. The economic era is about pleasing business and government buyers. Managed care firms view business and government as customers. Provider groups do as well. While the patient's desires must be considered, by no means does that mean care, service, and choice will be available on demand. That concept is already an anachronism for most Americans, political statements to the contrary notwithstanding.

There are other proximate causes of this problem. Community hospitals tried to compete utilizing all of the latest and best that technology could offer. Physicians thrived on this concept and emulated hospitals. Indeed, they had to have it since patients in the fee-for-service arrangement demanded it and got it—or voted with their feet and went where it was available.

Federal policy contributed to this situation. Fee-for-service (FFS) was initially adopted for Medicare and Medicaid, although it is vastly changed today. Medicare started out with cost-plus reimbursement. Later, it merely paid cost. And now for many, Medicare pays below cost. However, even with the change, Medicare can still be a profit center.

In order to keep up technologically, hospitals turned to the bond markets in a major way. With practically guaranteed financial results through cost reimbursement, the bond markets eagerly responded with debt offering and, why not, a good time and great profits were to be had by all.

Equity markets responded in kind for hospital chains, managed care firms, and physician management companies, etc. Equity and market debt now promise ways to bring physicians more into ownership positions even as the field of practice is increas-ingly becoming a salaried practice under managed care firms, often both owned and operated by insurance firms.

In response to booming investments in hospitals and other health care entities, the industry built an infrastructure that is the envy of the marketplace. The industry can service much of the world with the capacity in place today. This excess capacity does, however, portend the next round of change, which will complete the cycle into the Economic Era. Excess capacity makes price competition among hospitals and specialty physicians not only possible but probably inevitable.

This overcapacity provides the basis for buyer-driven price competition. Simply put, when a commodity is in surplus, buyers can extract price concessions. We now have a buyer's market and buyers are soliciting bids. Price competition makes it possible for insurers and managed care firms to profit initially from price discounting without changing much in the manner care is actually delivered. After extracting initial gains from price discounting, more selective contracting and the increasing use of rationing devices to control patient use of resources will be required. Thus, the new era dawns.

---

*After extracting initial gains from price discounting, more selective contracting and the increasing use of rationing devices to control patient use of resources will be required.*

---

All of the tools of the marketplace are being rolled into place to move the industry into a much more competitive mode. Managed care firms and aggressive corporate buyers will drive the early stages. As hospitals and physicians realize their fate is to be cost centers, they will move to develop the ability to eliminate the middlemen and to sell their services, and they will do a better job of managing care. This puts hospitals and physicians in two camps: in one they benefit from fee-for-service, and in the other they benefit from rationing access to services. One pays for resource use, the other for nonuse of resources. A tough balancing act, indeed.

The insurers and providers are all seeking to position themselves to take advantage of this market shift. Johnson makes much of the difference between (1) sellers that will own and operate the risk-taking operation, the providers, and the marketing infrastructure, and (2) those hospitals and physicians who are merely contractors to managed care organizations that seek to manage entire networks through contracts only.

Since managed care firms will benefit from mere price discounting from those entities that own hard assets (e.g., hospitals), such entities face the prospect of an ever-increasing and downward price spiral. Worse yet, the managed care firm can give bonuses and preferred prices to primary care physicians whose practice inclination is to minimize the use of hospital and specialty resources. This puts the hospital in a unique bind when their former colleagues have become their rationing agents for their services. Such practices can be especially hard on specialists and hospitals. No wonder so many are beginning to realize that they can hang together or separately. Either way, they are being hung out today with the transition to the Economic Era.

## PATIENT RESPONSIBILITY

Johnson makes much of the idea that in this managed care era patients will have less responsibility. It is true that the capitation method places a heavy responsibility on providers to effectively ration care to patients. However, a variety of financial incentives also confronts users of managed care. Many HMOs have disincentives to utilize services such as copays and deductibles in addition to their other methods of rationing services. And, for those systems that allow patients to go outside the plan (point of service option), there may be a copayment of 50 percent or even higher.

Managed care patients face even greater behavioral modification exercises. Such patients learn early on that an advice nurse (at times an LPN) intercedes to check things out initially. Past the advice nurse may be a nurse practitioner or physician assistant. Since most patients present themselves to physicians with self-correcting problems, this may be the primary contact with the system for many. The way the advice nurse controls the encounter is by offering sympathy and advice to take ibuprofen and by asking the patient to come in for an office visit scheduled about two to three weeks later. Why so long? By the time one waits this long, the self-correcting problems have resolved and no visit is necessary. That is just fine when the problem is self-correcting, but problematic when it is not. Too bad, but this type of access rationing is required to lower resource use and to make it possible

for the HMOs to staff for real need and not for every patient-perceived need.

Over time, of course, patients learn how to game the advice nurse and move up in the queue if necessary, but this is not accomplished without a new level of burden of proof on the part of patients. Being the one at the wrong end of the rationing decision is not fun. I know, because I have been there.

In the early iterations of these new managed care products, and even among old-line health plans, the insured often pays based upon a percentage of billed charges, while the insurer or managed care plans pay their portion as a percentage of negotiated discounts. After deducting the full amount of the copayment, as ridiculous as this may sound, some insureds, through their copayments, have actually ended up paying 60–100 percent of what the providers actually receive for their services.

## CAPITATION

Johnson provides an excellent overview of some of the motivating forces under capitation, but in some spots his analysis lends itself more to what might happen short term rather than long term.

He points out that under capitation physicians might well find ways to generate what they consider to be sufficient profits by not providing services or providing them through physician extenders. This advances the long-held belief that capitation provides incentives for withholding care rather than providing care. A straightforward analysis of behavior would suggest that physicians might take more leisure and work fewer hours since no additional fees are generated by working longer hours. On the other hand, any organization that has workers whose workload is reduced by technology (managed care methodologies) will take steps to reduce the number of people in that work force. Fewer encounters per physician ultimately means fewer physicians needed.

Many of the managed care firms capitate the primary care physician and require them to regulate access to specialists, who may or may not be capitated in turn. Specialists who get hired for such jobs will be the lucky ones; far fewer of them will be hired or given sufficient members on their panel to make much of a living. The idea that physicians will be getting paid for less and less work is simply too good to be true.

There seems to be universal acceptance of the idea that we have a surplus of specialized physicians, but a shortage of primary care physicians. Remember the drive of managed care is profit, the drive of buyers is reduced cost, and the interest of physicians is to practice what they learned to do. As rationing to patients takes hold, managed care firms will have to lower prices to buyers who want their cost to go down. As this occurs, managed care firms will be forced to cut cost further to keep profits up. And guess who is out at the logical end of that downward pressure: physicians and hospitals that will be pushed for greater and greater productivity while being denied the opportunity to perform more and more procedures.

One might logically ask why physicians would work long hours for managed care firms under capitation when it seems to offer fewer incentives than fee-for-service does for similar effort. One major reason this might be the case is because managed care firms will own the right to assign patients to physicians. In other words, physicians will only be able to find work in managed care firms. Private practice, fee-for-service will disappear under the scenarios envisioned herein. Just as the managed care firms adjust downward the reimbursement to hospitals as they become more efficient, so too will managed care firms adjust upward the number of patients on a panel as the methods for rationing care to patients is perfected.

There is, of course, much more than this to capitation. The principle behind capitation is to shift the incentive from resource use on demand to utilization based upon health status. However, in the early stages of managed care as we know it, price competition has been more of a driver than any real attempt to manage health status. The theory of capitation calls for increasing the resources for prevention and wellness. To make this happen, long-term contracts will need to replace short-term contracts to make it financially possible for one managed care firm to reap results from such efforts. With some preventive measures taking years to pay off, this may be an elusive dream. In order to get managed care firms to invest in the long term, it might be necessary to pool some percentage of fees to be paid out based upon long-term efforts to improve the health of entire populations, not just members of one plan.

To date, it would appear that capitation and managed care has mostly been about providing less costly, more efficiently delivered, and deliberately rationed access to reasonably good quality medical services. Aside from the group and staff model capitated arrangements, this theory has yet to be fully tested. In prepaid group practices, this concept can and does work quite well.

When used properly, capitation results in a shift in the emphasis from early and extensive use of physicians, including specialists, to the exclusion of or rationed use of specialists. The resulting difference in cost is huge. This lower cost can and does at times result in large profits for employers who self-insure and for managed care firms that take capitated risk and then shift the risk to its providers.

## HUGE PROFIT POTENTIAL KICKS OFF RACE FOR CONTROL OF PREMIUMS

The potential for profits from this shift has kicked off a major race for control over the premium dollar. The opportunities for those who might be in a position to profit from changing over from FFS to capitation is huge. No wonder the race is on to control the premium dollars at a time when cut-rate prices can be negotiated from a market glutted with providers, thus making it possible for managed care to ratchet down costs and usage resulting in windfall profits to pioneers in every region of the country with the exception, perhaps, of those states which in some manner regulate or control profits.

This Economic Era will fundamentally and forever change medical practice in this country. In this shift, physician practice styles, their business, and their autonomy are all under siege. Physician integration with other providers poses threats along with some opportunities. Most big hospitals and health care systems seek to establish partnerships utilizing PHOs, MSOs, and/or wholly owned practice groups. Insurers are also seeking to build a primary care base while, at the same time, seeking to limit their contracts with hospitals and specialists. Hospital-based integrated systems usually suffer from too many specialists while, at the same time, insurer-based systems may suffer from a restricted panel of specialists.

Many insurers will not survive this transformation and those that do will be forever changed. Insurer organizations are at risk if they do not vertically integrate throughout their regions and/or medical markets. Traditional hospitals are at risk if they are not part of a regional system and affiliated with as many primary care physicians as possible.

Physicians seem to be at risk from both sides. Those physicians who move to group practices with a primary case base of 50 percent or more and who expand regionally to serve contiguous markets have tremendous leverage potential. One of the groups in California bought a small hospital, expanded their covered lives to 100,000 plus, and contracted for specialty services from a university hospital on a fixed rate for 10 beds plus services. Imagine, only 10 specialty beds per 100,000 population. That is only 100 such beds for a population of 1,000,000. Over an approximately 10 year or so period, The Lovelace Clinic doubled its number of covered lives and physicians while keeping bed capacity at the same level. Lovelace is now owned by an insurance firm but evolved from a group practice and not-for-profit hospital. Both became larger organizations to acquire access to capital markets necessary for expansion and the growth in managed care. Physicians and hospitals throughout the country are now doing the same thing. Many physician owners need additional equity market capital for a chance to eventually cash out. Equity markets provide liquidity, and physician investors ultimately need liquidity. Many locally owned not-for-profit firms have too little interest in providing physicians with the kinds of return their assets might command in a public market.

## JOINT VENTURES CHANGE POWER RELATIONS BETWEEN HOSPITALS AND PHYSICIANS

The PHO movement seems logically to provide hospitals and physicians a chance to realign ownership of revenue and profit streams into a joint venture that compensates physicians more highly than they are now. The fact that hospitals provide for more substantial assets to the joint venture does not necessarily mean that community hospitals will end up with control of the evolving health system. Some new entities may evolve in an attempt to control these new markets.

In a typical hospital, physicians constitute 20 percent or less of hospital boards, but in PHOs they often comprise 50 percent. It is this jointly owned and operated firm that negotiates for prices with buyers and managed care firms. This intimate arrangement should, over time, allow physicians to move their prices up a notch and shift the hospital's down a notch or two. The primary basis for this shift will be that physicians are the ultimate decision makers regarding just how much of the hospital's resources will go into any patient care. If both are on capitation, the physicians determine nearly all of the hospital's costs through their individual utilization patterns. No wonder many hospitals are buying up primary care prac-

tices so that they can put the right amount of pressure on specialists to avoid just such a squeeze.

## ASSET OWNERSHIP AND CONTROL

Ownership of assets may become less important than control of revenue streams. If the power to strike a deal moves upstream where it is shared equally by physicians, then over time the base of power and revenue allocation will shift to that level. This is essentially why PHOs will shift power to physicians, provided they are independent of the hospital. In some public hospitals, as well as community hospitals, these PHOs are placed under some subsidiary organization. In an earlier article, Johnson correctly pointed out that this new organization would increasingly be the place where all of the important decisions get made. This clearly moves governance into a professionally dominated (managers and physicians) arena. Under such circumstances, voluntary boards are at risk of becoming appendages presiding over the husk of an outmoded business enterprise.

In a market with surplus assets, the power to control goes to those with premiums but no assets to protect. In these markets, buyers dominate and realize the largest profits by forcing asset owners to grant price discounts.

---

*As market forces cause hospital failures and consolidation of hospitals into dominant players, the balance between buyers and sellers will shift again.*

---

As market forces cause hospital failures and consolidation of hospitals into dominant players, the balance between buyers and sellers will shift again. At that point some providers will acquire the insurance function and some insurers will acquire the provider function. More likely, we will begin to see mergers between the insurer-managed care firms and major provider firms. At this point in history, perhaps five years out, the nation will have fully vertically integrated firms serving all major markets. Whether this leads to oligopoly pricing and control or more competition remains to be seen. In the short run, hospitals, insurers, and multispecialty groups will compete aggressively to buy up the primary care capacity in order to gain power and leverage with the other players.

## CAPITAL FORMATION

With physician-owned organizations, it would seem that power would eventually be shifted to a publicly owned corporation since very few, if any, physician groups (the large not-for-profit Mayo and others are exceptions) have amassed sufficient capital reserves necessary to fund a move to managed care. Thus, where physicians move aggressively and early into ownership roles, the corporations they establish will ultimately become publicly owned corporations.

Physician-driven entities will make their money from the physicians' practices, from lowering the portion of premiums allocated to hospitals, and from owning and rationing other services. By progressively squeezing hospitals, they will eventually be in a position to acquire one or more hospitals that will permit them to maximize their control over their practices, revenues, and profits from hospital ownership as well. Still, physician entities will ultimately need outside capital to grow and that will most likely come from deep-pocket insurers and shareholders. Only the hospital systems that are able to provide physicians with an ownership interest in the overall operation will be attractive to physicians as they sell equity stakes in the entities they create and seek to recapture profit from their investments. Once the initial round of physician movement into salaried positions occurs, new physicians coming into the field will take salaried practices. Why? Patients will be "owned" by managed care firms and will only be available to physicians who join their networks and/or organizations. Established entities will merely employ future generations, since those new entrants will be unable to establish a practice outside of managed care.

Ultimately this Johnson/Brown dialogue must be judged by the readers and the marketplace. The issues which need to be addressed include questions such as the following:

- Is this scenario on target? Can we reasonably predict the eventual demise of the solo public and community not-for-profit hospital as well as the hospital systems that cannot or will not aggressively transform themselves into health systems with a strong bent toward tightly managed care?

- If managed care is fully integrated with physicians and capitated reimbursement becomes the norm, can we also predict the gradual assumption by physicians of the top executive functions in such systems? While this does not eliminate the position of hospital administrators, does it not mean that hospitals as cost centers, whose utilization is physician and protocol driven, will increasingly come under the overall management and/or direction of physicians? The theory for this postulate is a much broader one which predicts that when a profession is overtaken by bureaucracy, the professionals will seek to control that bureaucracy and thus their own destiny. Physicians demanding equality in governance are an example of this tendency.

- Does this lurch whereby market capital increasingly flows into physicians' practices, managed care entities, and investor-owned hospitals spell the eventual dominance of for-profit enterprises in health care? A number of teaching hospitals are contemplating joint ventures that call for converting their hospitals into for-profit entities. Lovelace went this route 10 years ago.

- If more and more of the business is for-profit, does this not present an increased potential for the loss of tax-exempt status for many hospitals? The theory behind this is that government increasingly will look favorably on those who pay taxes and will scrutinize carefully the tax-exempt status of those who do not.

- If we couple all of these factors with the premise that health reform moves toward universal coverage, will the not-for-profits have even less of an argument for a preferred status?

- Since physicians can legally hold a piece of the action only if they are, in some fashion, equity holders, will they not pressure more and more community hospitals and others to spin off their hospital business to allow them an ownership interest? No doubt the Columbia strategy benefited greatly from this pressure in certain markets. Consulting firms are already offering up models that spin off the hospital, convert the assets to for-profit status, and sell the physicians' equity interests in the newly created entity.

- How far up the chain, from community hospital to teaching hospital to academic medical center, is this change likely to go? Will we see the large physician groups like Scripps, Mayo, and Cleveland shift from not-for-profit to for-profit in order to maintain market share and to share in the rewards that will initially come from tightly managed care?

Clearly, the major rewards for tightly managed care will be in the early years. Buyers will, over time, exert more and more downward pressure as they see windfall profits resulting from this shift in medical practices. No doubt they know this will be the result, and there should be little doubt that when the shift becomes irreversible, they will seek to cut their own costs even further. Whether that will happen depends upon whether we can maintain an adequate degree of competition in the marketplace for health care while the system ratchets down. If we do not, then some monopoly profits may remain available for some time to come.

## UNANSWERED QUESTIONS

No one can argue that capitation will solve all of the major problems driving health care cost. A review of some of these should help put this discussion in perspective.

The attendant health care–related problems associated with poverty, drug addiction, homelessness, and hanging cultures are unlikely to yield to a system that stresses rationing of access to services. Children having children inundate the health system with problems. Mothers who fail to obtain adequate prenatal care often have troubled pregnancies, have children born prematurely, and, equally dangerous for the long term, may provide so little stimulation and nurturing during the child's early years that the stimulation necessary to sustain a normal productive life fails to take place. Placing these one-parent families in an HMO of the traditional kind will do little to change this outcome. Merely controlling the cost through rationing of access to this population may even make matters worse.

Education and research particularly are at risk in a cost-driven system. Cost-driven networks will not readily pick up the support of research and education. These programs now benefit from a variety of cross subsidies. Fee-for-service payments from patients free to choose physicians and services at academic health science centers help subsidize other patients and other work. Disproportionate payments for taking care of unsponsored patients provides additional help. The Veterans Administration sites many of its facilities near such centers and adds support and referrals.

Long-term disabilities like Alzheimer's disease present problems that require long-term care, home care, respite care, and the like. Such services fall outside the usual HMO contract. While it remains true that many elderly and disabled persons remain at home and out of long-term care facilities, more attention is needed to encourage the kind of physical fitness that could prevent even greater use of long-term care.

Lifestyle changes required for longer-term, high-level wellness do not lend themselves to the kind of year-to-year payoff and performance measures utilized by most HMOs. There are many interventions that could help. Recently, the Department of Agriculture announced a change in the fat content requirements for school lunches several years from now. This shift can help save lives and prevent disability. So, too, could a national emphasis on physical fitness. Most of these types of policies are favorable to controlling health care cost but are outside the normal scope of HMOs, unless they establish public policy departments with agendas of this nature clearly in mind. Johnson argued strongly that cost of prevention and, we think by extension, lifestyle changes should *not* be in the budget of hospitals and physicians who contract with HMOs. His reasoning is that they get paid to fix and that preventing might even deprive the vendors of a business opportunity. To be fair, Johnson is not against this happening, but he sees capitation as driving out any possibility of having it in the hospital budget.

Some of these issues are more properly called social problems and perhaps should not be loaded onto the back of the health care delivery system. On the other hand, health care institutions by law must provide the services once people present themselves at emergency rooms for care. The burden of taking care of such people will be borne disproportionately by large public hospitals and teaching hospitals. They will need help to do this.

Public health advocates often have faulted the medical care system, including hospitals, with not being sufficiently interested in some of the issues outlined above. Prevention is mostly a token program for most organizations. HMOs might be expected to take a more visible role. But will they? Will they do it only for their defined populations? Will investor-owned HMOs use corporate profits for long-term, more problematic, and questionable outcomes?

Over the past few years some of the hospitals that have taken on advocacy and involvement in community development may have found themselves being squeezed by cost-driven contracts with little option but to cut into those programs in order to survive. These and many other such problems and issues may well be part of the price we pay for driving the bulk of the health care system into price competition, free market style.

•    •    •

The health care system which serves most of the insured population is being shifted into a managed care mode. If Congress expands health insurance to the uninsured and small firms, Medicaid and, increasingly, Medicare may also be pushed into the same risk pools. This approach to care will help satisfy the buyers (read customers) who pay the bills. Cost containment is the goal. Some seek value (a calculation of cost-benefit), but for most it is lower prices. Increasing the amount paid by the insured and rationing access keep patients from using resources unnecessarily. This relies on the self-correcting nature of many problems and the willingness and ability of people to live with discomfort. It also relies on creating efficiencies in doing what is ultimately needed by those patients who come through the rationing screen.

The kinds of institutions and organizations that can do this well will probably need to be invented. Something new may well be required so that the new forms may fit more logically with the business mentality of the Wall Street–financed enterprise geared to customer needs than they do with the warm, compassionate, and resource-based community service enterprise geared to patient needs. Like the buggy manufacturer who was replaced by the automobile firm, community institutions will likely yield to tough-minded business management of the Wall Street–financed firm. Some community enterprises will transform themselves, but many will more likely fail.

Congress will ultimately exempt academic health science centers from the fray, but not all of them, and not in the fashion they might like. Many social service organizations will receive aid to help with the non–HMO services needed by multiproblem clients who will not respond well to the rationing of service mode of HMOs.

This transformation is going on now and will likely be reinforced by whatever comes out of the reform effort in Washington. How will the American people like these changes? We suspect that they will be accepted in theory but ultimately resented in practice.

Johnson suggests that we will know who the winner and losers will be in 10 years or so. For those who like to stay ahead of the learning curve, finding out after the fact is of little consequence. Now is the time to place bets, pick sides, and do something about your favorite policy direction. Which way will it all go?

PART II

# STATE OF KNOWLEDGE: SUCCESS AND FAILURE OF INTEGRATION

# Alliances in health care: What we know, what we think we know, and what we should know*

Howard S. Zuckerman,
Arnold D. Kaluzny,
and
Thomas C. Ricketts, III

*Alliances are the organizations of the future. This article builds on the lessons from industry identifying important areas requiring definition and basic understanding of alliance structure, process, and outcome in health care services.*

*Health Care Manage Rev*, 1995, 20(1), 54–64

Companies are beginning to learn what nations have always known—in a complex uncertain world, filled with dangerous opponents, it is best not to go it alone.

—Kenichi Ohmae[1]

**In an increasingly turbulent environment,** companies around the globe and across a multitude of industries are turning to alliances as cooperative, interorganizational mechanisms for adaptation. Such alliances are designed to achieve strategic purposes not attainable by a single organization, providing flexibility and responsiveness while retaining the basic fabric of participating organizations. This article assesses the development and operation of alliances in industry and their applicability to health care. Specifically, what do we know about alliances from industry, what do we think we know, and what should we know about alliances as they emerge and function within health care?

## WHAT WE KNOW ABOUT ALLIANCES: EXAMPLES FROM INDUSTRY

Alliances are legion. In the airline industry, for example, Air Canada, a midsize airline, has formed alliances with carriers in the United States, Europe, and Asia.[2] To cut costs and increase market position, Air Canada provides maintenance services for Continental and shares schedules, reservation codes, and frequent flyer benefits with United. Similar approaches to cooperation are evident in the automobile industry.

*This article draws heavily from Kaluzny, A., Zuckerman, H., and Ricketts, T. (eds). *Partners for the Dance: Forming Strategic Alliances in Health Care.* Ann Arbor, Mich.: Health Administration Press, 1995. Adapted with permission.

Key words: *health care alliances, strategic alliances, internal organizational structure and process*

**Howard S. Zuckerman,** *Ph.D., is Professor, School of Health Administration and Policy, and Director, Center for Health Management Research, College of Business, Arizona State University, Tempe, Arizona.*

**Arnold D. Kaluzny,** *Ph.D., is Professor, Department of Health Policy and Administration, School of Public Health, and Senior Fellow, Cecil G. Sheps Center for Health Services Research, University of North Carolina at Chapel Hill, Chapel Hill, North Carolina.*

**Thomas C. Ricketts, III,** *Ph.D., is Assistant Professor, Department of Health Policy and Administration, School of Public Health, and Senior Fellow, Cecil G. Sheps Center for Health Services Research, University of North Carolina at Chapel Hill, Chapel Hill, North Carolina.*

For example, Jaguar-Ford and Saab-Scania-General Motors have formed alliances to ward off Japanese competition in Great Britain. Daimler-Benz is beginning joint activities to build busses with companies in China, thus providing the Chinese with needed production technology while enabling Daimler-Benz to expand its presence in Asia.[3] General Motors, Ford, and Chrysler, in a significant policy departure, are exploring an alliance to design pollution-free, technologically advanced cars, building on research links among the three automobile companies and governmental laboratories.[4]

The communication and media industries likewise may be characterized by a wave of alliances as telephone, cable, and computer hardware/software companies seek to be at the forefront of rapidly developing technological breakthroughs. Pushed by changing technology, rising competition, and a European economic common market (EEC) deadline for ending all state monopolies, European telephone companies are forming international partnerships.[5] Emerging are alliances linking British Telecommunications with MCI; France Telecom with Deutsche Budespost Telekom (Eunetcom); and Dutch, Swedish, and Swiss companies (Unisource). AT&T is considering allying with major cable companies to bring its customers into one interactive multimedia network, tying the current disparate cable systems into an integrated network of common switching and transmission functions.[6] The evidence is clear that many companies in many industries, including former and present competitors, are entering into a variety of alliances.

## What are alliances designed to achieve?

Alliances arise out of mutual need and a willingness between and among organizations to share risks and costs, to share knowledge and capabilities, and to take advantage of interdependencies to reach common objectives.[7] The basic aims of alliances are to gain competitive advantage, leverage critical capabilities, increase the flow of innovation, and improve flexibility in responding to market and technology changes. For example, alliances allow participation in highly volatile industries, where knowledge spreads rapidly, at substantially lower investment and risk than would be the case for a single organization.[8] Alliances also enable partners to enhance flexibility and accelerate getting to the market by taking advantage of complementary strengths and capabilities in areas such as production, marketing and distribution, and technology.

The influence of new knowledge and technologies on interorganizational structures, coupled with the need for new ways to coordinate the complexity that comes with alliances, will be continuing themes in organizational relations. Figure 1 summarizes the benefits and costs of interorganizational cooperation.

## How do alliances seek to achieve their goals?

Alliances are established along a variety of lines—joint ventures, marketing and distribution agreements, consortia, or licensing arrangements. Alliances require thinking in terms of "combinations" of firms. For example, Japanese firms often cooperate in order to penetrate new markets, which has often proven to be a key step to market dominance.[7] International companies often ally with local companies to yield successful entry into new markets, drawing on the

---

## FIGURE 1

---

BENEFITS AND COSTS OF
INTERORGANIZATIONAL COOPERATION[13]

**Benefits**

Develop opportunities to learn and adapt new
    competencies
Gain resources
Share risks
Share cost of product and technology development
Gain influence over domain
Gain access to new markets
Enhance ability to manage uncertainty and solve complex
    problems
Gain mutual support and group synergy
Respond rapidly to market demands and technological
    opportunities
Gain acceptance of foreign governments
Strengthen competitive position

**Costs**

Lose technical superiority
Lose resources
Share the costs of failure
Lose autonomy and control
Lose stability and certainty
Experience conflict over domain, goals, methods
Experience delays in solutions due to coordination
    problems
Experience government intrusion and regulation

knowledge and customer bases of the local company, in conjunction with the capital and technological resources of the international firm. Working with competitors often is the basis for an alliance against a common enemy. Newspapers often share facilities to compete with television, auto dealers compete yet share advertising, and pharmaceutical companies use each other's sales forces.[7] Joining forces is further desirable in the face of difficult economic conditions or the combined power of other alliances. Alliances may also be useful in enhancing flexibility, innovation, and performance in customer–supplier relationships. Captive supply units, not subject to market pressures, tend to develop cost, quality, and technology gaps. Alliances may thus be able to secure the benefits of vertical integration, without the drawbacks associated with ownership.

Successful alliances appear to have several key ingredients, beginning with shared objectives among the participants. Commitment is based on mutual need; the alliance will endure only so long as mutual need exists.[9] Risk sharing completes the bond, creating a powerful incentive to cooperate for mutual gain. It is important to note, however, that mutual reliability means mutual vulnerability. Relationships matter a great deal in alliances, the success of which requires mutual trust, cooperation, and understanding.[8]

Alliances have been labeled as "virtual corporations," seen as temporary networks of companies that come together to exploit fast-changing opportunities.[10] Such corporations share costs, skills, and access to global markets. Their key attributes are identified as technology and information networks; excellence, as each partner brings distinctive competencies; opportunism in meeting specific market opportunities, trust, as partners share a destiny; and borderlessness, as suppliers, competitors, and customers cooperate. The key is flexibility—absent hierarchies and vertical structures, as alliances enable companies to broaden offerings or produce sophisticated products less expensively.

### What problems face alliances and how are they managed?

Alliances must be carefully entered into, with clear objectives, a realistic appraisal of an organization's skills and resources, and knowledge of the strengths of each partner.[11] Alliances should be approached carefully and systematically; it is often critical that potential partners share common or compatible cultures, and similar approaches to issues and problems. Part-

---

*In many ways, the notion of alliances, and the underlying premise of strength through cooperation, are hard for American companies and managers to accept.*

---

ners must understand their motivation in entering an alliance. Alliances are designed to create competitive strength or augment a strategic position, not hide weaknesses.[12] As such, they are seen by many as anticipating long-term relationships, established for strategic purposes. Furthermore, alliances must generate tangible value, leading to win–win relationships. It has been found useful in organizations to have a "champion," or "boundary spanner,"[13] whose personal objective it is to see the alliance succeed. In many ways, the notion of alliances, and the underlying premise of strength through cooperation, are hard for American companies and managers to accept. The sense of individualism, desire for control, and "not invented here" syndrome often make American companies uncomfortable with alliances.[14] The close bonds required by alliances are inconsistent with traditional American business practices. For example, the IBM–Apple alliance will be successful only if the two companies are willing to place their need for this alliance above other priorities.[15] They must learn to appreciate and adjust to each other's views, rely on each other's information, and respect each other's need to maintain their own internal cultures.

### How have alliances performed?

Surveys indicate that chief executive officers (CEOs) of American companies tend to be much less positive about the results of alliances as compared to their European and Asian counterparts.[14] Joint ventures appear to be especially problematic. In examining why alliances are seen as unsuccessful, the following reasons have been suggested:

- alliances are judged by short-term financial results rather than long-term strategic objectives
- there is a lack of trust among the partners
- an uneven commitment and imbalance of power exist
- individuals at lower operating levels (who must make it work) are not informed about or involved in the alliance
- there is an absence of clear understanding of partners' respective motivations and expectations

- there is a lack of mutually accepted performance measures[16,17]

Thus, lessons from other industries and countries suggest that alliances provide the opportunity and potential to add value to organizations, but that many challenges need to be addressed in their development and operation. At issue now is how the concept of alliances applies in health care.

## WHAT WE THINK WE KNOW: ALLIANCES IN HEALTH CARE

Alliances in health care function in a larger environment, and that larger environment is likely to influence the development and performance of alliances. As described by Zuckerman and Kaluzny:

> In health care, much of the development of alliances can be traced to changes in the environment. As access to needed resources is threatened and new challenges are presented to health services providers, organizations seek to reduce their dependencies on and their uncertainty about the environment by banding together. . . . While there is clearly a growing degree of interdependency, there also remains a substantial amount of organizational independence and autonomy not possible under other interorganizational arrangements such as horizontal and vertical integration. Alliances appear to offer flexibility and responsiveness, with limited effects on the structure of participating organizations. In recent years, we have seen these new organizations become institutionalized as a form of organizational cooperation involving organizations heretofore considered autonomous, if not competitive, entities.[18,p.5]

These conditions apply to all parts of the American health care industry. Health care providers enter into alliances in order to gain economies of scale and scope, enhance the acquisition and the retention of key resources, expand their revenue and service bases, increase their influence, and improve market position.[19] Alliances, transcending existing organizational arrangements, permit activities not otherwise possible, link organizations through shared strategic purpose, provide access to technologies previously unavailable, and capitalize on the growing need for organizational interdependence.[20,21] Alliances make it possible to gain access to resources without owning them, encouraging organizations to look outward as well as inward as they struggle with how to do more with less.

### What are the types of alliances in health care?

Alliances in health care may be categorized into two general types. The first may be described as "lat-eral," or "service alliances,"[22] in which similar types of organizations, often with similar needs or dependencies come together to achieve benefits such as economies of scale, enhanced access to scarce resources, and increased collective power.[19] For example, alliances have formed among hospitals based on common religious preferences, particular types of hospitals, or geographic distribution. These alliances serve to take advantage of pooled resources, thereby expanding the strength and capabilities of any single members to benefit the entire membership. Their domain can be extensive, including group purchasing, insurance, information sharing, and human resource management, among the array of programs and services.

The second type may be described as "integrative," in which organizations come together for purposes largely related to market and strategic position and securing competitive advantage. Many of the attributes of such alliances are incorporated in Kanter's[22] formulation of "stakeholder alliances," emphasizing linkages among buyers, suppliers, and customers; Johnston and Lawrence's[23] "value-adding partnerships"; and Alter and Hage's[13] notion of "systemic networks." These alliances may be illustrated by the emergence of "corporate partnerships," linking providers and suppliers through long-term agreements and close relationships. Of particular interest will be the role of alliances as a mechanism to build integrated delivery and financing systems.[24] Such systems are defined as regional, market-based organizations, serving the health care needs of a defined population.[25] These systems are being developed to achieve vertical as well as horizontal integration, clinical as well as administrative integration, and integration of financing as well as delivery. How such systems achieve integration is a key issue. There is reason to believe that alliances will play an important role in their evolution, representing a mechanism to achieve integration without the necessity of ownership and/or control of each of the key components. These integrative alliances will likely prove especially important in the context of an already changing environment.

### How do alliances form?

The formation of health care alliances may be described in terms of stages of development or a life-cycle model. Each of the stages or each step in the life cycle has important implications for successful development of the alliance. For example, the Kanter[26] formulation, which appears quite applicable, proposes that alliance formation moves through stages defined as "selection or courtship," "engagement," "setting up housekeeping," "learning to collaborate," and "changing within." The first stage requires each organization to undertake a realistic appraisal of itself, as well as of each of the potential partners. After developing the basic agreement in the engagement stage, partners next begin to experience the difficulties in making the transition to a new form and relationship. They experience problems with coordination of resources, cultural differences, opposition to the alliance, lack of understanding, and dissimilarities in operating styles. Thus, the learning stage calls for building mechanisms—strategic, tactical, cultural, interpersonal, and operational—to bridge these gaps and overcome the barriers, while the final stage involves the internal changes needed to sustain the relationship over time.

In a comparable approach, Forrest[27] proposes three stages: "prealliance," "agreement," and "implementation." Like Kanter, Forrest emphasizes the importance of careful appraisal and selection of an appropriate partner, calling for a close fit in terms of expectations, values, goals, interdependence, trust, and commitment. The agreement stage serves to specify the terms and conditions of the alliance—its scope, objectives, resource requirements, management structure, mechanisms for conflict resolution, exit terms, and performance measures. In the implementation stage, emphasis is on open communication, timely decision making, ongoing review of objectives to ensure consistency with a changing environment, and strengthened mutual commitment.

Viewing the development of alliances in terms of a life cycle, steps along the way may be portrayed as "emergence," "transition," "maturity," and "critical crossroads."[28] Perhaps most applicable to the "lateral" alliances noted earlier, alliances among organizations that share ideology or resource dependencies emerge in response to environmental threats or uncertainty. Seen as a less costly organizational alternative and providing an opportunity to reduce dependency, members early on develop purposes, expectations, and criteria for participation. In the transition, mechanisms for control, coordination, and decision making are established, and trust and commitment are heightened, setting the foundation to enable the members to secure anticipated benefits as the alliance matures and grows. In reaching the critical crossroads, members face demands for greater commitment, more centralized decision making, and more dependence upon the alliance for needed resources, which are, to some ex-

tent, counter to the reasons for initially forming the alliance, thereby raising the specter of withdrawal or creating a more hierarchical type of organization.

Moreover, public policy is likely to greatly influence the stages of the life cycle.[29] For the past decade, public policies have stimulated the growth of alliances as they have forced health care systems into greater efficiency or at least into imposing lower costs on public and private sector purchases of their environment. These policies have presented serious threats to some health care organizations, as illustrated by the efforts of the federal prospective payment system for reimbursing Medicare services, as well as state policies restricting capitation expansion in the industry.

Much of the alliance activity of recent years may have been stimulated by threats to continued success of organizations, or at least by the perception that these threats existed or would soon exist within their environments. These policy initiatives may change over time from essentially negative to more positive. This shift will likely stimulate even faster growth of the alliance phenomena in the next few years. One clear example of a policy shift toward such supportive effort is found in the possible changes in antitrust laws. The Clinton proposal for health care reform, for example, included specific attention to the effect of existing antitrust laws on the shift to vertically integrated delivery systems. As these systems move into place, initially conforming to the cooperative spirit characterizing alliances, other forces pushing for stability and accountability will influence the nature of these relationships, thus moving toward a more permanent interorganizational relationship based on ownership among former alliance participants. As such, we may well witness the influence of public policy shifting focus from a "lateral" to an "integrative" arrangement.

### How are alliances operated?

Sustaining alliances over time requires constant vigilance. It is clear that the relationships within alliances are fragile and characterized by constant change. Members must believe that they are stronger together than they would be separately, and that ongoing commitment of time, energy, and resources is needed to secure the anticipated benefits. Indeed, in contrast with the long-standing control model of organizations, alliances are more appropriately defined in terms of a commitment model. As Kanter suggests, ". . . if an increasing amount of economic activity con-

*It is seen as essential that participating members or partners of an alliance are rigorous in analyzing themselves and each other as to compatibility and complementarity of goals, purposes, vision, and values, and possession of clear indications and interdependency.*

tinues to occur across, rather than within, the boundaries defined by the formal ownership of one firm, managers will have to understand how to work with partners rather than subordinates. . . ."[22,p.192] Such a model underscores the importance of designing and communicating common purposes; developing realistic expectations; and clearly framing the domain, scope, and activities of an alliance. As the purposes of an alliance may shift over time, the operating domain and the membership, too, may need to be reassessed. For example, as many hospital alliances evolved from "association" type efforts toward a "business" focus, areas of activity and criteria for members had to be reassessed. Likewise, as noted by Weinstein,[30] as member organizations address their attention to building vertically integrated health care systems, the role and contribution of their national alliances likely will be reassessed. Managing these potentially profound changes and balancing the interests of multiple constituencies are delicate and difficult tasks, testing the commitment, openness, and willingness of members to share resources and information, and challenging the alliance to add value and provide strategic benefit continually.

In assessing how alliances are sustained over time, several key themes emerge. First, is the critical nature of the selection of an appropriate partner(s). It is seen as essential that participating members or partners of an alliance are rigorous in analyzing themselves and each other as to compatibility and complementarity of goals, purposes, vision, and values, and possession of clear indications of interdependency. Second, is the underlying "glue" of alliances—trust and commitment. Partners must be candid, open, and fair in the workings of the alliance, and able to recognize that continued nurturing is needed to maintain the alliance over time. In fact, the fragile nature of alliances leaves open the question of whether they will prove to be temporary or permanent organizational phenomena.

In large part, the willingness of members to remain will depend on their perception as to the extent to which the alliance is crucial to the long-term viability of their organization. Third, the terms and terrain of the alliance must be clear, the operating rules explicit, and expectations mutually understood and agreed upon. Fourth, partners must learn from and be strengthened by the alliance. Alliances are seen by many as mechanisms to supplement and complement the core capabilities and knowledge of an organization, not as substitutes for internal development.[31] Indeed, as Lewis notes, "there is no reason to cooperate unless you grow stronger by the experience."[7,p.50]

### How effective are health care alliances?

Defining and assessing the effectiveness or performance of alliances are subjects of serious attention in many quarters. The performance of alliances may be viewed along either or both of two dimensions—performance as seen by those who are key internal stakeholders within the alliance and by those who are external stakeholders, outside but affected by or otherwise interested in the alliance and its impact. To date, attention has been devoted primarily to performance or effectiveness as perceived by those within the alliance. For example, Kanter[22] suggests that effective alliances are those characterized by the "six I's":

1. The alliance is seen as Important, with strategic significance, and getting adequate resources and management attention.
2. The alliance is seen as a long-term Investment, from which members will be rewarded relatively equally over time.
3. The partners in the alliance are Interdependent, maintaining an appropriate balance of power.
4. The alliance is Integrated, in order to manage communication and appropriate points of contact.
5. Each alliance member is Informed about plans for the alliance and for each other.
6. The alliance is Institutionalized, with supporting mechanisms that permeate Interorganizational activities and facilitate the requisite trust relationships among the members.

The effectiveness of health care alliances can be considered in terms of both a variance and process perspective.[32] The variance perspective focuses on outcomes, seeking to identify variables that explain variation in alliance performance. For example, are there identifiable changes in market share or financial performance attributable to alliance membership? This perspective is appropriate for analyzing the effects of an alliance on various indicators of performance and/or factors that account for specific stages of the adoption process. The process perspective, on the other hand, focuses on particular conditions, events, or stages in the overall development process. For example, are problems faced in the early stages of alliance development different from those experienced in later stages? This perspective is appropriate in considering the interaction among various factors as alliances and participating organizations adapt over time. Furthermore, application of both the variance and process perspectives occurs at two levels, the first being the alliance as a whole and the second being the organizations comprising the alliance. A related approach views performance in terms of an alliance's ability to achieve stated objectives, acquire needed resources, satisfy key stakeholders, and add value to the membership.[19] Performance would be judged in the context of an economic dimension (e.g., economies of scale, new sources of revenue and capital), an organizational dimension (e.g., market position, human resource management), and a social/political dimension (e.g., access to care, availability of services).

## WHAT WE SHOULD KNOW ABOUT ALLIANCES

While lessons can be learned from industry, and alliances are a reality in health care, the future will demand greater insight in the development and operation of alliances in health care. The issue of effectiveness will take on greater meaning and impact. With major structural and strategic changes already underway in the marketplace, the role of alliances as a key component in the development of integrated health care systems will be scrutinized carefully. These emerging integrated systems will be held broadly accountable for their performance, not only internally but externally as well. Such organizations will continue to evaluate themselves in order to enhance operating performance, and thus they will continue to assess financial performance, changes in market share, employee satisfaction, and so forth. However, they will also find increased accountability in the context of public and social demands, and will be assessed in terms of such factors as access to care, availability of services, and improvements in the health status of a defined population. Furthermore, the unit of analysis will shift to a broader perspective, centering on epi-

sodes of care and indicators defined on a per capita basis. Health care managers and providers are entering a new era of defining and assessing the characteristics and performance of alliances.

## What is, and how do we measure, an alliance?

Alliances, as emerging realities, present some fundamental challenges. Their lack of definition, dramatic development, and need for measurement all suggest that attention needs to be given to fundamental questions of definition and measurement.

### Definition of an alliance—the need for a taxonomy

When we see new forms of organizations emerging, how we cognitively describe them is important in itself. The process of naming social activity creates bounds and a context for understanding and expectations. As Scott (1993) suggests, "old dichotomies have failed,"[33] citing organization–environment and markets-hierarchies as the two that are most inappropriate in a world of alliances. We need to develop a more sensitive scale and determine if there are directional effects or multiple, organic systems that can explain and predict.

Alliances can and do take on very different forms while adhering to a general concept. That general concept of independent organizations collaborating for common goals is too general to allow comparison with other forms of production. One useful set of dimensions to describe alliances is based on strategic intent, scope of activities, and degree of control.[34]

A taxonomy is key to understanding a system of structures as they change. New and old versions of an alliance are different from alternative types of alliances; maturing alliances may become yet another type. The naming of types reflects the differences we can see and represents the distillation of our assessment of an organization.

### Indicators of alliance performance and operations across varying forms

A major requirement is to understand the range and mix of outcomes of alliances and how they both differ from and are like outcomes from other organizational forms. We must be able to scale and quantify outcomes that are multiple and potentially conflicting. Obviously, there are conflicting goals among alliance members as they enter networks or agreements, and successful alliances begin to develop a feeling of consensus over the outputs of the arrangements, while those that fail cannot agree. This process is important in and of itself, but the measurement of whatever is agreed to be an alliance and its output is the necessary condition for comparing and measuring their effectiveness.

## What are the managerial challenges?

Effective management requires basic understanding of structure, process, and outcomes, as well as developmental process. There are many substantive questions that should be asked about alliances and their effectiveness within the context of health services. Below, specific questions corresponding to the process, structure, and outcomes of alliances, as well as their development, are presented.

### Outcomes

Outcomes of the alliances are of key interest because these describe the social goals of organizations, and their future depends on the quality and relevance of these outputs. Outcomes are the basis for measures of the effectiveness, efficiency, and productivity of alliances, and how we define outcome is crucial to performance.

- What alliance forms are most effective? For example, are the same forms that have proven useful for short-term, temporary alliances, proven equally useful for longer-term, permanent alliances? Similarly, are there differences among alliances organized informally, or via contractual arrangements or equity positions? Clearly, we must find the most efficient and effective forms to promote in policy and to guide practitioners toward implementation. This process rests heavily on the decisions we make about outcomes measurement.
- Can performance influence structure? It is equally clear that the structures of alliances have evolved as a reaction to conditions that demand rationalization of effort and superior performance, and may cause changes in the rules that guide structure. It is important to predict how much of this does happen and can happen.
- What feedback loops are available? Alliances require significant investments in information transfer for the maintenance of the alliance itself,

and this maintenance burden may overwhelm any planning, review, and modification process.
- Does prior alliance experience or prior relationship among partners predict success in future alliances?
- What alliance forms are most effective for implementation? Implementation is a necessary, but not sufficient, condition for effective performance. Are different alliance forms more easily implemented—yet have only marginal effect—versus forms that are more difficult to implement, but have more substantive effect? Consideration needs to be given to the breadth of relationships among participants, degrees of commitment, exclusivity, and the authority of alliance to act on behalf of members.
- Is there learning in alliances as in other institutions? For example, do alliances serve to shorten the product development cycle? Do alliances reduce capital requirements in product development?

### Structure and process

Alliance structure and process are of interest because they focus on the mechanics and activities and represent the potential leverage points for the development of policy and management options.
- What are the organizational and environmental predictors of alliance success and performance—legal, geographic, cultural experience, governance scale, and traditional network characteristics such as centrality and dominance? For example, cultural differences have been cited as barriers to effective alliance performance. Complementarity among participants has been suggested as a key variable. Degree of dependency may be another important factor associated with alliance success—supplementing and complementing, not substituting for, competencies. Degrees of trust and commitment among parties are continuously referenced as factors related to success.
- How does the structure and size of an alliance relate to the types of services and resources shared across the alliance? Are there negotiation process and conflict resolution strategies that are effective, and under what conditions?
- How can we effectively create governance structures that take into consideration the needs of rural components who have relatively fewer re-

sources to bring to an alliance, but that demand equal voice and influence?

- What information systems and transfer mechanisms can best cope with the demands for quality, sharing, and accountability? What mechanisms can be put into place to ensure technology transfer among participating organizations, and how does the alliance assume that existing information technology is used?
- How do alliances develop their products and services and get them to the market? Do alliances serve to shorten the product development cycle and/or reduce capital requirements?
- What are the antitrust issues alliances face? Specifically, do the cooperative structures that characterize alliance activities interfere with competition? For example, do alliances seek to engage in dividing up markets, fixing prices, or limiting competition? This will be of particular concern where organizations in the same market seek to build an integrated system using the alliance as a connecting mechanism.

### Formulation

Alliances are not static, but involve a dynamic interchange with a larger environment providing resources for their various activities. Resources include funds, information, and personnel, all of which shape the way in which the alliance functions.

- What competencies are required in alliances that we do not have in adequate supply? This relates directly to several observations that we will need more boundary-spanning workers who can process paradoxical and conflicting organizational goals and who also understand the diverse needs of rural and urban members.
- What is the role of needs assessment in the allocation of resources? How does the approval process differ with an alliance configuration? This is especially relevant when there are imbalances tied to geography.
- How do we develop a standard of effectiveness and quality that can be used for accreditation of alliances, taking into consideration size and location? Perhaps more basic is whether the concept of accreditation is relevant to the alliance form.
- Are there transference skills that are effective in horizontal and not in vertical alliances and vice versa?

*Alliances are not static, but involve a dynamic interchange with a larger environment providing resources for their various activities.*

- How do you manage alliances in such a way as to accommodate political and policy influences? Many policy differences exist between urban and rural constituencies based on differences in their economies; these differences spill over into institutional arrangements and must be considered.
- What is the proper role of academic medical centers in alliances? Particular emphasis is needed on vertical dimensions—what is the role of academic health centers in building integrated delivery systems? How well can academic health centers integrate into clinical teaching and research functions within such systems without adversely affecting overall cost structure of the system? How can academic health centers link with rural communities to provide access to technology, as well as ensure a systematic flow of patients?

●　　●　　●

Alliances have come to health care and while we are learning from their development in other industries, the future lies in developing an alliance between both the research and practice communities, better determining what we "should know," and distinguishing that from what "we think we know." A strong working relationship between the health services research community and the practice community benefits all parties. The practice community, concerned with the rapid and chaotic changes in health care and its own markets, wants to know what will work "on Tuesday," not in 1997. Managers are entering into uncharted territory for their organizations. They are looking at financial incentives that have shifted completely, seeing former competitors as possible partners, and are beginning to realize that their organizations may have to take on a radically different form if they are to survive and fulfill their missions. They are desperate for some guidance, history, and indication that they are on the right track.

The research community is anxious to understand the changes that are taking place, the incentives that are driving them, and what changes are successful. They need real world laboratories and input to make this research relevant and useful. This curiosity is born out of a wish to know what the future will bring. This desire to know what will happen is not unique to the research community; providers need to know what the future will be like in order to adjust in time and anticipate changes that will affect their ability to perform. Effective action, however, requires that we distinguish what we know from what we think we know and what we should know.

## REFERENCES

1. Ohmae, K. "The Global Logic of Alliances." *Harvard Business Review* 89 (1989): 143–54.
2. Chipello, C.J. "Midsize Air Canada Plots Survival in Industry of Giants. Continental Bid is Example of Alliances Sought to Secure Carrier's Future." *The Wall Street Journal*, November 12, 1992: B4.
3. "Daimler-Benz Sets Plan to Expand Asia Presence." *The Wall Street Journal*, August 27, 1993: A3, B5.
4. Behr, P., and Brown, W. "In Policy Departure, U.S. Joins Detroit in Industrial Alliance." Washington Post Service, *Washington Post*, September 29, 1993, F1.
5. Hudson, R.L. "European Phone Companies Reach Out for Partners." *The Wall Street Journal*, September 30, 1993: B4.
6. Keller, J.J. "AT & T, Cable-TV Firms Discuss Linking Their Customers in Multimedia Network." *The Wall Street Journal*, August 27, 1993: A3.
7. Lewis, J.D. *Partnerships in Profit: Structuring and Managing Alliances.* New York: The Free Press, 1990.
8. Badaracco, Jr., J.L. *The Knowledge Link: How Firms Compete Through Alliances.* Boston: Harvard Business School Press, 1991.
9. Henderson, J.C. "Plugging Into Strategic Partnerships: The Critical IS Connection." *Sloan Management Review* 31 (Spring 1990): 7–18.
10. Byrne, J.A. "The Virtual Corporation." *Business Week*, February 8, 1993: 98–103.
11. Wysocki, Jr., B. "Cross-Border Alliances Become Favorite Way To Crack New Markets. Mitsubishi and Daimler Are Just the Latest to See Gain In Swapping Know-How." *The Wall Street Journal*, March 26, 1990: A1, A12.
12. Hamel, G., Doz, Y.L., and Prahalad, C.K. "Collaborate With Your Competitors—And Win." *Harvard Business Review* 89 (1989): 133–9.
13. Alter, C., and Hage, J. *Organizations Working Together.* Newbury Park, CA: Sage Publications, 1993.
14. Modic, S. "Alliances: A Global Economy Demands Global Partnerships." *Industry Week* (October 3, 1988): 46–52.
15. Lewis, J.D. "Manager's Journal—IBM and Apple: Will They Break the Mold?" *The Wall Street Journal*, July 31, 1991: A10.
16. Sherman, S. "Are Alliances Working?" *Fortune*, September 21, 1992: 77–78.
17. Bowersox, D.J. "The Strategic Benefits of Logistics Alliances." *Harvard Business Review* 90 (1990): 36–45.
18. Zuckerman, H.S., and Kaluzny, A.D. "Strategic Alliances in Health Care: The Challenges of Cooperation." *Frontiers of Health Services Management* 7, no. 3 (1991): 3–23.
19. Zuckerman, H.S., and D'Aunno, T.A. "Hospital Alliances: Cooperative Strategy in a Competitive Environment." *Health Care Management Review* 15, no. 2 (1990): 21–30.
20. Kaluzny, A.D., et al. "Predicting the Performance of a Strategic Alliance: An Analysis of the Community Clinical Oncology Program." *Health Services Research* 28, no. 2 (1993): 159–82.
21. Luke, R.D., Began, J.W., and Pointer, D.D. "Quasi-Firms: Strategic Inter-Organizational Forms in the Healthcare Industry." *Academy of Management Review* 14 (January 1989): 9–19.
22. Kanter, R.M. "Becoming PALS: Pooling, Allying, and Linking Across Companies." *Academy of Management Executive* 3 (August 1989): 183–93.
23. Johnston, R., and Lawrence, P.R. "Beyond Vertical Integration—The Rise of Value-Added Partnerships." *Harvard Business Review* 88 (1988): 94–101.
24. Dowling, W.L. "Alliances as a Structure for Integrated Delivery Systems." In *Partners for the Dance: Forming Strategic Alliances in Health Care*, edited by A. Kaluzny, H. Zuckerman, and T. Ricketts. Ann Arbor, Mich.: Health Administration Press, 1995.
25. Shortell, S.M., et al. "The Holographic Organization." *Healthcare Forum Journal* 36 (March–April 1993): 20–6.
26. Kanter, R.M. "Collaborative Advantage: The Art of Alliances." *Harvard Business Review* 72 (1994): 96–108.
27. Forrest, J.E. "Management Aspects of Strategic Partnering." *Journal of General Management* 17, no. 4 (1992): 25–40.
28. D'Aunno, T.A., and Zuckerman, H.S. "A Life-Cycle Model of Organizational Federations: The Case of Hospitals." *The Academy of Management Review* 12 (1987): 534–45.
29. Longest, B. "Strategic Alliances in Health Care." *Association of University Programs in Health Administration.* San Diego, CA, June 11, 1994.

30. Weinstein, A. *Comments at the National Invitational Conference on Strategic Alliances.* Chapel Hill, N.C., 1993.

31. Montgomery, R. "Alliances—No Substitute for Case Strategy." *Frontiers of Health Care Services Management* 7, no. 3 (1991): 25–8.

32. Kaluzny, A., and Zuckerman, H. "Alliances: Two Perspectives for Understanding Their Effects on Health Services." *Hospital & Health Services Administration 37,* no. 4 (1992): 477–90.

33. Scott, W.R. "Commentary." In *Partners for the Dance: Forming Strategic Alliances in Health Care,* edited by A. Kaluzny, H. Zuckerman, and T. Ricketts, Ann Arbor, Mich.: Health Administration Press, 1995.

34. Shortell, S.M. "Commentary." In *Partners for the Dance: Forming Strategic Alliances in Health Care,* edited by A. Kaluzny, H. Zuckerman, and T. Ricketts, Ann Arbor, Mich.: Health Administration Press, 1995.

# Owned vertical integration and health care: Promise and performance

Stephen L. Walston,
John R. Kimberly,
and
Lawton R. Burns

*This article examines the alleged benefits and actual outcomes of vertical integration in the health sector and compares them to those observed in other sectors of the economy. This article concludes that the organizational models on which these arrangements are based may be poorly adapted to the current environment in health care.*

*Health Care Manage Rev, 1996, 21(1), 83–92*
© 1996 Aspen Publishers, Inc.

**Vertical integration in** health care appears to be an idea whose time has come.[1] Vertical integration, the combination or coordination of different stages of production, may be achieved in a variety of ways such as contracts, relationships, or ownership. Although the potential benefits of vertically integrated systems in health care have been touted by various federal and private commissions for more than 70 years[2], current interest can be attributed to increasing pressures from employers and insurers to control costs and the advent of managed care. In an attempt to adapt their organizations to these demands, health care providers are experimenting with a variety of mechanisms to restructure, integrate, and better coordinate their services and provision of care.

Indeed, vertically integrated structures have come to be widely viewed as the solution to a host of problems in the health care industry, much as Shortell predicted several years ago.[3] Among the anticipated benefits are economies of scale, more efficient care, reduced duplication of services, reduced administrative costs, greater coordination of services, and increased market influence. Providers anticipate an increased ability to survive and prosper, while society and businesses anticipate lower costs and higher quality of care.

Major innovations in any industry are invariably accompanied by overly optimistic expectations and unanticipated problems. While most observers presume that new vertically integrated structures will yield significant societal and organizational benefits, there is no guarantee that these objectives will be met. Indeed, recently several prominent health care strategists have come to question the wisdom of using ownership as the vehicle for vertically integrative strategy (owned vertical integration).[4-6] Presently there is little empirical evidence to support the promised benefits with any type of vertical integration. In fact, the lim-

Key words: *market power, organizational efficiencies, ownership, vertical integration*

***Stephen L. Walston***, *M.P.A., F.A.C.H.E., is a doctoral candidate, Wharton School, University of Pennsylvania, Philadelphia, Pennsylvania.*

***John R. Kimberly***, *Ph.D., is a Professor, Wharton School, University of Pennsylvania, Philadelphia, Pennsylvania.*

***Lawton R. Burns***, *Ph.D., is an Associate Professor, Wharton School, University of Pennsylvania, Philadelphia, Pennsylvania.*

ited empirical evidence and the recent experience of a small number of owned vertically integrated systems, such as Kaiser, suggest that greater inefficiencies and organizational problems may actually be created.

Given the limited research regarding vertical integration in health care, managers and researchers might wish to consider evidence from firms in other industries that have vertically integrated. Automobile, steel, oil, forest products, and aluminum producers have all vertically integrated (and divested) over the past century. Their experience might be instructive as the fascination with integration in health care deepens.

This article explores the anticipated benefits of owned vertical integration in general and in health care specifically, and reviews the empirical evidence. The article then discusses special contextual factors in health care that influence the success of integrated structures, as well as other types of vertical integration that may be more effective. We conclude with a discussion of the implications of vertical integration for managers and policy makers.

## THE PROMISE OF VERTICAL INTEGRATION

Before exploring the results of vertical integration, it is important to first understand its promise. Knowing the anticipated outcomes provides a basis to compare actual empirical results and more fully understand the correlation between the results and prior objectives.

### Non–health care sector

Owned vertical integration promises cost efficiencies by means of economies of internal control and coordination, economies of information, and technology.[7,8] Costs of monitoring and negotiation are also reduced as integration creates mutual dependencies and trust.

Vertical integration also augments the firm's market power.[8] Consolidating upstream suppliers and/or downstream distributors moves a firm closer to monopoly or quasi-monopoly power. This power enables the firm to become a price maker.[9] This additional market power is further associated with increased bargaining power and increased entry and mobility barriers that augment the ability to raise prices.[7,10–14] Vertical integration may also permit the avoidance of regulatory costs[11,14] and the ability to more easily retire outmoded market assets.[15] While increased market power may yield short-term ben-

efits to the individual firm, it may not benefit society. Instead, reduced services at higher costs may be the ultimate consequence.

Vertical integration through ownership may also allow a firm to better adapt to environmental pressures. Particularly when organizations are characterized by ambiguous outputs, inputs, and technologies, organizational form may become a proxy for quality and/or efficiency.[16] DiMaggio and Powell[17] suggest the institutional pressures to adopt new organizational forms may stem from legal requirements, the threat of uncertainty that leads to imitation, or the force of the industry's professional opinion. The institutional environment rewards those organizations that adopt the appropriate structural form by governmental license, increased ability to contract, public acceptance, and/or augmented legitimacy.

In summary, organizations may be motivated to vertically integrate in order to obtain increased efficiencies and/or market power. Vertical integration may also be encouraged by the institutional environment.

### Health care

The health care literature echoes the strategic management literature regarding the promised benefits of vertical integration. Efficiencies (both clinical and administrative), increased market power, and environmental acceptance are commonly expressed benefits (see Table 1). Most authors also assume that vertical integration will improve the health status of the population.[2,4,18–20] Such improvements derive from clinical and administrative integration, creating improved marketplace efficiencies by reducing excess capacity, eliminating unnecessary care, and concentrating responsibility for a continuum of care.[19,21–23]

---

*The health care literature echoes the strategic management literature regarding the promised benefits of vertical integration.*

---

It is also widely assumed that increased market power will result from vertical integration. Mick[24] sees vertical integration forestalling physician competition. Peters,[22] Conrad and Dowling,[20] and Dowling[1] see vertical integration increasing the organization's power to negotiate with suppliers, managed care companies, and others. Johnson[4] states that vertical

**TABLE 1**

SUMMARY OF PRESUMED BENEFITS OF VERTICAL INTEGRATION IN HEALTH CARE

| | Lowering costs and eliminating unneeded services | Economics of scale | Increased market and negotiating power | Profit and market share gains | Better recruitment and retention of MDs | Environmental acceptance |
|---|---|---|---|---|---|---|
| Findlay (1993) | X | X | X | | | |
| Coddington (1994) | X | | | X | X | |
| Shortell (1989) | X | | X | | | |
| Peters (1994) | X | X | X | | X | |
| Fox (1989) | | | X | | | |
| Ackerman (1992) | X | X | | | | |
| Gillies (1993) | X | | | | | |
| Conrad (1993) | X | | | | | |
| Wirth (1993) | | | X | | | |
| Wheeler (1986) | X | | | X | | |
| Johnson (1993) | X | | X | | | |
| Conrad & Dowling (1990) | X | | X | | | |
| Zuckerman & D'Aunno (1990) | | | | | | X |
| Brown & McCool (1986) | X | X | | X | | |

integration facilitates market domination, while Conrad and Dowling[20] argue that it facilitates the avoidance of regulation.

Another benefit of vertically integrated systems is public and professional acceptance. Zuckerman and D'Aunno[25] argue that health care organizations gain legitimacy and subsequent support by meeting external norms or expectations. As the spate of recent health care literature in Table 1 suggests, vertical integration has fast become an expected, almost normative strategy to pursue. Almost all proposals for health care reform assume some type of owned integrated health system. Indeed, much of the current vertical integration frenzy can be seen as the response to the possibility of future governmental reform, be it at the national or state level.

## THE PERFORMANCE OF VERTICALLY INTEGRATED ORGANIZATIONS

### Non–health care sector

A review of empirical studies suggests that owned vertical integration does *not* generally produce significant efficiency gains. In one of the most thorough, recent studies, D'Aveni and Ravenscraft compared owned vertically integrated and nonintegrated firms.[26] Using Federal Trade Commission (FTC) data, they reported increases in production costs along with greater decreases in general and administrative costs among highly integrated firms. However, in industries with unstable demand, production costs increased with *no* saving in overhead expenses. Also, those firms that primarily implemented backwards integration incurred higher overall costs and lower profits. They conclude that ownership of vertically integrated organizations succeeds best when coordination, production scheduling, and planning are relatively easy, when demand is certain and growing, and the industry has a few very large plants.

Other research has likewise demonstrated that increased inefficiencies may result from vertically integrated organizations. D'Aveni and Ilinitch[27] examined the effect of owned vertical integration in the forest products industry during a period of turbulent environmental and competitive changes. They found that fully integrated firms had higher systematic and bankruptcy risks in turbulent product markets. Other researchers report that ownership and backwards integration create exit barriers that "trap" firms in industries that may cause destructive competition and reduced profits.[28] Similar research on mergers, which combines both vertical and horizontal acquisitions, indicates that profitability declines significantly following mergers.[29,30] Decreased growth and profitability among merged firms subsequently fosters a high incidence of divestiture of acquired firms. Overall, research on owned vertical integration suggests resultant firm inefficiencies, not efficiency gains.

The empirical research above is also supported by a number of academic reviews of the literature. Martin[13] finds no evidence to support any social benefit from mergers. Koch[31] states that all research has shown firms generally to be less profitable following mergers. Greer[32] suggests that only big firms with relatively large market shares generally find owned vertical integration to be profitable, due to their use of vertical integration in anticompetitive ways to increase price. Clarkson[14] points out that if owned vertically integrated arrangements were actually beneficial, more and more firms over time would vertically integrate. Yet, he and others[33–35] find "no discernible trend of increased vertical integration by ownership over time."[14(p.342)] Owned integration has been found, however, to occur in cyclical, perhaps faddish, waves for the past 60 to 100 years in the U.S., Europe, and Japan. Mueller[36] attributes such cycles to mimetic behavior. For all of these reasons, Williamson[37] and Stuckey and White[10] suggest owned vertical integration only as a structural form of last resort.

In sum, a review of the literature outside health care leads to two surprising conclusions. First, the amount of empirical research regarding the impact of owned vertical integration is quite small. Second, almost all findings suggest negative effects of owned integration on performance (see Table 2).

### Performance in health care

Many researchers acknowledge that systematic empirical research on vertical integration in health care does not yet exist.[1,2,5,19,23,24,38] A few ongoing research projects such as the Health Systems Integration Study have now produced some preliminary results. Shortell et al.[39] report that integration is positively associated with financial performance, total net revenue, and productivity. However, these findings are based on the perceived integration reported by organizational members, not on ownership and/or nonownership, and do not take into account other factors that may influence system performance. Mick notes that efforts to link separate health care functions under a single organizational structure have often been scuttled after unrealistic expectations of producing all or most services internally were not met.[24]

A reasonable amount of evidence has accumulated on the performance of multihospital systems and hospital mergers, however. While these studies do not directly report on the results of vertical integration, they do focus on many of the dynamics involved in vertical integration and, thus, may provide some information on the potential results of vertical integration in health care. Shortell,[3] Zuckerman,[40] and Ermann and Gabel[41] each conducted research on the performance of multiinstitutional hospital systems. Shortell[3] reports little if any economic or service "value added" generated by affiliation. His findings are consistent with Zuckerman's[40] conclusion of mixed evidence supporting economic benefits at the institutional level, and little evidence for community benefit. Ermann and Gabel[41] also find little evidence of efficiencies and community price benefits from multihospital systems. Dranove and Shanley[42] also found no evidence of lower costs in hospital systems. They conclude that horizontal integration does not reduce production costs, but does reduce the system's search/reputational costs and improve its marketing success.

Two recent studies do report efficiency gains following hospital mergers. The Hospital Research and Education Trust found that merged hospitals reduce acute care services, lower costs, and reap higher profits.[43] Similarly, the Health Care Investment Analysts found that hospital costs decline postmerger; however, hospitals retained the increased profits and did not pass the savings on to consumers.[44]

### Summary of effects of vertical integration

Owned vertically integrated arrangements do not appear to significantly reduce organizational costs or yield other efficiencies. On the contrary, research suggests higher production costs and exit barriers and, when unstable demand exists, higher administrative costs as well. In health care the potential costs may

---

*Increased bargaining power and the ability to augment price may be important strategically for such systems in order to pass on the increased production and administrative costs.*

**TABLE 2**

SUMMARY OF ORGANIZATIONAL EFFECTS DUE TO MERGERS AND OWNED VERTICAL INTEGRATION

| | Finding | Industry | Market event |
|---|---|---|---|
| *Empirical evidence* | | | |
| D'Aveni & Ravenscraft (1994) | Slight gains overall, consistent increases in production costs, inefficient with unstable demand and backward integration. | General | Vertical integration |
| D'Aveni & Illinitch (1992) | Fully owned firms have higher systematic and bankruptcy risks in turbulent product market environments. | Forest products | Vertical integration |
| Harrigan (1985) | High degrees of ownership and backward integration erect exit barriers that may result in destructive competition and reduced profits. | General | Vertical integration |
| Harrigan (1986) | Successful firms used forms of control less than full ownership. Unsuccessful firms purchase too often from owned companies. | General | Vertical integration |
| Ravenscraft & Scherer (1989) | Acquired companies tend to be highly profitable pre-merger. Following mergers profitability declines with a high degree of divestiture. Questions claims that mergers on the average are efficiency enhancing. | General | Mergers |
| Borg, Borg & Leeth (1989) | Evaluated mergers during the unregulated 1920s. Found consistent results that postmerger performance declined indicating substantial shareholder loss. | General | Mergers |
| *Opinions and Summaries* | | | |
| Martin (1993) | No evidence to support social benefits of mergers. | General | Mergers |
| Koch (1980) | All research has shown firms to be generally less profitable following mergers. | General | Mergers |
| Greer (1980) | Generally only big firms with relatively large market shares tend to benefit from owned vertical integration as can use their market power to raise prices. | General | Vertical integration |
| Clarkson (1982) | No increase in vertical integration over time in industries. | General | Vertical integration |
| Williamson (1991) | Owned vertical integration generally considered the choice of last resort. | General | Vertical integration |
| Stuckey & White (1990) | Ownership risky, hard to reverse. Vertical integration should be used only as a last resort. | General | Vertical integration |

even be greater as the industry's complexity and instability far surpass most other industries. Overall, these kinds of arrangements may actually create higher costs.

Owned vertically integrated arrangements do create the potential for greater market power, however. Increased bargaining power and the ability to augment price may be important strategically for such systems in order to pass on the increased production and administrative costs. However, market power may be transitory as a result of regulation and/or changes in the competitive market. As an industry moves closer to an oligopolistic or monopolistic struc-ture the probability of greater governmental regulation increases.

## INSTITUTIONAL PRESSURES FOR VERTICAL INTEGRATION

Although health care managers' reasons for pursuing integration by ownership are varied, the industry is now adopting models of vertical integration that have been recognized in the past as highly successful. Organizations such as Kaiser and Group Health Co-operative of Puget Sound have been generally accepted as highly successful forms of vertically integrated systems. Goldsmith[5] states that many organizations in California such as Sharp in San Diego, Sutter in Sacramento, and UniHealth in Los Angeles have begun to model their systems after Kaiser. Indeed, under high uncertainty, we might expect that health care managers will attempt to reconfigure their organization in ways which emulate models that have been successful in the past.

New laws reforming health care are yet another stimulus for reconfiguration, and often specify recommended or required organizational forms. For example, Minnesota's new health reform law specifically calls for the formation of integrated service networks (vertically integrated systems) that offer capitated care in order to compete as a health care provider.[45] Other states such as Washington have also fomented widespread integrative efforts as a result of state-level health care reform legislation. Health care managers have commented numerous times to the authors that many of their efforts in creating IDSs are responses to anticipated state and federal laws. These laws, even if never fully enacted, have created massive realignments of providers, and new integrated structures have proliferated.

Within the realm of state and/or federal reform, many health care systems are following the anticipated legitimate form by creating owned vertical integrated arrangements. It might be argued, then, that health care systems are responding to the current uncertainty mimetically by adopting an institutional form that they believe the majority is also selecting. Indeed, they may be behaving in a fashion consistent with Palmer's observation:

> ... (Organizations) adopt forms that are considered legitimate by other organizations in their field, regardless of these structures' actual efficiency. There is often substantial uncertainty about the efficacy characteristics of alternative structures. Restricting attention to legitimated structures allows firms to identify efficient satisfying (as opposed to maximizing) solutions to organizational problems while conserving time and effort.[46(p.104)]

Many organizations euphorically "jump on the band-wagon"[24] and reorganize because others are doing so and because it has become the expected norm. The sheer number of organizations adopting a new structure can cause others to adopt the innovation, especially when the innovation's results are ill-defined and organizations fear that their competitors may gain an enduring strategic advantage by its adoption.[47] Hospitals may fear the loss of referral sources as competitors appear prepared to steal members of their medical staff.

Convinced that competitors will soon adopt the new structure, individual organizations act to protect themselves. The decision of a small critical mass of hospitals to begin purchasing components of vertically integrated systems creates an escalating competitive contest as systems vie over physicians' practices and other components of integrated systems. Hospital managers have expressed concerns of "being left behind" if they are locked out of favorable market arrangements. This purchase frenzy may result in the overpricing of assets (e.g., physician practices) and result in a "winner's curse" such that the high bidder and winner of the assets is strategically weakened by assuming the assets now priced above their market value.

Emulating past successful models is a logical choice under stable environmental conditions. However, environmental factors contributing to the past success of these owned vertically integrated models may have changed enough to make these models the wrong choice for the industry's future environment. Kaiser, for example, has failed to expand its membership since 1991, has a cost disadvantage compared to other HMOs, and has recently been slow to respond and innovate.[48] Goldsmith[5] cautions that Kaiser may now be too integrated. Health care managers, in a sense, may be choosing the best railroad for an environment that now requires air travel.

## INHERENT DIFFERENCES OF THE HEALTH CARE INDUSTRY

The health care industry is inherently different from other industries. Outputs are ambiguous and difficult to measure. Much of its production is of an emergency or semi-emergency nature. There is little tolerance for error and the work entails a high degree of specialization. Organizational participants are highly professionalized with primary loyalty to their profession. Weak organizational control exists over the chief decision-making provider, the physician.[49,50]

Economists have long recognized the market imperfections in health care, including imperfect and asymmetrical information, high levels of insurance coverage, and third party payment for services. Consumers lack pertinent knowledge and have difficulty determining quality. Clinical decisions are made and health care services are provided by a fragmented, disjointed system. Insurance coverage and third party payment leads consumers to seek higher than optimal levels of services.[51,52]

On the other hand, health care has come to resemble other industries in recent years by virtue of adopting many of their managerial techniques and tools. Hospitals in particular have adopted structures and tools such as matrix management, management by objectives, total quality management, and reengineering in an effort to become more efficient and to compete more effectively in local markets. Thus in a broad sense, it could be argued that many of the managerial differences between health care and other sectors are narrowing.

Some analysts argue that the inherent differences of health care may allow the industry to recombine and produce greater efficiencies in large, owned systems. Some observers, in fact, believe that *only* owned vertically integrated systems will provide cost-efficient services that will remain sustainable over time.[53] Do the unique features of health care themselves provide a basis for the creation of efficiencies through owned vertical integration when such arrangements have generally not met with success in other settings? Little or no research exists to support this position. Perhaps, the inherent complexities of health care and the continuing turbulence in health care markets may lead to greater inefficiencies than in other industries. Early research by Lawrence and Lorsch[54] demonstrated that greater differences in group orientations produce greater conflict. Health care is rendered by distinct professional groups whose efforts must be combined and coordinated to provide a full continuum of care in an owned vertically integrated system. Health care is also heavily labor intensive compared to other industries. The greater relational densities and potential for conflict, combined with the difficulties in monitoring, coordinating production, and transferring costs (transfer pricing) in health care, may actually create deeper managerial problems when they are joined through common ownership. These concerns have been factors in Goldsmith's and Johnson's warnings regarding owned vertically integrated health systems.[4,5]

## NONOWNED VERTICAL INTEGRATION OPTIONS

A number of alternatives to full ownership may capture the advantages of integration without the potential liabilities of ownership. These include long-term contracts, partial equity investments, and joint ventures. However, these alternative structures have their own limitations, and their performance remains uncertain. As Sofaer and Myrtle correctly note:

> Few empirical studies have been conducted on interorganizational relations in health care. Those that have been done have emphasized the strategic motivations for organizational interactions, rather than . . . their observed consequences. . . . Managerial beliefs about expected consequences (motivations) are often confused with experienced consequences.[55(p.403)]

Nevertheless, a few studies suggest that benefits can be gained through alternatives to owned integration. Fottler[56] reviews prior research indicating that increased communication and coordination improves clinical quality and patient satisfaction. Lawrence and Lorsch[43] report that firms exhibiting greater intrafirm integration also demonstrate better performance. Dyer and Ouchi,[57] studying Japanese supplier relationships, report that improved economic performance results from greater interorganizational trust and goal congruence (forms of integration). Such benefits may not be available to owned vertically integrated firms, but rather result from long-term relationships with frequent and open communication, mutual assistance, and consistent trust-building practices. These extended efforts ultimately produce organizational goal congruence and significant market competitive advantages. Little empirical research is available on non–fully owned integration and organizational performance. Absent more research, the consequences of vertical integration remain uncertain but, perhaps, more promising than ownership.

## IMPLICATIONS FOR MANAGERS

Managers should carefully weigh the advantages and disadvantages of owned vertically integrated arrangements. If vertical integration is deemed necessary, managers should first seek contractual, non–owned mechanisms to accomplish their objectives and avoid the increased bureaucratic costs of ownership. D'Aveni and Ravenscraft suggest that "true competitive advantage may be gained by replacing vertical integration [ownership] with vertical relationships."[26(p.1196)] Contractual methods may provide greater flexibility[4] and more numerous opportunities for production sharing.[58]

These "new models of integration"[5] are not asset based models, but include agreements, protocols, and incentives. Such models are not created instantaneously, but take extensive effort, time, and experience to develop.

Managers should also be aware of the increased probability of regulation if large, owned vertically integrated systems are established. According to Conrad,[18] 58 percent of the U.S. population lives in areas that would have at most two owned vertically integrated health care systems. If health care systems become dominant in their markets, they will undoubtedly face tighter regulation. Johnson warns that health care systems may become the "Blue Crosses and Blue Shields of the 21st century with all of the management, governance, and regulatory problems that the worst of the Blues are experiencing, and then some."[4(p.2)]

Providers should also organize to halt legislative attempts to mandate or encourage owned integrated delivery systems. Legislators should instead be asked to fund relevant research and base health care laws on factual findings rather than anticipated promises. Health care industry leaders have significant opportunities to mold legislation as states position themselves to fill the void created by the failure of federal legislative reform. Health care managers must seek to assist and direct their legislators to carefully craft appropriate legislation.

## SUMMARY

Health care researchers and practitioners should acknowledge and learn from other industries' experiences with vertical integration. Empirical evidence from outside health care suggests that the cost efficiency benefits of owned integrated structures are at best exaggerated and, perhaps, do not exist. In fact, results from other industries suggest that owned vertically integrated arrangements may actually produce negative effects and create more inefficient, less flexible systems. The recent health care literature promises significant efficiency and effectiveness gains for vertically integrated systems. Currently however, no reasonable evidence exists in the health care literature confirming these gains. Moreover, the models upon which owned vertically integrated systems are based are now beginning to experience severe problems.

These well-intentioned promises, reinforced by real cost pressures, are promoting a rush by providers to reorganize and reaffiliate and by state and federal legislators to enact legislation encouraging or mandating integrated system. As Nurkin aptly states

The process of change (vertical integration) is a reaction to cyclical forces. The depth and breadth of this change is related to the length, depth, and breadth of public dialogue regarding the issues rather than the specifics of quality, dollars per capita expended or access to care.[59(p.68)]

In the midst of the current rush to promote vertical integration, practitioners and policy makers alike should consider the experience of other industries, be prepared to experiment broadly, encourage careful evaluation of these experiments, and move forward better informed and hence better able to focus efforts to mold health care's new configuration more effectively.

## REFERENCES

1. Dowling, W. "Strategic Alliances as a Structure for Integrated Delivery Systems." In *Partners for the Dance: Forming Strategic Alliances in Health Care*, edited by A.D. Kaluzny, H.S. Zuckerman, and T.C. Ricketts. Ann Arbor, Mich.: Health Administration Press, 1995.
2. Brown, M., and McCool, B. "Vertical Integration: Exploration of a Popular Strategic Concept." *Health Care Management Review* 11, no. 4 (1986): 7–19.
3. Shortell, S.M. "The Evolution of Hospital Systems: Unfulfilled Promises and Self-Fulfilling Prophesies." *Medical Care Review* 45, no. 2 (1988): 177–214.
4. Johnson, D.E.L. "Integrated Systems Face Major Hurdles, Regulations." *Health Care Strategic Management* 11, no. 10 (1993): 2–3.
5. Goldsmith, J. "The Illusive Logic of Integration." *Healthcare Forum Journal* 37, no. 5 (1994): 26–31.
6. Slomski, A. "Maybe Bigger isn't Better After All." *Managed Care Economics* 72, no. 4 (1995): 55–60.
7. Porter, M.E. *Competitive Strategy: Techniques for Analyzing Industries and Competitors.* New York: Free Press, 1980.
8. Vickers, J., and Waterson, M. "Vertical Relationships: An Introduction." *The Journal of Industrial Economics* 39, no. 5 (1991): 445–49.
9. Varian, H. *Microeconomic Analysis.* New York: Norton and Company, 1992.
10. Stuckey, J., and White, D. "When and When Not to Vertically Integrate." *Sloan Management Review* 34, no. 3 (1993): 71–83.
11. Mahoney, J. "The Choice of Organizational Form: Vertical Financial Ownership versus Other Methods of Vertical Integration." *Strategic Management Journal* 13 (1992): 559–84.
12. Lieberman, M. "Determinants of Vertical Integration: An Empirical Test. *Journal of Industrial Economics* 39, no. 5 (1991): 451–66.

13. Martin, S. *Advanced Industrial Economics*. Boston: Blackwell Publishers, 1993.

14. Clarkson, K., and Miller, R. *Industrial Organization: Theory, Evidence, and Public Policy*. New York: McGraw-Hill, 1982.

15. Dutz, M. "Horizontal Mergers in Declining Industries: Theory and Evidence." *International Journal of Industrial Organization* 7 (1989): 11–33.

16. Meyer, J.W., and Rowan, B. "Institutional Organizations : Formal Structure as Myth and Ceremony." *American Journal of Sociology* 83 (1977): 340–63.

17. DiMaggio, P., and Powell, W. "The Iron Cage Revisited: Institutional Isomorphism and Collective Rationality in Organizational Fields." *American Sociological Review* 48 (1983): 147–60.

18. Conrad, D. "Coordinating Patient Care Services in Regional Health Systems: The Challenge of Clinical Integration." *Hospital and Health Services Administration* 38 (Winter 1993): 491–505.

19. Gillies, R., et al. "Conceptualizing and Measuring Integration: Findings from the Health Systems Integration Study." *Hospital and Health Services Administration* 38, no. 4 (1993): 467–89.

20. Conrad, D., and Dowling, W. "Vertical Integration in Health Services: Theory and Managerial Implications." *Health Care Management Review* 15, no. 4 (1990): 9–22.

21. Coddington, K., Moore, K., and Fischer, E. "Cost and Benefits of Integrated Healthcare Systems." *Healthcare Financial Management* 48, no. 3 (1994): 28–30.

22. Peters, G. "Integrated Delivery Can Ally Physician and Hospital Planning." *Healthcare Financial Management* 45, no. 12 (1991): 21–28.

23. Ackerman, K. "The Movement Toward Vertical Integrated Regional Health Systems." *Health Care Management Review* 17, no. 3 (1992): 81–88.

24. Mick, S.S. "The Decision to Integrate Vertically in Health Care Organizations." *Hospital and Health Services Administration* 33, no. 3 (Fall 1988): 345–60.

25. Zuckerman, H., and D'Aunno, T. "Hospital Alliances: Cooperative Strategy in a Competitive Environment." *Health Care Management Review* 15, no. 2 (1990): 21–30.

26. D'Aveni, R., and Ravenscraft, D.J. "Economies of Integration Versus Bureaucracy Costs: Does Vertical Integration Improve Performance?" *Academy of Management Journal* 37, no. 5 (1994): 1167–1206.

27. D'Aveni, R., and Ilinitch, A. "Complex Patterns of Vertical Integration in the Forest Products Industry: Systematic and Bankruptcy Risks." *Academy of Management Journal* 35, no. 3 (1992): 596–625.

28. Harrigan, K. "Exit Barriers and Vertical Integration." *Academy of Management* 28, no. 3 (1985): 686–97.

29. Ravenscraft, D., and Scherer, F.M. "The Profitability of Mergers." *International Journal of Industrial Organizations* 7 (1989): 101–16.

30. Borg, J.R., Borg, M.O., and Leeth, J.D. "The Success of Mergers in the 1920s: A Stock Market Appraisal of the Second Merger Wave." *International Journal of Industrial Organization* 7 (1989): 117–31.

31. Koch, J. *Industrial Organization and Prices*. Englewood Cliffs, N.J.: Prentice-Hall, 1980.

32. Greer, D. *Industrial Organization and Public Policy*. New York: Macmillan, 1980.

33. Adelman, M.A. *Concept and Statistical Measurement of Vertical Integration: Business Concentration and Price Policy*. Princeton, N.J.: Princeton University Press, 1955.

34. Laffer, A.B. "Vertical Integration by Corporations: 1929–1965." *Review of Economics and Statistics* 51 (February 1969): 91–93.

35. Tucker, I., and Wilder, R. "Trends in Vertical Integration in the U.S. Manufacturing Sector." *The Journal of Industrial Economics* 26, no. 1 (1977): 81–94.

36. Mueller, D. "Mergers: Causes, Effects and Policies." *International Journal of Industrial Organization* 7 (1989): 1–10.

37. Williamson, O. "Comparative Economic Organizations: The Analysis of Discrete Structural Alternatives." *Administrative Science Quarterly* 36 (1991): 269–96.

38. Wheeler, J., Wickizer, T., and Shortell, S. "Hospital–Physician Vertical Integration." *Hospital and Health Services Administration* 31, no. 2 (1986): 67–80.

39. Shortell, S.M., Gillies, R., and Anderson, D.A. "The New World of Managed Care: Creating Organized Delivery Systems." *Health Affairs* 38, no. 4 (1994): 46–64.

40. Zuckerman, H. *Multi-Institutional Systems: Their Promise and Performance*. Chicago: Hospital Research and Educational Trust, 1979.

41. Ermann, D., and Gabel, J. "Multi-Hospital Systems: Issues and Empirical Findings." *Health Affairs* 3, no. 1 (1984): 51–64.

42. Dranove, D., and Shanley, S. "Cost Reductions or Reputation Enhancement as Motives for Mergers: The Logic of Multihospital Systems." *Strategic Management Journal* 16 (1995): 55–74.

43. Burda, D. "Study—Mergers Cut Costs, Services, Increase Profits." *Modern Healthcare* 23, no. 46 (15 November 1993): 4.

44. Greene, J. "Merger Monopolies." *Modern Healthcare* 24, no. 49 (5 December 1994): 38–48.

45. Findlay, S. "How New Alliances are Changing Health Care." *Business and Health* 11, no. 12 (1993): 28–33.

46. Palmer, D.A., Jennings, P.D., and Zhou, X. "Late Adoption of the Multidivisional Form by Large U.S. Corporations: Institutional, Political, and Economic Accounts." *Administrative Science Quarterly* 38 (1993): 100–31.

47. Abrahamson, E., and Rosenkopf, L. "Institutional and

Competitive Bandwagons: Using Mathematical Modeling as a Tool to Explore Innovation Diffusion." *Academy of Management Review* 18, no. 3 (1993): 487–517.

48. *Wall Street Journal*, December 2, 1994, p.1.

49. Shortell, S.M., and Kaluzny, A.D. *Health Care Management: Organization Design and Behavior*. Albany, N.Y.: Delmar Publishers, 1994.

50. Kimberly, J. "Managerial Innovation and Health Policy: Theoretical Perspectives and Research Implications." *Journal of Health Politics and Law* 6, no. 2 (1982): 637–52.

51. Danzon, P. "Consolidation and Restructuring in the Health Care Industry." Working paper, University of Pennsylvania, August 1994.

52. Arrow, K. "Uncertainty and the Welfare Economics of Medical Care." *American Economic Review* 53 (1963): 941–73.

53. Cave, D.G. "Vertical Integration Models to Prepare Health Systems for Capitation." *Health Care Management Review* 20, no. 1 (1995): 26–39.

54. Lawrence, P., and Lorsch, J. *Organization and Environment: Managing Differentiation and Integration*. Homewood, Ill.: Richard D. Irwin, 1969.

55. Sofaer, S., and Myrtle, R. "Interorganizational Theory and Research: Implications for Health Care Management, Policy, and Research." *Medical Care Review* 48, no. 4 (1991): 371–409.

56. Fottler, M. "Health Care Organizational Performance: Present and Future Research." *Journal of Management* 13, no. 2 (1987): 367–91.

57. Dyer, J., and Ouchi, W. "Japanese-style Partnerships: Giving Companies a Competitive Edge." *Sloan Management Review* 35, no. 1 (1993): 51–63.

58. Barrayre, P.Y. "The Concept of 'Impartition' Policies: A Different Approach to Vertical Integration Strategies." *Strategic Management Journal* 9 (1988): 507–620.

59. Nurkin, H. "The Creation of a Multi-Organizational Healthcare Alliance: The Charlotte-Mecklenburg Hospital Authority." In *Partners for the Dance: Forming Strategic Alliances in Health Care*, edited by A.D. Kaluzny, H.S. Zuckerman, and T.C. Ricketts. Ann Arbor, Mich.: Health Administration Press, 1995.

# Trends and models in physician–hospital organization

Lawton R. Burns
and
Darrell P. Thorpe

*Physicians and hospitals have developed new models for aligning their incentives and integrating their activities. These models serve numerous purposes, including unified contracting with managed care organizations, improved access to capital and patients, and strengthened competitive position. The more advanced models carry the added potential of providing comprehensive, community-based care with less duplication of services. The new models raise several important issues that providers need to consider before embarking on these strategies.*

*Health Care Manage Rev*, 1993, 18(4), 7–20
© 1993 Aspen Publishers, Inc.

**There has been** a great deal of interest in physician–hospital relationships over the past few years. Surveys to assess the attitudinal climate, governance involvement, and employment relationship between hospitals and their medical staffs have been conducted by academics, professional societies, and consultants.[1-5] Most recently, the Prospective Payment Assessment Commission initiated a survey of hospitals' ability to influence cost-effective practice behavior on the part of their physicians. All these studies focus on internal relationships between a hospital and members of its medical staff.

Competitive economic forces are driving the health care industry to develop new models of physician–hospital relationships, however. These relationships are different in that they are formally organized, contractual, and/or corporate in character and include physicians outside the boundaries of the medical staff. Such relationships are known as physician–hospital organizations (PHOs), management service organizations (MSOs), foundation models, and integrated health organizations (IHOs). These relationships have been described frequently in the medical group management and group practice literatures. With few exceptions, however, the new organizational models have not received much attention in the hospital administration literature.[6,7]

The article outlines the new competitive forces that are encouraging the formation of these new models from the perspectives of the parties involved: physicians and hospitals. It also describes the competitive strengths and competencies of the parties that are harnessed in these new arrangements. The article next describes the structural features of these new organizational models. It concludes with a discussion of the issues and implications that these models pose.

*Lawton R. Burns*, M.B.A., Ph.D., is in the Department of Management and Policy and the School of Public Administration and Policy, College of Business and Public Administration, University of Arizona, Tucson.

*Darrell P. Thorpe*, M.D., M.P.H., is Senior Vice-President for Strategic Services at the Tucson Medical Center, Tucson, Arizona.

This article was written while the first author was supported by the Hospital Research and Educational Trust and the Edwin L. Crosby Memorial Fellowship. The views expressed here are those of the authors. The authors wish to thank Geoffrey Baker and Ross Stromberg for their assistance in compiling some of the information contained in this article as well as Monty Brown and Alexandra Polydefkis for their consultation on the legal elements of the physician–hospital models. The authors also thank Jim Begun, Henry Golembeski, and Bob Hurley for their comments on an earlier draft.

## COMPETITIVE FORCES FOSTERING THE NEW MODELS

### Competitive forces facing physicians

The health care marketplace has become an increasingly unfamiliar, uncertain, and unfriendly environment for physicians. Changes in physician reimbursement in both the public and the private sectors and other environmental changes have significantly affected the ability of physicians to set and maintain their own levels of annual income.

Reimbursement under Medicare is increasingly fixed, and the implementation of the Resource-Based Relative Value Schedule (RBRVS) is lowering levels of payment for specialists while raising levels for primary care physicians (PCPs) in relative, but not absolute, terms. Medicaid payments in most states have become so meager as to discourage many physicians from participating in that program at all. Private payers are limiting the ability of physicians to shift the cost of public programs onto the private sector by expanding the use of managed care and other discounted and/or fixed-fee arrangements for their beneficiaries.

Efforts by physicians to make up for reductions in payment per unit of service by increasing the number of units of service provided are being inhibited (and prohibited) in both the public and the private sectors through utilization review and other monitoring programs. Finally, attempts by physicians to tap alternative sources of revenue through the establishment of in-office ancillary services are discouraged by tighter licensing and other regulatory restrictions and by managed care companies that specify in their contracts where such services are to be provided.

At the same time that physicians are experiencing these limitations on their practice revenues, they are also facing increased costs of operating their practices. The costs of medical malpractice insurance, medical supplies, office occupancy, and nonphysician personnel are all increasing at a rate greater than the increase in practice revenues, resulting in a flattening out of professional net income.[8] The net effect of these new economic realities for many physicians is that financial expectations are not being met and long-term economic security is of increasing importance.

The economics of medical practice is only one source of consternation for today's physicians. The impact of managed care on the practice of medicine itself is perhaps even more important. The physician is no longer the exclusive agent of the patient, determining where the patient should be treated and how much care should be ordered.[9] Instead, the physician is confronted by managed care imperatives such as prior certification for hospital admission and surgery, continued stay review, and case management.

PCPs are being asked to be gatekeepers, that is, to provide care themselves for a broader range of medical conditions and to refer to specialists less and then only when absolutely necessary. Patterns of referral are increasingly dictated by managed care contracts, causing many PCPs to switch from specialists to whom they have historically referred. Some specialists consequently may get fewer referrals and often must seek permission from the gatekeeper or from a utilization management person before performing diagnostic and/or therapeutic procedures or scheduling follow-up visits. Selective contracting arrangements with hospitals may further curb their autonomy.

Finally, physicians are confronted by increasing administrative complexity (popularly known as the hassle factor) in dealing with multiple plans and insurers, each with its own unique administrative and paperwork requirements. In addition to creating the discomfort that comes with significant change, all these factors contribute to the increased cost of operating a medical practice.

---

*Today's practice environment requires more sophisticated systems, including information systems and in-office medical technology, as well as personnel with managed care contracting, marketing, and other advanced management expertise.*

---

The forces and stresses described above have special impact on solo practitioners and small groups. Today's practice environment requires more sophisticated systems, including information systems and in-office medical technology, as well as personnel with managed care contracting, marketing, and other more advanced management expertise. Solo and small group practices do not have the financial wherewithal to acquire and maintain these capabilities. They may also lack the capital needed to recruit partners and expand services. Consequently, physicians increasingly favor group practice settings, as gauged by the number of groups (16,500 in 1988), the percentage of active nonfederal physicians within them (one third in 1988), and their increasingly large average size.[10] Of course, the growing size of group practices also reflects their growing attractiveness to physicians. Groups appeal to the increasing percentage of female physicians who want to balance family and career goals. Groups also appeal to younger physicians who want to balance their personal and professional lives.[11]

Group practices, although better able to deal with many of the challenges facing physicians than their solo colleagues, have a number of unique concerns. Because of growing size, group practices face barriers to entry and exit. Larger size means a greater valuation of the group's tangible and intangible assets and thus a prohibitive cost for prospective members to buy into the group. The greater valuation of intangible assets makes it more difficult to sell them off piecemeal for members who wish to depart the group.[12]

Groups also wish to minimize or share the financial risks incurred in their capitated arrangements with managed care plans. In such arrangements, the physicians may be capitated while the hospital receives a negotiated per diem. Not wishing to assume risk for variables beyond their full control (such as case management, discharge planning, test and procedure scheduling, etc.), all of which can increase patient stays and costs, physicians often prefer hospitals to share the risk associated with these arrangements.

Finally, groups are typically unwilling and/or unable to invest greater internally generated resources into needed administrative and information systems. For example, group physicians may be skeptical of the need to pay higher administrative salaries or to fund greater administrative expenses. There may be considerable pressure to pay out the group's earnings in the form of higher physician salaries and bonuses than in the form of capital or administrative investments.[12,13] Similarly, group members are unable to qualify for tax-exempt financing and frequently are unwilling to access needed capital through personally guaranteed bank loans.

### Competitive forces facing hospitals and hospital-based specialists

Like physicians, hospitals face more uncertain revenue streams as a result of the prospective payment system (PPS) and managed care. Hospitals are feeling the long-term effects of PPS, such as a decrease in inpatient volume and a shift to outpatient settings, and are concerned about maintaining and building census. In particular, hospitals need to protect their internal medicine and surgical specialists and thus stabilize their medical staffs. These specialists are concerned about the hospital's PCP base and adequate clinical work to support their hospital practice and to protect their earnings. To protect their specialists, hospitals need to protect and broaden their physician referral base, which acts as a feeder system to the institution.

Hospitals are thus seeking to design structures and ventures that reward loyal physicians on staff yet do not anger other physicians but allow them to participate in other mechanisms. They also seek ways to shore up the practices of aging solo practitioners on staff, which may be deteriorating in both size and value. Finally, hospitals recognize that managed care plans use PCPs as gatekeepers to the hospital system and thus the need to establish linkages with them. This issue is particularly important for urban and suburban hospitals that are heavily laden with specialists and have relatively little inpatient contact with PCPs.

Hospitals, like physicians, also face growing competitive threats to their market share and profitable product lines. This competition comes not only from other hospitals but also from large multispecialty groups practices and physicians on staff who set up diagnostic and therapeutic facilities outside the hospital to escape from the RBRVS and hospital control. The PPS and competition threaten to dismantle the hospital's traditional profit centers, transfer them to the ambulatory care market, and thereby curb the hospital's capacity to cross-subsidize services.[14] Hospitals facing this threat seek to gain some measure of control over physicians' ambulatory care business and to preempt competitive initiatives from outsiders.

Finally, hospitals are confronted by the imperatives of managed care contracting: Cut costs, control utilization, and document/improve quality of care. Hospitals are also being pushed to assume more risk in these arrangements, such as the use of single pricing contracts for hospital and medical services. Hospitals wish to educate their physicians about managed care and to share with them the financial risks of managed care. They also want to increase their leverage over managed care firms. One strategy is to pool their contracting activities with other providers to achieve economies and efficiencies. Another strategy is to create alternative contracting vehicles to attract employers directly.

### STRENGTHS AND COMPETENCIES FOR DEVELOPING THESE MODELS

#### Solo physicians

According to the latest American Medical Association statistics, solo practice still represents the single largest practice setting among U.S. physicians. By virtue of their numbers and the fact that many are practitioners of primary care, solo physicians constitute an important, although fragmented, block of providers to include in any new model of physician–hospital relationships. The most popular way of organizing them during the past decade has been through independent practice association (IPA) model health maintenance organizations (HMOs). IPA-HMOs have experienced the most rapid growth among all HMO types in terms of numbers of plans, enrolled members, and participating physicians.[15] Their popularity stems from their relatively inexpensive start-up costs, the ability of physicians to remain in private practice in their own offices, their protection of fee-for service reimbursement, and the ability of patients to retain their customary physicians.[16] Most hospital administrators unfortunately lack information about the practices of solo physicians who work primarily in their own offices; such information is needed to harness quickly the IPA HMO potential.

### Group practice physicians

Group practices offer different competitive strengths in the development of new physician–hospital models. An obvious advantage is their strength in numbers.[11,17] The growing number and average size of group practices increase their salience to hospitals as attractive coalition partners and their voice in the governance structures of these arrangements. By virtue of their larger size, groups of physicians can offer a more comprehensive range of services at multiple sites and thus can increase their attractiveness to managed care organizations (MCOs). Their size may also appeal to HMOs and preferred provider organizations (PPOs) that look for provider groups with sufficient numbers to assume risk. At the same time, groups of physicians can present an organized front to managed care organizations and third party payers, thereby augmenting their bargaining position in contract negotiations. As a final advantage of size, groups can band together and meet the competitive threat posed by large networks and systems of other providers, such as Kaiser Health Plan in California.

In addition to their size, group practices enjoy competitive advantages in attracting patients. Groups are better situated than solo practitioners to meet patient demands and preferences for care that is centralized in one site, convenient to access, and comprehensive in the scope of services provided.[11] Groups also enjoy brand recognition (e.g., the Mayo Clinic and the Cleveland Clinic) and a marketplace perception of quality.

Research suggests that quality of care may be higher in groups settings as a result of greater professional interaction and surveillance.[16,18] Indeed, some analysts suggest that purchasers prefer contracting with groups because of their ability to manage quality and cost.[9]

Finally, in contrast to solo physicians, group practices have sufficient patient volume to permit diversification into ancillary services and ambulatory care businesses.[9] As a result, they may be capable of generating a much higher return on investment. They may also be better situated to take on more risk as well as to self-insure.

### Hospitals

Hospitals contribute a different set of strengths to new physician–hospital arrangements. In contrast to physicians, hospitals have greater access to capital because of their nonprofit status and larger scale. Such capital is required to expand service offerings and delivery sites. Hospitals also possess the administrative leadership necessary to develop and guide these new arrangements as well as the required technical capabilities such as management information systems, data processing, finance, and marketing.

Hospitals may possess another critical advantage over other providers as a result of their prior experience with managed care contracting. As a result, hospitals have greater experience with utilization review, practice profiles, contract negotiation, and pricing. Some hospitals are already offering contract review and advisory services to their medical staffs. They also have greater knowledge of competitors' strategies/offerings and physician referral patterns.

### Summary

Physicians and hospitals face an increasingly competitive and uncertain environment. They are confronted with a series of challenges, some common to both parties and some unique to each. Perhaps the greatest common challenge is posed by the shift from a non–managed care to a managed care environment, in which they are at greater financial risk. Physicians and hospitals recognize their mutual interdependence in managing these risks as well as their mutual advantage in combining forces to operate within a managed care marketplace. The two parties thus have the incentive to seek closer cooperation. They also have the opportunity. Physicians and hospitals each possess competitive strengths that make them mutually attractive as partners in a coalition that pools their resources to gain greater leverage in a managed care environment. The new models of physician–hospital organization described below constitute different formats for organizing these coalitions.

## NEW MODELS OF PHYSICIAN–HOSPITAL ORGANIZATION

There are at least four different models of new physician–hospital arrangements that have been described in case studies in the group practice literature. These include the PHO, the MSO, the foundation model, and the integrated health organization (IHO). Because each model has a number of variants, this classification should be considered a rough typology. There is some indication that physician–hospital arrangements develop from one model to the next. In this process of development, the arrangements foster much higher integration between the two parties. According to the Leadership Institute, such integration involves shared risk through common ownership, governance, revenue/capital, planning, and/or management.[19] The four basic models are described below.

### Physician–hospital organization

A PHO is a joint venture between one or more hospitals and physicians. The physicians may participate in the joint venture as individuals or, more often, as members of a physician organization such as an IPA or professional corporation (PC).

The PHO may be organized for a single purpose, such as acting as a single agent for managed care contracting. More often, the PHO is organized for multiple purposes. It serves as the single agent for contracting with multiple HMOs and/or PPCs as well as directly with employers. It may also own a managed care plan (HMO or PPO), own and operate ambulatory care centers or ancillary services projects, and provide administrative or other services to physician members.

---

*If the PHO is used for contracting, the two parties can exert greater bargaining leverage as well as respond to purchaser preferences for a single, bundled price.*

---

If the PHO is used for contracting, the two parties can present a united front and exert greater bargaining leverage as well as respond to purchaser preferences for a single, bundled price. To be effective, however, this coalition must be viewed by purchasers as a potential cost-

control strategy. The PHO therefore requires active utilization management, sophisticated utilization information, and intensive involvement of physicians in developing standards of care and monitoring utilization. Given the contentiousness and complexity of economic credentialing, it should be evident that the PHO offers distinct advantages over the hospital medical staff structure as a lean, mean, contracting machine.

To avoid concerns of antitrust, the PHO cannot exist solely to negotiate contracts but must also contain significant elements of risk sharing between the two parties and the integration of operations for some legitimate purpose. Depending upon that legitimate business purpose, the PHO may also need to comply with safe harbors regulations (see below). These regulations are especially pertinent to potential PHO projects involving ancillary medical services, where physician members of the PHO can also be a major source of its patient referrals.

In additional to contracting, PHO responsibilities typically include utilization review and quality assurance, physician credentialing and claims processing, marketing, and the development of fee schedules. The PHO may also serve as an educational vehicle to teach practitioners about the economics of managed care and the economic needs of the hospital.

The PHO model allows alignment of the interests of the hospital(s) and important physicians and provides for the sharing of risk between the parties. That risk is shared, however, only as it relates to those projects/activities that are conducted through the PHO. Each party continues to conduct and carry the risk for the remainder of its non-PHO activities.

### Management services organization

The MSO is a corporation (for profit or nonprofit) that may be freestanding or, for purposes of this discussion, owned by a hospital or a physician–hospital joint venture. It provides management services to one or more medical practices (usually sizeable group practices) and serves as a framework for joint planning and decision making in the business affairs of the practice. If forming a new relationship with an existing PC, the MSO purchases the tangible assets of the PC at fair market value to avoid concerns of private inurement (Figure 1). These assets are then leased back to the PC as part of a full-service management agreement, under which the MSO employs all nonphysician staff and provides all supplies and administrative systems required by the group in exchange for either a flat fee or a set percentage of group revenues. The practice con-

---

**FIGURE 1**

---

MSO/PC MODEL: COMMON FEATURES

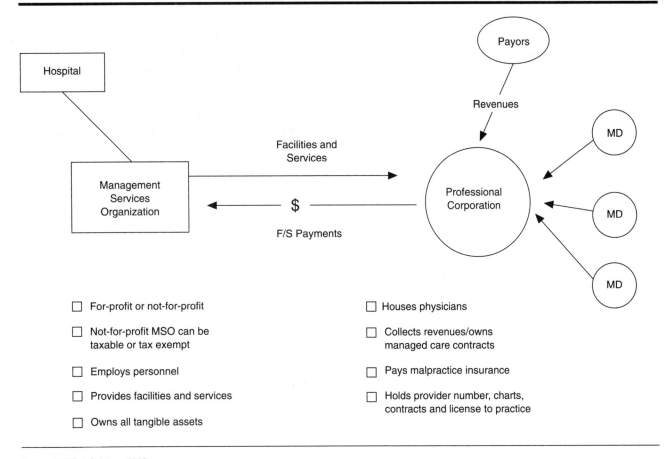

☐ For-profit or not-for-profit

☐ Not-for-profit MSO can be
  taxable or tax exempt

☐ Employs personnel

☐ Provides facilities and services

☐ Owns all tangible assets

☐ Houses physicians

☐ Collects revenues/owns
  managed care contracts

☐ Pays malpractice insurance

☐ Holds provider number, charts,
  contracts and license to practice

---

*Source:* BDC Advisors, 1992.

---

tinues to be owned by the PC and the provider number used is that of the PC. In California, some MSO examples include Alta Bates and Mercy–San Diego.

This brief description conveys three of the main attractions of the MSO to physicians. First, the MSO serves as a vehicle to transfer hospital capital to the group of physicians, which can be used to develop a group as well as to expand existing clinical services, staff, and/or operations. Second, the MSO provides administrative systems that may not be affordable by the individual physicians in the PC. Third, the MSO may provide comprehensive ambulatory and inpatient services through an integrated business entity that manages that care and assumes financial risk.

The MSO resembles the PHO in several respects. The physicians' PC retains its autonomy and acts as the provider of patient care services. The MSO may also provide for shared governance between the hospital and the PC. Finally, the hospital must comply with antifraud and safe harbors regulations, for example by granting only limited subsidies to the MSO if it operates at a loss and thus avoiding private inurement of physicians, by demonstrating that the MSO furthers the hospital's charitable purpose and benefits the community, and by negotiating the purchase of the PC's tangible assets at arms' length.

Unlike the situation in PHOs, in MSOs the PC is typically the entity that executes contracts with payers and MCOs. Thus all managed care revenues flow to the PC, not the MSO. Another difference between the PHO and the MSO is the amount of risk shared between the hospital and physicians. In the PHO risk is shared only for those activities in which the PHO is engaged, generally a limited part of any physician's practice. In the MSO, the full risk of the practice is shared between the PC and the owners of the MSO. Alignment of interests and incentives is thus more complete in the MSO than in the PHO.

### The foundation model

The foundation is a corporation, usually nonprofit, that is organized either as an affiliate of a hospital with a common parent organization or as a subsidiary of a hospital. In this model the foundation owns and operates one or more practices, including their facilities, equipment, and supplies. The foundation employs all nonphysician personnel and contracts with a physician-owned entity (usually a PC) to provide the medical services for the practice (Figure 2). Some of the more prominent examples of existing foundations in California include UniHealth America, Mercy Medical Foundation, Sharp Rees–Stealy, Palo Alto Medical Foundation, Sutter Health, and, most recently, Friendly Hills Healthcare Foundation.

Foundations can qualify for tax-exempt status under 501(c)(3) of the Internal Revenue Code by adhering to two main statutory requirements[20]:

1. *Organizational/operational tests:* The foundation must primarily engage in activities that serve charitable purposes, such as promotion of health and provision of health care services to the broader community with no limitations based on ability to pay, educational activities, or medical research. The foundation must also be able to demonstrate that it is not organized and operated for the benefit of private interests (i.e., its board and the board of the medical group do not substantially overlap).

## FIGURE 2

FOUNDATION MODEL: COMMON FEATURES

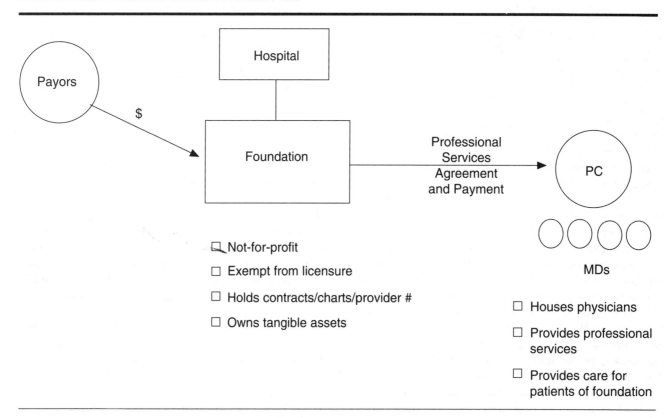

*Source:* BDC Advisors, 1992.

2. *Private inurement proscription:* The foundation's net earnings may not inure to the benefit of any private shareholder, member, or other interested person (i.e., a physician). This requires that all compensation payable by the foundation to physicians be reasonable in amount, be the result of arms' length negotiation, and not be a device to distribute the foundation's operating surplus. Similarly, the acquisition of physician assets by the foundation must bear a reasonable relationship to the foundation's exempt purposes, be purchased at fair market value, be negotiated at arms' length, and not result in more than an insubstantial private economic benefit to physicians in relation to the public benefit that will be conferred from the foundation's activities.

In some states, a medical foundation requires exemption from clinic licensing and application of the corporate practice of medicine rule. In California, for example, where they originated, foundations are explicitly exempt from the former and implicitly exempt from the latter if they contract with a group of physicians (a PC) that numbers at least forty, whose members practice in at least ten specialties, where two thirds of the physicians practice within foundation facilities, and that conducts medical research and health education.[20,21]

In this model, the physician group owns no assets, either tangible or intangible. This makes it much easier for new physicians to buy into the group and for retiring physicians to leave. Moreover, as in the MSO, the transfer of assets from the group to the foundation enables the group to expand services and to recruit additional providers, both PCPs and specialists.

Under this model, the foundation becomes the formal provider of health care but negotiates a professional services agreement with physicians to provide services to foundation patients. As payment, the PC receives either a percentage of the foundation's revenues/collections or a lump sum. The PC retains its autonomy and remains self-governing. It employs or compensates all physicians, conducts all credentialing, and performs utilization review activities.

For its part, the foundation provides the clinic premises, provides all administrative/financial/marketing services, employs all nonmedical personnel, and serves as a vehicle to accumulate and retain surpluses that can be used to finance new equipment, facilities, and operations. In the tax-exempt nonprofit foundation, unlike the MSO, such surpluses are not taxed.[22] In addition, unlike the MSO, the foundation may qualify for tax-exempt financing under certain conditions.

These include limitations on the number of contracting physicians who may serve on the foundation's board of directors to one of every five members (the 80–20 rule) and restrictions on the length, compensation features, and termination clause in physician service contracts.[20] Tax-exemption enhances the foundation's access to capital. Tax-exempt foundations, with sufficient cash flow and assets, can get rated by bond rating agencies. These agencies may give higher ratings to more integrative physician–hospital arrangements. Foundations can thus obtain substantial amounts of capital in the form of tax-exempt debt on favorable terms as well as avoid sales and income taxes.[23] As a tax-exempt affiliate of the nonprofit hospital, the foundation may also be able to access additional (hospital) capital via transfers of funds from one hospital affiliate to another with less risk of private inurement.[24]

The foundation also engages in all contracts with payers and managed care firms. This model allows the hospital and physicians to present themselves as a combined contracting unit. Usually both the physicians and the hospital will be capitated in these arrangements. The capitation rate paid by the managed care organization will be divided into a physician capitation pool (cap pool) and a hospital cap pool. In addition, the physicians and the hospital will negotiate a per diem to be charged to the hospital cap pool that should cover monthly expenses on a break-even basis. Both parties have an incentive to conserve resource utilization to ensure that the hospital cap pool shows a surplus that can then be shared. The risks of capitation (i.e., instances where the hospital cap pool shows a deficit) are likewise shared. Other shared incentives to promote efficiency stem from marketplace demands to reduce costs and managerial controls exerted by both the hospital and the medical leadership of the PC.

For hospitals, the foundation constitutes one method for developing the network of providers essential for a vertically integrated system. Hospitals also engage in such arrangements to develop new sources of admissions, to increase market share and their primary care base of patients, to protect their specialists' incomes, and to generate referrals to other parts of the system. Physi-

---

*Physicians view the medical foundation as relief from the administrative hassles of practice and freedom to focus on clinical considerations.*

cians view the foundation as relief from the administrative hassles of practice and freedom to focus on clinical considerations.[24] Physician groups also view the foundation as a means to access capital—whether borrowed externally through operations—without having to borrow it themselves. Such capital can be used to expand to meet growing outpatient demand. Physicians may also view the model as their entree to the managed care market controlled by the hospital or as an accommodation with a potential competitor in a turbulent ambulatory care market.

Organizationally, the foundation and the hospital are on a level plane. Each is free to concentrate on its own special projects or operating issues. The foundation is governed by a combination of representatives from the PC, the hospital, and/or the community. Physicians representation in foundation governance is limited by Internal Revenue Service (IRS) regulations to no more than 49 percent of practitioners in the medical group because of IRS reluctance to exempt physician-controlled entities from taxation.[22] The majority of board members are required by the IRS to be nonpaid community leaders and/or nonphysician hospital representatives.

Of course, not every foundation exhibits all the above features. Foundation models vary in terms of state regulations governing the corporation practice of medicine, the existence of a separate legal entity, the managerial and legal commitment made by hospitals and the PC, and the degree of risk assumed by the two parties.[25]

The foundation model offers most of the advantages over PHO arrangements that are offered by MSOs and results in a high degree of alignment of incentives and sharing of risk. It offers a potential additional advantage over the MSO model in the availability of tax exemption and thus access to cheaper capital and avoidance of taxation on foundation surpluses and property values. It carries with it, however, a major disadvantage for physicians compared with the MSO, particularly if tax exemption is sought. Because physician participation in governance is limited in the foundation and not in the MSO, there is a relative loss of physician control. Even so, physicians can maintain significant influence over the foundation's operation through the terms of the professional services agreement between the foundation and the PC.

### Integrated health organization

The IHO model involves the development of a separate legal entity (a parent corporation) that typically controls three main subsidiaries: a hospital corporation, a medical services corporation, and an educational and research foundation. Conceptually, the IHO could be either for profit or nonprofit. From a practical point of view, IHOs are usually organized such that the parent and its subsidiaries are all tax-exempt, nonprofit corporations. Some prominent examples of IHOs include Virginia Mason in Seattle (Figure 3) and Ramsey HealthCare in St. Paul.

The parent board of the IHO comprises representatives of the subsidiary boards along with lay members from the community. The hospital corporation is generally a community hospital organization with a board of directors. The medical services corporation is unique in that it is a tax-exempt, nonprofit entity with a physician-controlled board and employed physicians who provide services to patients of the parent. Because physicians are salaried, the nonprofit medical corporation does not face the same IRS constraints regarding physician representation in governance. To qualify for tax-exempt financing, however, the IHO must conform to the 80–20 rule.

In terms of the division of labor, the parent governing board ratifies the budgets of the subsidiaries, reviews their strategic plans, and acts as arbiter in the event of disputes. The medical subsidiary employs all physicians, provides adequate specialty and geographic coverage across the network of delivery sites (satellite clinics), and performs quality assurance, utilization review, and peer review functions.[25] The hospital subsidiary performs most administrative services (e.g., marketing, finance, and management information systems), provides capital for expansion, and provides the systems to integrate administrative with utilization data. It also relieves physicians of the administrative hassle of medical practice.

The IHO can, and frequently does, sponsor its own managed care activities such as an HMO or PPO. It can do this through the parent, but more typically it does this through a joint venture of the MSOs and hospital organizations. These managed care companies can be either for profit or nonprofit in their legal form. In this manner, the IHO develops a set of insurance products that enable it to merge the financing and delivery of health care.

There are several advantages to this model of physician–hospital linkage. First, it enables the corporation to design and control its own delivery systems, benefit programs, and contracts. Coordination among hospital, physician, and especially insurance activities is handled through internal transfer pricing rather than through market transactions. Second, it enables providers to compete with existing integrated systems,

## FIGURE 3

VIRGINIA MASON MEDICAL CENTER GOVERNANCE STRUCTURE, 1992

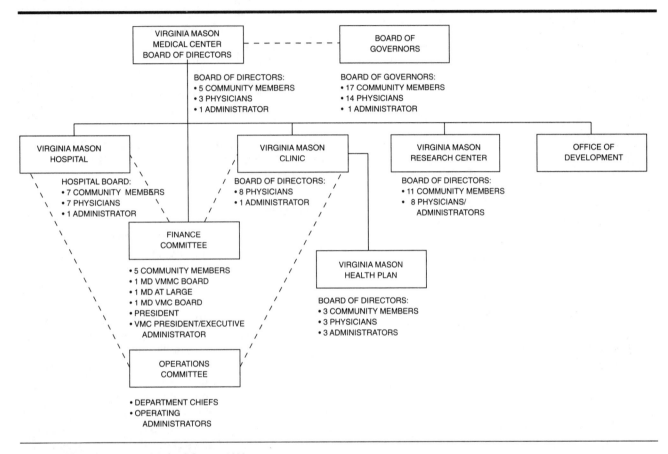

Courtesy of Virginia Mason Medical Center, 1992.

such as Kaiser and the Mayo Clinic. Third, it enjoys greater leverage over managed care contracts external to the system. Increased leverage over payers is facilitated by the system's extensive network of providers (e.g., satellite clinics), the enhanced collection and integration of operating statistics, the resulting enhancement of utilization review activities and cost-control capability, and the new image of united, coordinated providers resulting from their joint marketing effort.

Finally, the IHO provides the highest degree of alignment of interests and incentives between physicians and hospitals. It therefore enjoys the potential to develop a comprehensive, community-based system of health care services that is integrated in design and absent of duplication, what some analysts describe as the seamless delivery of care.[26] Through its network of hospitals and physician groups, the IHO can develop a single strategic plan to deliver comprehensive services to the community. Instead of duplicating expensive services and facilities to compete with other providers, the system can focus on needed services and channel patients to the appropriate service provider in this network. Some systems are currently developing a common patient registration system and computerized medical record that will permit the system to track patients across its multiple provider sites.[27] Such community-based networks form a cornerstone of the National Health Care Reform plan proposed by the American Hospital Association.[28] They are also compatible with the Certified Health Plans proposed by the Washington state legislature and with the Accountable Health Plans described in the managed competition proposal currently being drafted by the Clinton administration.[29]

This movement has several important implications for national health reform. As its health care and insurance services become more comprehensive, the system will collect a premium for each patient and then manage that patient's care, and the risks for that care, along a broad continuum of services. The system will assume the guise of a large supermarket of health care services in which employers shop for their employees. The traditional third party insurer/broker role will be pared down or eliminated. Capital outlays in the system may then be allocated more freely to areas of community need, health promotion, and prevention. In such a system, the managerial emphasis will shift from revenue generation to the conservative management of premium dollars collected. The ideal IHO sketched here, however, will come to fruition only with greater rationality and integration on the purchaser side (such as contained in the Washington state reforms).

### Other models

In the interest of brevity, we have omitted mention of two other physician–hospital models that have grown in number over the past few years. One is physician ownership of hospitals. Such a model is certainly not novel. Physicians established and owned many hospitals in the late nineteenth century and have been quite prominent in the ownership and control of several proprietary hospital chains. Since the 1960s, groups of physicians have assumed equity positions in hospitals, at first on a piecemeal basis by leasing radiology and laboratory departments and later developing joint ventures involving surgical suites, specialty operations, and finally the entire facility. A common vehicle is for a hospital corporation to purchase the assets of another facility as a general partner; physician investors serve as limited partners.[30] Physicians may also purchase the hospital's assets themselves and lease back the operations.

Such ventures are more attractive to physicians than other businesses that proved either unprofitable or undercapitalized. They also enable physicians to gain control over hospital management. Hospital corporations expect that such strategies will foster greater physician utilization of the facilities.

The second model is the establishment of hospital-affiliated or hospital-owned group practices. The hospital may contract with a group through a professional services agreement to operate a group practice program as the outpatient department, or it may incorporate the group as a group practice division of the hospital, in which physicians are employees of the division. The advantages to the hospital include enhanced market image, improved quality assurance and utilization review for outpatient care, improved recruitment of new PCPs and improved leadership development among the medical staff. These groups may also compete with external groups in the community, promote physician loyalty to the hospital, permit expansion into new markets, and strengthen practice management and development activities in physician offices.

## ISSUES FOR HOSPITALS AND PHYSICIANS IN DEVELOPING THESE NEW ORGANIZATIONAL MODELS

### Legal issues

There are two sets of legal issues that hospitals must consider before developing these new relationships with physicians. One set revolves around the IRS's General Counsel Memorandum 39862, which deals with problems surrounding joint ventures.[31] Put simply, the IRS looks disapprovingly on ventures that entail no public benefits. Problematic ventures, for example, do not further the hospital's charitable mission, expand existing health care resources, create new providers, or result in improved treatments or reduced costs.[32] New physician–hospital models must be capable of documenting their community benefit in terms of access, cost, and/or quality. These models must also distribute risk equally across hospitals and physicians and tie rewards to the level of risk assumed. Finally, these models should structure in safeguards to keep at arms' length any transactions involving the purchase of physician practices or revenue flows.[32]

A second set of legal issues revolves around fraud and abuse problems.[33] These issues stem from the Medicare and Medicaid statute that prohibits payments for referrals (antikickback statute). In July 1991, the Department of Health and Human Services released its safe harbors regulations, which exempted eleven activities from this statute. One such activity involves the famous 60–40 rule for investments of less than $50 million of net tangible assets related to Medicare and Medicaid services. According to the rule, this investment activity falls within the safe harbor, and thus is exempt from fraud and abuse problem, if no more than 40 percent of the investment is made by those in a position to refer patients to it and if no more than 40 percent of revenues come from referrals generated by the investors. Other safe harbors that are germane to new physician–hospital models involve space and equipment rentals and the sale of practices.

According to legal analysts, the safe harbors are quite narrow in definition and leave much gray area separating exempt activities from fraudulent ones. They therefore recommend several guidelines to reduce the risk of violating the fraud and abuse statute through physician–hospital joint ventures.[34] These include recruiting physician investors regardless of their potential to make referrals, avoiding any linkage between investment and referral obligations, making risk and reward commensurate with investment, incorporating quality assurance and utilization review components, and documenting any agreements in writing. For other types of arrangements, hospitals are advised not to guarantee physician income levels or to provide services, loans, or space to physicians at below market rates. Because the statute exempts any payments made to individuals under a bona fide employment relationship, hospitals are encouraged to hire new physicians and employees.

### Organizational issues

The new physician–hospital models generate a host of managerial issues that need resolution. First, the closer integration of the two parties involves the merger of quite different cultures. The physician group and hospital typically have different organizational and political structures, different legal structures, different incentive systems, different types of governance, and different time horizons that require harmonization. Even more important, perhaps, the people involved in these new relationships have different personalities and ways of doing things based upon differences in their training and experience. Physicians characteristically have been taught to function independently in problem solving and to be action oriented. Hospital people, on the other hand, are trained to function in a collaborative and more deliberate manner. Thus key success factor will be a common vision and shared goals between the physicians and the hospital. A related success factor will be strong physician and administrative leadership to promote the shared vision and goals.

Second, the formation of a unified contracting unit of physicians and hospitals to negotiate with managed care firms involves the merger of their revenue streams. The unified contracting unit receives a capitated payment that must then be split between the parties. The organization must determine the proper mix of fees, incentive, and/or penalties to ensure that both parties receive fair compensation and manage utilization effectively. In so doing, the organization (not the purchaser) has a greater

*The people involved in these new relationships have different personalities and ways of doing things based upon differences in their training and experience.*

opportunity to develop new payment methods for physicians and the hospital.

Third, the new organization must develop business plans and negotiate agreements that are attractive to all members.[35] There must be not only adequate physician representation in the governance of the new organization to foster collaborative decision making but also flexibility to allow each side to engage in ventures that may benefit only one of the parties but will make that party stronger as a partner for the other.

Finally, the management of these new forms of health care organizations requires administrators that have different educational backgrounds, sets of skills, and attitudes than those of most administrators who are currently in the field. Executives of PHOs, MSOs, medical foundations, and IHOs must have a broader understanding of the health care enterprise, must be expert in their knowledge of managed care, and must be skilled in facilitating collaboration between physicians and hospital personnel. These executives are liable to come from the ranks of hospital, medical group, and managed care administration as well as from among physicians. In each case, formal preparation beyond that previously experienced will be needed for them to be successful in this new area of management. Additionally, the managed care focus on these entities will demand other people skilled in the administration of utilization and quality management programs. These managers will usually be health care providers, physicians and nurses who have special interest and capability in these management activities. Most important, executives must be attitudinally prepared to cede real power to physicians in these arrangements. Rather than view such models as potential opportunities for administrative control and victory over the medical staff, executives should be prepared to accept supporting and facilitating roles in systems built around new collectivities of physicians.[36]

### Professional issues

The new physician–hospital models must be sensitive to the issue of professional autonomy at both aggregate and individual levels. Considering the aggregate of physicians, the new models should be sensitive to and respect the medical group's control over medical practice and quality assurance activities.[37] Participating physicians may also be concerned about the degree to which their practice is locked in by their contract with the new organization.[35] For their part, hospitals wish to develop closer bonds with participating physicians but may need to avoid the appearance of imposing restrictive covenants that prohibit activities that compete with the new venture. Thus new models should carefully document the roles and expectations of both parties. Hospitals that seek to restrict the practices of participating physicians may need to work indirectly through the PC to have such covenants imposed.

At the individual physician level, the new models should be sensitive to physician suspicions regarding bureaucratic control, fears over declining autonomy, and apprehension regarding practice in unfamiliar, organized settings. Physicians may need considerable time, significant involvement, and strong medical leadership to get acclimated to the new arrangements.[36] Such arrangements should not be simply imposed from above. Slightly less caution may be needed with younger generations of physicians, who appear to be more mentally prepared to practice in managed care environments.[38,39]

In addition to the issue of autonomy, the new models will need to confront the professional issue of collegiality. In our atomized and competitive health care system, collegiality has become a forgotten term both among physicians and between physicians and administrators. Goldsmith defines collegiality as shared professional values, trust, and collaboration among all parties.[36] He suggests that collegiality will serve as the primary organizing principle in these new arrangements. Such collegiality will enable physicians and hospitals successfully to share financial risks and achieve integration.

Finally, nonparticipating physicians on the hospital's medical staff may be concerned about their exclusion from the new arrangement. They may perceive that the hospital is favoring some physicians over others, helping some of the competitors to succeed, and/or taking away some of their patients.[21] This issue can be resolved by involving the excluded physicians in other arrangements, such as a medical staff IPA.

Indeed, most of the advanced health care systems are actively engaged in linking independent physicians to their integrated physician networks. For example, HDI with its Good Samaritan Medical Foundation incorporates a medical group and an IPA under the foundation with both sets of physicians on the board. Similarly, UniHealth and Sharp have vehicles to tie independent physicians closely with the system and its medical groups via managed care contracts.

## IMPLICATIONS FOR EDUCATORS AND RESEARCHERS

These trends in PHOs also have important implications for education and research in health care management. For educators, greater emphasis must be placed in the classroom on understanding the professional activities of physicians: their training and socialization, their interests and incentives, and their practice concerns. Attention should be paid to the life cycle of medical practice and how physician practice needs change over time.[40] Heavy emphasis must also be placed on managed care contracting, utilization and quality management, the development of systems and networks, the formation of groups, and the legal barriers in such arrangements. To facilitate this training, health programs may wish to consider structuring part of their curricula around entrepreneurship issues and new venture formation.

In the new term, many, if not most, administrators of the new integrated health care organizations will be individuals with diverse backgrounds who are currently in the health care field and who need additional education and training not previously received. Programs in health administration may need to think about structuring offerings for part-time students, meeting in the evening and on weekends, and becoming more flexible in their content to meet the needs of these individuals.

For researchers, the task is not only to understand the structure and formation of these new models but also to document their process and outcomes. Physician–hospital models have enormous potential not only for aligning provider incentives to control health care costs but also for fostering the development of integrated systems to provide comprehensive care at the community level. It is important to determine which of the various models are most successful in this regard and to identify those specific characteristics of the most successful models that contribute to that success. Researchers from several universities associated with the Western Network Health Management Research Consortium are currently developing a project to study these issues.

## REFERENCES

1. Alexander, J.A., et al. "Effects of Competition, Regulation, and Corporatization on Hospital–Physician Relationships." *Journal of Health and Social Behavior* 27 (1986): 220–235.
2. Burns, L.R., et al. "The Effect of Hospital Control Strategies on Physician Satisfaction and Physician–Hospital Conflict." *Health Services Research* 25 (1990): 527–560.

3. Shortell, S.M. *Effective Hospital–Physician Relationships.* Ann Arbor, Mich.: Health Administration Press, 1991.

4. Joint Commission on Accreditation of Healthcare Organizations (Joint Commission). *Report of the Joint Commission Survey of Relationships among Governing Bodies, Management, and Medical Staffs in U.S. Hospitals.* Chicago, Ill.: Joint Commission, 1988.

5. Touche Ross. *U.S. Hospitals: The Future of Health Care—A Survey of U.S. Hospital Executives and Presidents of Medical Staffs on the Challenges They Face in an Environment of Enormous Change.* City: Touche Ross, 1988.

6. Shortell, S.M. "The Medical Staff of the Future: Replanting the Garden." *Frontiers of Health Services Management* 1 (1985): 3–48.

7. Shortell, S.M. "Revisiting the Garden: Medicine and Management in the 1990s." *Frontiers of Health Services Management* 7 (1990): 3–32.

8. American Medical Association (AMA), *Socioeconomic Characteristics of Medical Practice 1990/91.* Chicago, Ill.: AMA Center for Health Policy Research, 1991.

9. Benvenuto, J., et al. "From 12 Solo Practices to a Hospital-Based LSMG in 100 Easy Steps." *Medical Group Management Journal* 38 (1991): 84–92.

10. Havlicek, P. *Medical Groups in the U.S.* Chicago, Ill.: American Medical Association, 1990.

11. Schryver, D. "Group Practice/Hospital Relations." *Medical Group Management Journal* 38 (1991): 20–23.

12. Korenchuk, K. "Making the Choice: A Close Look at the Joint Venture Option." *Medical Group Management Journal* 38 (1991): 12–22.

13. Peters, G. "Integrated Delivery Can Ally Physician and Hospital Plans." *Healthcare Financial Management* 45 (1991): 21-32.

14. Barnett, A. "The Integration of Health Care as a Model for the Future." *Medical Group Management Journal* 38 (1991): 16, 18.

15. Christianson, J., et al. "The HMO Industry: Evolution in Population Demographics and Market Structures." *Medical Care Review* 48 (1991): 3–46.

16. Wholey, D., and Burns, L. "Organizational Transitions: Form Changes by Health Maintenance Organizations." *In Research in the Sociology of Organizations* edited by S. Bacharach. Greenwich, Conn.: JAI Press, 1993.

17. McCarthy, G. "Strength in Numbers." *Health Progress* 72 (1991): 50–53.

18. Burns, L., and Wholey, D. "Differences in Access and Quality of Care Across HMO Types." *Health Services Management Research* 4 (1991): 32–45.

19. BDC Advisors. *Physician/Hospital Integration Models.* San Francisco, Calif.: BDC, 1993.

20. Stromberg, R.E. *Medical Foundation and Management Service Organizations: Legal and Regulatory Issues.* Irvine, Calif.: Jones, Day, Reavis & Pogue, 1991.

21. Perry, L. "California Hospital Systems Use Not-for-Profit Foundations in Pursuit of Physician Practices." *Modern Healthcare* 21 (1991): 32.

22. Golembesky, H., et al. "Physician/Hospital Medical Foundations: A Future Model for Integrated Health Care." *Medical Group Management Journal* 39 (1992): 96–104.

23. Lindeke, J. "The 'Foundation Model' as a Hospital–Physician Organizational Structure: Panacea, Fad, or . . . ?" *Health Care Law Newsletter* 7 (1992): 9–12.

24. Stromberg, R.E. *Hospital-Affiliated Medical Group Practice: The Use of Medical Foundations and Management Service Organizations.* Irvine, Calif.: Jones, Day, Reavis & Pogue, 1991.

25. Baker, G. "Hospital Physician Organizations: Models for Success." *Group Practice Journal* 39 (1990): 4–22.

26. Burda, D. "Seamless Delivery." *Modern Healthcare* 22 (1992): 38, 40, 42.

27. Gardner, E. "Shared Information Could Revolutionize Healthcare." *Modern Healthcare* 22 (1992): 30–36.

28. American Hospital Association (AHA). *National Health Care Reform: Refining and Advancing the Vision.* Chicago, Ill.: AHA, 1992.

29. Shortell, S.M. "State Health Policy Reform: A Basis for National Reform." Paper presented to Irving B. Harris Graduate School of Public Policy Studies, University of Chicago, March 1993.

30. Hudson, T. "Hospital–MD Joint Ventures Move Forward Despite Hurdles." *Hospitals* 65 (1991): 22–26, 28.

31. Bromberg, R. "Hospital–Physician Joint Ventures: New, Menacing IRS Stance." *HealthSpan* 9 (1992): 3–12.

32. Herman, A. "IRS Memorandum Limits Joint Ventures." *Healthcare Financial Management* 46 (1992): 49, 51–52.

33. MacKelvie, C. "Fraud, Abuse, and Inurement." *Topics in Health Care Financing* 16 (1990): 49–57.

34. MacKelvie, C., et al. "The Impact of Fraud and Abuse Regulations." *Healthcare Financial Management* 46 (1992): 26–33.

35. O'Gara, N. "Charging Forward: Hospital–Physician Relations in Managed Care." *Healthcare Executive* 7 (1992): 22–25.

36. Goldsmith, J.C. "Driving the Nitroglycerin Truck." *Healthcare Forum Journal* 36 (1993): 36–44.

37. Johnsson, J. "Dynamic Diversification: Hospitals Pursue Physician Alliances, 'Seamless' Care." *Hospitals* 66 (1992): 20–26.

38. Baker, L.C., and Cantor, J.C. "Physician Satisfaction under Manager Care." *Health Affairs,* 12 (1993): 258–270.

39. Huonker, J., and Burns, L.R. "Factors Affecting Physician Choice between Managed Care and Fee-for-Service Settings, and the Effect of that Choice on Physician Autonomy and Satisfaction." Paper presented at the annual meeting of the Association of University Programs of Health Administration, Atlanta, April 1992.

40. Super, K.E. "Services Should Be Linked to Practices' Life Cycles." *Modern Healthcare* 10 (1987): 57–58.

# The problematic fit of diagnosis and strategy for medical group stakeholders— Including IDS/Ns

John D. Blair,
Terence T. Rock,
Timothy M. Rotarius,
Myron D. Fottler,
Gena C. Bosse,
and
J. Matthew Driskill

*This article extends stakeholder management theory using data from 270 medical practice executives to identify key stakeholders and determine the "fit" between stakeholder diagnosis and stakeholder management strategy. Four optimal and 12 suboptimal situations are identified.*

*Health Care Manage Rev*, 1996, 21(1), 7–28
© 1996 Aspen Publishers, Inc.

**No health care system** in the world has undergone as much structural change as has that of the United States over the past 3 decades. It was suggested by Shortell[1] that the extent and swiftness of structural change are unprecedented in post/industrial society. This process of structural change has accelerated in the 1990s in response to increased competition, sophistication and demands of health care consumers, public and private regulation, public and private demands for information, and health care reform within the industry (even in the absence of federal government legislation). An increased range of services is now being provided outside of traditional hospitals in ambulatory settings, home care, long-term care, and others.

The previous cottage industry of individual freestanding providers has become a complex web of systems, alliances, and networks. The evolution of the system has been from individual units to multiprovider units to the emergence of integrated multi-

Key words: *integrated delivery system, medical group, stakeholder, strategy*

*John D. Blair, Ph.D., is Professor of Management and Health Organization Management, Senior Research Fellow, The Institute for Management and Leadership Research, College of Business Administration, Texas Tech University, Lubbock, Texas.*

*Terence T. Rock, B.Comm., is a doctoral student in International Strategic Management, and Research Associate, The Institute for Management and Leadership Research, College of Business Administration, Texas Tech University, Lubbock, Texas.*

*Timothy M. Rotarius, M.B.A., is a doctoral student in Health Care Strategic Management, and Project Director, The Institute for Management and Leadership Research, College of Business Administration, Texas Tech University, Lubbock, Texas.*

*Myron D. Fottler, Ph.D., is Professor of Management and Director, Ph.D. Program in Administration—Health Services, School of Health Related Professions, University of Alabama at Birmingham, Birmingham, Alabama.*

*Gena C. Bosse, M.B.A. (H.O.M.), is Director of Operations, Diagnostic Clinic of San Antonio, San Antonio, Texas.*

*J. Matthew Driskill, B.B.A., is Executive Director, Methodist Medical Group, Lubbock Methodist Hospital System, Lubbock, Texas.*

Winner of the 1995 "Best Health Care Management Theory to Practice Paper" Award given by the Health Care Administration Division of the Academy of Management and sponsored by *Health Care Management Review.*

provider systems addressing the continuum of health care needs at a local or regional level.[2]

As the U.S. health care system has restructured over time, the key (i.e., nonmarginal) stakeholders for these evolving organizations must also change over time.[3] From the perspective of health care executives, a failure to redefine key stakeholders as organizations evolve and restructure will result in a failure to respond to the opportunities and threats posed by new stakeholders.[4]

If health care executives of the focal organization correctly identify the new key stakeholders, they may still fail to recognize that some of their original key stakeholders are no longer "key." Even if the new key stakeholders are correctly identified and some of the original key stakeholders redefined as "marginal," they may still not be managed appropriately. This means the strategy may not be appropriate for the stakeholder's new classification.

The latter refers to the matching of stakeholder categorization (based on the stakeholder's potential for cooperation and potential for threat) and generic stakeholder management strategies. As we will discuss in detail later in this article, according to Blair and Whitehead[5] (and further confirmed by Blair and Fottler[3]), health care executives should:

1. Collaborate with mixed blessing stakeholders;
2. Involve supportive stakeholders;
3. Defend against nonsupportive stakeholders; and
4. Monitor marginal stakeholders.

These prescriptions for managerial action (and propositions for future research) were based upon qualitative data generated from interviews with health care executives drawn from a wide variety of health care organizations.[3] The data reflected what were "best practices" by successful executives but did not systematically examine what happens when the "correct" strategies were not used.

From a theoretical perspective, an understanding of what health care executives actually do to manage stakeholders who are categorized (or given a summary "diagnosis") in each of the four categories above would be a contribution to the literature. There have been no empirical data in the health care industry or elsewhere regarding how closely actual stakeholder management strategies match the above four categories of stakeholders.

If there is a lack of "fit" between stakeholder category (i.e., summary "diagnosis") and the generic stakeholder management strategy, are the implications always negative as implied by the theory? Are

some types of "suboptimal fit" more appropriate or more common than others? What is the probability of development of integrated delivery systems given the current and future stakeholder management strategies? Answers to such questions will allow the authors to refine the existing theory and provide practical guidelines for health care executives as well.

While there is considerable literature on multi-hospital systems, multiprovider systems, and alliances[2,6–10] relatively little is known about integrated delivery systems that embrace all levels of care including primary, secondary, tertiary, and rehabilitative.

The present article reviews the theoretical and practitioner literature of stakeholder management and integrated delivery systems, identifies the significant research questions, and discusses the sample of medical group practice experts used in this study and the study methodology. Then we will provide an analysis of how well the proposed management strategies in 1994 and 1999 fit each stakeholder's diagnostic category as well as the implications for various types of suboptimal fits. The article concludes with a discussion of the theoretical and managerial implications of the research as well as research issues for the future.

## THEORETICAL BACKGROUND AND RESEARCH QUESTIONS

The theoretical basis of the present study is the conceptual framework of stakeholder diagnosis and generic stakeholder management developed by Blair and Whitehead[5] and elaborated by Blair and Fottler.[3] Earlier contributions in this area were made by Mason and Mitroff[11] and Freeman.[12] This theoretical framework was developed on the basis of qualitative interviews with practicing health care executives. It has also shown its utility outside of the health care industry in understanding airline stakeholder management.[13] The basic typology shown in Figure 1 shows how health care executives can "diagnose" their organization's stakeholders in a summary way through a joint examination of both a stakeholder's potential for threat and potential for cooperation. These two overall dimensions take into account issues such as relative power, control over resources, likelihood of forming coalitions, and so forth.[3]

Also, in Figure 1 four types of generic strategies are presented that can be used to manage stakeholders. Each of these strategies best serves one or more organizational priorities—to reduce stakeholder threat or

**FIGURE 1**

STRATEGIC STAKEHOLDER MANAGEMENT
PROPOSITIONS: FINDING THE "OPTIMAL FIT"
OF DIAGNOSES AND GENERIC STRATEGIES FOR
KEY ORGANIZATIONAL STAKEHOLDERS*

**The generic strategy that best "fits"
each diagnostic type of
key organizational stakeholder**

Stakeholder's potential for
threat to the organization

|  | High | Low |
|---|---|---|
| **High**<br><br>**Stakeholder's potential for cooperation with the organization** | Strategic stakeholder management proposition 1:<br><br>**The optimal fit is to collaborate with the mixed-blessing stakeholder** | Strategic stakeholder management proposition 2:<br><br>**The optimal fit is to involve the supportive stakeholder** |
| **Low** | Strategic stakeholder management proposition 3:<br><br>**The optimal fit is to defend against the nonsupportive stakeholder** | Strategic stakeholder management proposition 4:<br><br>**The optimal fit is to monitor the marginal stakeholder** |

*Typology adapted and extended from J. Blair & M. Fottler, *Challenges in Health Care Management: Strategic Perspectives for Managing Key Stakeholders*. San Francisco: Jossey-Bass, 1990, p. 133.

to enhance stakeholder cooperation. Figure 1 provides the underpinning of how these health care executives should manage stakeholders diagnosed as being one of the four types based on their potential for threat and cooperation.

*Collaborate* and *involve* are two strategies described by the original authors that can be easily confused and should be clarified here. Involvement differs from collaboration in that involvement further activates or enhances the supportive capability of an already supportive stakeholder. This strategy attempts to capitalize on an already existing high potential for cooperation by converting even more of that potential into actuality. By contrast, collaboration involves more give and take and even has a defensive element

to protect the organization against potential threat. For example, collaboration is more likely to involve formal, highly specified contracts that are not necessary with fully supportive stakeholders who can be involved with a higher level of trust (and lack of risk) on the part of the organization.

In this figure, we elaborate the earlier strategic stakeholder management models by making explicit the fundamental propositions presented by Blair and Whitehead[5] and Blair and Fottler.[3] For each of the four categories of stakeholders there is an optimal strategic choice that in turn provides the optimal fit between diagnosis and strategy. Figure 1 shows these optimal fits of diagnosis and stakeholder management strategy for each of the four types of stakeholder situations that can face organizations.

**RESEARCH QUESTIONS**

In this article we address several research questions—both theoretically and empirically. In each case, there is a very general research question (not necessarily focused on health care organizations) that will be addressed, in part, through new theoretical development. This is coupled with very specific questions that look at medical groups and rely on data from the "Facing the Uncertain Future" study that is described later. The research questions are:

1. Who are the key stakeholders for particular types of organizations?
   1a. Who are the current key stakeholders of medical groups based on expert perceptions?
   1b. Who will be the key stakeholders of medical groups in the future based on expert predictions?
2. Do organizations manage their stakeholders as suggested by Blair and Fottler?[3]
   2a. How are medical groups currently managing their stakeholders based on experts' perceptions?
   2b. How will medical groups manage their stakeholders in the future based on experts' predictions?
3. What are the implications of managing key organizational stakeholders optimally or, alternatively, suboptimally?
   3a. What are the implications of experts' perceptions of how optimally or suboptimally medical groups are currently managing their key stakeholders?

3b. What are the implications of experts' predictions of how optimally or suboptimally medical groups will manage their key stakeholders in the future?

## THE PROBLEMATIC FIT OF DIAGNOSIS AND STRATEGY: EXTENDING STRATEGIC STAKEHOLDER MANAGEMENT THEORY

Although Blair and Whitehead[5] and Blair and Fottler[3] focused clearly on what their qualitative research indicated were the best fits between diagnosis and strategy, they did not specify any typology that clarifies the range of situations where there is a "lack of fit" or "suboptimal fit" and the implications of each.

Suboptimal fits can (and do) occur for a variety of reasons. Three possible ways to end up with suboptimal diagnosis/strategy fits are:

1. An organization initially misdiagnoses a stakeholder and then uses the strategy that would have been appropriate had the diagnosis been correct (e.g., misdiagnose a marginal stakeholder as supportive and then use an involving strategy, instead of the appropriate monitoring strategy).
2. The stakeholder purposefully misleads the organization so the stakeholder is misdiagnosed (e.g., a nonsupportive stakeholder acts very supportive, which leads the organization into using an involving strategy, instead of the appropriate defensive strategy).
3. The organization's management has developed as a strategic strength one particular stakeholder management strategy. Therefore, they manage all types of stakeholders with the same strategy. For example, if an organization desires to have their stakeholders view the organization as a "good guy," management may use an *involving* strategy regardless of the diagnosis of the specific stakeholder. Or, if management believes all relationships should be (or can be) win–win, they may exclusively use a *collaboration* strategy with all stakeholders. In addition, if the organization's management is overly cautious, very risk averse, and quite distrusting of everyone, they may rely only on the *defensive* strategy. Finally, if the organization believes in the "wait and see" approach and, therefore, is reluctant to initially commit any resources to stakeholder management, the organization will likely use the *monitoring* strategy in all their dealings with any stakeholder.

In initially analyzing the data we describe later in this article, it became necessary to elaborate the original four-fold typology in order to interpret fully the results. Although optimal fit situations were empirically important, the patterns of findings related to suboptimal situations suggested that they were not only common but might well represent very different managerial realities.

Figure 2 represents an extension of the original theory required by identifying a total of 16 situations (4 stakeholder diagnostic categories by 4 generic stakeholder management strategies) representing all possible combinations of diagnosis/strategy fits—optimal and suboptimal. We use this model to analyze the data and interpret the empirical findings later in this article. This interaction between quantitative data analysis and theory development provided a key iteration in the theory-building process and together provide the findings in this article.

We argue that there are four basic types of fit with quite different implications for the organization:

1. Situations with optimal fit between stakeholder diagnosis and strategy. Situations 1, 6, 11, and 16 are optimal fit situations.
2. Situations with Type 1 suboptimal fit between stakeholder diagnosis and strategy resulting in "the organization missing opportunities." Situations 2, 3, 4, 7, and 8 represent this type of suboptimal situation.
3. Situations with Type 2 suboptimal fit between stakeholder diagnosis and strategy resulting in "the organization being at risk." Suboptimal situations 5, 6, 8, 10, and 12 illustrate where the organization is put at risk.
4. Situations with Type 3 suboptimal fit between stakeholder diagnosis and strategy resulting in "the organization focusing its attention and resources on low-potential stakeholders," as shown in suboptimal Situations 13, 14, and 15, where the organization is wasting resources (including management time and attention) by focusing on stakeholders low in either potential for cooperation or threat.

The descriptions of the determinants of these four basic types of optimal and suboptimal fit are detailed in Table 1.

The classification of each situation shown in Figure 2 and described in Table 1 is based on six key pieces of information. This information is put together to deter-

**TABLE 1**

OPTIMAL AND SUBOPTIMAL FITS OF DIAGNOSIS AND STRATEGY

| Situation | Stakeholder potential for threat | Organization's priority on reducing threat | Stakeholder potential for cooperation | Organization's priority on enhancing cooperation | Should organization focus on this stakeholder? | Organizational allocation of resources | Implications |
|---|---|---|---|---|---|---|---|
| *Situations with optimal fit between diagnosis and strategy* | | | | | | | |
| Situation 1: involve a supportive stakeholder | Low | Low | High | High | Yes, high potential | Appropriately high | Organization has focused on a high potential for cooperation stakeholder and has used appropriately high resources to implement the strategy designed to enhance cooperation. |
| Situation 6: collaborate with a mixed-blessing stakeholder | High | High | High | High | Yes, high potential | Appropriately high | Organization has focused on a high potential for both threat *and* cooperation stakeholder and has used appropriately high resources to implement the strategy designed to both reduce threat and enhance cooperation. |
| Situation 11: defend against a nonsupportive stakeholder | High | High | Low | Low | Yes, high potential | Appropriately high | Organization has focused on a high potential for threat stakeholder and has used appropriately high resources to implement the strategy designed to reduce threat. |
| Situation 16: monitor a marginal stakeholder | Low | Low | Low | Low | No, low potential | Appropriately limited | Organization has not focused on either cooperation or threat stakeholder and has used appropriately limited resources to implement the strategy designed neither to significantly reduce threat nor to enhance cooperation but only to monitor the stakeholder to be aware of the potential for either cooperation or threat to increase. |
| *Situations with type 1 suboptimal fit between diagnosis and strategy: the organization misses opportunities* | | | | | | | |
| Situation 2: collaborate with a supportive stakeholder | Low | High | High | High | Yes, high potential | Those focused on reducing threat are wasted and may be counter-productive, e.g., reduce cooperation. | Suboptimal because the organization's priority is on both cooperation and reduction of threat, when the stakeholder does not pose any threat. The resources focused on reducing threat are wasted, since there is no threat. The strategy sets up constraints on cooperation, and is thus counterproductive. |

*continues*

# TABLE 1

## CONTINUED

Medical Group Stakeholders

The Problematic Fit of Diagnosis and Strategy for Medical Group Stakeholders 101

| Situation | Stakeholder potential for threat | Organization's priority on reducing threat | Stakeholder potential for cooperation | Organization's priority on enhancing cooperation | Should organization focus on this stakeholder? | Organizational allocation of resources | Implications |
|---|---|---|---|---|---|---|---|
| Situation 3: defend against a supportive stakeholder | Low | High | High | Low | Yes, high potential | Those focused on reducing threat are wasted and may be counterproductive, while not enough are focused on enhancing cooperation. | Suboptimal because the organization's priority is on reduction of threat, when the stakeholder does not pose any threat. The resources focused on reducing threat are wasted, since there is no threat. The strategy sets up constraints on cooperation, instead of trying to encourage it, and is thus counterproductive. |
| Situation 4: monitor a supportive stakeholder | Low | Low | High | Low | Yes, high potential | There are inadequate resources devoted to enhancing cooperation. | Suboptimal because the organization's priority is not on cooperation, when the stakeholder has a lot of potential for cooperation. Therefore, the organization is losing an opportunity to gain an ally. |
| Situation 7: defend against a mixed-blessing stakeholder | High | High | High | Low | Yes, high potential | There are inadequate resources devoted to enhancing cooperation. | Suboptimal because the organization's priority is only on reduction of threat, when the stakeholder is high in potential for threat, yet also has high potential for cooperation. The resources devoted to enhancing cooperation are inadequate and the resources focused on reducing threat are potentially wasted, since they do not allow for the potential for cooperation with the stakeholder. The strategy focuses on setting up constraints on cooperation, and is thus potentially counterproductive. |
| Situation 8: monitor a mixed-blessing stakeholder* | High | Low | High | Low | Yes, high potential | There are inadequate resources devoted to reducing threat and enhancing cooperation. | Suboptimal because the organization's priority is not on cooperation or reduction of threat, when the stakeholder has a lot of potential for both. Therefore, the organization is losing an opportunity to gain an ally, while overlooking the possibility of damage from a threatening or hostile stakeholder. |

**TABLE 1**

**CONTINUED**

*Situations with type 2 suboptimal fit between diagnosis and strategy: the organization is at risk*

| Situation | Stakeholder potential for threat | Organization's priority on reducing threat | Stakeholder potential for cooperation | Organization's priority on enhancing cooperation | Should organization focus on this stakeholder? | Organizational allocation of resources | Implications |
|---|---|---|---|---|---|---|---|
| Situation 5: involve a mixed-blessing stakeholder | High | Low | High | High | Yes, high potential | There are inadequate resources devoted to reducing threat. | Suboptimal because the organization's priority is only on cooperation, when the stakeholder is high in potential for cooperation, yet still poses a threat. Resources devoted to reduce potential threat are inadequate, and the resources focused on cooperation are potentially wasted, since the stakeholder could still threaten the organization. The strategy sets up no recourse in the case of threat, and could therefore be counterproductive. |
| Situation 8: monitor a mixed-blessing stakeholder* | High | Low | High | Low | Yes, high potential | There are inadequate resources used to reduce threat and to enhance cooperation. | Suboptimal because the organization's priority is not on cooperation or reduction of threat, when the stakeholder has a lot of potential for both. Therefore, the organization is losing an opportunity to gain an ally, while overlooking the possibility of damage from a threatening or hostile stakeholder. |
| Situation 9: involve a nonsupportive stakeholder | High | Low | Low | High | Yes, high potential | There are inadequate resources devoted to reducing threat and wasted resources focused on enhancing cooperation. | Suboptimal because the organization's priority is on cooperation, when the stakeholder is low in potential for cooperation. The resources devoted to cooperation are wasted, since there is little potential for cooperation. The strategy does not put constraints on the relationship, and in fact opens the organization up to a potential "enemy," and is thus counterproductive. |
| Situation 10: collaborate with a nonsupportive stakeholder | High | High | Low | High | Yes, high potential | There are wasted resources focused on enhancing cooperation. | Suboptimal because the organization's priority is on both cooperation and reduction of threat, when the stakeholder does not have significant potential for cooperation. The resources focused on cooperation are wasted, since there is low potential for cooperation. The strategy is potentially counterproductive, since it partially opens the organization to a potentially threatening stakeholder. |

*continues*

**TABLE 1**

CONTINUED

| Situation | Stakeholder potential for threat | Organization's priority on reducing threat | Stakeholder potential for cooperation | Organization's priority on enhancing cooperation | Should organization focus on this stakeholder? | Organizational allocation of resources | Implications |
|---|---|---|---|---|---|---|---|
| Situation 12: monitor a nonsupportive stakeholder | High | Low | Low | Low | Yes, high potential | There are inadequate resources focused on reducing threat. | Suboptimal because the organization's priority should be on reducing threat, since the stakeholder has high potential for threat. Therefore, the organization is overlooking the possibility of damage from a threatening stakeholder and is failing to devote resources to protect itself. |

*Situations with type 3 suboptimal fit between diagnosis and strategy: the organization is focused on low-potential stakeholders*

| Situation | Stakeholder potential for threat | Organization's priority on reducing threat | Stakeholder potential for cooperation | Organization's priority on enhancing cooperation | Should organization focus on this stakeholder? | Organizational allocation of resources | Implications |
|---|---|---|---|---|---|---|---|
| Situation 13: involve a marginal stakeholder | Low | Low | Low | High | No, low potential | There are wasted resources focused on enhancing cooperation. | Suboptimal because the organization is expending resources to cooperate with a stakeholder who is low in potential for cooperation. The is a waste of resources that should probably be devoted to managing high-potential stakeholders. |
| Situation 14: collaborate with a marginal stakeholder | Low | High | Low | High | No, low potential | There are wasted resources focused both on reducing threat and enhancing cooperation. | Suboptimal because the organization is expending resources to cooperate with a stakeholder who is low in potential for cooperation, as well as expending resources to reduce the threat of a stakeholder who is low in potential for threat. This is a waste of resources that should probably be devoted to managing high-potential stakeholders. |
| Situation 15: defend against a marginal stakeholder | Low | High | Low | Low | No, low potential | There are wasted resources focused on reducing threat. | Suboptimal because the organization is expending resources to reduce the threat of a stakeholder who is low in potential for threat. This is a waste of resources that should probably be devoted to managing high-potential stakeholders. |

*Note: Situation 8: monitoring a mixed-blessing stakeholder involves both "at risk" and "missed opportunities."

**FIGURE 2**

THE PROBLEMATIC FIT OF DIAGNOSIS AND STRATEGY FOR ORGANIZATIONS AS THEY "MANAGE" THEIR KEY STAKEHOLDERS—IMPLICATIONS FOR OPPORTUNITIES, RISK, AND USE OF RESOURCES IN STRATEGIC STAKEHOLDER MANAGEMENT

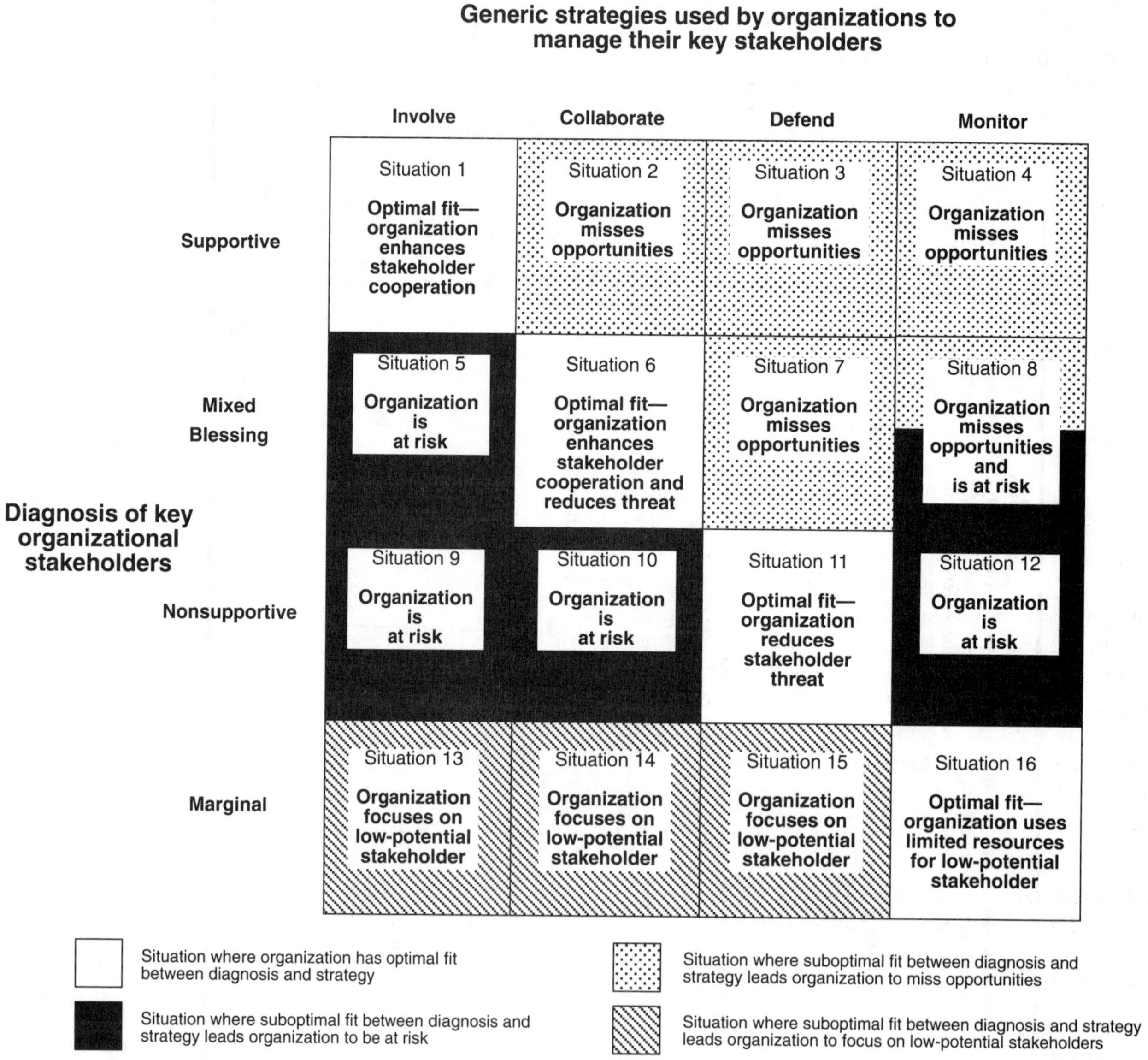

**Generic strategies used by organizations to manage their key stakeholders**

|  | Involve | Collaborate | Defend | Monitor |
|---|---|---|---|---|
| **Supportive** | Situation 1 — Optimal fit—organization enhances stakeholder cooperation | Situation 2 — Organization misses opportunities | Situation 3 — Organization misses opportunities | Situation 4 — Organization misses opportunities |
| **Mixed Blessing** | Situation 5 — Organization is at risk | Situation 6 — Optimal fit—organization enhances stakeholder cooperation and reduces threat | Situation 7 — Organization misses opportunities | Situation 8 — Organization misses opportunities and is at risk |
| **Nonsupportive** | Situation 9 — Organization is at risk | Situation 10 — Organization is at risk | Situation 11 — Optimal fit—organization reduces stakeholder threat | Situation 12 — Organization is at risk |
| **Marginal** | Situation 13 — Organization focuses on low-potential stakeholder | Situation 14 — Organization focuses on low-potential stakeholder | Situation 15 — Organization focuses on low-potential stakeholder | Situation 16 — Optimal fit—organization uses limited resources for low-potential stakeholder |

**Diagnosis of key organizational stakeholders**

- Situation where organization has optimal fit between diagnosis and strategy
- Situation where suboptimal fit between diagnosis and strategy leads organization to be at risk
- Situation where suboptimal fit between diagnosis and strategy leads organization to miss opportunities
- Situation where suboptimal fit between diagnosis and strategy leads organization to focus on low-potential stakeholders

mine whether there is optimal or suboptimal fit. The separate information items are:

1. the diagnosis of stakeholder potential for threat ("high" or "low");
2. the organization's priority on reducing stakeholder threat ("high" or "low");
3. the diagnosis of stakeholder potential for cooperation ("high" or "low");
4. the organization's priority on enhancing stakeholder cooperation ("high" or "low");
5. the question of whether the organization should focus its managers' attention and the organization's resources on this stakeholder ("yes, because the stakeholder is high potential"—either in threat or cooperation or both—or "no, because the stakeholder is low potential"); and
6. whether the organization's allocation of resources is appropriate or not ("appropriately high," "appropriately limited," "resources are wasted in a certain way," or "there are inadequate resources devoted to a particular strategic priority"). The organizational implications for opportunities, risk, and use of resources within each of the 16 diagnosis/strategy fit situations are described in detail in the last column on the right.

The first, albeit partial, answers to the research questions posed earlier are found in the extended theoretical model presented above and its accompanying table, which includes the implications of different types of diagnosis/strategy fit. Having presented in Figure 2 and Table 1 the theoretical findings related to our research questions, we will now move to empirical findings from data on the stakeholders of a particular type of organization—the medical group. These quantitative data will supplement earlier qualitative data and continue to facilitate the grounded theory-building process.

## METHODOLOGY FOR EXAMINING THE EXTENDED THEORETICAL MODEL

### Description of the data

The data used in this article come from the *Facing the Uncertain Future (FUF)* Delphi project. The FUF project is managed and administered by the joint team of the Medical Group Management Association (MGMA), including its subsidiaries the Center for Research in Ambulatory Health Care Administration (CRAHCA) and the American College of Medical Practice Executives (ACMPE), and Texas Tech University (TTU), through the Institute for Management and Leadership Research (IMLR) and the M.B.A. and Ph.D. Programs in Health Organization Management. The FUF project is sponsored by Abbott Laboratories, Abbott Park, Illinois.

Questionnaires were mailed to health care industry experts classified as medical practice executives (MPEs). The FUF project received 270 completed instruments from the sample of 752 MPEs. After adjusting these numbers for bad addresses and those who declined to participate, our response rate came out to 41 percent. Almost all of the respondents were either Fellows or Candidates of MGMA's ACMPE.

---

*The first, albeit partial, answers to the research questions posed earlier are found in the extended theoretical model presented above and its accompanying table, which includes the implications of different types of diagnosis/ strategy fit.*

---

Since Delphi techniques focus on panels of experts in a given industry or field of study, results from Delphi studies tend to be somewhat ungeneralizable to those who are not experts in their industry or field. Even though the FUF project used a modified Delphi technique, the FUF results also tend to suffer from this ungeneralizability phenomenon. In other words, since the FUF Delphi project queried medical practice *experts*, the results may be somewhat limited in their generalizability to all medical practice managers. We are, however, confident that the results of the FUF project do represent the views of leading MPEs; that is, those MPEs who set the standards against which all other MPEs are measured.

### Rationale for studying medical groups and medical practice executives

This study focuses on strategic stakeholder management for medical groups, including solo practices, single-specialty, and multispecialty practices. Medical groups were studied because, regardless of their exact organizational form, they will be very integral components to the emerging integrated delivery systems. To be a fully integrated delivery system, integrated delivery networks require participation by hospitals, medical groups, and managed care organizations.

As part of our theory-building process regarding optimal and suboptimal diagnosis–strategy fits, and to understand the implications of choosing suboptimal stakeholder management strategies, we focused on those 270 MPE respondents. Since we are focusing on medical groups at the organizational level of analysis, we felt it would be important to understand medical groups from the point of view of their executive and operational managers.

Integration of medical groups with other medical groups is just now beginning to be realized on a large scale.[14] Medical group integration into an integrated delivery system is also occurring at an unprecedented pace.[15] Therefore, this study's focus on medical groups should provide valuable insight to researchers and practitioners who need to understand the complexity of how medical groups manage their integrated delivery system stakeholders. Specifically, we are interested in the effects the changing health care industry will have on medical groups, vis-a-vis their stakeholders and the strategies medical groups use currently and will use to manage these stakeholders in the still uncertain future.

## FINDINGS RELATED TO THE EXTENDED THEORETICAL MODEL

This section of our article will use the data collected in the *Facing the Uncertain Future* study to examine how medical practice executives view the stakeholders of medical groups now and in 1999. Two simple, yet powerful data analysis steps were conducted. First, the key stakeholders of medical groups now and in the future were explicitly identified, and became the focus of this analysis. A *key stakeholder* is one identified as important by 25 percent or more of the respondents. Second, a simple cross-tabulation was conducted, comparing each respondent's diagnosis of the key stakeholders with the strategy he or she felt medical groups are using now, or will be using in 1999. The overall frequencies were calculated, and these figures were summed, as will be demonstrated, to draw conclusions about how certain stakeholders are (or will be) managed.

To ensure a clear and meaningful analysis, as well as to demonstrate the power of the expanded theoretical model, we will look at Integrated Delivery Systems/Networks [IDS/Ns] in detail, with summary data presented for the remaining key stakeholders. We will take the reader step-by-step through the analysis, showing the current perceptions of the re-

spondents, moving to predictions for the future, and finally showing what changes are predicted to occur.

It is important to keep in mind that the data presented represent the perceptions and predictions of medical practice executives about the stakeholders of medical groups in general, now and in 1999. We are treating the data as the opinions of experts—those who deal with these stakeholders on a day-to-day basis. The conclusions drawn do not reflect the respondents' own organizations; rather they are intended to show a "picture" of all stakeholders in the environment.

### Key stakeholders of medical groups

Figure 3 shows the key and marginal stakeholders of medical group practices in 1994 and 1999. The key stakeholders are shown in rectangular boxes in the upper portion of each figure while marginal stakeholders are shown in rounded circles in the lower portion of each figure.

These data indicate that there are eight key stakeholders of medical groups in both 1994 and projected for 1999. There were only two important changes in stakeholder classification over the 5-year period. First, *independent hospitals* are a key stakeholder (37 percent) of medical groups in 1994 but only a marginal stakeholder (5 percent) in 1999. Second, IDS/Ns are only a marginal stakeholder (18 percent) in 1994, but a key stakeholder (82 percent) in 1999.

The shaded area of the 1999 diagram indicates stakeholders that have been identified in the literature as potential components of IDS/Ns as well as the IDS/Ns themselves.[15–18] Shortell, Gillies, Anderson, Mitchell, and Morgan[19] label the stakeholders in the 1999 shaded area "organized delivery systems." An organized delivery system is a "network of organizations that provides or arranges to provide a coordinated continuum of services to a defined population and is willing to be held clinically and fiscally accountable for the outcomes and health status of the population served."[19(p.448)] It will also own or be closely aligned with an insurance product.

Throughout this article, our use of the "integrated delivery system/network" label for this configuration of organizational components is consistent with their "organized delivery system" conceptualization. If the expert panel is right, these data indicate that half of the important medical group stakeholders in 1999 are potential components of an IDS/N. This finding provides the impetus to look in detail at IDS/Ns as particularly key stakeholders of medical groups.

**FIGURE 3**

THE SHIFTING MEDICAL GROUP PARADIGM—A STAKEHOLDER PERSPECTIVE (PERCEPTIONS AND PREDICTIONS BY MEDICAL PRACTICE EXECUTIVE EXPERTS)

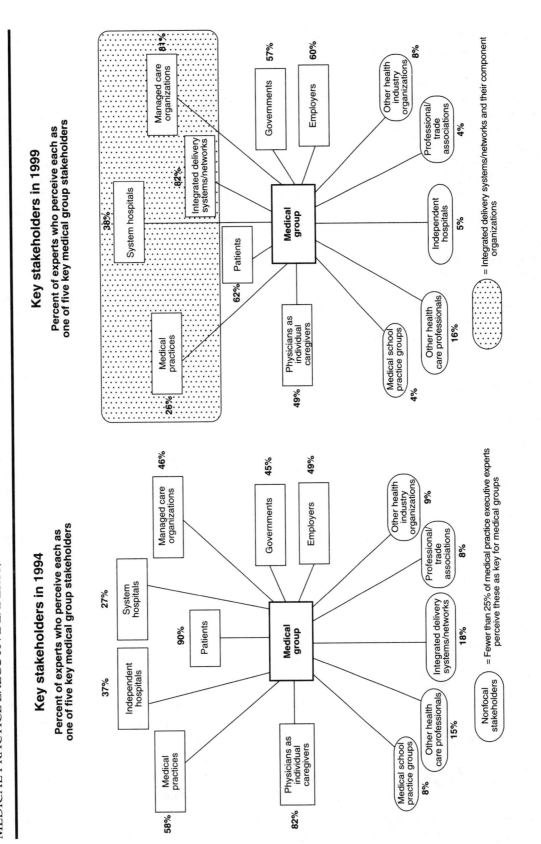

**Key stakeholders in 1994**

Percent of experts who perceive each as one of five key medical group stakeholders

**Key stakeholders in 1999**

Percent of experts who perceive each as one of five key medical group stakeholders

Other interesting findings from Figure 3 include the decreasing number of respondents who felt that patients and physicians as individual caregivers will be important medical group stakeholders in 1999 (90 percent to 62 percent; 82 percent to 49 percent, respectively). Additionally, we see the increasing importance of managed care organizations [MCOs] (46 percent to 81 percent). These results all indicate that there are some dramatic changes occurring among the stakeholders of medical groups. The next part of our analysis looks at these changes in further detail using stakeholder diagnosis and strategy theory as developed by Blair and Fottler[3] and expanded on in this article.

## MEDICAL GROUP OPTIMAL FITS OF DIAGNOSIS AND STRATEGY

The arguments developed earlier are now put to use to analyze our respondents' perceptions and predictions of the *types* of stakeholders facing medical groups, as well as *how they are (will be) managed (the strategy used)*, now and in the future. We will begin the analysis with a look at the situations defined as optimal by Blair and Fottler.[3]

### The situation of optimal fit

In Figures 4 and 5, we show four situations where a stakeholder is *managed optimally*; where the strategy used to manage the stakeholder fits with the diagnosis. The current study allows us to examine whether or not the panel of experts perceive that the stakeholders of medical groups are being managed optimally.

In the sections to follow, we will look at optimal fits. First, we examine the specific situations for IDS/N stakeholders. Then we look in summary form at all nine of the key medical group stakeholders.

### Optimal fit findings for integrated delivery system/ network stakeholders

Focusing on IDS/Ns as current stakeholders of medical groups (Figure 4), we can see that overall, 40 percent of the respondents feel that medical groups are managing IDS/Ns optimally. Most often (23 percent), the respondents feel that IDS/Ns are *mixed-blessing* stakeholders that are being managed with a *collaborative* strategy. Ideally, we would hope that the diagonal of the expanded theoretical model (the "optimal fit" category) would make up the bulk of the responses. Since these four cells represent 25 percent of the total possible responses, a test of significance will

be a test of whether the proportion of responses in the "optimal fit" category is greater than 25 percent. In the case of IDS/Ns, there is a high probability ($p <$ .0001) that respondents were intentionally choosing the "optimal fit" category.

For IDS/Ns in 1999 we see similar results, with a shift away from *monitoring* IDS/Ns as *marginal* stakeholders to *involving* them as *supportive* stakeholders. This shift is accounted for by IDS/Ns greatly increasing in importance (Figure 1)—they are no longer *marginal* stakeholders of medical groups. Medical practice executives perceive a need for medical groups to attempt to enhance the cooperation potential of IDS/Ns, be they *mixed-blessing* or *supportive* stakeholders.

### Optimal fit findings for all nine key stakeholders

Table 2 is a summary of the information presented in Figure 4 for all nine of the stakeholders identified as key for medical groups either now or in 1999. We see that in all cases, except for *independent hospitals*, a significant number of respondents perceive or predict that stakeholders are or will be managed optimally. We see that IDS/Ns and their organizational components tend to be managed with the *collaborate with mixed-blessing* stakeholder strategy. Physicians and patients are the only stakeholders who are generally being managed with the *involve a supportive stakeholder* strategy. Governments, on the other hand, are seen as *nonsupportive* stakeholders who are best managed with a *defend* strategy.

## MEDICAL GROUP SUBOPTIMAL FITS OF DIAGNOSIS AND STRATEGY

In the sections to follow, we look at suboptimal fits. First, we examine the specific situations for IDS/N stakeholders. Then we look in summary form at all nine of the key medical group stakeholders.

### Suboptimal fit findings for IDS/N stakeholders

Figure 5 presents the remaining possible situations for IDS/Ns. We can add together the various related situations, resulting in an overall percentage of respondents who have suggested situations of medical groups at risk, missing opportunities, or wasting resources.

### *Medical group misses opportunities with IDS/Ns*

A medical group could miss opportunities if it spends too much time and too many resources de-

**FIGURE 4**

MANAGING INTEGRATED DELIVERY SYSTEMS/NETWORKS (IDS/Ns) STRATEGICALLY—NOW AND IN THE FUTURE: MEDICAL PRACTICE EXECUTIVES' PERCEIVED AND PREDICTED "OPTIMAL FITS" OF STAKEHOLDER DIAGNOSES AND STRATEGIES

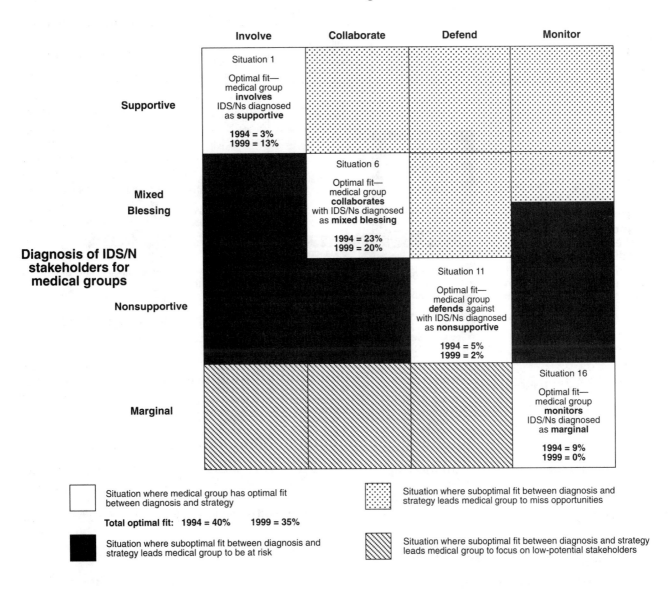

## FIGURE 5

CURRENT AND FUTURE IMPLICATIONS OF USING "SUBOPTIMAL" STRATEGIES TO MANAGE INTEGRATED DELIVERY SYSTEMS/NETWORKS (IDS/Ns): PERCEPTIONS AND PREDICTIONS BY MEDICAL PRACTICE EXECUTIVES OF "SUBOPTIMAL FITS" BETWEEN STAKEHOLDER DIAGNOSES AND STRATEGIES

**Generic strategies used by medical groups
to manage IDS/N stakeholders**

|  | Involve | Collaborate | Defend | Monitor |
|---|---|---|---|---|
| **Supportive** | Optimal fit | Situation 2<br>Medical group misses opportunities<br>1994 = 16%<br>1999 = 7% | Situation 3<br>Medical group misses opportunities<br>1994 = 4%<br>1999 = 2% | Situation 4<br>Medical group misses opportunities<br>1994 = 4%<br>1999 = 0% |
| **Mixed Blessing** | Situation 5<br>Medical group is at risk<br>1994 = 3%<br>1999 = 36% | Optimal fit | Situation 7<br>Medical group misses opportunities<br>1994 = 8%<br>1999 = 3% | Situation 8<br>Medical group misses opportunities and is at risk<br>1994 = 6%<br>1999 = 2% |
| **Nonsupportive** | Situation 9<br>Medical group is at risk<br>1994 = 1%<br>1999 = 2% | Situation 10<br>Medical group is at risk<br>1994 = 4%<br>1999 = 6% | Optimal fit | Situation 12<br>Medical group is at risk<br>1994 = 2%<br>1999 = 2% |
| **Marginal** | Situation 13<br>Medical group focuses on low-potential stakeholder<br>1994 = 1%<br>1999 = 4% | Situation 14<br>Medical group focuses on low-potential stakeholder<br>1994 = 4%<br>1999 = 0% | Situation 15<br>Medical group focuses on low-potential stakeholder<br>1994 = 5%<br>1999 = 0% | Optimal fit |

**Diagnosis of IDS/N stakeholders for medical groups**

☐ Situation where medical group has optimal fit between diagnosis and strategy

▦ (dotted) Situation where suboptimal fit between diagnosis and strategy leads medical group to miss opportunities

**Total "missed opportunities" fit:  1994 = 36%   1999 = 13%**

■ Situation where suboptimal fit between diagnosis and strategy leads medical group to be at risk

▧ (hatched) Situation where suboptimal fit between diagnosis and strategy leads medical group to focus on low-potential stakeholders

**Total "at-risk" fit:  1994 = 14%   1999 = 47%**

**Total "focus on low-potential" fit:  1994 = 10%   1999 = 4%**

**TABLE 2**

"MANAGING" THE KEY STAKEHOLDERS OF MEDICAL GROUPS STRATEGICALLY—NOW AND IN THE FUTURE: SUMMARY OF MEDICAL PRACTICE EXECUTIVES' PERCEIVED AND PREDICTED "OPTIMAL FITS" OF STAKEHOLDER DIAGNOSES AND STRATEGIES

| | | Involves a supportive stakeholder | Collaborate with a mixed-blessing stakeholder | Defend against a nonsupportive stakeholder | Monitor a marginal stakeholder | Total optimal fit | $p$-value for $H_0$ total optimal fit <= 25% |
|---|---|---|---|---|---|---|---|
| *IDS/N & organizational components* | | | | | | | |
| IDS/N | 1994 | 3 | 23 | 5 | 9 | 40 | 0.001 |
| | 1999 | 13 | 20 | 2 | 0 | 36 | 0.005 |
| Managed care organizations (MCOs) | 1994 | 2 | 20 | 16 | 1 | 39 | 0.001 |
| | 1999 | 6 | 33 | 6 | 1 | 46 | 0.001 |
| Medical practices | 1994 | 14 | 18 | 6 | 5 | 43 | 0.001 |
| | 1999 | 18 | 17 | 3 | 1 | 39 | 0.001 |
| System hospitals | 1994 | 2 | 15 | 8 | 8 | 33 | 0.025 |
| | 1999 | 7 | 23 | 4 | 1 | 35 | 0.01 |
| *Other providers* | | | | | | | |
| Independent hospitals | 1994 | 2 | 9 | 8 | 13 | 31 | 0.075 |
| | 1999 | 6 | 8 | 4 | 11 | 29 | 0.175 |
| Physicians | 1994 | 21 | 11 | 3 | 5 | 40 | 0.001 |
| | 1999 | 27 | 10 | 2 | 3 | 42 | 0.001 |
| *Third party payers* | | | | | | | |
| Governments | 1994 | 0 | 6 | 37 | 3 | 46 | 0.001 |
| | 1999 | 0 | 13 | 32 | 2 | 47 | 0.001 |
| Employers | 1994 | 6 | 10 | 5 | 11 | 32 | 0.05 |
| | 1999 | 11 | 24 | 1 | 4 | 39 | 0.001 |
| *Patients* | | | | | | | |
| Patients | 1994 | 26 | 9 | 1 | 4 | 41 | 0.001 |
| | 1999 | 24 | 13 | 1 | 3 | 41 | 0.001 |

fending against the IDS/N. If the medical group perceives the IDS/N as a powerful, nonsupportive stakeholder that is high on potential for threat, the medical group will likely fail to recognize and capitalize on situations that could be very beneficial to itself. For example, if the medical group's physicians are given the opportunity to invest in and become partners in the IDS/N (i.e., the physicians are treated as supportive stakeholders by the IDS/N), but they fail to do so, then they have missed an opportunity to not only have more input into the direction and scope of the IDS/N, but they have also missed an investment opportunity that could potentially be very financially beneficial to the medical group and physicians if the IDS/N is successful. In reality, the IDS/N is a mixed-

blessing stakeholder to both the medical group and physicians, which was not managed with the appropriate collaboration strategy.

Adding together situations 2, 3, 4, 7, and half of situation 8, yields a total of 36 percent of respondents who perceive a situation of medical groups missing opportunities with IDS/Ns now. They are particularly missing opportunities now since, in 1999, only 13 percent of the respondents make a similar prediction.

### Medical group is at risk from IDS/Ns

In the future, as more and more medical groups become associated with IDS/Ns, the medical groups will be forced to give up some of their autonomy and decision making in order to be a part of the large IDS/N system. In the beginning, as these IDS/Ns form, the IDS/N will be a mixed-blessing stakeholder for the medical group (although they may be supportive later). If the medical group involves the IDS/N from the beginning, assuming the IDS/N is overly supportive, the medical group will be put at risk. For example, if the medical group gives up all its negotiating power and entrusts the IDS/N to negotiate contracts on the medical group's behalf, then the IDS/N could enter into contracts that might be beneficial for the IDS/N as a whole, but not specifically beneficial for the medical group as an individual entity.

These negotiated contracts could include the introduction of capitation into the IDS/N. The insurance company, the hospital providers, and the physician providers will all be struggling to get the maximum amount possible from the capitation dollar. If the medical group has involved the IDS/N too much and/or surrendered too much of their power, then the medical group could risk not getting a fair percentage of this capitation dollar. In this latter case, the IDS/N (or some of the system's other partners) could be basically nonsupportive.

Adding together Situations 5, 9, 10, 12, and half of Situation 8, we get a total of 14 percent of respondents who perceive a situation of medical groups being at risk from IDS/Ns now. (Situation 8 comprises a situation where the organization is both at risk and misses opportunities. Please note that to prevent confusion due to percentages adding to more than 100%, the frequency of responses in Situation 8 is split between "at risk" and "misses opportunities.")

Medical groups in this situation are at risk because the stakeholder management strategy they are pursuing fails to protect the organization from potential threats by the stakeholder. In 1999, the same five situations result in a total of 47 percent of the respondents predicting an "at-risk" situation.

### Medical group focuses on IDS/Ns as a low-potential stakeholder

If the medical group continues to spend a lot of time and effort on developing collaborative alliances with independent hospitals (who the medical group's managers believe are key, mixed-blessing stakeholders), the medical group will be wasting resources. In the past, physicians and medical groups have spent valuable resources developing relationships with many independent hospitals and then played these hospitals off one another. However, in the future, as IDS/Ns develop, independent hospitals will be mar-

ginal stakeholders to the medical groups and physicians. If a medical group fails to recognize that independent hospitals have moved to the marginal category, they will spend too much time working with the hospital.

In addition, if a medical group is focused on continuing to develop relationships with independent hospitals (a low-potential stakeholder), it is likely to miss opportunities to affiliate with large IDS/N systems. If, in the long term, the medical group continues to collaborate or involve these marginal stakeholders (i.e., independent hospitals), and does not collaborate or involve with an IDS/N (a supportive or mixed-blessing stakeholder), the medical group faces the risk of being completely left out of all IDS/Ns that are developed in the market area (i.e., the IDS/N has all the physicians it needs and does not want to add any additional physicians to the panel).

---

*These negotiated contracts could include the introduction of capitation into the IDS/N.*

---

Looking at Situations 13, 14, and 15, we see 10 percent of respondents feel that medical groups are wasting resources by taking action for or against IDS/Ns now. In 1999, however, this number falls to only 4 percent of all respondents. They are currently wasting resources because IDS/Ns are not key now. In 1999, they are predicted to be key stakeholders by the vast majority of respondents. Therefore, resources used to manage them will not be wasted since their potential for both cooperation and threat will be much greater.

### The changing importance of IDS/Ns as stakeholders of medical groups

The power of the expanded theoretical model is demonstrated when we look at all three of the possible suboptimal situations together with the optimal situations. The first thing we notice is that those respondents who saw IDS/Ns as being managed optimally, saw them in one of two situations: (a) collaborating with the mixed-blessing stakeholder situation, or (b) moving toward involving the supportive stakeholder by 1999. In both of these situations, the organization's priority is, at least in part, on enhancing cooperation with IDS/Ns.

A second trend that is forecast by the responses of the MPEs is the move away from situations of *missing opportunities* toward situations of being *at risk*. This move shows a perceived need for medical groups to work with IDS/Ns. Medical groups will have to use less defensive strategies than they are currently using if they hope to capitalize on the potential of IDS/Ns in 1999. The number of responses to this study that fall into the *medical group is at risk* in 1999 (47 percent) shows that it may be prudent to add an element of caution to these movements.

## Suboptimal fit findings for all nine key stakeholders

We have already seen in Table 2 that there is a general, nonrandom pattern indicating that approximately 40 percent of experts feel that medical groups will be managing their stakeholders optimally. We will now take an overall look at the nine key stakeholders of medical groups (Table 3), focusing on areas of suboptimal strategy choice.

### Medical group misses opportunities

Table 3 shows that if the perception is that medical groups are not managing stakeholders optimally now, they are likely managing in a way that results in missed opportunities (i.e., using a strategy that does not address the stakeholder's potential for cooperation). This result is most prominent in the case of independent hospitals (31 percent optimal, 42 percent

---

**TABLE 3**

CURRENT AND FUTURE IMPLICATIONS OF USING "NONOPTIMAL" STRATEGIES TO MANAGE STAKEHOLDERS: SUMMARY OF MEDICAL PRACTICE EXECUTIVES' PERCEIVED AND PREDICTED "NONOPTIMAL FITS" OF STAKEHOLDER DIAGNOSES AND STRATEGIES

| | | Optimal strategy | Medical group at risk | Medical group misses opportunities | Medical group focuses on low potential | Total (%) |
|---|---|---|---|---|---|---|
| *IDS/N & organizational components* | | | | | | |
| IDS/N | 1994 | 40 | 14 | 36 | 10 | 100 |
| | 1999 | 36 | 47 | 13 | 4 | 100 |
| Managed care organizations | 1994 | 39 | 17 | 36 | 9 | 100 |
| | 1999 | 46 | 35 | 15 | 2 | 100 |
| Medical practices | 1994 | 43 | 18 | 32 | 8 | 100 |
| | 1999 | 39 | 31 | 22 | 9 | 100 |
| System hospitals | 1994 | 33 | 16 | 42 | 11 | 100 |
| | 1999 | 35 | 40 | 19 | 7 | 100 |
| *Other providers* | | | | | | |
| Independent hospitals | 1994 | 31 | 11 | 42 | 15 | 100 |
| | 1999 | 29 | 17 | 30 | 25 | 100 |
| Physicians | 1994 | 40 | 19 | 33 | 9 | 100 |
| | 1999 | 42 | 21 | 23 | 15 | 100 |
| *Third party payers* | | | | | | |
| Governments | 1994 | 46 | 18 | 25 | 10 | 100 |
| | 1999 | 47 | 26 | 22 | 5 | 100 |
| Employers | 1994 | 32 | 21 | 39 | 9 | 100 |
| | 1999 | 39 | 32 | 21 | 9 | 100 |
| *Patients* | | | | | | |
| Patients | 1994 | 41 | 18 | 37 | 4 | 100 |
| | 1999 | 41 | 23 | 25 | 11 | 100 |
| **Average for 1994** | | 38 | 17 | 36 | 9 | 100 |
| **Average for 1999** | | 39 | 30 | 21 | 10 | 100 |

missed opportunities) and system hospitals (33 percent optimal, 42 percent missed opportunities). In fact, for all key stakeholders now, missed opportunities account for the first or second most often reported perception. Moving to 1999, the bulk of the predictions are that the stakeholders will not be managed such that medical groups will miss opportunities (most are 25 percent or lower). Some prominent exceptions include independent hospitals (30 percent) and patients (25 percent).

### Medical group is at risk

In Table 3, we can see that most respondents do not perceive that medical groups are at risk now, with the range from 11 percent (independent hospitals) to 21 percent (employers). However, there is a big change as we look at predictions for 1999. We have already noted the large amount of risk associated with IDS/Ns. We also see that 40 percent of the respondents see medical groups using strategies that do not address the potential threat posed by system hospitals in the future—35 percent for MCOs and 32 percent for employers.

### Medical group focuses on low-potential stakeholders

In general, both now and in the future, medical groups are not perceived or predicted to be wasting resources on marginal stakeholders. This is due in most part to the focus of this article being on key stakeholders as identified in an earlier section of the questionnaire. However, independent hospitals do

become marginal stakeholders in 1999. The data show that medical groups are likely to be wasting resources on independent hospitals, with 25 percent of respondents predicting a strategy other than *monitor* when they diagnosed them as marginal stakeholders. In the first part of our analysis, we also saw that patients and physicians declined significantly in importance from now to 1999. This phenomenon also shows up here. In both cases, the category of wasting resources on marginal stakeholders increases (physicians: 9 percent to 15 percent; patients: 4 percent to 11 percent).

### The changing nature of medical group stakeholders

Up to this point in our analysis, we have focused on individual stakeholders. However, by grouping the stakeholders into IDS/Ns, organizational components, other providers, third party payers, and patients, we can get a general sense of the challenges facing those who are actually managing medical group stakeholders. Table 4 presents mean summaries of the data previously presented, grouped by categories of stakeholders.

The most striking trend apparent in Table 4 is the overall move away from a situation of missing opportunities toward a situation where the medical group is at risk. Much of this move is accounted for by the increased risk posed by IDS/Ns and organizational components (from 16 percent now to 38 percent in 1999). Apparently, the perception is that this group of stakeholders is increasing in potential for threat to medical groups, but medical group executives are not taking steps to protect against this threat. Instead, the

---

## TABLE 4

SUMMARY OF MEDICAL PRACTICE EXECUTIVES' PERCEIVED AND PREDICTED FITS OF STAKEHOLDER DIAGNOSES AND STRATEGIES: MEANS OF ALL STAKEHOLDERS AND FOUR STAKEHOLDER CATEGORIES WITH DIFFERENCES BETWEEN 1994 AND 1999

|  | Optimal fit | | | Medical group at risk | | | Medical group misses opportunities | | | Medical group focuses on low potential | | |
|---|---|---|---|---|---|---|---|---|---|---|---|---|
|  | 1994 | 1999 | Diff | 1994 | 1999 | Diff | 1994 | 1999 | Diff | 1994 | 1999 | Diff |
| IDS/N & organizational components | 39 | 39 | 0 | 16 | 38 | 22 | 37 | 17 | −20 | 9 | 6 | −3 |
| Other providers | 35 | 35 | 0 | 16 | 19 | 3 | 38 | 27 | −11 | 12 | 20 | 8 |
| Third party payers | 39 | 43 | 4 | 20 | 29 | 9 | 32 | 22 | −10 | 10 | 7 | −3 |
| Patients | 41 | 41 | 0 | 18 | 23 | 5 | 37 | 25 | −12 | 4 | 11 | 7 |
| Mean for all key stakeholders | 38 | 39 | 1 | 17 | 30 | 13 | 36 | 21 | −15 | 9 | 10 | 1 |

priorities of medical groups are becoming more oriented toward enhancing cooperation. While now they are too defensive, in the future they will be too open. Other important predicted trends shown in Table 4 include wasting resources on other providers and patients. Additionally, we see somewhat of an increased at-risk situation with third party payers.

## SUMMARY AND DISCUSSION

The present study is the first to address the evolution toward integrated delivery systems from a stakeholder management perspective. The focus was on medical group practices as an important component of the emerging integrated delivery systems, their nine key stakeholders now and in 1999, strategies for managing these key stakeholders, and the "fit" between the diagnosis of each stakeholder and the strategy being used to manage this stakeholder. Data were derived from a panel of medical group practice experts.

Seven of eight key stakeholders were the same in 1994 and 1999: physicians as individual caregivers, other medical practices, system hospitals, patients, managed care organizations, governments, and employers. Over the next 5 years, our respondents expected system hospitals, managed care organizations, governments, and employers to increase in importance while physicians as individual caregivers, other medical practices, and patients are expected to decline in importance. In addition, integrated delivery systems (not perceived by medical practice executives to be a current key stakeholder) are expected to increase significantly in importance and become key stakeholders while independent hospitals will become marginal stakeholders.

As regards the fit between the experts' diagnosis of each stakeholder and the strategy for management perceived or predicted by expert medical practice executives, all nine were seen as being optimally managed by anywhere from 33 to 48 percent of the respondents. There was not much change in the level of fit from 1994 to 1999. Wasting resources on marginal stakeholders was generally less of a problem than lost opportunities and failure to protect the organization from key stakeholder threats. Lost opportunities are the major cause of lack of fit now, but failure to protect against threats is expected to be the major problem in 1999.

### Implications for health care executives

The managerial implications of these data are that medical group practice executives and other health care executives need to identify their own key stakeholders in the emerging integrated systems of which they will be a part. Then they need to allocate time, effort, and economic resources to diagnosing and managing relationships with these stakeholders. In particular, they need to develop strategies to better defend against nonsupportive key stakeholders and collaborate with mixed-blessing stakeholders.

The expected rise of integrated delivery systems poses both opportunities and threats to medical practices. The opportunity is to provide patients to secondary and tertiary facilities in exchange for economic and managerial support from these facilities. The threat is that control of resources and inflexible policies on the part of the individuals controlling the system will reduce the autonomy of medical practitioners. This may reduce physician satisfaction, flexibility, and quality of care at the delivery site. Steps should be taken now to defend against or collaborate with the network (depending upon how the system is diagnosed). More specifically, managers should consider a range of alternatives including education, participation, facilitation, negotiation, cooperation, and coercion.[20] The important point is that the solution should match the nature of the actual or potential threat posed by a particular key stakeholder perceived by a particular medical group practice executive.

The study by Shortell and colleagues[19] examined 12 integrated systems in order to determine the obstacles or challenges to achieving greater levels of integration. Some of the most important of these obstacles have clear implications for management of key stakeholders—one of which is the medical group. Medical groups are key stakeholders for a specific integrated system, since they can be an existing component of the system, a potential member or strategic partner, or even a competitor (or part of a competing integrated system).

Many of the barriers to development of fully integrated health care delivery systems identified by Shortell and his colleagues[19] stem from a failure to accurately identify, assess, and appropriately manage stakeholders who are key to the success of the effort. Too much time, effort, and money is being spent on managing stakeholders who are marginal in terms of the development of integrated delivery systems.

At the same time, new opportunities are lost due to a failure to identify these opportunities and the stakeholders who are key to their implementation. Our study indicates that the reciprocal can be true for medical groups themselves—looking at integrated systems or networks, such as those studied by Shortell et al.[19] as *their* stakeholders.

Perhaps the most important finding from our study is the clear perception by experts that (a) the stakeholders that make up integrated systems or networks and their component organizations are increasing in potential for threat to medical groups but (b) medical group executives are not taking steps to protect against this threat. Instead, the priorities of medical groups are becoming more oriented toward enhancing cooperation. Note that our expert panel is predicting that medical groups will be focusing too much on enhancing cooperation, leaving themselves open to the threats posed by IDS/Ns and their components. While now they are too defensive, in the future they will be too open.

### Implications for future research

From a theoretical perspective, our analysis has contributed to the literature by identifying and providing some preliminary data regarding the fit between diagnosis and strategy for managing key stakeholders. Sixteen cells were identified. All cells are classified as either optimal, missed opportunity, at risk, or focus on low-potential stakeholders. Our data indicate that suboptimal strategies are currently being used and will continue to be used in the future by most respondents.

Future research should address the linkage between fit or various types of lack of fit (noted above) on organizational performance as measured by economic and noneconomic outcomes. The former might include profits, market share, and survival, while the latter might include data on satisfaction of various key stakeholders such as patients, employers, and managed care organizations.

In situations where there is a lack of fit, there are two possible outcomes: (a) negative outcomes as measured by the above criteria or (b) positive outcomes associated with the movement of key stakeholders from the less positive to a more positive diagnostic category (e.g., nonsupportive to mixed blessing or mixed blessing to supportive).

In-depth, longitudinal case studies of specific organizations should help probe these relationships as they manage their stakeholders not only optimally but also suboptimally. For example, if an organization involves—rather than collaborates with—a mixed-blessing stakeholder, will that mixed-blessing stakeholder, in fact, become supportive or will the organi-

zation just be putting itself at risk from potential threat that has not been confronted strategically?

For example, Blair and Whitehead[5] and Blair and Fottler[3] regard stakeholder diagnosis to be influenced by the strategy implementation itself, and they focus particularly on the mixed-blessing stakeholder by showing that diagnostic type with a large question mark indicating its likely instability. They also show two arrows—one pointing from mixed-blessing to supportive and one from mixed-blessing to nonsupportive to both encourage and caution executives as they attempt to manage this particularly volatile stakeholder.

Hence, this article suggests two additional future research questions. Since a longitudinal study is required to examine the actual outcomes of managing a stakeholder with an optimal or nonoptimal strategy, the first question is this: "Is the choice of any strategy a self-fulfilling prophecy?" In other words, if an organization's executives manage a stakeholder as if it were nonsupportive (with a defensive strategy) will it eventually become nonsupportive? Does an involvement strategy not only enhance the cooperation potential of a mixed-blessing stakeholder, but could it also reduce the potential for threat? These questions could be addressed in a longitudinal, outcome-based study. Additionally, some of Ring and Van de Ven's[21] propositions regarding the dynamics of cooperative interorganizational relationships, especially those dealing with the effects of time and types of contracts, would also benefit from this research.

The second question to be dealt with in depth is: "What is the role played by uncertainty in the diagnosis of stakeholders?" This article suggests that conservative managers would deal with uncertain stakeholders using strategies that tend to miss opportunities, while risk takers would use the strategies that tend to put the organization at risk. Is one better than the other? Is there a risk–reward dimension to stakeholder management?

We encourage other researchers to test and extend the strategic approach presented in this study through both empirical and conceptual research. The strategies suggested throughout this article are open to further empirical investigation and should be thought of as theoretical propositions to be tested. The strategies are consistent with the existing stakeholder management literature and the qualitative data that have grounded the theory building to date on these topics. However, the link between these different types of diagnosis–strategy fits and the outcomes proposed to result from the optimal or suboptimal fits are a special focus of this paper. This link will need considerable systematic empirical research, in addition to the initial quantitative data presented here, to supplement the original qualitative approach of Blair and Fottler.[3]

## REFERENCES

1. Shortell, S.M. "The Evolution of Hospital Systems: Unfulfilled Promises and Self-Fulfilling Prophesies." *Medical Care Review* 45, no. 2 (1988): 177–214.

2. Fottler, M.D., and Malvey, D. "Multiprovider Systems." In *Health Care Administration: Principles, Practices, Structure and Delivery*, edited by L. Wolper. Gaithersburg, Md.: Aspen Publishers, 1995.

3. Blair, J.D., and Fottler, M.D. *Challenges in Health Care Management: Strategic Perspectives for Managing Key Stakeholders.* San Francisco: Jossey-Bass, 1990.

4. Blair, J.D., Rotarius, T.M., Shepherd, K.B., Whitehead, C.J., and Whyte, E.G. "Strategic Stakeholder Management for Health Care Executives." In *Health Care Administration: Principles, Practices, Structure and Delivery* edited by L. Wolper. Gaithersburg, Md.: Aspen Publishers, 1995.

5. Blair, J.D., and Whitehead, C. "Too Many on the Seesaw: Stakeholder Diagnosis and Management for Hospitals." *Hospitals and Health Services Management* 33, no. 2 (Summer 1988): 153–156.

6. Luke, R.O. "Local Hospital Systems: Forerunners of Regional Systems?" *Frontiers of Health Services Management* 9, no. 2 (1992): 177–214.

7. Shortell, S.M., Morrison, E.M., and Friedman, B. *Strategic Choices for America's Hospitals: Managing Change in Turbulent Times.* San Francisco: Jossey-Bass, 1990.

8. Zuckerman, H.S., and D'Aunno, T.A. "Hospital Alliances: Cooperative Strategy in a Competitive Environment." *Health Care Management Review* 15, no. 2 (1990): 21–30.

9. Zuckerman, H.S., and Kaluzny, A.D. "The Management of Strategic Alliances in Health Services." *Frontiers of Health Services Management* 7, no. 1 (1991): 3–23.

10. Kaluzny, A.D., and Zuckerman, H.S. "Strategic Alliances: Two Perspectives for Understanding Their Effects on Health Services." *Hospital & Health Services Administration* 37 (1992): 477–90.

11. Mason, R.O., and Mitroff, I.I. *Challenging Strategic Planning Assumptions.* New York: Wiley, 1981.

12. Freeman, R.E. *Strategic Management: A Stakeholder Approach.* Marshfield, Mass.: Pitman Publishing, 1984.

13. Savage, G.T., Nix, T.W., Whitehead, C.J., and Blair, J.D. "Strategies for Assessing and Managing Stakeholders." *Academy of Management Executives* 5, no. 2 (1991): 61–75.

14. Burns, L.R., and Thorpe, D.P. "Trends and Models in Physician-Hospital Organization." *Health Care Management Review* 18, no. 4 (1993): 7–20.

15. Coddington, D.C., Moore, D.D., and Fischer, E.A. *Integrated Health Care: Reorganizing the Physician, Hospital and Health Plan Relationship.* Englewood, Colo.: MGMA, 1994.

16. Coddington, D.C., Moore, D.D., and Fischer, E.A. "Integrated Health Care Systems: The Key Characteristics." *Medical Group Management Journal* (November/December 1993): 76–80.

17. Conrad, D.A., and Hoare, G.A. (Eds.). *Strategic Alignment: Managing Integrated Health Systems.* Ann Arbor, Mich.: Health Administration Press, 1994.

18. Kongstvedt, P.R., and Plocher, D.W. "Integrated Health Care Delivery Systems." In *Essentials of Managed Care* edited by P.R. Kongstvedt. Gaithersburg, Md.: Aspen Publishers, 1995.

19. Shortell, S., Gillies, R., Anderson, D., Mitchell, J., and Morgan, J. "Creating Organized Delivery Systems: The Barriers and Facilitators." *Hospital & Health Services Administration* 38, no. 4 (1993): 447–66.

20. Zajac, E.J., and D'Aunno, T.A. "Managing Strategic Alliances." In *Health Care Management: Organization Design and Behavior* (3rd ed.) edited by S.M. Shortell and A.D. Kaluzny. Albany, N.Y.: Delmar Publishers, 1994.

21. Ring, P.S., and Van De Ven, A.H. "Developmental Processes of Cooperative Interorganizational Relationships." *Academy of Management Review* 19, no. 1 (1994): 90–118.

# PART III

# MAKING ALLIANCES WORK

# Implementing organized delivery systems: An integration scorecard

Kelly J. Devers,
Stephen M. Shortell,
Robin R. Gillies,
David A. Anderson,
John B. Mitchell,
and
Karen L. Morgan Erickson

*Organized vertically integrated health systems are in a key position to play a major role in present health care reform efforts. To demonstrate a competitive advantage in the new health care environment, however, integration efforts must be successful. Based on a national study of nine organized delivery systems, this article develops measures of three types of integration that occur in vertically integrated health systems— functional, physician-system, and clinical. These measures can be used as a "scorecard" to assess progress toward achieving integration objectives.*

*Health Care Manage Rev*, 1994, 19(3), 7–20
© 1994 Aspen Publishers, Inc.

**Over the past several** decades, health care providers, payors, and policy analysts have expressed a growing interest in organized delivery systems. This interest arises from the developing consensus that such systems represent an innovative organizational form that may be capable of meeting the challenges of the emerging health care environment. These challenges include (1) new payment arrangements to contain rising costs, (2) an aging population with chronic illnesses which require services that the current system is ill-equipped to provide, (3) rapid advances in technology which increase length of life and raise costs (confounding previously mentioned problems) while providing new delivery opportunities (e.g., outpatient surgery), and (4) potential health care human resource shortages.[1-4] Traditional health care delivery organizations have not effectively met these chal-

Key words: *organized delivery systems, functional integration, physician-system integration, clinical integration*

***Kelly J. Devers***, *Ph.D., is a Robert Wood Johnson Foundation Post-Doctoral Fellow at the University of California–Berkeley and was Project Coordinator, Health Systems Integration Study, Northwestern University.*

***Stephen M. Shortell***, *Ph.D., is A.C. Buehler Distinguished Professor of Health Services Management and Professor of Organization Behavior, J.L. Kellogg Graduate School of Management and the Center for Health Services Policy Research, Northwestern University.*

***Robin R. Gillies***, *Ph.D., is Research Assistant Professor, Center for Health Services and Policy Research, Northwestern University, and Project Director, Health Systems Integration Study.*

***David A. Anderson***, *C.P.A., M.B.A., is Partner-in-Charge at KPMG Peat Marwick, Management Consulting, National Health Care Strategy Practice.*

***John B. Mitchell***, *J.D., M.H.A., is Partner at KPMG Peat Marwick, Management Consulting, National Health Care Strategy Practice.*

***Karen L. Morgan Erickson***, *M.H.A., is Manager at KPMG Peat Marwick, Management Consulting, National Health Care Strategy Practice.*

The authors gratefully acknowledge the participation of the nine systems in the Health Systems Integration Study (HSIS) who funded this research and assisted in the development of the measures described in this paper. They are Baylor Health Care System (Dallas), EHS Health Care (Oakbrook, Ill.), Fairview Hospital and Healthcare Services (Minneapolis), Franciscan Health System (Aston, Penn.), Henry Ford Health System (Detroit), Sharp HealthCare (San Diego), Sisters of Providence (Seattle), Sutter Health (Sacramento), and UniHealth America (Burbank, Calif.). They also wish to thank Alice Schaller for her assistance with manuscript preparation.

lenges. As a result, patients, payors, and providers have become increasingly open to new relationships and approaches.

An organized delivery system (ODS) is a network of organizations (e.g., ambulatory care clinics, physician groups, diagnostic centers, hospitals, nursing homes, home health care agencies) usually under common ownership which provides, or arranges to provide, a coordinated continuum of services to a defined population and is willing to be held clinically and fiscally responsible for the health status of that population. These systems often own, or are closely aligned with, an insurance product.[5] As the definition suggests, organized delivery systems are primarily pursuing a vertical integration strategy (often in a defined geographic region), and, therefore, are frequently referred to as vertically integrated (regional) systems. While organized delivery systems utilize horizontal integration strategies as well, vertical integration strategies are emphasized to differentiate them from multihospital systems or other chains providing services at a single stage of the delivery process (e.g., psychiatric hospitals, laboratories). Through a variety of integrative mechanisms, it is argued that systems can provide care more efficiently and effectively than if individual operating units were to carry out tasks independently or if purchasers were to bundle services together.

Several researchers have developed models and frameworks for categorizing and assessing vertically integrated health systems.[1,4,5,6–9] Building on these approaches, we have developed a model which identifies three key forms of integration: functional integration, physician-system integration, and clinical integration (see Figure 1). As Figure 1 indicates, these forms of integration are conceptualized as occurring sequentially, with functional and physician-system integration promoting clinical integration.

Clinical integration is defined as the extent to which patient care services are coordinated across various functions, activities, and operating units of a system.[9] It is viewed as the most important form of integration because it is the primary means by which organized delivery systems are able to provide cost effective, quality care in a managed care environment, particularly under capitated payment structures. Physician-system integration is defined as the extent to which physicians benefit economically through their affiliation with the system, are committed to using the system, and have substantive administrative involvement with the system. Functional integration is defined as the extent to which key support functions and activities (such as financial management, human resources, information management, quality assurance/improvement, strategic planning, and marketing) are coordinated across operating units.

## FIGURE 1

FRAMEWORK FOR EXAMINING INTEGRATION*

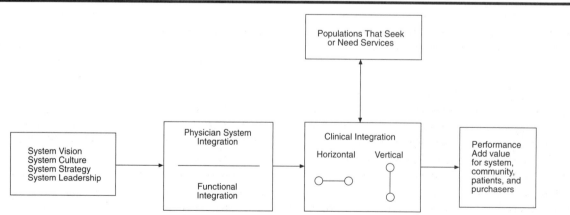

*These factors will also be influenced by certain context variables such as each system's market environment, geographical distribution of facilities, length of time each unit has been with the system, and the historical evolution of the system.

Adapted with permission from Gillies, R., et al. "Conceptualizing and Measuring Integration: Findings from the Health Systems Integration Study." *Hospital and Health Services Administration*, 1993.

The purpose of the present article is to

- examine the challenges associated with measuring the above dimensions of integration;
- propose some tested measures based on three years of research involving nine organized delivery systems around the country; and
- suggest the development of an integration scorecard which can be used to chart progress toward achieving integration objectives.

## ISSUES IN MEASURING INTEGRATION

Integration measures can be grouped into three areas: (1) measures of the precursors of integration, (2) measures of intermediate outcomes or internal process variables which assess the level of systemwide activity in key areas which are the means to achieving ultimate goals, and (3) outcomes measures which assess the extent to which systems are in fact fulfilling their ultimate purpose. Since others have identified indicators of the precursors of integration[9] and potential outcomes,[10] the present paper focuses on intermediate outcome or process measures. There are a number of issues associated with the development of such measures.

First, developing measures of organized or vertically integrated system activity requires a shift to systems thinking.[11,12] An organizational system is a set of interdependent parts that relate in the accomplishment of a common goal.[13] The shift from freestanding hospitals to organized or vertically integrated health systems means that interdependencies and common goals be emphasized and measures be redesigned to reflect this shift. For example, assessments of individual operating units and/or relationships between operating units must be viewed not only in terms of their individual performance but how and what they contribute to the "system" as a whole.

The shift to integrated systems and systems thinking, however, is often difficult to make as there are a variety of barriers to overcome, including overemphasis on acute care, the entrepreneurial interests of successful hospitals, and the lack of incentives for achieving systemwide objectives.[5,14] We argue, however, that systemwide measurement itself may help overcome these barriers and aid the development of systems thinking. The development, collection, and feedback of systemwide indicators can help systems explicitly examine the relationships between system operating units, as well as foster an operating unit's reconceptualization of its activities in system terms.

For example, "overcoming the hospital paradigm" (a common barrier to integration) may be easier if the hospital's role vis-a-vis other operating units (e.g., owned insurance product, outpatient clinics, physician groups, other hospitals) is explicitly assessed.

A second, closely related, point involves methodological challenges that are raised by shifting the focus of analysis from the hospital (or individual operating unit) to the system. In brief, how should one measure system activity and performance when there are a diversity of operating units performing somewhat unique tasks? Should operating unit integration activity be scored relative to its size and strategic importance to the system (in which case one or two large operating units may have a disproportionate effect on the "system" score) or should each operating unit be weighted equally? Should different types of operating units be compared relative to another and how is this possible if the system only has one operating unit of a particular type? These represent statistical, methodological (i.e., aggregation, measurement), and conceptual issues that often arise in social science research.

In the current study, we examined system performance in three ways: (1) we computed an overall percentage which would proportionately score operating units, (2) we computed an average of operating unit scores (in which case each system operating units' integration scores are equally weighted), and (3) we examined measures by type of operating unit. Computing the measures in these three ways provided added insight into the measures themselves as well as the systems, even though the measures varied only slightly by the computation method employed. The data reported in this paper are computed by the second method (the system score is equal to the average scores of its operating units) because it is less sensitive to effects of one or two large system operating units that have high levels of integration (e.g., flagship hospitals and clinics).

Finally, as systemwide data are gathered, issues of comparability and compatibility of system operating unit records must be addressed. To efficiently collect data and draw meaningful conclusions, operating unit records may need to be modified so they are comparable and/or new data collected. Experience from the present study suggests that the quality of data varied within individual system operating units (as well as across systems) and that some effort was required to convert data for systemwide measurement. This was particularly true when systems had minority ownership of an operating unit (e.g., a physician group or managed care plan) and had difficulty obtaining data.

In sum, lack of systems thinking, methodological challenges, and the availability and comparability of data made measurement of system integration activity challenging. Systems were, however, able to collect the data and reported learning a great deal from both the process and the results.

## MEASURES OF FUNCTIONAL, PHYSICIAN-SYSTEM, AND CLINICAL INTEGRATION

Based on a review of the literature, interaction with the study research advisory group committee, and two- to three-day site visits made in summer 1991, measures of functional, physician-system, and clinical integration were developed. While perceptual data were collected and are reported elsewhere, the present paper focuses on "objective" measures.[9] Data were collected on the objective measures through a questionnaire that was completed by appropriate personnel in the system and operating unit offices (e.g., the physician-system integration section was completed by personnel in the corporate physician affairs office, staff in physician groups, etc.). Data were cleaned and coded, input, checked for completeness and accuracy using standard techniques (e.g., ensure values are in possible ranges, response is logical, etc.), and then fed back to the research advisory group member for further clarification and final approval. Data reported here are for the 1991 fiscal year.

### Functional integration

As previously noted, *functional integration* is defined as the extent to which key support functions and activities (such as financial management, human resources, information management quality assurance/ improvement, strategic planning, and marketing) are coordinated across operating units. One approach to examining coordination is to assess the extent to which the above functions are standardized across operating units (i.e., the extent to which all operating units within a system use the same approaches, policies, practices, and/or guidelines in carrying out functions and activities).

Standardization of functions are evaluated using a questionnaire that was completed by each of the system strategic planners. The degree of standardization was determined from a series of 49 yes/no questions related to selected functional support areas including culture, financial management, support services, human resources, information systems, other (i.e., managed care contracting, administrative practices, new product and service development), quality assurance/improvement, and strategic planning (see the Appendix for the complete list of items). For each functional area, a percentage of "yes" responses was computed, with 0 percent meaning that none of the items were standardized and 100 percent meaning that all items were standardized throughout the system.

As Table 1 indicates, 42 percent of the functions overall are standardized throughout systems, ranging from a low of 22 percent for information services to 72 percent for financial management. These findings are consistent with field interviews and with the perceptual data where information systems integration was perceived as among the least integrated areas ($\overline{X}$=2.49, on a 1 [low] to 5 [high] scale), and financial management (operating policies) was the most highly integrated ($\overline{X}$=3.47).

### Measures of physician-system integration

As noted, physician-system integration is defined as the extent to which physicians benefit economically through their affiliation with the system, are committed to using the system, and have substantive administrative involvement with the system. In the model, it is argued that physician-system integration is a key factor influencing the ability of a system to clinically

## TABLE 1

DEGREE OF STANDARDIZATION OF FUNCTIONS PERCENTAGE OF FUNCTION ITEMS STANDARDIZED

| Functional area | Percent of function items standardized |
|---|---|
| Human resources | 32 |
| Financial management | 72 |
| Support services | 50 |
| Quality assurance/improvement | 26 |
| Strategic planning | 55 |
| Information services | 22 |
| Culture | 33 |
| Other | 43 |
| Average percent standardized over 8 functional areas | 42 |

integrate services in a local market. Not only is physician input needed to assess areas where clinical integration efforts may be most successful, but also physicians ultimately decide how patients are treated. To achieve clinical integration, systems will need mechanisms to tie physicians' interests and activity more closely to the systems objectives.

There are four major subcomponents of the physician-system integration concept: (1) economic involvement, (2) administrative involvement, (3) group practice formation, and (4) shared accountability. Figure 2 illustrates these four components of physician-system integration and the specific measures of each are described below.

*Economic involvement*

Economic involvement has four subcomponents related to physician utilization activity, the extent of joint venture activity between physicians and the system's facilities, the extent to which the system provides physicians with benefits for themselves and their employees, and the extent to which hospital-based contracts are shared throughout the system.

In regard to *physician utilization activity in various system settings*, eight measures were developed: (1) the percent of total active staff physicians at system operating units who admit 10 or more patients to system facilities; (2) the percent of active staff physicians

**FIGURE 2**

COMPONENTS OF PHYSICIAN-SYSTEM INTEGRATION AND ASSOCIATED MEASURES

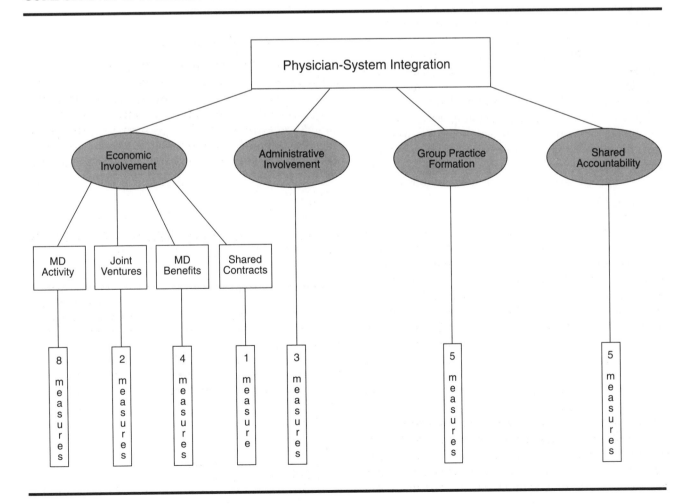

at system operating units who account for 75 percent or more of the operating unit's admissions or outpatient visits; (3) the percent of physicians at system operating units who admit 10 or more patients to two or more system affiliated operating units; (4) the percent of active staff physicians at system operating units who see 50 or more patients per year in an outpatient setting, wholly or partially owned by the system operating unit; (5) the percent with offices in a system-owned or campus-related medical office building; (6) the percent of physicians at system operating units who have offices in a system-owned or campus-located medical office building and who are among those doctors accounting for 75 percent or more of the operating unit's admissions or outpatient visits; (7) the percent of physicians at system operating units that have practices managed by or affiliated with the system; and (8) the percent of physicians at system operating units with practices managed by or affiliated with the system who constitute physicians that account for 75 percent or more of the operating unit's admissions or outpatient visits.

There are two measures of *joint venture activity:* (1) the percent of physicians at system operating units who are involved in joint venture activity, and (2) the percent of joint venture activity physicians who are among those doctors that account for 75 percent or more of an operating unit's admissions or outpatient visits.

There are four measures of *physician benefits:* (1) the percent of total active staff physicians in system operating units for whom the system provides benefits for either the physician or the physician's employees—these benefits include health care insurance, disability insurance, and pensions; (2) the percent of total active staff physicians in system operating units who are provided practice management support services such as billing, recruiting, and marketing assistance; (3) the percent of total active staff physicians in system operating units who are provided electronic linkage; and (4) the percent of physicians in system operating units who receive any of the above benefits that are among those physicians accounting for 75 percent or more of the operating unit's admissions or outpatient visits.

There is also one measure of *shared physician contracts* defined as the average percent of the system's operating units with a shared physician contract out of all possible opportunities for a shared contract involving 12 clinical specialty areas including anesthesiology, cardiology, cardiovascular surgery, critical care/intensive medicine, emergency room, neonatology, oncology (medical), oncology (radiation), pathology, perinatology, radiology, and trauma.

### Administrative involvement

Under the administrative involvement subcomponent of physician-system integration, there are three specific measures: (1) the percent of five administrative involvement mechanisms used by system operating units (the five mechanisms examined include having at least one or more physicians involved as an elected governing board member, at least half of the governing board committees have at least one physician member, at least one physician who is a senior manager, physicians are regularly invited to participate in strategic planning retreats, and physicians serve on systemwide committees or task forces); (2) the percent of physicians at system operating units who are also active staff physicians that are paid for administrative responsibilities; and (3) the percent of paid physicians at system operating units who have responsibilities across two or more operating units of the system.

### Group practice formation

There are five specific measures of the third subcomponent of physician-system integration, group practice formation. These include (1) the percent of total active staff physicians at system operating units who practice in groups; (2) the percent of the physicians in groups at the system operating units that practice via single-specialty groups; (3) the percent of the physicians in groups at system operating units that practice via multi-specialty groups; (4) the percent of the physicians practicing in groups at system operating units that account for 75 percent or more of the operating unit's admissions or outpatient visits; and (5) the percent of the physicians practicing in groups at system operating units that practice via *primary care* single-specialty groups.

### Shared accountability

The fourth subcomponent of physician system integration is shared accountability mechanisms. There are five measures of shared accountability, including (1) the percent of a system's operating units with a common medical staff organization, (2) the percent of a system's operating units with a common credentialing process, (3) the percent of a system's operating units with a common quality assurance/improvement program, (4) the percent of a system's operating units that share common patient care diagnostic and/or treatment protocols, and (5) an overall measure of the percent of the four shared accountability mechanisms listed above that are shared by system operating units.

Table 2 provides descriptive statistics for these physician-system integration measures. Perhaps most striking about the data is the relatively high degree of physician involvement in management and governance activities at the individual operating unit level (i.e., 72.2 percent of units have such involvement) but

---

**TABLE 2**

DESCRIPTIVE SUMMARY OF PHYSICIAN-SYSTEM INTEGRATION MEASURES

| Concept/Measure | Mean | Standard Deviation | Range |
|---|---|---|---|
| **Economic Involvement** | | | |
| *Physician Utilization Activity* | | | |
| Percent admitting 10+ patients | 76.5 | 13.7 | 52.8–99.1 |
| Percent accounting for 75+ admissions or outpatient visits | 44.2 | 11.0 | 34.3–66.8 |
| Percent admitting to 2+ operating units | 9.3 | 8.7 | 0.0–25.9 |
| Percent with 50+ outpatient visits in a system-owned facility | 33.0 | 27.5 | 2.0–79.8 |
| Percent with offices in system-owned or campus-related medical office building (MOB) | 29.9 | 20.5 | 4.0–69.4 |
| Percent of those in a MOB who help account for 75%+ admissions | 58.8 | 15.9 | 30.0–86.6 |
| Percent of physicians in a system-managed or affiliated practice | 6.6 | 6.7 | 0.0–18.3 |
| Percent of those in a system-managed/affiliated practice who help account for 75%+ admissions | 41.7 | 27.1 | 0.0–70.8 |
| *Joint Venture Activity* | | | |
| Percent involved in a joint venture (JV) | 3.9 | 5.1 | 0.0–14.1 |
| Percent of those in a JV who help account for 75%+ admissions or outpatient visit | 46.3 | 29.2 | 9.5–100.0 |
| *Physician Benefits* | | | |
| Percent receiving benefits for self and/or employees | 9.9 | 20.5 | 0.0–60.1 |
| Percent receiving practice management support services | 16.6 | 22.8 | 0.0–63.4 |
| Percent receiving electronic linkage of clinical/financial data | 14.7 | 20.6 | 0.0–60.0 |
| Percent receiving any of above benefits who help account for 75%+ admissions or outpatient visits | 35.5 | 17.3 | 0.0–62.6 |
| *Shared Contracts* | | | |
| Percent of hospital-based operating units involved in shared physician contract opportunities | 17.1 | 15.4 | 0.0–45.8 |
| **Administrative Involvement** | | | |
| Percent operating units involving physicians in selected set of administrative/governance responsibilities | 72.2 | 12.3 | 53.3–88.6 |
| Percent active staff physicians paid for administrative responsibilities | 6.7 | 5.1 | 1.3–17.4 |
| Percent of paid physicians with responsibilities at two or more units | 8.2 | 10.5 | 0.0–29.2 |
| **Group Practice Formation** | | | |
| Percent physicians practicing in groups | 45.5 | 19.0 | 16.0–76.0 |
| Of those in groups, percent that are single specialty | 70.2 | 27.9 | 14.5–100.0 |
| Of those in groups, percent that are multispecialty | 29.8 | 28.0 | 0.0–85.5 |
| Of those in groups, percent that are *primary care* single specialty | 32.0 | 26.0 | 3.0–100.0 |
| Of those in groups, percent who help account for 75%+ admissions | 31.9 | 26.1 | 2.6–100.0 |
| **Shared Accountability** | | | |
| Percent of operating units (OU) sharing a common medical staff organization | 7.3 | 14.3 | 0.0–42.9 |
| Percent of OUs sharing a common physician credentialing process | 24.4 | 38.2 | 0.0–100.0 |
| Percent of OUs sharing a common quality assurance/improvement program | 49.4 | 46.7 | 0.0–100.0 |
| Percent of OUs sharing at least one common patient care diagnostic and/or treatment protocol | 27.7 | 37.6 | 0.0–100.0 |
| Overall percent of OUs involved in shared accountability mechanisms | 26.9 | 21.5 | 0.0–66.7 |

the relatively low degree of physician administrative involvement that cuts across two or more operating units (i.e., of the 6.7 percent of physicians who are paid, only 8.2 percent have administrative responsibilities at two or more operating units). In brief, most efforts at administratively integrating physicians into the system are taking place at the individual operating unit level as opposed to systemwide involvement and responsibilities. It is also of interest to note that only 16.6 percent of active staff physicians are receiving practice management support services such as billing, office management assistance, and managed care contracting help. Further, while 45.5 percent of physicians are practicing in groups, the majority of those (70.2 percent) are practicing in single-specialty groups rather than multispecialty groups, which have greater potential for integrating services across different levels of care.

Preliminary data analysis suggests these measures not only provide insight into physician-system integration activity itself but also the way in which physician-system integration is linked to both clinical integration and some aspects of financial performance. Specifically, greater physician administrative involvement is associated with many other dimensions of physician-system integration, such as the percent of physicians in system-managed or affiliated practices and the percent of physicians practicing in multispecialty groups, which suggest that in order to make progress in this area physicians must be involved administratively. In addition, many aspects of physician-system integration are correlated with greater clinical integration (discussed below), as the model suggests. Finally, selected measures of physician-system integration, while primarily working through increased clinical integration, are significantly correlated with select measures of financial performance, such as increased system productivity (adjusted admissions per full time equivalent [FTE] personnel, $r=.50$ to $r=.71$), greater system net revenue ($r=.49$ to $r=.74$), and higher system operating margin ($r=.51$). In sum, preliminary data analysis suggests that the physician-system integration measures have predictive validity in relation to clinical integration and selected measures of system financial performance.

## Measures of clinical integration

*Clinical integration* was previously defined as the extent to which patient care services are coordinated across various functions, activities, and operating units of a system. Six major dimensions of clinical integration were examined including (1) clinical protocol development, (2) medical records uniformity and accessibility, (3) clinical outcomes data collection and utilization, (4) clinical programming and planning efforts, (5) shared clinical support services, and (6) shared clinical service lines. Figure 3 illustrates these six components of clinical integration and the specific measures of each are described below.

Two specific measures of *clinical protocol development* were assessed: (1) the average number of standard treatment protocols or clinical practice guidelines developed at system operating units, and (2) the percent of standard treatment protocols or clinical practice guidelines shared with at least one other system operating unit.

Five measures of *medical records accessibility* were utilized. The first measure is the percent of medical records features that either are available to other operating units in the system or are shared by other system operating units. For example, electronic access is available *between* system operating units, not simply within a single operating unit. The second measure of medical records accessibility is the average time that is required to obtain information from a medical record from other system operating units. The third measure of medical records accessibility assessed the percent of operating units using a common numbering system of all possible opportunities. The fourth measure involved the percent of operating units having shared electronic access out of all possible opportunities. Finally, the fifth measure of medical records accessibility is the average percent of system operating units using an integrated record with a problem-oriented flow sheet.

The first measure of *clinical outcome data* utilization was the overall percent of fifteen clinical outcomes (e.g., hospital acquired infections, unplanned admissions following ambulatory procedures) that were collected and shared among all possible operating unit sharing opportunities. The second measure assessed the average number of outcomes data collected and shared per system operating unit.

*Shared programmatic and planning efforts* were assessed using four measures. The first is the average percent of six programs and assessment tools (e.g., medical staff planning, collection of common patient satisfaction scores) used by system operating units. The second measure is the percent of physician-hospital organizations (PHOs) shared by system operating units and the third measure is the percent of system

**FIGURE 3**

COMPONENTS OF CLINICAL INTEGRATION AND ASSOCIATED MEASURES

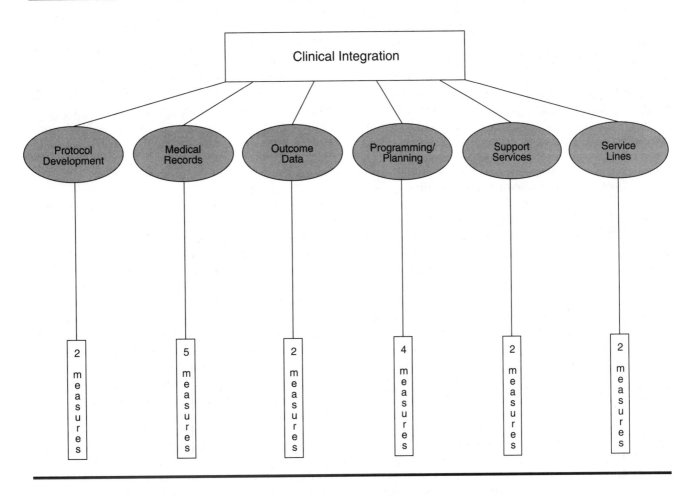

operating units that have a PHO that is exclusive to the unit. The fourth measure is the average number of the programs and assessment tools utilized by each system operating unit.

Sharing of *clinical support services* among system operating units was measured by the average percent of nine support services (e.g., pharmacy, laboratory, physician therapy) shared at system operating units out of all possible support services shared and by the average number of support services shared by each system operating unit.

Finally, two measures of *shared clinical services* were developed. The first measure is the average percent of 10 clinical service lines (e.g., behavioral health, oncology, cardiology) shared at system operating

units out of all possible clinical services. The second measure assesses the magnitude of sharing at system operating units by calculating the average number of clinical service lines shared per operating unit.

Table 3 provides descriptive statistics on these measures of clinical integration. The data indicate relatively low to moderate levels of integration across the various dimensions. For example, an average of only 2.9 clinical protocols are developed per operating unit; only 11.4 percent of operating units share a common inpatient and outpatient ID number; an average of only 1.9 clinical outcome measures are collected and shared among the units; an average of only 1.4 clinical support service, such as laboratory or radiology, is shared; and an average of only 1.3 clinical

## TABLE 3

### DESCRIPTIVE SUMMARY OF CLINICAL INTEGRATION MEASURES

| Concept/Measure | Mean | Standard Deviation | Range |
|---|---|---|---|
| **Clinical Protocol Development** | | | |
| Number of protocols per operating unit (OU) | 2.9 | 4.9 | 0.0–16.0 |
| Percent protocols shared with at least one other OU | 61.5 | 31.7 | 25.0–100.0 |
| **Medical Records Uniformity and Accessibility** | | | |
| Percent of medical records features shared | 10.9 | 15.2 | 0.0–48.2 |
| Availability of medical records information | 2.3 | 0.8 | 1.0–3.0 |
| Percent ID features shared | 11.4 | 17.8 | 0.0–44.4 |
| Percent of OUs with electronic access to at least one other OU | 9.5 | 17.3 | 0.0–42.9 |
| Percent OUs using an integrated record with a problem-oriented flow sheet | 5.0 | 16.6 | 0.0–55.0 |
| **Clinical Outcomes Data Collection and Utilization** | | | |
| Percent of 15 clinical outcomes collected and shared | 16.3 | 28.4 | 0.0–81.3 |
| Average number of 15 clinical outcomes collected and shared | 1.9 | 3.3 | 0.0–9.3 |
| **Clinical Programming and Planning Efforts** | | | |
| Percent of 6 programs used by OUs | 34.6 | 25.9 | 0.0–86.4 |
| Percent of OUs sharing a PHO | 12.8 | 29.4 | 0.0–100.0 |
| Percent of OUs sharing a recruitment plan | 42.3 | 47.0 | 0.0–100.0 |
| Average number of 6 programs used | 2.1 | 1.6 | 0.0–4.9 |
| **Shared Clinical Support Services** | | | |
| Percent of 9 support services shared by at least one other OU | 17.6 | 17.3 | 0.0–49.4 |
| Average number of 9 support services shared by at least one other OU | 1.4 | 1.4 | 0.0–4.0 |
| **Shared Clinical Service Lines** | | | |
| Percent of 10 clinical services shared with at least one other OU | 15.2 | 19.8 | 0.0–61.1 |
| Average number of 10 clinical service lines shared with at least one other OU | 1.3 | 1.7 | 0.0–5.0 |

service line is shared across operating units (e.g., oncology, cardiovascular, behavioral, women's health). This is to be expected as systems are only beginning to make concerted efforts at clinical integration having first laid the groundwork in terms of functional and physician-system integration as previously discussed.

As noted previously, analysis suggests that physician-system integration activity is associated with greater clinical integration, particularly in regard to physician administrative involvement, the percentage of physicians in multispecialty group practice and common credentialing of physicians. In addition, selected measures of clinical integration activity is associated with increased system productivity (measured by adjusted admissions per FTE, r=.50 to r=.54), greater debt coverage (r=.54 to r=.58), and availability of capital (r=.54 to r=.59).

Further research is needed on the relationship between clinical integration and other dimensions of system performance such as patient satisfaction, clinical and functional health status outcomes, communitywide health status indicators, cost per enrolled life, efficiency of utilization, and related measures.

## DEVELOPING A SYSTEM INTEGRATION SCORECARD AND WAYS TO USE IT

Measuring these key areas of integration fosters systems thinking, helps identify the mechanisms and implementation activities that enhance overall system performance, and provides a "measuring stick" with which to gauge progress. There are a number of ways in which systems can use these measures to achieve these goals.

First, a systemwide committee or task force can be formed to discuss the measures proposed in this article (and others believed to be beneficial), oversee the collection of relevant data (perhaps on a selected subset of measures of greatest interest), and assess the results. The very process of determining which measures will be useful, and the gathering of data on those measures, is a learning process for both corporate and operating unit staff. The process encourages system and operating unit executives to explicitly consider systemwide relationships, particularly the ways in which relationships between operating units can reduce transaction costs[8,15] and/or create synergies.[16] In addition, the process helps system and operating unit executives assess their internal data resources and identify gaps in knowledge about systemwide activity. Ongoing discussion about these measures and the results within the committee may enhance current discussions about what integration means and how strategic plans may be implemented.

Second, we suggest that an integration scorecard be developed as a tool to track system progress (See Table 4 for a sample scorecard). The scorecard can be used to set concrete goals and assess progress toward those goals. The indicators and the baseline scores can be listed down the first two left columns (as shown). The scorecard then should set a target and a time frame (where we want to be in one year), specific activities that the system will pursue (action steps), and determine who is primarily responsible for progress in that area. Systems may also want to form subgroups or sub–task forces to work on focused areas of integration interest. This includes examining the relationship between integration indicators and improved productivity, financial viability, increased cross operating-unit referrals, increased number of covered lives, clinical outcomes, functional health status, and patient status.

In addition, we encourage systems to begin considering ways the integration scorecard can be used with key *external groups,* such as employers, payors, and consumer groups. While the integration scorecard is primarily designed for charting progress and identifying the mechanisms associated with improved performance, it may also be used to demonstrate to outside parties that the system is succeeding in its integration efforts. A key concern for purchasers and health policy analysts is the extent to which systems can overcome the barriers to integration and actually deliver on their promises. For example, data pertinent to purchasers may include provider mix (e.g., percent of physicians in multispecialty groups), in-system referral patterns (e.g., percent of physicians referring patients to two or more system facilities), administrative efficiency (e.g., number of physicians with administrative responsibilities at two or more system facilities, reduced billing costs), and quality of care indicators (outcomes measures used in selected areas). In this way, the integration scorecard becomes part of an overall performance profile or "balanced scorecard" for the system, similar to those developed

## TABLE 4

### INTEGRATION SCORECARD (EXAMPLES)

| Integration Category/Item | Where We Are Now | Where We Want To Be Next Year | What We Plan To Do— Action Plan | Who's Responsible |
|---|---|---|---|---|
| (FOR EXAMPLE) 1. Percent of physicians in groups | 35% | 50% | 1. Purchase two groups 2. Subsidize group practice formation efforts | Vice President for Clinical Affairs |
| 2. Percent of physicians in multispecialty groups | 15% | 30% | Appoint a task force to consider merging primary care and specialty groups | Vice President for Clinical Affairs and systemwide medical director |
| 3. Percent of operating units sharing common clinical protocols | 50% | 100% | Appoint cross-system task forces in those areas where protocols are already used in some units (e.g., cardiovascular) | Vice President for Clinical Affairs and Manager of CV surgery line |

by companies in other industries.[17,18] Further, a modified scorecard may be used by systems to initiate dialogue with key outside parties (e.g., purchasers, business coalitions, policy analysts) about aspects of system integration and performance of particular interest. This demonstrates both leadership and a willingness on the part of systems to be held accountable for the care of defined populations.

Finally, the task force should disseminate scorecard results throughout the system. A key aspect of this process is to ascertain the extent to which perceptions within the system do, or do not, match integration scores in various areas. Perceptions are important because people often act on them. If perceptions and measures of actual system activity seem incongruous, however, discussions should begin to discern reasons for this difference. Systems may be more or less integrated in these areas than they thought, basing decisions and carrying out actions on inaccurate information.

• • •

The measures developed and examined in this article and the suggestions for the ways systems may use them are a starting point for assessing key aspects of organized, vertically integrated, delivery systems. As further experience is gained with these and related measures, it should become possible to more readily identify those areas of greatest leverage for achieving more integrated delivery of care. Such indicators enable systems to track integration efforts and their effects through time. An important factor in a system's ability to achieve its ultimate goals is the identification of activities that enhance (or impede) performance *during the process*. To do this, a system must be able to track integration activity in various areas and make adjustments, "learning" from experience which activities do and do not produce desired results.

## REFERENCES

1. Ackerman, F.K. "The Movement Toward Vertically Integrated Regional Health Systems." *Health Care Management Review* 17, no. 3 (1992): 81–8.
2. Conrad, D.A., and Dowling, W.L. "Vertical Integration in Health Services: Theory and Managerial Implications." *Health Care Management Review* 15, no. 4 (1990): 9–22.
3. Brown, M., and McCool, B.P. "Vertical Integration: Exploration of a Popular Strategic Concept." *Health Care Management Review* 11, no. 4 (1986): 7–19.
4. Shortell, S.M. "The Evolution of Hospital Systems: Unfulfilled Promises and Self-Fulfilling Prophesies." *Medical Care Review* 45, no. 2 (1988): 177–214.
5. Shortell, S.M., et al. "Creating Organized Delivery Systems: The Barriers and Facilitators." *Hospital and Health Services Administration* 38, no. 4 (1993): 447–66.
6. Conrad, D.A., et al. "Vertical Structures and Control in Health Care Markets: A Conceptual Framework and Empirical Review." *Medical Care Review,* 45, no. 1 (1988): 49–100.
7. Fox, W.L. "Vertical Integration Strategies: More Promising than Diversification." *Health Care Management Review* 14, no. 3 (1989): 49–56.
8. Mick, S.S. "The Decision to Integrate Vertically in Health Care Organizations." *Hospital and Health Services Administration* 33, no. 3 (1988): 345–60.
9. Gillies, R.R., et al. "Conceptualizing and Measuring Integration: Findings from the Health Systems Integration Study." *Hospital and Health Services Administration* 38, no. 4 (1993): 467–89.
10. Nerenz, D.R., and Zajac, B.M. *Indicators of Performance for Vertically Integrated Health Systems.* Ray Woodham Visiting Fellowship Program Project Summary Report. The Hospital Research and Educational Trust and the Section for Health Care Systems of the American Hospital Association, AHA Catalog No. C-154725, 1991.
11. Ackoff, R.L. *On Purposeful Systems.* Chicago, Ill.: Aldine-Atherton, 1972.
12. Senge, P.M. *Fifth Discipline: The Art and Practice of the Learning Organization.* New York, N.Y.: Doubleday/Currency, 1990.
13. Bedian, A.G., and Zammuto, R.F. *Organizations: Theory and Design.* Chicago, Ill.: Dryden Press, 1991.
14. Hurley, R.E. "The Purchaser-Driven Reformation in Health Care: Alternative Approaches Leveling Our Cathedrals." *Frontiers of Health Services Management* 9, no. 4 (1993): 5–35.
15. Williams, O.E. *The Economic Institutions of Capitalism: Firms, Markets, Relational Contracting.* New York, N.Y.: Free Press. 1985.
16. Porter, M.E. *Competitive Advantage: Creating and Sustaining Superior Performance.* New York, N.Y.: Free Press, 1985.
17. Kaplan, R.S., and Norton, D.P. "The Balanced Scorecard-Measures That Drive Performance." *Harvard Business Review* (January–February 1992): 71–9.
18. Kaplan, R.S., and Norton, D.P. "Putting the Balance Scorecard to Work." *Harvard Business Review* (September–October 1993): 134–47.

# APPENDIX

SYSTEM NAME

TO BE COMPLETED BY SYSTEM PLANNERS AND RETURNED TO SITE VISITORS AT TIME OF VISIT

For each of the items below, please circle yes or no. Please add any comments to further explain your choice. This is to be returned directly to the site visitors during the upcoming visit. Thank you.

| | Item or Characteristic | Yes | No | Functional Area |
|---|---|---|---|---|
| 1. | Common statement of values and mission visibly posted in all operating units. | 1 | 2 | CULTURE |
| 2. | The systemwide strategic plan and annual goals are distributed to all units. | 1 | 2 | STRATEGIC PLANNING |
| 3. | There is an orientation program for all system employees emphasizing the system's values. | 1 | 2 | CULTURE |
| 4. | The same approaches, policies, and guidelines are used by all operating units in their supervisory training programs. | 1 | 2 | HUMAN RESOURCES |
| 5. | The same approaches, policies, and guidelines are used by all operating units in their management development programs. | 1 | 2 | HUMAN RESOURCES |
| 6. | The same approaches, policies, and guidelines are used by all operating units in evaluating management performance. | 1 | 2 | HUMAN RESOURCES |
| 7. | There exists systemwide financial targets in addition to unit level financial targets for compensating top managers. | 1 | 2 | FINANCIAL MGMT. |
| 8. | The same approaches, policies, and guidelines are used by all operating units for orienting new governing board members. | 1 | 2 | CULTURE |
| 9. | A profitability target exists for the system as a whole. | 1 | 2 | FINANCIAL MGMT. |
| 10. | Profitability targets exist for each operating entity. | 1 | 2 | FINANCIAL MGMT. |
| 11. | There exists systemwide cash management. | 1 | 2 | FINANCIAL MGMT. |
| 12. | There exists systemwide debt management. | 1 | 2 | FINANCIAL MGMT. |
| 13. | There exists systemwide capital budgeting and approval processes. | 1 | 2 | FINANCIAL MGMT. |
| 14. | Operating unit budgets are first developed within the context of systemwide guidelines. | 1 | 2 | FINANCIAL MGMT. |
| 15. | Operating budgets require system office or regional office approval. | 1 | 2 | FINANCIAL MGMT. |
| 16. | A single systemwide financial staff works with the operating units under the direction of the systemwide chief financial officer. | 1 | 2 | FINANCIAL MGMT. |
| 17. | The same approaches, policies, and guidelines are used by all operating units for determining incentive compensation. | 1 | 2 | HUMAN RESOURCES |
| 18. | The same approaches, policies, and guidelines are used by all operating units in conducting technology assessment. | 1 | 2 | STRATEGIC PLANNING |
| 19. | There is a single systemwide chart of accounts. | 1 | 2 | FINANCIAL MGMT. |
| 20. | Payroll, accounts payable, and reimbursement are consolidated in the system or regional office. | 1 | 2 | FINANCIAL MGMT. |
| 21A. | Systemwide strategic planning and marketing staff are assigned to the operating units. IF YES TO 21A: | 1 | 2 | STRATEGIC PLANNING |
| 21B. | These systemwide strategic planning and marketing staff report directly to the system office executives in these areas. | 1 | 2 | STRATEGIC PLANNING |
| 22. | There is extensive physician involvement in the development of the systemwide strategic plan. | 1 | 2 | STRATEGIC PLANNING |
| 23. | The systemwide strategic plan and financial plans are well coordinated and integrated among each other. | 1 | 2 | STRATEGIC PLANNING |
| 24. | A systemwide human resource policy manual exists that is used by all operating entities. | 1 | 2 | HUMAN RESOURCES |
| 25. | There exists a systemwide collective bargaining labor management committee. | 1 | 2 | HUMAN RESOURCES |

| Item or Characteristic | Yes | No | Functional Area |
|---|---|---|---|
| 26. There exists a systemwide full time equivalent reporting system. | 1 | 2 | HUMAN RESOURCES |
| 27. The same approaches, policies, and guidelines are used by all operating units for purposes of wage and salary administration. | 1 | 2 | HUMAN RESOURCES |
| 28. There exists systemwide employee recognition programs. | 1 | 2 | HUMAN RESOURCES |
| 29A. System office human resources staff are assigned to the operating units. | 1 | 2 | HUMAN RESOURCES |
| IF YES TO 29A: | | | |
| 29B. These system office human resources staff report directly to the system office VP for human resources. | 1 | 2 | HUMAN RESOURCES |
| 30. There is systemwide or regionwide computerized job posting. | 1 | 2 | HUMAN RESOURCES |
| 31. There exists a systemwide plan for identifying existing and future staffing needs throughout the system. | 1 | 2 | HUMAN RESOURCES |
| 32. There exists a single systemwide management information system. | 1 | 2 | INFORMATION SYSTEMS |
| 33A. There exists a systemwide materials management program. | 1 | 2 | SUPPORT SERVICES |
| IF YES TO 33A: | | | |
| 33B. This systemwide materials program is characterized by direct reporting to a single system office person. | 1 | 2 | SUPPORT SERVICES |
| 34. There exists systemwide group purchasing. | 1 | 2 | SUPPORT SERVICES |
| 35. There exists systemwide or regionwide market research analysis. | 1 | 2 | SUPPORT SERVICES |
| 36. There exists systemwide or regionwide managed care contracting. | 1 | 2 | OTHER |
| 37. There exists a systemwide or regionwide mechanism for identifying and sharing "best administrative practices" by each unit. | 1 | 2 | OTHER |
| 38. There exists a systemwide or regionwide plan for new product and service development. | 1 | 2 | OTHER |
| 39. There exists systemwide physician credentialing and assessment of privileges. | 1 | 2 | QA/QI |
| 40. The same approaches, policies, and guidelines are used by all operating units in developing quality assurance/improvement programs and policies. | 1 | 2 | QA/QI |
| 41. There exists systemwide Joint Commission survey coordination. | 1 | 2 | QA/QI |
| 42. The same approaches, policies, and guidelines are used by all operating units in doing case management. | 1 | 2 | QA/QI |
| 43. There exists a systemwide quality leadership educational program. | 1 | 2 | QA/QI |
| 44. There exists a single systemwide quality measurement, monitoring, and improvement system. | 1 | 2 | QA/QI |
| 45. There exists a systemwide common comparative severity measurement system. | 1 | 2 | QA/QI |
| 46. There exists a single combined business office that does all billing and collections, accounts receivable, and insurance management. | 1 | 2 | FINANCIAL MGMT. |
| 47. There exists a systemwide centralized laundry. | 1 | 2 | SUPPORT SERVICES |
| 48. There exists a systemwide centralized food service. | 1 | 2 | SUPPORT SERVICES |
| 49. There exists a single systemwide or regionwide internal audit and legal service function. | 1 | 2 | SUPPORT SERVICES |

# Developing interorganizational relationships in the health sector: A multicase study

James B. Thomas,
David J. Ketchen, Jr.,
Linda Klebe Trevino,
and
Reuben R. McDaniel, Jr.

*Because of the wide diversity among health care organizations, interorganizational relationships (IORs) among them are difficult to manage. This article describes three case studies that, taken together, suggest that IOR performance is related to IOR development processes. Specifically, IOR performance is related to the way managers process information to manage uncertainty and ambiguity.*

*Health Care Manage Rev*, 1992, 17(2), 7–19
© 1992 Aspen Publishers, Inc.

**In light of the** turbulent state of the health care industry, many hospitals are developing interorganizational relationships (IORs).[1] IORs are the enduring transactions, flows, and linkages that occur between two or more hospitals or other organizations.[2] Examples include federations, systems, joint ventures, and joint programs that have been developed to integrate and improve services while at the same time reducing costs.[3]

Hospital chief executive officers (CEOs) and boards of directors have established IORs to gain certain benefits. These include maintaining or gaining market share by being more competitive, increasing access to needed capital, and getting exposure to new ideas.[4] Despite the growing number of hospitals entering into IORs, these arrangements have not produced the expected benefits.[5] For example, a recent study of 959 hospitals found little evidence to suggest that hospitals that are part of multihospital systems enjoy the anticipated advantages relative to free-standing hospitals.[6]

It has been suggested that the failure of health care IORs to produce expected results may be due to a lack of (1) commitment among member organizations to a common culture and underlying mission, (2) planning regarding financial concerns, strategy, and human resources of the IOR, (3) integrated decision and input support systems, and (4) IOR-wide quality assurance and physician credentialing.[5] Jemison and Sitkin suggest that researchers should also examine the IOR development *process* for clues to creating predictive models of IOR performance.[7] This article presents the linkages between IOR development processes and subsequent IOR performance and suggests guidelines for managing them. These relationships are explored

*James B. Thomas, Ph.D., is Assistant Professor of management and a Faculty Associate with the Center for Health Policy Research at The Pennsylvania State University.*

*David J. Ketchen, Jr., is a doctoral candidate in the program in management and organization at The Pennsylvania State University.*

*Linda Klebe Trevino, Ph.D., is Assistant Professor of organizational behavior at The Pennsylvania State University.*

*Reuben R. McDaniel, Jr., Ed.D., is the Charles and Elizabeth Prothro Regents Chair in Health Care Management and is Professor of Management at The University of Texas at Austin. Dr. McDaniel is on the board of trustees at Seton Medical Center in Austin, Texas, and is a column editor for* Health Progress.

This research was supported by a grant from the Smeal College of Business Administration, The Pennsylvania State University.

through an investigation of three efforts to construct IORs in the health sector.

The fundamental assumption guiding this study is that during the development process, health care IOR participants must process complex information and divergent viewpoints from multiple sources (e.g., administration, physicians, boards of trustees). This divergence is pronounced because stakeholders are very different in terms of their backgrounds, power, emotions, and expectations of the IOR.[8] Information processing under these circumstances is difficult due to the limitations of human cognition[9] and the potential for disagreement among key participants.[10] Given this information-processing perspective, we assume that a crucial challenge facing managers guiding health care IOR development efforts is to develop information-processing mechanisms capable of coping with extremely high levels of uncertainty and ambiguity.

## UNCERTAINTY AND AMBIGUITY IN IOR DEVELOPMENT

All hospitals developing IORs encounter uncertainty. The three most common definitions of uncertainty are (1) an inability to assign probabilities to future events, (2) a lack of information about cause/effect relationships, and (3) an inability to accurately predict outcomes of a decision.[11] These definitions converge on the notion that under conditions of uncertainty, decision makers lack information.[12] Thus, the uncertainty surrounding IOR development is best dealt with by reducing the information gap between what is known and what needs to be known in order to make decisions. Indeed, normative guidelines for IOR development suggest that hospital managers direct attention to the collection, analysis, and communication of program, market, and financial data to determine the IOR's ability to enhance financial or service goals.

Many health care organizations involved in IOR development must also cope with ambiguity. Ambiguity means the existence of multiple and conflicting interpretations among decision makers and stakeholders.[13] Unlike uncertainty, ambiguity does not denote a lack of information. Rather, it suggests that those involved in decision making interpret existing information differently. For example, an acquisition may be viewed by the acquiring organization as an opportunity while the targeted organization may see the relationship as a threat. Therefore, the information processing associated with ambiguity reduction must be aimed at de-

veloping a shared understanding of the situation among IOR participants.[14]

In any industry, the management of ambiguity is likely to be important during IOR development efforts because IORs bring together multiple parties from different organizations with different interpretations of IOR goals. The importance of managing ambiguity is magnified in the health sector because the groups involved in health care IORs (e.g., payors, managers, providers, and clients) often have particularly divergent perspectives. If these perspectives are not reconciled, problems with IOR implementation may arise.[15] Therefore, managing ambiguity is a critical element for success in developing health care IORs.[16]

## MANAGING UNCERTAINTY AND AMBIGUITY THROUGH MEDIA CHOICE

An important aspect of managing the uncertainty and ambiguity surrounding IOR development is understanding the key role that the choice of communication media plays. These media can be differentiated along a continuum from rich to lean based upon their ability to effectively transit different types of information.[17]

The richest media, such as face-to-face encounters, are those that have a high capacity to resolve ambiguity by bringing together multiple and conflicting interpretations and frames of reference. These media transmit the verbal and nonverbal cues that convey shades of meaning and allow for rapid feedback and the exchange of ideas. Through these interactions, a common understanding among individuals can be created. Thus, rich media are best suited to reducing ambiguity.

Lean communication media, such as numeric and other written documents, are not effective for reducing ambiguity and reconciling different viewpoints. For example, a memo or newsletter cannot transmit shades of meaning, and simply conveying facts or data will oversimplify an ambiguous problem. Crucial interpretations may be overlooked. While lean media are limited in terms of the number of and types of cues transmitted and the immediacy of feedback, they are, however, highly efficient for reducing uncertainty through transmitting concrete facts and data.

Research has found that managers choose media based on the ambiguity or uncertainty of the situation,[18] suggesting that, in general, managers are sensitive to the need to match communication media to information-processing requirements. Because communication is a primary activity of managers, those who

---

*Managers who correctly match rich media to highly ambiguous messages and lean media to more routine messages have been found to be more effective performers.*

---

correctly match rich media to highly ambiguous messages and lean media to more routine messages have been found to be more effective performers.[17,18] Thus, sensitivity to this matching phenomenon appears to be an important component of managerial effectiveness.

Media choice is an important tool for health care managers building IORs. Because of the divergent backgrounds and desires of IOR participants (e.g., administrators, physicians, and technicians from different organizations), low levels of trust are likely to exist among them. Such lack of trust reduces the probability of IOR success. By using rich media in appropriate situations, managers can foster the high level of information exchange needed to overcome low levels of trust.[14,17] Lean media also play a role in IOR development. Managers can use lean media to quickly convey facts such as program usage, diagnosis related group (DRG) analysis, and financial and market information to IOR participants.[17,18]

This information-processing perspective—how communication media are matched to the information requirements of uncertainty and ambiguity during IOR development—was used as the organizing framework for our examination of the IOR development process and its link to performance.

## SELECTION OF IORs

The locations for this study were selected through consultation with a large, northeastern state's hospital association. Ongoing IOR development efforts were chosen to allow observation of at least part of the IOR development process and to avoid sole reliance on retrospective accounts.

Sites were selected based on the typology of health care IORs described by Longest.[3] Longest's typology is one of several offered in the literature that are relevant to health care. Other frequently cited typologies have been developed by Luke, Begun, and Pointer,[19] Oliver,[20] and Fottler et al.[21] In contrast, Fombrun has suggested that such typologies oversimplify the dynamic process of structuring that organizations undergo.[22] Despite this possible limitation, typologies remain a good tool for conceptualizing the systematic patterns of structure in IORs. Because we focus only on arrangements that are voluntary, Longest's typology, which differentiates between voluntary and involuntary IORs, is particularly well suited to our study.

In terms of Longest's typology, the three IORs examined here are all best described as *voluntary interorganizational relationship transactions*. This type of IOR involves voluntary actions by managers attempting to better manage their respective organizations' interdependencies. Voluntary IOR transactions can be further delineated into the specific strategies of co-opting, coalescing, quasi-firm, and ownership.

---

*Voluntary IOR transactions can be further delineated into the specific strategies of co-opting, coalescing, quasi-firm, and ownership.*

---

Co-opting involves the absorption of leadership elements from other organizations into a focal organization. The creation of a management contract is a simple example of co-opting. Placing representatives of interdependent organizations on the focal organization's board is another.

Coalescing is based upon two or more organizations partly combining their resources in order to pursue some objective. Activities such as joint ventures between hospitals and their medical staffs or groups of members of their medical staffs are examples of such relationships.

A quasi-firm is created when organizations develop enduring relationships such that some purpose of strategic importance to the participants can be better served. In such arrangements, the partner organizations remain independently owned, although they are heavily interdependent regarding the quasi-firm's activity. An example of a quasi-firm arrangement is an arrangement between an acute care general hospital, a skilled nursing facility, and an insurance carrier collaborating to provide a managed care product.

Ownership is the final category of voluntary interorganizational relationship transactions. The most obvious form of ownership involves voluntary mergers and acquisitions. An example of such a relationship is the creation of a new entity, called an umbrella organization (e.g., a regional health system), designed to span but not replace the health care organizations forming it.

The IORs examined in this study represent three of the above types. One example of each was found for coalescing, quasi-firm, and ownership (the fourth type, co-opting, is not discussed). Descriptions of all three sites are presented in Table 1.

## DATA COLLECTION

The study was done in four phases. The first phase involved an extensive interview process coupled with observations of various IOR development events including executive meetings and consultant presentations. The first phase also included the gathering of appropriate documents such as contracts, reports, and other analyses.

During this first phase, 23 interviews (n=7, 7, and 9 across the three sites) were conducted by two researchers with the top decision makers at each site (i.e., president, vice president of medical affairs, and chief financial officer) and other key stakeholders, such as prominent physicians. Reliability of data was promoted by having all organizations involved in each of the three IORs subjected to the same series of interview procedures and by gathering similar data for each organization. The interviews were audiotaped and transcribed to provide a basis for analysis.

The second phase was an analysis of the interview transcripts, observations, and documents from phase one. Nine doctoral students not involved in the data collection conducted a content analysis[23] of the ideas expressed by the presidents of the initiating institutions at all three IOR sites. Results of this analysis were discussed collectively with the authors. The authors performed a parallel analysis on all 23 transcripts.

In phase three, a survey questionnaire was developed to further examine certain key constructs that were identified from the content analyses in phase two. These constructs were operationalized by using existing theoretically based questionnaire items. They included political activity during the IOR development effort, the level of perceived ambiguity, and the IOR's structural capacity for information processing.[24]

In addition, IOR performance[25] was measured twice (18 months apart) at each site. All variables were measured with multi-item, seven-point Likert scales. For each variable scale, item scores were averaged to calculate a variable score. Cronbach alpha reliability measures for each scale were >.75. Questionnaire items are presented in the Appendix.

The questionnaire was pretested with 5 hospital executives and then mailed to all 23 interviewees; 17 responded. Responses at each site (n=6, 6, and 5 across the sites) were combined to represent the perceptions of the development process from each IOR.

## TABLE 1

### CHARACTERISTICS OF THE IORs

| | IOR | | |
|---|---|---|---|
| | **Alpha** | **Beta** | **Gamma** |
| Type of IOR: | Coalescing | Quasi-firm | Ownership |
| Size: | 515 beds | 431 beds | 573 beds |
| Location: | Urban | Urban | Suburban |
| Type: | General, non-profit teaching hospital | General, non-profit teaching hospital | General non-profit hospital |
| Linking Facility: | Physician groups—"medical mall" | Community Hospital | Memorial Hospital |
| Size: | 3289 outpatient procedures (1988) | 58 beds | 201 beds |
| Location: | Suburban | Suburban | Urban |
| Type: | Ambulatory-care facility/ out-patient surgery | General, non-profit hospital | General, non-profit hospital |

Phase four involved constructing a model of the IOR development process based on the interview analyses and the survey results. From the model, and earlier analyses, process guidelines for IOR development were devised.

## CASE DESCRIPTIONS

Following are descriptions of the three IOR development processes and results. The type of IOR represented in each case is noted in parentheses. All names are fictitious.

### Alpha IOR (coalescing)

In late 1983, Peter Cavanaugh, president of Alpha Hospital, became concerned with the increasing demand for outpatient surgery and other ambulatory care services. Cavanaugh proceeded to analyze market trends and Alpha's ability to keep pace. It became apparent that the hospital's in-house outpatient facility could not continue to process the increasing outpatient surgery load; however, Alpha and the various groups of physicians had different interpretations of the situation. Initially, these differences focused on whether the surgical overload constituted a threat to the hospital from potential competitors, an opportunity to meet community needs, a chance to create a competitive advantage, a medical education problem, or some combination.

Through a series of discussions, ideas were exchanged until a consensus was built around the perspective that the inadequate facility created a market opportunity that could be exploited by an outside provider if action were not taken. As Cavanaugh remarked, "This part of the [IOR development] process was not as much planning as it was a political sort of thing . . . . Different people had various views of what was going on and there were very strong political implications with various groups. It was a matter of getting these perspectives out so they could be integrated."

This agreed-upon interpretation led to the need for information about the market, potential locations, as well as surgical and administrative needs. Once these facts were gathered, differing views again developed over the types of facilities that should be considered. At the direction of Cavanaugh, key participants debated the different possibilities, including in-house expansion, a stand-alone surgical center, and multiple ambulatory care sites. A synthesis of perspectives developed into the idea of an off-site surgical center that would involve shared ownership among the hospital and interested physicians and physician groups. This was followed by a business plan designed to provide the information needed for board support.

By early 1986, the plan for the joint venture developed beyond anyone's expectations. A "medical mall" was envisioned that would include an outpatient surgery center, a pharmacy, physical therapy, laboratories, a nutrition center, and physicians' offices. In late 1986, Alpha's board approved the venture, mall space was sold to physician groups, and construction of the facility began. Recently opened, the medical mall is considered by all stakeholders to be a success.

### Beta IOR (quasi-firm)

In 1987, John Griner became president of Beta Health System (BHS), an organization representing a number of health care facilities including Beta Hospital, the system's flagship. For many years, Griner's predecessors at BHS had been seeking to develop a relationship with Community Hospital, a smaller, financially troubled hospital located in a potentially profitable market somewhat geographically removed from BHS. While both BHS's and Community's medical staffs had been interested in developing linkages to enhance health care delivery for some time, the board of directors at Community discouraged the idea until mid-1987 when their financial difficulties became overwhelming. At that time, a trial relationship was established where Community retained its autonomy while BHS played an advisory role and provided some financial assistance.

By early 1989, BHS had provided well over $1 million to keep Community operational. In order for Community to become profitable, Griner and his staff believed that the health care delivery program had to center around ambulatory care. This would replace the focus of Community as a general hospital; a change that the Community board, various physicians, and others were not ready to accept.

Griner focused communication on ambiguity reduction throughout most of the IOR development process. Rich media such as group and two-way discussions were emphasized in an attempt to bring divergent perspectives together concerning numerous IOR issues (e.g., credentialing and contractual ties). Facts and figures were collected occasionally during the IOR development process but were rarely used. As Griner remarked, "We had analyses done but I asked the people involved [in the IOR development] to forget all that . . . I wanted debate and group meetings for team building . . . . Facts and figures were used later."

Griner engaged in proactive political activity in an effort to exchange ideas with and to influence other key stakeholders. As Griner suggested, "I define 60 percent of my job [in this IOR development process] as politics. There are a lot of people who can put these joint programs together, but keeping them glued together is the role of politics." Eventually, differences in how the critical issues surrounding the IOR were interpreted were reconciled, facilitated by Griner's efforts. Today, the mission of Community Hospital has been redefined to focus on outpatient surgery, and the facility has earned a profit for the first time in many years.

### Gamma IOR (ownership)

George Jameson, president of Gamma Hospital for 35 years, had dreamed of forming a comprehensive health care federation in Gamma County. All of the financial and market analysis that he had done indicated that the federation was a rational move for all concerned. After years of work, Gamma Health System (GHS) was formed in early 1987 with Jameson as president.

Having convinced other health care delivery institutions to be involved in the federation, Jameson pursued an affiliation with Memorial Hospital, a smaller, financially troubled institution. In late 1987, a one-year trial agreement was entered into between Gamma Hospital and Memorial Hospital while issues concerning funding, ownership, and programs remained to be resolved. Although key actors from Gamma and Memorial held widely divergent viewpoints of the situation, Jameson used fact-laden memos to present his case. Jameson steadfastly refused to exchange ideas and interpretations with other key players. As he remarked, "The facts should speak for themselves . . . . However, there were many people who were not influenced by my fact sheets."

In 1988, as the hospitals moved toward the end of the trial period, factions (e.g., physicians, administrators, and boards of directors) with different perspectives on issues facing the IOR (e.g., physician certification, funding, and mission) balked at entering into a permanent relationship. In an attempt to reconcile the differences, Jameson conducted a last ditch effort by holding group meetings with key actors. During these encounters, however, Jameson presented the financial and market data analysis that supported his positions while ignoring others' ideas. Further, as Jameson re-

marked, "In between these meetings I didn't solicit support. If you come to meetings, you will get everything you need to know—no politicking is necessary."

As perceptual gaps widened, he began to pressure the various factions to rapidly establish a permanent affiliation between Gamma and Memorial. Despite Jameson's efforts to force closure, the hospitals' boards of directors voted to disband the relationship in late 1988. Shortly thereafter, Jameson took an early retirement.

## RESEARCH FINDINGS AND DISCUSSION

### Information-processing requirements—Uncertainty and ambiguity

Our analysis of the interview and survey data suggests that both uncertainty and ambiguity reduction were important information-processing needs in all three IORs. First, survey respondents at all three research sites viewed ambiguity as relatively high (>4.6 on a 7-point scale). In addition, interviewees at all three sites discussed the multiple interpretations and divergent viewpoints that characterized the information-processing needs of the developing IORs: "Different people had various views of what was going on" (Alpha IOR); "People over there have a very different view of the world than people over here" (Beta IOR); and "The ambiguity of the thing is that our board saw it from one perspective, theirs saw it from another" (Gamma IOR).

Against this backdrop of ambiguity, uncertainty also arose, requiring the collection and dissemination of facts and figures to support particular interpretations and decisions. Consistent with the literature, the IORs in this study were all prompted by desires to reduce uncertainty about resource flows and exchanges and to improve efficiency.[20] Thus, we observed similarity across the research sites in terms of their information-processing needs. What appears to have differed, however, was how these needs were managed.

### Managing information processing and IOR performance

Table 2 presents the performance measures from each site obtained from the surveys conducted in phase two of the research project. The following observations on the linkage between the management of information processing and IOR performance are offered. They relate to the initiating organization and its CEO's ability to manage information processing by (1) matching media to the changing information-processing needs of the de-

## TABLE 2

SURVEY RESULTS*

| | IOR | | |
|---|---|---|---|
| | Alpha | Beta | Gamma |
| Performance Measures (1988/1990) | | | |
| a. Meeting service needs of community | 5.3/6.0 | 2.5/5.5 | 2.1/na[†] |
| b. Extent to which reputation for quality enhanced | 5.3/5.5 | 2.0/4.5 | 2.5/na |
| c. Financial performance | 4.9/5.2 | 2.9/4.0 | 1.3/na |
| d. Meeting physician needs | 4.2/4.2 | 2.8/6.0 | 2.0/na |
| e. Overall (all measures combined) | 4.9/5.2 | 2.6/5.0 | 1.9/na |
| Variables | | | |
| a. Level of perceived ambiguity | 4.6 | 5.0 | 5.2 |
| b. Structural capacity for information processing | 5.2 | 4.8 | 4.1 |
| c. Amount of political activity | 3.9 | 3.7 | 4.3 |

*Measures represent mean on a 7-point scale ranging from 0 to 6.
[†] Gamma was disbanded in late 1988.

veloping IOR, (2) managing process momentum, (3) creating an information-processing structure with the capacity to handle ambiguity, and (4) using political activity positively to manage ambiguity.

### Alpha IOR

Alpha IOR was clearly the most successful of the three IORs. We attribute this success, at least in part, to Peter Cavanaugh's ability to appropriately handle information-processing needs. First, Alpha had an information-processing structure that was capable of handling ambiguity. In our survey, we measured information-processing capacity along three dimensions: (1) the ability of key managers and stakehold-

*High participation, high interaction, and low formality indicated a high capacity for processing information needed to reduce ambiguity.*

ers to *participate* in the IOR development process, (2) the managers' *interaction* during the process, and (3) the use of *formal* rule-oriented processes. High participation, high interaction, and low formality indicated a high capacity for processing information needed to reduce ambiguity. As Table 2 demon-

strates, Alpha was rated highest in terms of capacity for ambiguity reduction.

At Alpha, Cavanaugh focused on uncertainty and ambiguity in a cyclical reduction process. Originally faced with uncertainty about the market and Alpha Hospital's ability to keep pace, relevant facts were gathered. When these facts were presented to stakeholders, differences in interpretation (ambiguity) arose. Groups were formed to work out these differences. Once they were resolved, it became apparent that a new set of facts was needed to support the developing interpretation. Individuals were dispatched to collect the needed data. This sequential processing of uncertainty and ambiguity, matched to appropriate media, continued over a long period of time as the IOR was successfully implemented. As a result, divergent interpretations were effectively brought together and supported by relevant facts when needed.

Cavanaugh did not seem to have a strong preference for a particular communication medium. He used committees as he felt they were needed. "We used these [committee meetings] to discuss what the issues were and the various solutions." Cavanaugh did not rush these groups to make premature decisions. He explained, "I think there were enough ambiguities that I thought we really needed the time to sort it out." Thus, groups were given the time they needed to discuss their perspectives and arrive at a common interpretation.

In addition, Cavanaugh was very aware of the highly political nature of the IOR effort. He approached politics as a natural part of the ambiguity reduction effort. "Politics is a big part of everything we do. There were very strong political implications with the medical staff and with the surgeons. That's why we got them involved [in committees]." Cavanaugh used committee membership strategically and politically. Individuals whose views and perspectives were key to the ultimate success of the IOR effort were placed in important committee roles so that their views would become part of the ultimate plan. Nevertheless, despite a great deal of emphasis on ambiguity reduction, Cavanaugh also valued the role of facts, data, and documentation when appropriate: "We developed a business plan to include financial aspects, feasibility, and resources required."

### Beta IOR

The performance of Beta IOR was low on all dimensions when performance was first measured near the beginning of the IOR implementation. Overall, the performance rating was 2.6 on a 7-point scale. During the early stages of the IOR development process, Griner emphasized ambiguity reduction through the use of rich communication media (i.e., group meetings and one-on-one, face-to-face interactions) almost exclusively. These communication media choices were consistent with his strongly held belief that meetings and discussions among stakeholders were key to strategic decision-making success.

Like Cavanaugh, Griner believed that politics was an important factor. But, for him, it seemed to be the most important factor. "It all boils down to politics. I define 60 percent of my job as . . . politics." In terms of media use, Griner rarely used lean media and paid little attention to the information transmitted through these media. "In our business, the human element craps all over the facts . . . . One has to work hard to make sure that the relationships are in place. . . . We had analysis done . . . but I asked people to forget all that. [Written media] are only important as a matter of creating a record . . . I wanted a lot of debate to go on to bring people together." In addition, Griner deliberately slowed the momentum of the IOR development process because of his belief that more time was needed to reach consensus.

After 18 months had elapsed, perceptions of performance had greatly improved, increasing from 2.6 to 5.0. While ambiguity reduction was the focus of information processing during most of the IOR develop-

ment process, after initial performance proved to be lower than expected, Griner shifted his information-processing focus to incorporate sharing figures and data conveyed through staff and consultant reports. "I brought a consultant in at the end to present the facts and figures." A heavy focus on ambiguity reduction may have been appropriate given the highly ambiguous nature of this particular IOR development effort. Nevertheless, a focus on ambiguity reduction to the total exclusion of uncertainty reduction could have had disastrous consequences. These may have been averted, in part, because of Griner's ability to alter his information-processing style when performance figures demonstrated the need to do so.

### Gamma IOR

Gamma IOR demonstrated poor performance in the short run (all dimensions < 2.6 on a 7-point scale) and disastrous performance in the long run (i.e., the relationship was disbanded). Despite the high ambiguity surrounding the IOR, information processing focused almost exclusively on uncertainty reduction through the use of lean media (i.e., fact sheets, memos, and reports) to the exclusion of ambiguity reduction. This focus was a very direct reflection of the top manager's introspective and authoritarian management style. "Introspection, that's my style. I figure things out. Then I communicate it. The facts speak for themselves."

In our interviews, Jameson made very clear his strong belief that facts and figures should have the power to influence people and build commitment to the IOR. "We used newsletters to inform . . . strategic plans. . . . We educated at every board meeting . . . . About a week before we signed the affiliation agreement, we did a fact sheet that was sent to the medical staff . . . . We tried to get commitment through all kinds of written communication." In addition, Jameson was disdainful of any activity that smacked of politicking. "In between meetings, I didn't solicit support. If you come to the meetings, you will know everything—no politicking."

Jameson never successfully reduced the high level of ambiguity involved in the IOR development effort. He dealt with ambiguity as if it were uncertainty, responding to divergent perspectives predominantly with newsletters and fact sheets. This information-processing approach is consistent with Gamma's low rating on information-processing structure (see Table 2). The nearly exclusive focus on lean media contributed to the increasing divergence of perspectives and interpretations. Stakeholder frustration is evident in this comment from a physician, "The skeleton was presented to us [through these fact sheets] but nobody showed us the meat or what the faces looked like." Another comment from the president of Memorial Hospital suggests that fact sheets were not going to be enough to gain commitment: "But even with the fact sheets, the politics of the situation was that no one wanted to believe those facts."

As the divergence increased, Jameson became aware that his approach was not working. "There were many people who were not influenced by my fact sheets." His concern led him to escalate the momentum by pressing for a permanent affiliation. As part of this effort, he made an ill-fated attempt to alter his preferred communication style by planning a group retreat that would bring together important stakeholders to discuss the IOR effort. This belated attempt at ambiguity reduction was ineffective, however, because Jameson was unable to take advantage of the potential for richness in a group meeting. Rather than being a forum to discuss and bring together different views, the president used the meeting as an opportunity once again to transmit his own vision. "I *presented* [emphasis added] my views . . . managers discussed them after the meeting." Communication was one-way rather than interactive. The meeting became a free-for-all, with discussions deteriorating into arguments and complaints. Thus, given the highly ambiguous nature of the IOR development effort, focusing exclusively on uncertainty reduction and lean media may have had disastrous consequences.

## GUIDELINES

Our observations and analysis of the three cases suggest seven specific guidelines for managers of health care organizations faced with the difficult task of developing interorganizational relationships:

*Guideline one: During the IOR development process, the levels of uncertainty and ambiguity need to be diagnosed continuously.* The results of this study suggest that the health care manager who is attempting to shepherd organizations through an IOR development process must be keenly aware of uncertainty and ambiguity levels and how they change over time. The manager should expect to be faced with high uncertainty and high ambiguity. It is possible that both will be simultaneously high; however, it is more likely that uncertainty and ambiguity will cycle as they did at Alpha IOR. Data and facts will give rise to multiple interpretations that must be resolved. These interpretations will then demand more facts that will lead to the need for more interpretations, and so on.

*Guideline two: Health care managers should match their choice of communication media to the information-processing requirements of the situation.* As observed in this study, choice of communication media for information processing has important implications for the success of IOR development efforts. At Gamma Health System, George Jameson used lean media, such as memos and fact sheets, to deal with an IOR development process that was high in ambiguity. Ambiguity was not reduced. Rather than coming together, interpretations diverged even further, followed by a lack of commitment to the affiliation of Gamma and Memorial hospitals by key stakeholders and a collapse of the federation. Also, John Griner's almost exclusive use of rich media, even when uncertainty was high, was accompanied by lower than expected initial performance at Beta Health System.

In contrast, Alpha's Peter Cavanaugh used media that matched the information-processing needs of the circumstances. When faced with uncertainty, Cavanaugh employed lean media. When dealing with ambiguity, Cavanaugh relied on rich media. As noted above, Cavanaugh's IOR outperformed those of Jameson and Griner.

*Guideline three: In order to conduct needed information processing, health care managers must use a medium correctly.* It is not sufficient to correctly choose a medium to fit the situation. One must also use it correctly in order to have productive information processing. For example, just prior to the collapse of GHS, Jameson attempted to use a potentially rich medium, group meetings, to solve some communication problems surrounding the development of the IOR. Jameson used these meetings as forums to present his views, however, rather than using them to conduct an exchange of perspectives. He did not take advantage of the interactivity available in group meetings. As a result, ambiguity was not reduced despite the choice by Jameson of a potentially rich medium.

*Guideline four: Health care managers involved in IOR development must effectively manage momentum to prevent premature closure of important issues.* Factors such as secrecy, overconfidence, and resistance tend to escalate momentum. This can lead to premature closure of key IOR decisions, create a narrow focus on completing the process at all costs, and draw attention away from crucial integration issues.[7]

The present study reveals the importance of managing momentum. The IOR development process at Gamma, the least successful IOR, can be characterized as an effort to speed momentum and force closure. In this sense, the process of IOR development took on a life of its own, fueled by the president's fear that delay would destroy the IOR's chance to become a permanent union. As one of the IOR participants observed, "I think we could have succeeded had we done it in a more protracted fashion . . . . Both medical staffs could have been brought along but it had to be slow . . . [Jameson] just moved too fast."

In contrast, at both Alpha and Beta, process momentum was more restrained. These managers intentionally sought delays to allow time for ambiguities to be resolved. As Griner remarked, "I let things perk along for a sufficient amount of time to reduce the ambiguity and to get consensus . . . . You have to let the ball stay up in the air for a while." Providing time for the resolution of ambiguity enabled these managers to slowly, and successfully, undertake IOR development efforts.

*Guideline five: To facilitate successful IOR development, health care managers must develop information-processing structures with high capacities for ambiguity reduction.* Given the high levels of ambiguity present in all three IOR development processes, a high capacity to process information seems important. Recall that the highest performer, Alpha, also had the highest capacity to process information (5.2 on a 7-point scale).

The implication for managers is that managing IOR development includes paying attention to the design of information-processing structure. Effective reduction of ambiguity may be difficult if not impossible given a structure that is high in formalization (rules and regulations) and low in participation and interaction. For ambiguity to be effectively reduced, managers and stakeholders must feel free to participate and interact in an environment that is open and accepting of their views. Normative decision-making techniques such as decision analysis can help create such an environment.[26]

*Guideline six: Political activity can help IOR development to the extent that it is used as a way to resolve ambiguity.* According to survey respondents, political activity was relatively high at all three sites. This political activity reflects the highly political nature of IOR development efforts in general. At both Alpha and Beta, the top managers viewed the political arena as a forum to exchange perspectives and influence developing interpretations of IOR issues. Cavanaugh made strategic appointments to committees so that key stakeholders could influence others and be influenced. Griner engaged in a great deal of political behavior himself, meeting one-on-one with many stakeholders to exchange perspectives and influence developing interpretations of the IOR. Thus, the political arena was used as an opportunity for ambiguity reduction by these managers. It enabled them to build consensus and commitment to the developing IORs.

In contrast, Jameson looked on politics with disdain. His resistance to acknowledging the importance of political activity and his total unwillingness to participate in the political process, however, left him out of touch with the developing conflict and dissensus. Political activity actually increased as a result as groups continued in vain to try to influence developments in the direction of their own interests.

The message for health care managers is that political activity does not have to be viewed as negative. Rather, political activity can be viewed as a natural and manageable part of ambiguity reduction in the development of an IOR. The effective manager acknowledges the importance of political activity and creates opportunities for key decision makers and stakeholders to influence the decision-making process.

*Guideline seven: Health care managers must be prepared to alter their preferred communication style.* The managers at these three sites all had preferred communication styles that they had developed over a period of many years. This was most problematic for Jameson whose preferred style was introspective, authoritarian, fact-based, and lean media-oriented. This communication style had been quite successful in his many years as a hospital administrator. Nevertheless, it was much less effective in the more dynamic and ambiguous IOR development setting.

Ideally, managers should diagnose the information-processing needs of the IOR development effort and adapt their communication style as needed. However, if a manager finds it impossible to adjust, as Jameson did, it may be possible to delegate those communication tasks that are inconsistent with the manager's style, as Griner did when he relied on consultants to bring facts and data to the development process.

•    •    •

Those who study IORs in the health sector have been concerned primarily with the motivations or conditions for constructing IORs. Thus, IOR performance has been linked mainly with design aspects of IORs. The study presented here suggests that processes used in the development of health care IORs have a substantial impact on subsequent IOR performance. We have sought to enhance the understanding of the process/performance relationship by conceptualizing the development process as an information-processing ef-

## FIGURE 1

### THE THREE INTERORGANIZATIONAL RELATIONSHIPS BY TYPE AND PERFORMANCE

| Performance \ Type of IOR | Coalescing | Quasifirm | Ownership |
|---|---|---|---|
| Hi | Alpha | | |
| Med | | Beta | |
| Low | | | Gamma |

fort where the success or failure of attempts to manage uncertainty and ambiguity have important ramifications for IOR outcomes.

The guidelines presented here suggest that health care managers can take certain actions to increase the chances of conducting successful IOR development efforts. By diagnosing uncertainty and ambiguity levels, matching communication media to information-processing needs, effectively managing IOR development momentum, constructing high capacity information-processing structures, and using politics to reduce ambiguity, managers can increase their chances of realizing the expected benefits of IORs.

The case study method used here is gaining respectability as a technique of inquiry, particularly for theory building.[27] Case studies can help researchers to identify important concepts, to establish theoretical reasons for the relationships between them, and to suggest under what conditions these relationships might or might not be found.[28] Accordingly, our study has used three cases to uncover some key aspects of the process of building health care IORs and the links between them. The generalizability of our study, however, is limited in that only one example of each of three types of IORs (coalescing, quasi-firm, and ownership) was examined and only one example of high performing, medium performing, and low performing IORs was examined.

Because each type of IOR has been shown to be high performing in some situations, we did not believe that the level of performance was a function of type of IOR,

but of the way that the IOR was managed.[7] Nevertheless, future studies should be extended to cases in all nine of the cells shown in Figure 1. The study reported here isolates variables that help to explain performance characteristics of complex organizational relationships. Future authors may want to consider using a different research design in order to test the variables and relationship developed in our study.

## REFERENCES

1. Goldsmith, J. "A Radical Prescription for Hospitals." *Harvard Business Review* 67 (1989): 104–11.
2. Provan, K.G. "Interorganizational Cooperation and Decision Making Autonomy in a Consortium Multihospital System." *Academy of Management Review* 9, no. 3 (1984): 494–504.
3. Longest, B.B. "Interorganizational Linkages in the Health Sector." *Health Care Management Review* 15, no. 1 (1990): 17–28.
4. D'Aunno, T.A., and Zuckerman, H.S. "The Emergence of Hospital Federations: An Integration of Perspectives from Organizational Theory." *Medical Care Review* 44 (1987): 323–43.
5. Shortell, S.M. "The Evolution of Hospital Systems: Unfulfilled Promises and Self-fulfilling Prophesies." *Medical Care Review* 45, no. 2 (1988): 177–214.
6. Shortell, S.M., et al. *The Strategy, Structure and Performance of Multi-Hospital Systems.* Final Report to the National Center for Health Services Research and Health Care Technology Assessment, Rockville, Md.: National Center for Health Services Research, 1988.
7. Jemison, D.B., and Sitkin, S.B. "Corporate Acquisitions: A Process Perspective." *Academy of Management Review* 11 (1986): 145–63.
8. Alderfer, C.P. "An Intergroup Perspective on Group Dynamics." In *Handbook of Organizational Behavior*, edited by J.W. Lorsch. Englewood Cliffs, N.J.: Prentice Hall, 1987.
9. March, J.G., and Simon, J.P. *Organizations.* New York, N.Y.: Wiley, 1958.
10. Ashmos, D.P., and McDaniel, R.R. "Differences in Perception of Strategic Decision Making Processes: The Case of Physicians and Administrators." *The Journal of Applied Behavioral Science* 26 (1990): 201–218.
11. Milliken, F.J. "Three Types of Perceived Uncertainty About the Environment: State, Effect and Response Uncertainty." *Academy of Management Review* 12 (1987): 133–43.
12. Galbraith, J.R. *Designing Complex Organizations.* Reading, Mass.: Addison-Wesley, 1973.
13. Daft, R.L., and Weick, K.E. "Toward a Model of Organizations as Interpretive Systems." *Academy of Management Review* 9 (1984): 284–95.

14. Weick, K.E. *The Social Psychology of Organizing*. Reading, Mass.: Addison-Wesley, 1979.

15. Lord, C.G., Ross, L., and Lepper, M.R. "Biased Assimilation and Attitude Polarization: The Effects of Prior Theories on Subsequently Considered Evidence." *Journal of Personality and Social Psychology* 27 (1979): 2098–2109.

16. Lewin, A.Y., and Minton, J.W. "Organizational Effectiveness: Another Look and an Agenda for Research." *Management Science* 32 (1986): 514–538.

17. Daft, R.L., and Lengel, R.H. "Organizational Information Requirements, Media Richness, and Structural Design." *Management Science* 32 (1986): 554–71.

18. Daft, R.L., Lengel, R.H., and Trevino, L.K. "Message Equivocality, Media Selection, and Manager Performance: Implications for Information Systems." *MIS Quarterly* 11 (1987): 355–66.

19. Luke, R.D., Begun, J.W., and Pointer, D.D. "Quasi Firms: Strategic Interorganizational Forms in the Health Care Industry." *Academy of Management Review* 14, no. 1 (1989): 9–19.

20. Oliver, C. "Determinants of Interorganizational Relationships: Integration and Future Directions." *Academy of Management Review* 15, no. 2 (1990): 241–65.

21. Fottler, M.D., et al. "Multi-Institutional Arrangements in Health Care: Review, Analysis, and a Proposal for Future Research." *Academy of Management Review* 7, no. 1 (1982): 67–79.

22. Fombrun, C.J. "Structural Dynamics Within and Between Organizations." *Administrative Science Quarterly* 31 (1986): 403–21.

23. Spradley, J.P. *The Ethnographic Interview*. New York, N.Y.: Holt, Rinehart and Winston, 1979.

24. Thomas, J.B., and McDaniel, R.R. "Interpreting Strategic Issues: Effects of Strategy and the Information-Processing Structure of Top Management Teams." *Academy of Management Journal* 33, no. 2 (1990): 286–306.

25. Fottler, M.D. "Health Care Organizational Performance: Present and Future Performance." *Journal of Management* 13 (1987): 367–91.

26. Ketchen, D.J., and Thomas, J.B. "Breaking Down Complex Problems: The Use of Decision Analysis." *Health Progress* 71, no. 7 (1990): 64–67.

27. Eisenhardt, K.M. "Building Theories from Case Study Research." *Academy of Management Review* 14, no. 4 (1989): 532–50.

28. Snow, C.C., and Thomas, J.B. "Field Research Methods in Strategic Management: Contributions to Theory Building and Testing." *Journal of Management Studies*, forthcoming.

# APPENDIX

## VARIABLE MEASURES

*Performance*

To what extent have each of the following performance objectives of the relationship been met?
1. Long-term profitability
2. Net profit over the coming year
3. Growth
4. Prestige of the IOR participants
5. Innovation of medical care and delivery
6. Service to the community
7. Meeting the needs of the physicians
8. Increasing the range of services offered

*Perceived Ambiguity*

To what extent . . .
1. . . . were issues associated with the relationship open to subjectivity?
2. . . . was this an ambiguous situation?
3. . . . was the interpretation of the nature of the relationship unclear?
4. . . . were all the relevant variables known?
5. . . . was this an objective, well defined situation?
6. . . . was there confusion about the nature of the relationship?
7. . . . were there multiple interpretations among key players?

*Structural Capacity for Information Processing*

During the development process, to what extent . . .
1. . . . did you feel you had the opportunity to express your ideas about the relationship?
2. . . . did you feel that your views were included in the decision process?
3. . . . did you feel that others' ideas were imposed on you?
4. . . . were written rules and procedures followed?
5. . . . did individuals interact with each other on an informal basis?
6. . . . did committees, such as ad hoc task groups, form to deal with strategic issues?
7. . . . did one or two people dominate the handling of the development process?
8. . . . was there a free and open exchange of ideas?

To what extent can the development process be characterized as . . .
9. . . . formal and rule-oriented?
10. . . . participative?
11. . . . interactive?

*Amount of Political Activity*

To what extent . . .
1. . . . did coalitions form and change among decision actors over the relationship?
2. . . . was strategic decision making during the development process characterized by the "push and pull" of different interests?
3. . . . was conflict an accepted action during the process?
4. . . . was information used to influence the decision surrounding the issues associated with the relationship?
5. . . . was there a systematic search for information during the strategic decision making process?
6. . . . can the development process be characterized as an exercise in bargaining, negotiation, and compromise?

# Losing sight of the shore: How a future integrated American health care organization might look

Kenneth C. Cummings
and
Richard M. Abell

*American health care, both nationally and locally, has entered a time of uncertainty, yet with the certainty of change. In this article, the authors take a fresh look at patient/ community needs and propose a new level of integration of administration/ management, clinical services, education, and public health in the health care organization of the future.*

**We are living** in an era of profound global and national change. Simultaneously, we are forced to confront seemingly overwhelming issues of overpopulation and starvation, ethnic hatred and war, economic development and pollution, and on and on. In America, this is a time of considerable national self-doubt, a time of crisis in leadership with governmental, economic, educational, "competitiveness," and health care dimensions. It should be no great surprise that these are closely interrelated.

Regarding American health care, little prescience is required to conclude that the next decade will bring fundamental, painful, and possibly startling change. Over these last few years, much has been spoken and written concerning the deficiencies of our system of health care delivery, and a number of plans have been proposed to correct them. We believe it likely that a new health care system will emerge that retains current pluralistic and entrepreneurial elements.

In *Health Care Management Review* 18:1, Wolford, Brown, and McCool propose a health care delivery model that relates providers and insurers in vertically integrated, community-focused and chartered competitive entities. This approach retains strengths of our current delivery system but forces vertical integration and accountability to the community. These elements of integration and accountability will be critical to the success of whatever plan is adopted.

It is our presumption that, whatever the eventual system design, integration will be a key element. How can and should health care services be integrated? As health care professionals, we are accustomed to thinking somewhat narrowly regarding the continuum of services delivered. The doctor sees a patient with hip pain in his office; a hip joint replacement is eventually accomplished; a consultation from a rehabilitation medicine specialist is requested, followed by physical therapy and a patient questionnaire from the hospital. Across the country, many of our health care institutions have ongoing attempts to design continua of care but, because of economic, legal, structural, and competitive realities, significant integration of services in most instances has not been accomplished.

As we set about designing our new health care system, the authors have taken a few moments to dream.

***Kenneth C. Cummings**, M.D., is Vice President for Medical Affairs, Saint Joseph Health Center, Kansas City, Missouri.*

***Richard M. Abell**, M.A., M.H.A., is President and CEO of Saint Joseph Health Center, Kansas City, Missouri.*

*Health Care Manage Rev*, 1993, 18(2), 39–50
© 1993 Aspen Publishers, Inc.

Just as we must begin to think in new paradigms of organization, financing, and accountability, we must also revisit our communities' health needs and design services to meet these needs with integration, continuity, and effective resource utilization in mind. We have envisioned the integration of an idealized local health care system's array of services, which form a continuum of care that begins before birth and ends after death. The following is, by no means, a complete listing of services to be integrated but is intended to stimulate further thought and discussion.

## EDUCATIONAL OFFERINGS TO THE COMMUNITY

Though, by necessity, our new health care system will focus primarily on the provision of clinical services, in our view, community education and focused public health programs will be critical determinants for long-term community health and, thus, a successful system of health care provision. It has been well established that much human infirmity is preventable or, at least, controllable. The American lifestyle, so sought after from a social point of view, leaves much to be desired from a health care perspective. Our health care system of the future must place more accountability upon the members of the community as well as upon the providers of health care. But to do this will require community motivation, based not only upon financial implications of wise use of resources, but also upon a sound knowledge base regarding good health in all its dimensions.

Many of the following health educational programs are already extant across our country. The problem is that, for a multiplicity of reasons, they are rarely, if ever, locally arranged in a continuum and deeply and functionally integrated with clinical services. In the new system, not only would educational offerings and clinical continua of care be integrated, but these programs would be integrated into the local public health program and education system as well. Several of these are discussed in more detail below. (See the box entitled "Educational Programs" for a list of programs that might be included.)

### The art of living

The object of this program series is to bring about a more fulfilling, peaceful, happy and healthy life. Obviously, the issues that could be dealt with are numerous but, for the sake of discussion, we would include common elements of daily life such as work, home, mari-

---

### Educational Programs

Basic human physiology and pathophysiology
The art of living
Health maintenance
Stress management
Smoking cessation
Psychological and social adjustment
Family dynamics
Preparation for parenthood (prior to conception)
Single mothers-to-be
Addicted mothers-to-be
Prenatal course including preparing home and family for the baby and new marital dynamics, with a subprogram for couples pregnant for the first time
Postnatal course featuring early pediatric and family dynamic issues
Childhood programs—physical, psychological, developmental, and social
Programs for special children, including handicapped and gifted
Program to begin teaching children about health maintenance
Disease-specific programs both for the patient and family (e.g., arthritis, heart disease, diabetes, etc.)
Specific abbreviated programs for certain postoperative patients—radical prostatectomy, post-coronary surgery, postmastectomy, colostomy, etc.
Death and dying
Grieving
Financial programs dealing with specific financial matters related to health care or whatever the environment is at the time
Programs on various legal aspects of family, childhood, or community life
Nutrition
Spiritual development
Retirement—financial, legal, social, health, and other issues
Self-directed learning center

---

tal, or parenting stress; finances; and career alternatives. The program would delve into why happy people are happy. The series will probably be the entry point for other, more specific, offerings. For example, if a subscriber had interest in pursuing a program concerning career alternatives, this program would provide skills and abilities assessment and advice regarding preparing for a job change, constructing a resume, networking, and interviewing skills. Each of these programs should, in the long run, lead toward improved happiness and health.

### Preparation for parenthood (prior to conception)

It is rhetorical to say the ideal time to begin planning for parenthood is prior to parenthood, but, unfortunately, this appears to happen much too infrequently in our society. This series of discussions would focus on a number of important considerations, such as the health of the parents prior to conception, financial implications, and the relationship of the parents-to-be and their children and how it will change with a new addition to the family. A specific subfocus of the series would be first-time parents-to-be. When viewed over the long term, the positive effects for the future families would undoubtedly be substantial.

### Spiritual development programs

It is the authors' bias that provision of an array of programs concerning the various dimensions of spirituality would be efficacious. Though the medical literature is scant concerning the impact of spiritual belief on clinical outcomes, we believe it likely that such a positive relationship exists. At the very least, it is probable that patients who are knowledgeable of and content with their spirituality and at peace will be happier and will take their personal responsibilities for their health more seriously.

### Self-directed learning center

A key element in improving the long-term health of our community members will be their realization of their personal responsibility for their health. As efforts to bring this understanding about progress, it would be important for the local health care system to encourage continued self-directed learning related to health care topics. This could take many forms: audiotapes for loan or by telephone, videotapes for loan or via modem to a personal computer, printed material by mail, and a health care library. Additionally, a health bookstore could be a valuable resource.

### PHYSICIAN SERVICES

Though physician services are critical to the success of our new health care system, a discussion of how they will be organized is beyond the scope of this article. The authors believe that the present trends toward employed physicians and contracts with physician groups will continue and will intensify. Ultimately, physicians' remuneration will be significantly influenced by their resource utilization and clinical outcomes, and their access to patients will be usually determined by contract. Likewise, funding mechanisms for physicians and health care organizations of the future are not discussed.

### THE CONTINUUM OF CLINICAL SERVICES

The following are elements of an idealized continuum of clinical services, from before birth to after death. Where each of the activities occurs will depend on patient convenience, efficiency, and need for related services.

- Prenatal care.
- Birth. Various levels of maternal care, depending on the assigned clinical category of care needed, and various birthing environments would be available, from birthing facilities adjacent to the hospital to a high technology hospital delivery suite and associated operating facilities.
- The newborn would go either to a well-baby nursery contiguous with the birthing facility or to an adjacent, centralized neonatal intensive care unit (NICU) in the hospital.
- A "barely sick" unit would be available for children who are not seriously ill but who should not go to school (children of working parents). Excess hospital beds could be used initially, with an eventual separate structure, to decrease cost.
- Child development centers (as opposed to child care centers) would provide day care for children of the health care system and would begin the health care educational process.
- Pediatric outpatient clinic services.
- Pediatric inpatient services, with substantial visitor support facilities; hospital centralized NICU and pediatric ICU.
- Centralized child psychiatric inpatient and outpatient facilities.
- Adolescent medicine program for physical and psychological needs, inpatient and outpatient, centralized.
- Adult outpatient clinics—general, gynecologic, male, geriatric, specialty, and psychological services.

---

*A key element in improving the long-term health of our community members will be their realization of their personal responsibility for their health.*

---

- Outpatient diagnostic center and satellites.
- "Quick Care" facility for acute but not critical health problems.
- Intermediate care facility(ies) for adult and possibly pediatric medical/surgical in- and outpatient services, placed ideally in the community at a modest distance from the hospital. If the patient is in generally good health and the operative or diagnostic procedure is straightforward, the procedure would be performed in this outpatient facility with recovery beds for a several-day stay, including visitor support capability. Fewer high technology services would be immediately available. Certain orthopedic; ear, nose, and throat; gynecologic; general surgical; urologic; neurologic; plastic; ophthalmologic; and diagnostic (e.g., bronchoscopy) procedures could be performed in this facility. Medical patients with low risk factors or certain nonsurgical illnesses (pneumonia, chest pain, etc.) could be treated in an intermediate care facility, with nearby hospital beds and services available as needed. For patients whose treatment needs are less immediate or require less intensive observation, a "medical motel" would be available. Physician offices would be located nearby.
- Hospital adult intensive care unit, cardiac care unit, surgical intensive care unit, pediatric intensive care unit, monitored units, acute medical/surgical units, ventilator units, "transition" beds, emergency department, hyperbaric chamber(s).
- Outpatient infusion center.
- Cancer unit (stand-alone with radiotherapy capability and short-stay recovery beds).
- Rehabilitation services—orthopedic, neurological, cardiac, arthritis, speech, otologic, etc.
- Psychiatric services, some centralized and some in satellites, with specific subprograms for psychotics, day programs, counseling services (adult and adolescent), and detoxification.
- Home health nursing (newborn, pediatric, and adult), home therapy (pulmonary, chemotherapy, etc.), home safety assessment program, lifestyle assessment program.
- Skilled nursing facility, possibly nursing homes.
- Adult day care program.
- Respite program for caregivers of homebound pediatric and adult patients.
- Services for retirees living at home, including meals, visiting nurse and home health aides, electronic emergency call capability, cleaning, simple home maintenance.
- Hospice care and associated family services, including grieving/psychological counseling, legal assistance, financial counseling.

## INTEGRATION

With sufficient time, resources, and creative and technical expertise, the above educational and clinical programs can be developed. Many of these (particularly clinical services) already exist but are uncoordinated, under various for-profit and not-for-profit ownership arrangements, serving various community segments, and under varying quality of leadership. The restructuring of our health care system, particularly from legal, competitive, and community service points of view, will be a monumental undertaking. Once the new restructuring is philosophically embraced and under development, the administrative and clinical coordination of services and community-focused attitude readjustment will represent the next significant challenge.

Both from the community need and provider points of view, there are four major elements to be integrated in our new health care system: administration/management, educational programs, clinical services, and public health services. Of these, the most daunting may well be the integration of administration/management. The actual administration/management structure that each local health care provision entity adopts will depend on a multiplicity of factors with legal, local, competitive, and economic dimensions overlying whatever national health care policy has been adopted.

A detailed discussion of local health care organization administrative/management changes to come is beyond the intended scope of this article. However, the authors believe the administrative/management structures of the future will continue to flatten and will focus on optimal, seamless, quality outcome-defined functional efficiency as opposed to diffuse financial and management control objectives. Up to the present, administrative and management processes have been designed primarily for the convenience and business needs of the organization. Many boundaries are present, with many "turf" issues. These have led to poor communication, poor coordination, and suboptimal resource utilization. Patient inconvenience and lack of concern for the patient's sensitivities and involvement in the decision-making process have been more the rule than the exception. For our purposes, the authors will approach the issue of integration of administration/management narrowly from the point of view of the community: What is the need or want of the patient/community member and how best can these be addressed?

We envision a unified, computerized information system with a single entry point (from an organizational point of view) for the entire local health care entity. This will require that all elements of the provision entity be networked by computer, facsimile, and other communication technologies as they develop. A common, real-time interactive database will be necessary. The organizational information/referral center will have the resources necessary to answer most questions concerning services, benefits, and programs offered and will enroll the caller for educational programs. The caller could also be connected to the self-directed learning center. If the caller is in need of health services, a health care professional in the information center would receive the caller and, after a brief interview, make the appropriate disposition, including appointments.

Either via telephone information given to the information center/central registration or when the patient/consumer arrives for the appointment, the user would be specifically identified and logged into the computer database. A "credit card" with visible identification and magnetic information (or microfiche) could be used for this purpose and would be updated at each point of service or contact.

A computer database that integrates and provides correlation of clinical data and that is integrated with the administrative, demographic, and financial database would be extremely powerful. Software for several of the clinical database subelements have recently become available, but their impact within a comprehensive database can only be imagined. The clinical database of the future will allow correlation of many or all of the diffuse data elements of a patient's inpatient stay or outpatient experience. This will include physiologic and diagnostic data and correlation with medication effects and other therapeutic interventions. Computerized diagnostic algorithms and on-line, real time library search availability will aid physicians in reaching the desired clinical outcome as efficiently as possible.

*The clinical database of the future will allow correlation of many or all of the diffuse data elements of a patient's inpatient stay or outpatient experience.*

The integrated clinical database will allow true resource coordination. With the patient's data in the database, the system will automatically flag medication and nutritional interferences with ordered diagnostic tests and will inform appropriate ancillary services. The efficiency of the nursing service will be greatly enhanced, with aids such as miniaturized, hand-held terminals for patient data input; a hardcopy of patient status, changes in therapy and diagnostic procedures pending at the beginning of each work shift; current position of the patient's care in the diagnostic algorithm; flags for possible complications from current diagnostic and therapeutic interventions; and constant correlation of physiologic (and pathophysiologic) data to flag abnormal trends or impending complications. These patient reports will require an even higher level of function and independence from nursing personnel. With optimal clinical pathways established by diagnosis, utilization review will effectively begin even before the patient enters the facility, with the initial order set and diagnosis. Clinical outcome monitoring will increasingly include prospective action to alter projected suboptimal outcomes. Using continuously recomputed severity indices for each inpatient, worsening trends will be recognized even earlier, allowing earlier intervention and, hopefully, less morbidity and lower cost. Special care unit beds will be more optimally utilized.

The medical staff database will also be integrated into the main clinical database. It will allow an instant assessment of whether or not a physician has a certain clinical privilege and who is responsible for his patients in his absence. With the above integrated database, the medical administration staff will become much more effective in assessing physician competence by diagnosis, procedure, outcome, and resource utilization. This information will then form the basis for selected physician education or privilege modification.

For inpatients and certain outpatients (cancer therapy, rehabilitation or other circumstances requiring multiple services), we believe that a case manager will be assigned to each patient. The case manager will have a clinical background, administrative experience, and organizational knowledge and, using the computer aides as described above, will act as the ombudsman for the patient, facilitating and coordinating the diagnostic and treatment processes. Further, the case manager will be a source of information and comfort to the patient, who is uncomfortable and apprehensive at best. Finally, the case manager will be responsible for the completeness of the computer record of all activities relative to the patient. Though the database regarding the cost effectiveness of the case management approach as we envision it above is not large, we believe that this approach will be shown to be more cost effective than the present design.

With the database as described above, the local health system will be able to monitor and communicate with patients/consumers regarding Pap smears, breast examinations, colorectal examinations, prostate and other screening programs and will be able to follow up with reminders. It would be conceivable to build into the process disincentives if patients do not fulfill their part of the "contract." With this database, not only would a specific, portable health history be developed and maintained for each patient, but very useful information would also be obtained for planning and for evaluation of the efficacy of the program or services offered. Knowing the utilization characteristics of the various patient subsets within this closed system would allow more rational cost projections, and the clinical therapeutic/cost efficacy of new therapies, programs, and technologies would be more accurately assessed. Selected elements of these databases would be most useful regionally and nationally in comparing health care systems, their resource utilization versus outcomes, and in assessing the nation's health.

Early on, the authors foresee the local health care system coordinating its programs and services with local and state public health programs. However, at least in some locales, we see the likelihood and desirability of the local health system contracting to provide appropriate public health services. Whether or not this occurs, the distinction between public health services and those provided by the local health care system will blur.

Following are several examples of how patients might experience the integration of education, clinical, administrative/management, and public health services of the new local health system. Effort has been made to include only "value added" activities and opportunities from the patient's point of view, while controlling and coordinating resource utilization for the greatest clinical and social efficacy. In these examples, we have espoused an organizational philosophy whereby early clinical, educational, and social interventions are cost saving and health enhancing when considered in the long view (years).

### New parents-to-be

Mr. and Mrs. James are both 28 years old, college graduates, married for two years, new to the health care system, and desire to start a family. Having just recently enrolled in the program, they have answered detailed questionnaires that have been placed in the system database. Mrs. James has reviewed the detailed introductory materials provided her describing the health system and its offerings and has called the system information center regarding educational offerings and clinical care. She is told that she will be first connected with the education department and then will be transferred back to the information center. Her call is forwarded to the education center where she receives information regarding preconception classes and enrolls herself and her husband. Additionally, she and her husband are interested in the basic physiology and pathophysiology program and enroll in that series as well. She is then transferred back to the information center where she is connected with a clinical representative to whom she briefly describes her desire for pregnancy. The clinical representative then brings up the "doctor database" on her computer terminal and reviews the biographies of family practitioners and obstetricians for the patient's selection. After the patient makes the selection, the clinical representative makes contact with the physician's office and arranges the initial appointment for the patient.

The patient arrives for the appointment with the physician and has a checkup; basic information is entered into the system clinical database, both for recordkeeping and for future screening reminders. When the patient and her husband conceive, the patient returns to the physician for obstetric care. At the initial obstetric visit, the physician's office staff connects the patient to the system education center where the patient and her husband are enrolled in the "Parents-to-Be" class. As the patient progresses through her obstetric care, a home health nurse is available for advice and questions. At this time, a pediatrician or family practitioner is selected for care of the newborn, and an appointment is made to meet the physician prior to delivery. During the prenatal period, if the patient fails to appear for prenatal care, the system computer automatically identifies this and prompts the obstetrician's staff to determine if a follow-up telephone call or notice is needed. During the pregnancy, risk factors are assessed (e.g., twins, toxemia, diabetes, or cephalopelvic disproportion). Should complications arise, audio- and videotapes are available through the education center (lending library). If risk factors are present, the patient is admitted at the appropriate time to the hospital obstetric unit. If no risk factors are present, the patient is admitted to the adjacent birthing facility. When the infant is born, it will be cared for in either the newborn nursery of the birthing facility or a smaller newborn nursery in the hospital adjacent to the NICU (if the mother has been hospitalized). If fetal demise has occurred, psychological counseling and support are provided the family. If the infant has some abnormality, psychological counseling and support for the family are provided, plus other clinical or social services as necessary, and contact is made with the pediatric clinical services program and appropriate referrals made.

At the time of discharge of the mother and infant, appointments are made for postnatal obstetric follow-up and for the infant's first appointment with the pediatrician or family practitioner.

At the infant's first appointment, the clinical history established at birth will be updated in the information system, the database from which automatic reminders for well-baby visits, vaccinations, etc., will be generated. During the time from the date of discharge until the first postnatal and pediatric appointments, a visiting nurse visits the mother and new infant at home, answers questions, and ensures that mother and infant are doing well. After the postnatal obstetric follow-up visit, the patient is returned to her primary care physician, where her clinical care continues. She will routinely receive computer-generated reminders, via her physician's office, for Pap smears and breast exams for herself, vaccinations and other reminders for her children, and screening test reminders for her husband. Educational information will also be frequently provided. (Figure 1 presents a summary of these events and services.)

## An acute injury

Mike Johnson is a 17-year-old male, enrolled with his family in the health system. He has sustained an athletic injury to his right knee over the weekend. His parents transport him to the nearest "Quick Care" facility of the system, where his clinical history is brought onto the computer screen and a computer "flag" is placed in the computer terminal of his personal physician. He is seen by the physician on duty, who requests an orthopedic consultation. The orthopedist arrives and determines that the patient may have sustained ligament damage and requires a diagnostic arthroscopy. The patient is generally healthy (low-risk category) and is transported to the nearest system intermediate care facility, where a diagnostic arthroscopy is performed. The diagnostic procedure reveals the need for further orthopedic reconstructive

surgery, which is performed at that time. Postoperatively, the patient recuperates in the intermediate care facility for two days, and his mother is encouraged to stay in his room to give supportive care. (A convertible bed chair is provided, as well as generic toiletries in the private bath and extra meals.) Nursing personnel are very enthusiastic about the extra help. A rehabilitation consultation is obtained and durable medical equipment provided. Also, a videotape on sports injuries and how to avoid them is provided, the same videotape that is used in other educational programs of the system in its pediatric health care series. The patient is then discharged home with appointments for postoperative medical evaluation and rehabilitation. After these occur, the patient is returned to his primary care physician for routine follow-up. (Figure 2 presents a summary of these events and services.)

## A patient with cancer

Ethel Richards is a 68-year-old female, new to the health system, and a long-term cigarette smoker. She has completed the detailed health questionnaire upon enrollment in the health system and, if she does not contact the information center for entry into the system, she will be contacted. She does contact the information center and is connected with a clinical representative with whom she briefly discusses her clinical history and who then helps her select a physician from the doctor biographic database, with an appointment being made. At her first appointment, the examination reveals mild chronic obstructive pulmonary disease, and a baseline chest X-ray is requested from a system satellite diagnostic center located in the building. The chest X-ray is obtained and a radiologist at the central diagnostic facility identifies a pulmonary nodule in the image transmitted over telephone lines and calls the patient's physician while the patient is returning to his office. The primary care physician then arranges for a consultant, also in the building, to see the patient. The patient makes her way to the consultant's office in the building and is examined, and the chest X-ray image is transmitted via telephone line to his computer terminal and printer. The consultant recommends bronchoscopy and biopsies. These are performed the next day at a system intermediate care facility (the patient being in generally good health). Other specimens are obtained for laboratory work along with other X-rays while the patient is there during her overnight stay. During this time her husband elects to remain with her in her room, accommodations for a visitor's stay being routinely available. The next day, the diag-

## FIGURE 1

### SUMMARY OF EVENTS AND SERVICES IN THE NEW PARENTS-TO-BE SCENARIO

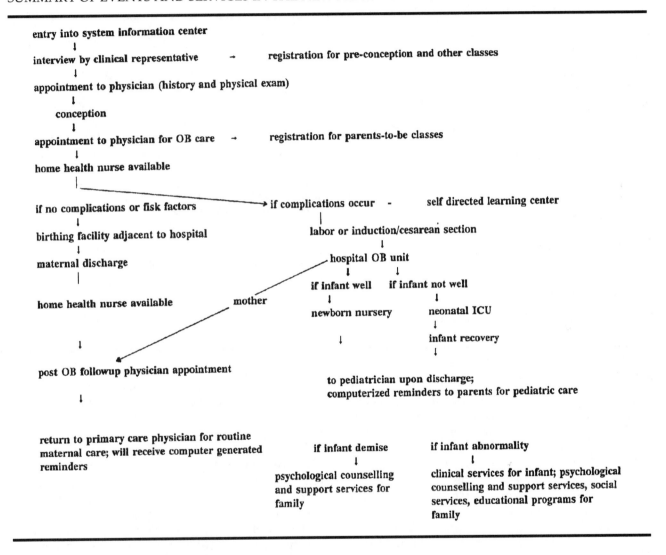

nostic work-up is complete, revealing a solitary squamous cell carcinoma without apparent metastases. This is discussed with the patient by the physician, and a videotape concerning lung cancer is made available to the patient and her husband. They elect surgery and postoperative irradiation. At the patient's convenience, she is admitted to the hospital and is greeted by her case manager, who facilitates her hospital stay. She is admitted to the hospital for the surgery because of the extent of surgery required and for the ancillary services that may be needed. Surgery is performed, and pulmonary, radiotherapy, and oncology consulta-

tions are obtained. After several days of convalescence in the hospital, the patient is transferred to the nearby skilled nursing facility, where she fully recuperates. When the patient is sufficiently healed, she goes to her appointment at the system cancer center where radiotherapy is initiated. During this period, the patient has frequent visits from the home health nurse. Following her postoperative visit to her surgeon and after release from her radiotherapist, she is returned to the care of her primary care physician.

Approximately one year later, Mrs. Richards presents to her primary care physician with lingering back pain.

---

**FIGURE 2**

---

SUMMARY OF EVENTS AND SERVICES IN THE ACUTE INJURY SCENARIO

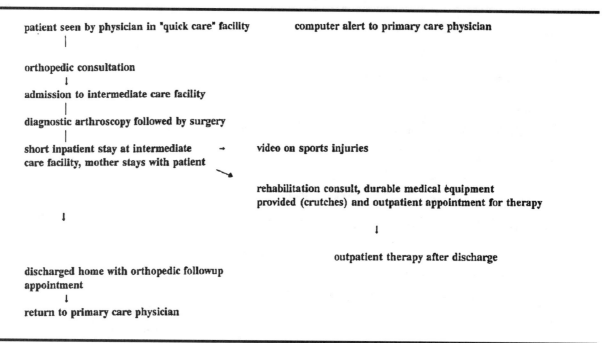

Diagnostic X-rays reveal lytic lesions in her spine and ribs, and an appointment is arranged with an oncologist. While at the oncologist's office, a videotape is available that provides information concerning chemotherapy. The patient elects to begin chemotherapy, and it is begun in the system cancer center that day.

After two days, the patient is discharged and an appointment is made at the system infusion center, where the patient will continue chemotherapy and nutritional consultation. During this period, home health nurse visits are available as needed. The home health nurse notes that the patient is not able to manage at home, and the patient elects admission to the hospice.

At the hospice, psychologic, spiritual, legal, and financial counseling are available to both the patient and her husband. A short time later, the patient expires.

The patient's husband is visited by the home health nurse and a social worker to determine his physical, emotional, and social status and to recommend and arrange his participation in the program dealing with grieving. "Meals on Wheels" are arranged, along with light housekeeping and light home maintenance, and his primary physician is notified for follow-up. When he is ready, he is encouraged to attend social activities sponsored by the health care system. (Figure 3 presents a summary of these events and services.)

**FOCUS OF SYSTEM**

As we envision the integrated local health care system, beyond clinical excellence, it is very patient focused, sensitive to patient concerns, and sensitive to the patient's understanding. The focus is on keeping patients well through education, early diagnosis and treatment, and efforts to gain realization of patient responsibilities for wellness. With the above, we expect patients to be ill less often, to be happier, and to be back to work and life more quickly.

From the health care system's point of view, systems and critical pathways must be established to ensure

---

*As we envision the integrated local health care system, beyond clinical excellence, it is very patient focused, sensitive to patient concerns, and sensitive to the patient's understanding.*

## FIGURE 3

### SUMMARY OF EVENTS AND SERVICES IN THE PATIENT WITH CANCER SCENARIO

entry into system information center
↓
interview by clinical representative
↓
selection of and appointment with physician
↓
first appointment, mild chronic obstructive
pulmonary disease diagnosed      →      self-directed learning center - information available
↓
physician orders chest x-ray at diagnostic center in building
↓
pulmonary nodule identified by radiologist, report to
primary physician
↓
consultation with thoracic surgeon      →      self-directed learning center - videotape available on bronchoscopy
↓
admission to intermediate care facility
↓
bronchoscopy, biopsies and metastatic workup
↓
diagnostic workup complete; diagnosis is solitary
epidermoid carcinoma without metastases
↓
surgeon discusses with patient      →      self-directed learning center - videotape available on lung cancer
                                                                          and treatment options
↓
decision is made for surgery and post-op irradiation
↓
admission to hospital
↓
surgery performed; respiratory therapy and radiotherapy
consultations obtained
↓
brief convalescence in hospital
↓
to skilled nursing facility
↓
upon discharge, to cancer center; radiotherapy initiated
↓
followup by home health nurse
↓
postoperative surgical appointment
↓
return to primary physician                                        *continues*

appropriate use of resources. Efforts must be focused on selecting technologies that provide the information needed in the safest manner for the least cost, again taking the long view. Our health care system will no longer be able to uncritically acquire extraordinarily expensive technology, support staff, and programs without seriously considering the incremental long-term health efficacy and cost benefits that that may or may not obtain.

We believe a major thrust of the future will be applying the most appropriate services in the most appropriate settings. In general, this will mean a significant move away from the highly centralized, high-service-intensity health care settings we cur-

---

## FIGURE 3

---

CONTINUED

---

[1 year later]

patient to primary physician complaining of back pain
↓
x-ray in diagnostic center reveals metastases
↓
consult oncologist                    →        self-directed learning center - videotape on chemotherapy
↓
chemotherapy begun at cancer center
↓
discharged home                       →        chemotherapy completed at outpatient infusion center
↓
patient doing poorly
↓
  hospice          →         psychological, legal, financial and spiritual counselling available for patient and family
↓
patient expires; husband receives visit from home
health nurse and social worker, enrolled in grief program
↓
receives meals, housekeeping, light home maintenance
↓
when ready, introduction to community social activities;
continues relationship with his primary care physician

---

rently have to a more decentralized but highly integrated structure. This will mean that more of our resources will be expended in lower intensity settings, will be more convenient for the patient, and will be aggregated in a more rational, functional manner both from the clinical and the patient's points of view.

One very exciting characteristic of the integration of educational programs and clinical services is that patients will move back and forth between general health education programs, clinical services, and specific education services. The patient would ideally be involved in a life-long series of health education programs, increasingly knowledgeable, increasingly aware of early symptoms, increasingly able to deal with small health problems before they become large, and increasingly accountable for health and resource utilization.

Ultimately, effective, seamless integration of administration/management, educational programs, and clinical and public health services will be required by the community. The extent to which the health care entity is successful in this integration will likely be a major determinant of whether its social and business contracts with the community continue.

•   •   •

Just as the time is right to reorganize our health care system, this is a propitious moment to revisit the services we offer and how we offer them. There are many in our country who, though unprepared by training or experience, are nonetheless eager to accomplish both of the above for us. Integration of our organizations, human resources, financial arrangements, and health care services will have great appeal to business, government, and our patients. A serious restructuring will require time, patience, flexibility, and foresight.

Even without fundamental changes in the financing or legal structure of our health care organizations or national health care reform, major elements of the above model can be accomplished. In years past, a hospital's impact on health care in its community was commonly equated with its bed capacity. This is no longer the case, and excess bed capacity has become the rule rather than the exception. Of course, community size and numbers of competing hospitals vary greatly, but the authors believe that financially stable hospitals with bed capacities of 250–350 are well positioned to establish integrated health care systems as described above. Health care organizations that successfully actualize the concepts and demonstrate the benefits of integration, continuity, effective resource utilization, and enthusiastic service will dominate, whatever the financial and structural alterations that eventuate.

We Americans are outstanding at solving problems, once we realize that we have a problem and understand the problem. It appears that we are well on our way to realizing that we have a problem in the provision of health services. Through discussion such as this, we must come to consensus regarding the boundaries and characteristics of the problem and possible solutions. But in order to approach what our health care *can* be, we must be willing to reconsider what our communities' health needs really are and how best to satisfy them. The French novelist André Gide said that, in order to discover new lands, we must be willing to lose sight of the shore. We have the provisions, we know how to operate the vessel, we have a vision of where we would like to land, and we are developing our map. We need to soon set sail.

# Vertical integration models to prepare health systems for capitation

Douglas G. Cave

*Health systems will profit most under capitation if their vertical integration strategy provides operational stability, a strong primary care physician base, efficient delivery of medical services, and geographic access to physicians. Staff- and equity-based systems best meet these characteristics for success because they have one governance structure and a defined mission statement. Moreover, physician bonds are strong because these systems maximize physicians' income potential and control the revenue stream.*

Health Care Manage Rev, 1995, 20(1), 26–39

**One in five people** with health insurance coverage is enrolled in a health maintenance organization (HMO).[1] Nationally, the number of people receiving care from HMOs grew 7% in 1992 and 9% in 1993.[2] At this rate, nearly one in three people will be enrolled in HMOs by the year 2000. In some states—such as Massachusetts, California, Minnesota, and Oregon—HMO enrollment already is over 30%.

Most HMOs capitate some or all medical services. Under capitation, a provider system receives from the HMO a sum of money per covered member, paid before any services are rendered. In exchange for the capitation payment, the provider system is obligated to deliver contracted services to covered members.[3]

Not surprisingly, capitation arrangements have increased with the growth in HMO enrollment. For example, approximately 5% of primary care physicians' (PCPs) payment was by capitation in 1980. This percentage grew to 9% by 1990.[4-7] Nationally, 25% or more of all provider payments may be in the form of capitation by the turn of the century. In some states, capitation might be 45% or more of all provider reimbursements.[3,8,9]

Physicians in solo and small single-specialty group practices have watched their fee-for-service practices shrink as HMO enrollment has increased. To protect their patient base, many physicians have formed strong alliances with large physician groups, clinics, or hospitals. Other physicians have sold their practices to one of these organizations. Already one in four physicians reports that he or she is an employee of another entity, as do one in two physicians under 36 years of age.[10] The result has been the formation of over 650 vertically integrated health systems that generally have one or more hospitals and over 100 physicians.[11-13]

The majority of health systems either contract with or are owned by HMOs. Many HMOs pay full-risk capitations to these systems, and the system provides to HMO members all primary care, specialty, and outpatient and inpatient facility services. Established health systems generally receive 20% to 25% of their revenues from capitation contracts. However, some

---

Key words: *vertical integration, capitation, primary care physician*

**Douglas G. Cave,** *Ph.D., M.P.H., is senior health policy analyst in the Managed Care Research Division of Hewitt Associates, Newport Beach, California.*

systems now secure 70% to 80% of their revenues through capitation.[14,15]

The purpose of this article is to present vertical integration models that will allow health systems to profit and grow under full-risk capitation. We begin by defining the characteristics of successful models. We then define the vertical integration models used today and discuss whether these models are sustainable in a capitated environment.

## CHARACTERISTICS OF SUCCESSFUL MODELS

Health systems will profit most under capitation if their vertical integration strategy provides operational stability, a strong primary care physician base, efficient delivery of medical services, and geographic access to physicians.[15] "Efficient" means that the health system physicians treat medical conditions with the least expensive level of medical care possible and still achieve the desired health outcome for the patient.

### Operational stability

Health systems with the following features are most likely to succeed over the long term.

#### Support of a single governance structure

One governance body is necessary to profit most under capitation (i.e., one board, one chief executive officer [CEO], and one set of financial statements). The single CEO oversees chief operating officers responsible for individual operation units.[16] The reason for one governance body is that health systems need to make difficult strategic decisions in a short period of time. For instance, systems need to determine the best way to allocate limited capital resources, compensate PCPs and specialists, and relocate or consolidate physician practices. Health systems that support many boards and CEOs often cannot develop one mission statement, resulting in competing interests and internal power struggles.

#### Strengthening of physicians' bond to system

Theories of change and common sense suggest that physicians will attempt to maintain their income and autonomy.[17,18] Therefore, health systems that maximize income potential are likely to retain physicians because other systems cannot offer better compensation to recruit physicians away.

Furthermore, health systems that purchase physicians' tangible assets (e.g., medical equipment, supplies, patient billings, information systems) and intangible assets (e.g., contract ownership, patient base, patient records, exclusivity agreements) directly control all physician revenues, keeping physicians financially tied to the health system.

In addition, physicians will cede more autonomy to health systems owned and operated by physician peers than to systems operated by hospitals or non–health professionals.[14,15]

#### Generation of revenues for physicians

Health systems generating new and ongoing physician revenues are most likely to be profitable and successful in the long term. Some health systems are not attractive to HMOs because the system's structure either does not include the whole continuum of care (e.g., integrated medical campuses, acute and tertiary hospital services, outpatient surgical departments, home health, durable medical equipment, hospice care) or does not permit efficient operations (i.e., unnecessarily high fixed administrative and variable patient care expenses).

HMOs will direct their contracts to health systems that offer full-service, cost-efficient medical care. These systems will receive a continuous flow of new capital, improving operational stability and growth opportunities.

### Strong primary care physician base

Health systems need to develop and own a cost-efficient PCP base to succeed under full-risk capitation. Findings show that PCPs are the principal care providers for 60% or more of covered patients' episodes of care (e.g., upper and lower respiratory tract infections, otitis media, abdominal pain, lower back pain, sprains and strains, hypertension, urinary tract infections, headaches).[8]

Furthermore, under the HMO system of care, PCPs generally are the first provider of care for patients with more complicated medical conditions (e.g., bronchitis, cancers, cholelithiasis, emphysema, glaucoma, hemorrhoids, seizure disorders, thyroid diseases). The PCPs triage these patients and direct them to the appropriate, cost-efficient medical resources.[8,19] In addition, the PCPs provide patient follow-up evaluations, monitor specialists' treatment plans, and oversee patients' compliance with recommended treatment plans.

The HMOs also entrust PCPs to provide established preventive care regimens and to perform appropriate screening tests for early detection of potentially fatal, high-cost diseases. These measures will enhance a system's cost efficiency by reducing preventable medical expenses. Health systems with the following characteristics are most likely to build a strong PCP base.

### Commitment to own PCP network

Systems that own PCP networks can directly invest in salaries and practices. Consequently, these systems can pay the highest compensation package in a health care market (i.e., salary, bonus based on performance, and an equity position) reducing the chance that PCPs will leave for a higher salary from a competitor system. Health systems that retain a select PCP network will profit most under full-risk capitation. Other systems will decline to less efficient, specialist-heavy networks.

### Infusion of capital for PCP network growth

Internal Revenue Service (IRS) inurement restrictions state that tax-exempt health systems and hospitals can only provide incidental monetary benefit to independent physicians.[20] These restrictions determine standards for community benefit, such as preventing undue private benefit to independent physicians. The private benefit restriction prevents many health systems both from subsidizing PCP incomes and from investing capital for PCP network growth. In addition, the Medicare fraud and abuse regulations prohibit health systems from investing in independent PCP practices in exchange for referrals of federally funded patients.[21]

However, health systems are largely exempt from inurement restrictions and fraud and abuse regulations once the affiliated physicians transfer their revenue stream to the system. That is, the health system purchases physicians' tangible and intangible practice assets, and physicians become employees of the system. The restrictions and regulations require physicians' assets to be purchased at fair market value in order to prevent undue private benefit and the buying of practices for referral purposes.

Once physicians are employed, the health system can subsidize PCP incomes and infuse capital into PCP network growth. The IRS and Department of Health and Human Services reason that employed PCPs now are part of the health system. Consequently, infusion of capital to the PCP network benefits the system and not independent physicians. Surveys show that health systems purchasing practices do infuse capital into their PCP networks. For example, employed PCPs' net income generally is $30,000 to $40,000 more than PCPs in solo and small-group practices. In addition, these systems deploy capital to buy new PCP practices, build new central campuses and satellite offices, upgrade office-based equipment, and purchase new information systems.[15,22]

### Assurance that PCPs' interests are in-line with system

Full-risk capitation provides health systems with the incentive to deliver efficient medical care. Therefore, PCPs must have an interest both in reducing practice pattern variations and in controlling increases in the volume (greater use of existing equipment and services) and intensity of services (shifts from less expensive to more expensive services). Research shows that health systems need to control a significant percentage of the physician's income (probably 50% or more) to alter patterns of treatment. Health systems that account for a small portion of a physician's revenues (between 10% and 30%) generally will not be able to impact practice patterns.[23–26]

### Reduction of administrative tasks

Overhead practice costs are approaching 70% of indemnity-based PCPs' net revenues.[11] These costs can be divided into five categories: office support services (e.g., front office personnel, medical staff, recruiting and hiring, training, benefits); information systems (e.g., computerized billing statements, reasonable and customary charge updates, contract monitoring and evaluation); patient billing and collection services; contract marketing and negotiations; clinical support systems (e.g., utilization review, pattern-of-treatment monitoring, case-mix adjustment, outcomes research); and direct practice costs (e.g., malpractice premiums, rentals/leases, utilities, supplies). Physicians generally spend 20% of total work hours on administrative tasks.[27]

Many PCPs want to reduce their administrative burdens and devote more time to patient care. One way to accomplish this goal is for PCPs to join or contract with health systems that provide centralized administrative services. To the extent the health system can decrease the time PCPs devote to administrative tasks, PCPs can increase income by generating new revenues (net of administrative contract charges) from more patient care. Alternatively, some PCPs may choose to maintain their present income and use the remaining "freed" time for leisure and an improved lifestyle.

Health systems are likely to retain a satisfied PCP base if they offer a comprehensive package of administrative services, and the system either subsidizes PCPs' income to reflect the increased productivity or allows PCPs to have more flexible work and call schedules.

## Efficient delivery of medical services

Many health systems will eventually receive the majority of revenues from capitation contracts. Annual capitation revenues for some larger systems already range from $150 million to $300 million.[8,15]

---

*Many health systems will eventually receive the majority of revenues from capitation contracts.*

---

These revenues are offset by overhead practice costs (i.e., fixed costs) and the variable expenses of patient care. Health systems providing quality, cost-efficient services profit most under capitated arrangements because they retain all payments not used on patient care. Efficient systems have the following characteristics in common.

### Selection of efficient physicians

Efficient health systems select physicians through a detailed credentialing process and then monitor physicians' performance on a regular basis. Health systems offering membership to all interested physicians generally are not efficient because the systems tend to become specialist-heavy and seldom invest the resources necessary to monitor practice patterns.[15,26]

The credentialing process should address both cost efficiency and quality of care. Technical analysis should measure the structure, process, and outcomes of care. Measures of "structure" reflect the physician's education and training (e.g., graduation from an accredited college of medicine, board certification appropriate to practice area, competence, and ethical character references from peers). Measures of "process" reflect activities of the physician in patient management (e.g., formal disciplinary actions by state medical boards, sanctions by U.S. Department of Health and Human Services, detailed malpractice history, past utilization patterns). "Outcome" measures

reflect the physician's results or impact of care (e.g., changes in patient health status, patient satisfaction survey ratings, adverse events, avoidable hospital admissions).[28]

### Retention of efficient physicians

The credentialing process alone will not ensure the selection of cost-efficient physicians because utilization and survey data often are not available. Furthermore, there is mounting evidence that shows physicians practice differently in an organized health system. For example, HMO-based physicians can treat similar health-risk patients approximately 25% less expensively than indemnity-based physicians. This difference is attributed to the HMO-based physicians' less hospital-intensive style of medical practice.[29–34]

Consequently, health systems need to develop and implement continuous quality improvement (CQI) programs that monitor patterns of treatment and identify physicians with unintended practice pattern variations. As importantly, the CQI program should address a process for affecting physician behavioral change. Empirical findings show that changing behavior is most successful when physicians receive individualized feedback based on their practice patterns as compared to a peer group both of the same specialty type and in the same patient catchment area. In addition, the physician feedback needs to address single clinical actions that a respected clinical leader presents in a face-to-face meeting on a regular basis.[26,35–40]

For example, isolating a physician's inappropriate laboratory test ordering for gastrointestinal disease will result in a more successful change effort than providing information that shows the physician's overall laboratory test ordering behavior is too high. Moreover, stating that the physician is ordering too many gastric acid specimens to help diagnose peptic ulcers will result in more successful change than stating that the physician is ordering too many laboratory tests for all gastrointestinal conditions.

Another way to reduce unintended practice pattern variations is to educate physicians on disease-management guidelines defined by expert opinion or scientific evidence.[41–44] Guidelines provide explicit criteria on how physicians and patients should act in specific clinical situations. Guidelines are used to reduce pattern-of-treatment variations attributed to physician factors (i.e., inadequate knowledge of pharmacology and alternative disease treatments, predispositions based on habits and beliefs, failure to follow up on abnormal signs and symptoms, and complications from initial treatments) and patient factors (i.e., lack of compliance with recommended treatments and demands for inappropriate services). In general, guidelines alone have been less successful than physician feedback programs in changing practice patterns.

Continued system membership should be based on the physician's willingness to reduce practice pattern variations identified by clinical leaders of the CQI program. As with any corporate entity, system leaders must have the power to dismiss repeated nonperformers. Health systems will thrive and grow under capitation when leaders can select and retain efficient physicians.

### Maintenance of proper PCP/specialist staffing levels

Physician work-force policies of staff/group model HMOs have been well documented.[8,9,11,45-49] One way HMOs achieve efficiencies over the indemnity system is by exercising private-sector, population-based health planning. Although physician hiring rarely is based on the level of resources required to maintain the health of covered members, the available evidence suggests that HMOs have the same outcomes as indemnity plans.[50-53] Consequently, HMO hiring rates often are used to forecast physician need.

The overall rate of full-time equivalent (FTE) nonadministrative physicians per 100,000 HMO members is approximately 122, with a range from 97 to 163 across HMOs. Current HMO staffing data for some specialists may be modestly underestimated because out-of-plan use may not be completely documented. On average, the HMO staffing levels show that 47% of HMO physicians are in primary care specialties (i.e., general and family practitioners, general internists, and pediatricians), with a range between 41% and 51%.

As a comparison, national data illustrate that there are about 180 nonfederal, nontrainee FTE physicians in active practice per 100,000 U.S. population.[11,54] Approximately 36% of these practicing physicians are PCPs, or 65 FTEs per 100,000 U.S. population. The national PCP rate is somewhat higher than the staff/group HMOs' average PCP rate of 57 FTEs per 100,000 members. However, the national specialist rate is over 75% higher than the staff/group HMOs' rate (i.e., 115 FTEs and 65 FTEs, respectively).

These results indicate there currently is not a PCP shortage, but a specialist surplus. While the staff/group HMOs' specialist staffing levels are compa-

rable to national rates for certain specialists (e.g., obstetricians/gynecologists, allergists, dermatologists, endocrinologists, oncologists, otolaryngologists), the national supply of other specialists appears to outstrip staff/group HMO hiring needs by at least 60% (e.g., cardiologists, gastroenterologists, general surgeons, neurosurgeons, ophthalmologists, psychiatrists, neurologists).

Furthermore, the staff/group HMOs use nonphysician providers (i.e., nurse practitioners, nurse midwives, and physician assistants) to deliver a significant proportion of primary care services. The average number of nonphysician providers per 100,000 members is approximately 23, with a range from zero to 67 across the HMOs.[47,55] For three large Kaiser Permanente HMO regions, the nonphysician provider rate was 23, with a range from 15 to 30. National data show the average number of nonphysician providers per 100,000 U.S. population can be estimated at 20.[55-57]

The findings show some variation in the hiring levels that staff/group HMOs use to meet their patients' health needs and demands. Nevertheless, the HMOs generally have the following work-force policies in common: (1) no HMO hires or contracts with more than 163 FTE physicians per 100,000 members; the most common range is between 120 and 130; (2) approximately 47% of staff/group HMO physicians are PCPs; this percentage is not less than 41%; and (3) the HMO hires or contracts with about 23 FTE nonphysician providers per 100,000 members; the most common range varies between 20 and 25. Health systems having similar work-force policies should be most efficient and sustainable under capitation.

## Geographic access to physician

Health systems will succeed over the long term when clinical leaders can relocate physician practices and rapidly expand the system.

### Relocation of physician practices

Health systems need to retain control over their physicians' practice locations. The system may require certain physicians to relocate their practices to ensure optimal access to care. A commonly used method for measuring geographic access is to match postal zip codes of enrolled members to health system physicians' service areas. A good match indicates that physicians are geographically located in the same areas as covered members.[58,59]

Other physicians may be asked to consolidate their practices to a fewer number of centralized locations. The latter request will help to reduce practice overhead costs.

### Expansion of system to meet demand

Adequate member access to providers requires the health system to hire or contract with a certain number of physicians and hospitals per 100,000 members. Members should have good access to network providers when provider rates are above the expected minimum level and providers have capacity to see new patients.[8,9,59]

As HMOs direct their contracts to health systems delivering cost-efficient medical care, health systems need to quickly add physicians to meet new patients' health needs and demands.[15,59] Otherwise, physician capacity issues will result in more member complaints and lower member satisfaction ratings. Moreover, overworked physicians may leave the health system for another system offering comparable income potential and more leisure time.

*Adequate member access to providers requires the health system to hire or contract with a certain number of physicians and hospitals per 100,000 members.*

## VERTICAL INTEGRATION MODELS

Figure 1 illustrates the predominant types of vertical integration models being used to form health systems. These are, in order of increasing cost efficiency and long-term sustainability: group practice without walls (GPWW), open physician-hospital organization (PHO), closed PHO, management service organization (MSO), foundation model, staff model, and equity model.[14–16,60]

### Group practice without walls

A popular form of vertical integration has solo practitioners and small-group practices forming and

---

**FIGURE 1**

VERTICAL INTEGRATION MODELS

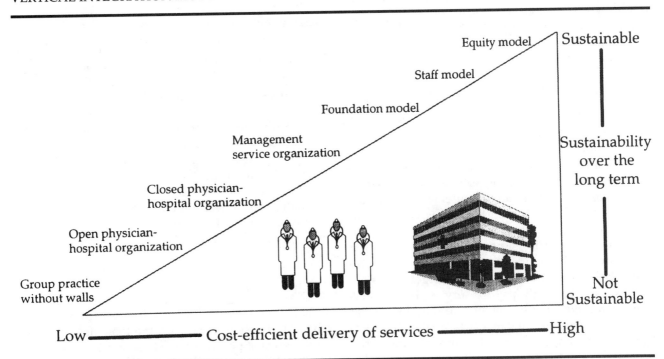

operating a central administration to reduce practice overhead costs. Functions of the administrative staff commonly include marketing the physician group to managed care payers, negotiating and monitoring contracts, performing patient billings and collections, and purchasing supplies. The administrative staff bills physicians for shared service expenses. Hospitals generally are not involved in forming GPWW-based health systems.

### Open physician-hospital organization

The open PHO generally is a partnership between a hospital and its medical staff, characterized by equal capitalization and ownership. All physicians are invited to participate, often resulting in specialist-heavy membership. The main responsibility of the open PHO's administrative staff is to establish hospital and physician services agreements that solidify terms for managed care contracting. Subsequently, the staff negotiates contracts with managed care payers.

### Closed physician-hospital organization

The closed PHO is similar to the open PHO with a few exceptions. Only a select group of efficient physicians is invited to join the PHO, resulting in more effective physician work-force policy. Moreover, ongoing membership is based on physicians' willingness to comply with established practice pattern and quality criteria. The primary role of the closed PHO's administrative staff is to negotiate contracts with managed care payers.

### Management service organization

Usually a wholly owned subsidiary of a health system (generally not-for-profit, but can be for-profit), the MSO purchases and manages the tangible practice assets of a select group of physicians. Physicians retain ownership of intangible assets, such as goodwill of practice (e.g., trade names, patient base, contract ownership, revenue stream), patient records, and physician billing numbers. The MSO's management services include office support, information system purchasing and operations, patient billings and collections, and contract marketing and negotiations.

Physicians generally pay for services by transferring a fixed monthly fee amount to the MSO, a flat percentage of net monthly revenues, a rolling percentage of net revenues (where the amount transferred decreases as net revenues increase), or a cost-plus

amount. The fixed fee and percentage of net revenue arrangements generally transfer between 45% to 55% of net monthly revenues.

### Foundation model

A foundation is a wholly owned subsidiary of a not-for-profit health system. Under this vertical integration model, the foundation purchases the tangible and intangible assets of physician practices. As well, the foundation enforces exclusivity agreements that state physicians in the group cannot compete for patients in the same geographic area. Exclusivity agreements generally are valid for up to 3 years.

The foundation negotiates contracts with managed care payers and retains ownership of the contracts. Therefore, the foundation controls all physicians' revenues. Because the foundation owns practices and controls the revenue stream, the health system can infuse capital into physician practices.

However, physicians are not employees of the foundation and remain part of a separate physician group entity. The physician group signs a professional services agreement with the foundation to provide professional services. Consequently, the physician group retains significant autonomy over practice pattern standards and professional service fee distributions to PCPs and specialists.

### Staff model

Health systems (generally not-for-profit) directly purchase the tangible and intangible assets of physician practices. Staff physicians usually are organized into clinics that have their own leadership. The health system negotiates with managed care payers and retains control of all contracts and physician revenues.

Because the health system employs physicians, the system can invest capital into physician practices. Moreover, the health system can directly subsidize PCP incomes and infuse capital into PCP network growth because decision making is made by a single corporate entity. The system also has significant leverage over staff physicians' patterns of treatment and productivity.

### Equity model

This for-profit health system is owned by physicians. The system purchases the tangible and intangible assets of physician practices and organizes physicians into clinics. Physicians are offered equity ownership in the system after several years. Alternatively, the health system may offer physicians an equity position in place of cash when securing practice assets.

Unlike other vertical integration models, hospitals generally are not involved in capitalizing or operating equity-based systems. Therefore, management philosophy is not influenced by inpatient occupancy rates, but instead on expanding investments in the higher-growth sectors, outpatient and ambulatory care. The health system generally contracts with hospitals to provide inpatient services.

As with the staff model, the health system negotiates with managed care payers and owns all contract revenues. The system also is free to directly invest in PCP salaries and practices to grow the PCP network. Furthermore, the system's clinical leaders can intervene in face-to-face meetings with physicians to influence practice patterns and productivity.

## SUSTAINABLE MODELS

We previously described the characteristics of health systems that will profit and grow under full-risk capitation. We next define the vertical integration models that meet these characteristics for success.

### Support of a single governance structure

A health system should have one controlling entity with a defined mission statement. Only the staff and equity models support a health system with a single governance structure (Table 1). The foundations model preserves many decision-making boards and CEOs, including one for the health system, one for each foundation, and one for every physician group. The same holds true for the MSO model.

For GPWW and PHO models, the health system and central administrations maintain separate governance boards. These boards have no clear authority over providers because physicians and hospitals maintain their revenue streams and practice autonomy.

### Strengthening of physicians' bond to system

Physician bonds are strongest when health systems maximize income, control revenues, and are owned and operated by physician peers. Health systems founded on the equity model meet all three objectives (Table 1). The for-profit and legal structures of the equity model allow physicians to maximize income through highly competitive salaries, bonuses, and equity positions. These physician-owned health systems purchase the tangible and intangible assets of physicians, thereby controlling all physician revenues.

The staff and foundation models also generate strong physician bonds by purchasing all physician assets, controlling the revenue stream, and paying highly competitive salaries and bonuses. However, the staff and foundation models' not-for-profit status prevents physicians from owning equity interest in the system. In addition, health systems based on these models are not exclusively owned by physicians—although clinic leaders generally are physicians. Under the foundation model, moreover, the physician group (not the health system) retains control over the distribution of salaries and bonuses. The group leaders may have competing interests to the health system, such as not desiring to maximize PCPs' income.

The MSO's legal structure does not allow health systems to deploy capital into physician salaries and practices. Therefore, MSO-based systems cannot offer the same competitive salaries as systems using the equity, staff, and foundation vertical integration strategies. Although physicians in an MSO relinquish some practice autonomy by selling their tangible assets, physicians retain ownership of patient revenues and managed care contracts. Consequently, the physician's bond to MSO-based systems is not strong.

Even weaker bonds exist between physicians and health systems using PHO and GPWW models. Legal structures do not allow these health systems to maximize physicians' incomes. This is because PHOs and GPWWs do not control physician revenues and, therefore, the IRS and Medicare do not consider physicians to be employees of the system. Consequently, PHOs and GPWWs cannot subsidize physicians' incomes. Physician bonds also are weak because these systems are not owned and operated by physicians; at least 50% of capitalization comes from hospitals.

### Generation of revenues for physician

Health systems need to generate a constant revenue stream to improve operational stability and growth opportunities. Over time, HMOs and other payers will direct their contracts to those systems providing quality, cost-efficient services (Table 1). As discussed below, the operational structures of equity and staff models provide the best opportunities for influencing physicians' practice-pattern efficiency, followed by foundation and MSO models. The structures of

**TABLE 1**

VERTICAL INTEGRATION MODELS FOR HEALTH SYSTEM FORMATION*

| Area of interest | Group practice without walls | Open physician-hospital organization | Closed physician-hospital organization | Management service organization | Foundation model | Staff model | Equity model |
|---|---|---|---|---|---|---|---|
| Operational stability | | | | | | | |
| Supports single governance structure | – | – | 0 | + | ++ | +++ | +++ |
| Strengthens physicians' bond to system | – | 0 | 0 | + | ++ | +++ | +++ |
| Generates revenues for physicians | 0 | 0 | + | ++ | ++ | +++ | +++ |
| Strong primary care physician base | | | | | | | |
| Commitment to own PCP network | – | – | 0 | + | ++ | +++ | +++ |
| Infuse capital for PCP network growth | – | – | – | – | ++ | +++ | +++ |
| Interests of PCPs in-line with system | – | – | + | + | + | +++ | +++ |
| Reduce administrative tasks | ++ | 0 | 0 | +++ | +++ | +++ | +++ |
| Efficient delivery of medical services | | | | | | | |
| Select efficient physicians | – | – | + | ++ | ++ | +++ | +++ |
| Retain efficient physicians | – | 0 | 0 | + | ++ | +++ | +++ |
| Proper PCP/specialist staffing levels | 0 | 0 | + | ++ | ++ | +++ | +++ |
| Geographic access to physicians | | | | | | | |
| Relocate physician practices | – | – | – | +++ | ++ | +++ | +++ |
| Expand system to meet demand | + | ++ | ++ | + | 0 | 0 | + |
| Model sustainable under full-risk capitation | – | 0 | + | + | ++ | +++ | +++ |

* Model effectiveness rating to allow health system profits under full-risk capitation:

+++ Extremely effective
++ Highly effective
+ Moderately effective
0 Slightly effective
– Not effective or not structurally possible with model

*Health systems need to generate a constant revenue stream to improve operational stability and growth opportunities.*

GPWW and PHO models provide little incentive for physicians to deliver efficient medical care.

## Commitment to own PCP network

Maintaining a select PCP network is essential for a health system's long-term sustainability. This means the system needs to purchase PCPs' tangible and intangible assets, pay highly competitive salaries, invest in practices, and improve PCPs' lifestyle by limiting practice hours and call schedules. The staff and equity models generally meet all criteria (Table 1).

However, the foundation model preserves physician group sovereignty, and the physician group retains control over the PCP network. Because the boards of foundations usually are dominated by specialists, physician group leaders may be reluctant to subsidize PCPs' incomes and capitalize the PCP network at the expense of specialists.

The remaining models do not buy all PCP practice assets. Therefore, capital cannot be directly invested in the PCP network. Moreover, the boards generally are specialist-heavy, and specialists will attempt to maintain income and prestige. This makes it politically difficult for health systems based on the GPWW, PHO, and MSO models to maintain an elite PCP network.

## Infusion of capital for PCP network growth

Health systems need to grow their PCP networks to succeed under full-risk capitation. The IRS and Medicare require that health systems purchase all physician assets before infusing capital into the PCP network. Systems based on foundation, staff, and equity models are exempt from inurement restrictions and fraud and abuse regulations (Table 1). Other models cannot legally invest in PCP network growth.

## Assurance that PCPs' interests are in-line with system

The principal interest of the health system under full-risk capitation is to deliver efficient medical care. Primary care physicians will have a similar interest when the system controls a significant percentage of PCPs' income, rewards PCPs for efficiency and productivity, and invests the necessary resources to develop and implement CQI programs. Health systems founded on the staff and equity models meet these objectives (Table 1). The systems control all PCP revenues and can pay PCPs up to a 20% performance bonus of base salary. Furthermore, because these systems own PCP networks, the systems are now free to direct capital investments toward the CQI program.

Foundations also control all physician revenues. However, leaders of the physician group may impede the health system's efforts to reward efficient PCP behavior. Moreover, leaders of the health system often cannot interact face-to-face with PCPs, but instead need to discuss PCP performance issues with the physician group's leaders. Investing in CQI programs is at the discretion of the physician group.

Health systems based on the MSO, PHO, and GPWW models do not control the majority of PCPs' revenues and cannot reward PCPs for good performance. Physicians retain ownership of contract revenues. Consequently, health systems have little control over PCPs' practice patterns, and PCPs have little interest in the system's efficiency objectives.

## Reduction of administrative tasks

Health systems need to reduce physicians' administrative burdens and allow physicians to devote more time to patient care. These actions increase productivity and lower fixed overhead costs because the system can hire or contract with fewer physicians to treat the same membership base. Physicians gain the added benefit of more flexible work and call schedules.

Table 1 illustrates that the GPWW, MSO, foundation, staff, and equity models are all effective in reducing physicians' administrative tasks. All have centralized administrations that can provide office support services, information systems, patient billings and collections, managed care contract marketing and negotiations, clinical support services, and supply purchasing. Health systems using the GPWW model usually do not provide clinical support services, such as utilization review and pattern-of-treatment monitoring systems.

On the other hand, PHO-based systems only establish provider service agreements that solidify terms for marketing and negotiating managed care contracts. Physicians continue to assume responsibility for other administrative functions.

### Selection of efficient physicians

Health systems need the ability to select physicians based on established efficiency and quality criteria. Otherwise, long-term sustainability will be jeopardized. Health systems based on staff and equity models typically hire physicians based both on established work-force policies and on explicit criteria that address physicians' structure, process, and outcomes of care (Table 1).

Likewise, health systems using MSO and foundation models often apply efficiency and quality selection criteria. MSOs evaluate individual physician's performance, while foundations target physician groups to purchase. However, the specialist-heavy boards of MSOs and foundations may not strictly enforce work-force selection policies, resulting in more specialists than are necessary.

The GPWW and open-PHO models invite all physicians to participate, regardless of the physician's efficiency and specialty. On the other hand, closed PHOs often have established efficiency criteria for membership. Once more, the specialist-heavy boards may not rigorously enforce work-force selection policies.

### Retention of efficient physicians

Efficient health systems invest the resources necessary to develop and implement CQI programs. These programs monitor physicians' practice patterns and provide physicians with the individualized feedback required to affect positive behavioral change. Systems based on foundation, staff, and equity models typically invest substantial capital to build CQI programs that fundamentally improve physicians' delivery of medical services in a nonadversarial manner (Table 1). Furthermore, clinical leaders of staff- and equity-based systems have the power to sanction or remove repeated nonperformers. Physician group leaders retain this power in foundation-based systems.

For MSO-based health systems, legal restrictions and regulations prohibit investing more in the CQI program than the system can expect to collect from physicians in administrative fees. The expense of CQI development and implementation often prevents MSOs from operating successful, ongoing programs. Most GPWW- and PHO-based systems are designed to market and negotiate managed care contracts, not to develop and operate effective CQI programs. Consequently, these systems will have difficulty identifying inefficient physicians and improving practice pattern efficiency.

### Maintenance of proper PCP/specialist staffing levels

The most sustainable health systems have work-force policies that hire or contract with between 120 and 130 FTE physicians per 100,000 members, 45% to 50% PCPs (and 50% to 55% specialists), and 20 to 25 FTE nonphysician providers per 100,000 members. The governance structure of staff- and equity-based health systems allows them to meet these hiring objectives. However, the specialist-heavy boards of foundations and MSOs often make the ideal PCP-to-specialist staffing levels politically impossible to achieve.

By definition, GPWWs and open PHOs are open to most physicians who want to join. Most often, the proper PCP-to-specialist mix is not realized, and the mix typically is 35% PCPs and 65% specialists. Staffing levels in closed PHOs are somewhat better, but generally the physician mix remains heavily weighted toward specialists.

### Relocation of physician practices

Health systems need to retain control over physicians' practice locations to ensure optimal access to care and reduce practice overhead costs. Physicians in systems based on the MSO, foundation, staff, and equity models can be asked to relocate or consolidate practices (Table 1). The system maintains this authority for MSO-, staff- and equity-based systems, while physician group leaders retain oversight of practice locations for foundation-based systems. Physician group leaders may impede efforts to optimize access to care.

For PHOs and GPWWs, physicians have control over their practice locations.

### Expansion of system to meet demand

Health systems need the ability to quickly add physicians as HMOs and other payers direct new managed care contracts to the systems. The PHO-based systems can expand most rapidly because the health system does not need to negotiate for either tangible or intangible practice assets. Moreover, a mission statement of PHOs is to expand the system through new managed care contracts.

The GWPP-based systems also have the ability to rapidly expand. However, their charge is not to plot system growth, but to form and operate a central administration that reduces physicians' practice overhead costs. System growth generally is not a declared mission statement.

Health systems based on foundation and staff models—generally, not-for-profit organizations—have the slowest short-term growth potential. One cause of this is the need to negotiate to purchase all physician assets. These discussions generally take 3 months or longer. Another reason considers IRS tax and Medicare penalties associated with legal violations of inurement restrictions and fraud and abuse regulations. Physicians' tangible and intangible assets must be appraised and purchased at fair market value. Otherwise, the IRS will view the purchase as benefiting a private party, and Medicare will view the sell as a monetary exchange for referral purposes.

Systems based on MSO and equity models have moderate-to-good, short-term growth potential. Most MSOs must consider inurement restrictions and fraud and abuse regulations. However, because MSOs only purchase more easily appraised tangible assets, there are fewer legal complexities. This allows MSOs to add physicians more rapidly than either the foundation- or staff-based systems.

When purchasing physician assets, equity-based systems are not subject to the same restrictions and regulations as not-for-profit systems. Consequently, these systems are not required to purchase intangible assets at fair market value, and instead can pay a price the highest alternative bidder is willing to pay. This significantly reduces negotiating time and legal complications. Moreover, health systems can trade an equity position for intangible assets, making expansion relatively cheap as compared to foundation and staff models.

•  •  •

Health systems will profit and grow under full-risk capitation if their vertical integration strategy provides operational stability, a strong PCP base, efficient delivery of medical services, and geographic access to physicians. Staff- and equity-based systems best meet these characteristics for success. These health systems are operationally stable in that there is one governance structure and a defined mission statement. Moreover, physician bonds are strong because staff- and equity-based systems maximize physicians' income potential and control the revenue stream. Physicians are employed by both systems.

Staff- and equity-based systems also are committed to owning elite PCP networks. Both health systems pay PCPs highly competitive salaries, invest capital in the PCP network, and improve PCPs' lifestyle by limiting practice hours and call schedules. Furthermore, these systems are structured to deliver efficient medical services. They select physicians through established work-force policies and a detailed credentialing process. As well, these health systems invest the resources needed to implement CQI programs and can remove repeated nonperformers.

Foundations and MSOs usually preserve many decision-making boards and CEOs. Because the boards are specialist-heavy, physician group leaders may not have the same commitment (as health system leaders of staff and equity models) to build elite PCP networks and develop CQI programs. While foundations can capitalize such programs, legal restrictions and regulations prohibit MSOs from investing more in the PCP network and CQI program than the system can expect to collect from physicians' administrative fees.

Moreover, the IRS and Medicare do not consider physicians to be employees of foundations and MSOs. For this reason, Medicare prevents foundation- and MSO-based systems from demanding that physician and hospital referrals remain inside the health system. Furthermore, physician group leaders (not health system leaders) retain the power to sanction and remove repeated nonperformers. These issues can impede progress toward improved health system efficiency.

Similar to foundations and MSOs, GPWW- and PHO-based systems support separate governance boards. However, GPWWs' and PHOs' boards have no real authority over providers because physicians and hospitals maintain their revenue streams and practice autonomy. In addition, most GPWWs and PHOs are developed to attract managed care contracts in the short term, and not to implement workforce policies or capital-intensive CQI programs. These systems are inefficient and their long-term sustainability is low.

Health systems based on equity, staff, and foundation vertical integration models will profit and grow under full-risk capitation. Systems founded on other models will not be sustainable in the long term, and either will be forced from the marketplace or will be reduced to becoming specialist-heavy subcontractors to successful, more efficient systems.

## REFERENCES

1. Group Health Association of America. *Patterns in*

*HMO Enrollment.* Washington, D.C.: GHAA Publications Department, June 1994.

2. Marion Merrell Dow/SMG Marketing Group. *Managed Care Digest: HMO Cost Analysis and Midyear Enrollment Update.* Kansas, Mo.: Marion Merrell Dow, December 1993.

3. Cave, D.G. "Incentives and Cost Containment in Primary Care Physician Reimbursement." *Benefits Quarterly* 3 (1993): 70–7.

4. Group Health Association of America. *HMO Industry Profile: 1988 Edition.* Washington, D.C.: GHHA of America Research and Analysis Department, 1988.

5. Group Health Association of America. *HMO Industry Profile: 1992 Edition.* Washington, D.C.: GHHA of America Research and Analysis Department, 1992.

6. Health Insurance Association of America. *Principal Methods of Reimbursing Physicians: Group Insurance.* Unpublished HIAA data (information obtained by phone conversation).

7. Hoy, E.W., Curtis, R.E., and Rice, T. "Change and Growth in Managed Care." *Health Affairs* 10, no. 4 (1991): 18–36.

8. Cave, D.G. "Analyzing the Content of Physicians' Medical Practices." *The Journal of Ambulatory Care Management* 17, no. 3 (1994): 15–36.

9. Weiner, J.P. "Forecasting the Effects of Health Reform on US Physician Workforce Requirements: Evidence From HMO Staffing Patterns." *Journal of the American Medical Association* 272, no. 3 (1994): 222–30.

10. Friedman, E. "Changing the System: Implications for Physicians." *Journal of the American Medical Association* 269, no. 18 (1993): 2437–42.

11. American Medical Association. *Physician Characteristics and Distribution in the United States.* Chicago, Ill.: AMA, 1993.

12. Group Health Association of America. *Number of Plans, Enrollees, and Percentage by Plan Characteristics, Year End 1992.* Washington, D.C.: GHAA Publications Department, 1993.

13. American Managed Care and Review Association. *Managed Healthcare Database.* Washington, D.C.: AMCRA Foundation, 1994.

14. Barnett, A.E., and Mayer, G.G. *Ambulatory Care Management and Practice.* Gaithersburg, Md.: Aspen Publishers, 1992.

15. The Governance Committee. *Vertical Integration Strategies for Physicians and Health Systems.* Washington, D.C.: The Advisory Board Company, 1993.

16. Shortell, S.M., et al. "Creating Organized Delivery Systems: The Barriers and Facilitators." *Hospitals and Health Services Administration* 38, no. 4 (1993): 447–66.

17. Bennis, W.G., et al. *The Planning of Change: Third Edition.* New York: Holt, Rinehart and Winston, 1976.

18. Greco, P.J., and Eisenberg, J.M. "Changing Physicians' Practices." *The New England Journal of Medicine* 329 (1993): 1271–3.

19. Cave, D.G. "Can Primary Care Physicians Really Contain Medical Care Costs?" *Compensation and Benefits Management,* 1994 (in press).

20. IRS Service Code Section 501(c)(3). *The Complete Internal Revenue Code: 1993 Edition.* Internal Revenue Service. New York, New York; 1993: 2320.

21. Department of Health and Human Services Medicare and Medicaid Guide, Paragraph 13,923 (prohibition against certain physician ownership and referral). *Medicare and Medicaid Guide: Fraud and Abuse.* Chicago, Ill.: Commerce Clearing House, 1994.

22. American Medical Association. *Physician Marketplace Statistics 1992.* Chicago, Ill.: AMA, 1992.

23. Epstein, A.M., Begg, C.B., and McNeil, B.J. "The Use of Ambulatory Testing in Prepaid and Fee-for-Service Group Practices: Relation to Perceived Profitability." *The New England Journal of Medicine* 314 (1986): 1089–94.

24. Luft, H.S. "How Do Health Maintenance Organizations Achieve Their Savings?" *The New England Journal of Medicine* 298 (1978): 1336–62.

25. Martin, A.R., et al. "A Trial of Two Strategies to Modify the Test-Ordering Behavior of Medical Residents." *The New England Journal of Medicine* 303 (1980): 1330–6.

26. Cave, D.G., and Geehr, E.C. "Analyzing Patterns-of-Treatment Data to Provide Feedback to Physicians." *Medical Interface* 7, no. 7 (1994): 117–28.

27. The Physician's Advisory. *Percentage of Practice Time Spent in Various Activities.* Washington, D.C.: The Advisory Board, 1992.

28. Cave, D.G. "Managed Care Network Quality: Employer Action Plans." *Compensation and Benefits Management* 9, no. 1 (1992): 1–8.

29. Cave, D.G. "Profiling Physician Practice Patterns Using Diagnostic Episode Clusters." *Medical Care,* 1994 (in press).

30. Cave, D.G., and Abel, J.D. "Who Treats Medical Conditions More Cost Efficiently?" *Medical Interface* 1994 (in press): 136–42.

31. Cave, D.G. "Pattern-of-Treatment Differences Among Primary Care Physicians in Alternative Systems of Care." *Benefits Quarterly* 10, no. 3 (1994): 6–19.

32. Manning, W.G., et al. "A Controlled Trial of the Effect of a Prepaid Group Practice on Use of Services." *The New England Journal of Medicine* 310 (1984): 1505–10.

33. Greenfield, S.G., et al. "Variations in Resource Utilization Among Medical Specialists and Systems of Care: Results From the Medical Outcomes Study." *Journal of the American Medical Association* 267 (1993): 1624–30.

34. Luft, H.S. "Assessing the Evidence on HMO Performance." *Milbank Memorial Fund Quarterly* 58 (1980): 501–36.

35. Eisenberg, J.M., and Williams, S.V. "Cost Containment and Changing Physicians' Practice Behavior: Can the Fox Learn to Guard the Chicken Coop?" *Jour-*

*nal of the American Medical Association* 246 (1981): 2195–201.

36. Billi, J.E., et al. "The Effects of a Low-Cost Intervention Program on Hospital Costs." *Journal of General Internal Medicine* 7 (1992): 411–7.

37. Anderson, O.W., and Shields, M.C. "Quality Measurement and Control in Physician Decision Making: State of the Art." *Health Services Research* 17 (1982): 125–55.

38. Everett, G.D., et al. "Effect of Cost Education, Cost Audits, and Faculty Chart Review on the Use of Ambulatory Services." *Archives of Internal Medicine* 143 (1983): 942–4.

39. Winickoff, R.N., et al. "Improving Physician Performance Through Peer Comparison Feedback." *Medical Care* 22 (1984): 527–34.

40. Sanazaro, P.J. "Determining Physicians' Performance: Continuing Medical Education and Other Interacting Variables." *Evaluation of Health Professionals* 6 (1983): 197–210.

41. Fowkes, F.R., et al. "Implementation of Guidelines for the Use of Skull Radiographs in Patients with Head Injuries." *Lancet* 2 (1984): 795–6.

42. Audet, A.M., Greenfield, S., and Field, M. "Medical Practice Guidelines: Current Activities and Future Directions." *Annals of Internal Medicine* 113 (1990): 709–14.

43. Kosecoff, J., et al. "Effects of the National Institutes of Health Consensus Development Program on Physician Practice." *Journal of the American Medical Association* 258 (1987): 2708–13.

44. Greco, P.J., and Eisenberg, J.M. "Changing Physicians' Practices." *The New England Journal of Medicine* 329 (1993): 1271–4.

45. Steinwachs, D., et al. "A Comparison of the Requirements for Primary Care Physicians in HMOs with Projections Made by the Graduate Medical Education National Advisory Committee." *The New England Journal of Medicine* 314 (1986): 217–22.

46. Mulhausen, R., and McGee, J. "Physician Need: An Alternative Projection From a Study of Large, Prepaid Group Practices." *Journal of the American Medical Association* 261 (1989): 1930–4.

47. Kronick, R., et al. "The Marketplace in Health Care Reform: The Demographic Limitations of Managed Competition." *The New England Journal of Medicine* 328 (1993): 148–52.

48. Cave, D.G. "Making Health Reform Work: Managed Competition Can Succeed, Even in Rural Areas." *Business Insurance* 3 (1993): 19–20.

49. Group Health Association of America. *Survey of HMOs' Staffing*. Washington, D.C.: GHAA Publications Department, 1993.

50. Luft, H.S. "Health Maintenance Organizations and the Rationing of Medical Care." *Milbank Memorial Fund Quarterly* 60, no. 2 (1982): 268–306.

51. Cave, D.G. "Improving Efficiency in the Health Plan Market." *Benefits Quarterly* 5, no. 2 (1989): 63–71.

52. Wennberg, J.E., et al. "Finding Equilibrium in U.S. Physician Supply." *Health Affairs* 12, no. 2 (1993): 89–103.

53. Miller, R.H., and Luft, H.S. "Managed Care Plan Performance Since 1980: A Literature Analysis." *Journal of the American Medical Association* 271 (1994): 1512–9.

54. American Osteopathic Association. *Osteopathic Physician Distribution*. Chicago, Ill.: AOA, 1993.

55. Clawson, D.K., and Osterweis, M. *The Role of Physician Assistants and Nurse Practitioners in Primary Care*. Washington, D.C.: Association of Academic Health Centers, 1993.

56. Bureau of Health Professionals. *Eighth Report to the President and Congress on the Status of Health Professionals in the U.S. Department of Health and Human Services*. DHHS publication HRS-POD-92-1. Washington, D.C.: Government Printing Office, 1992.

57. Weiner, J.P., Steinwachs, D.M., and Williamson, J.W. "Nurse Practitioners and Physician Assistant Practices in Three HMOs: Implications for Future US Health Manpower Needs." *American Journal of Public Health* 76 (1986): 507–11.

58. Cave, D.G., and Tucker, L.J. "Ten Facts About Point-of-Service Plans." *HRMagazine* 36, no. 9 (1991): 54–61.

59. Cave, D.G., and Moskowitz, M.N. "Is There a Doctor in the House?" *Business and Health* 9, no. 11 (1991): 86–94.

60. Griffin, R.B., "PHOs: The Past or the Future of Physician Alliance Strategies." *Health Care Strategic Management* 11, no. 12 (1993): 20–4.

# Physician–hospital networking: Avoiding a shotgun wedding

Charles Harris,
Lanis L. Hicks,
and
Bruce J. Kelly

*The erosion of the traditional market is forcing hospitals and physicians to reevaluate their historical relationships. One method for addressing the potential conflicts created by current pressures is the formation of physician–hospital networks. These entities are formed and function on the basis of mutual interests and responsiveness to change.*

*Health Care Manage Rev*, 1992, 17(4), 17–28
© 1992 Aspen Publishers, Inc.

**Traditional health care providers** are seeing their historical market erode as health care costs rise, regulations increase, technologies proliferate, patient expectations change, competition increases, managed care expands, and additional providers emerge. As the health services market continues to consolidate, individual and institutional practitioners will intensify their efforts to maintain their own financial viability. One potential response to such market pressures is the development of physician–hospital networks, which integrate hospital and physician interests.

The purpose of this article is fourfold:

1. to describe the historical structure of the relationship between physicians and hospitals and examine the major changes in the environment affecting this relationship, thus motivating change;
2. to describe the networking concept;
3. to present a step-by-step model for implementing such a network system; and
4. to discuss the potential benefits and pitfalls of such a system and provide illustrations of the actual implementation of networking systems.

## RELATIONSHIP BETWEEN PHYSICIAN AND HOSPITAL

### Historical relationship

During the years of relatively unlimited resources, physicians and hospitals developed a unique, symbiotic relationship that maximized the independence and autonomy of the physician. This professional autonomy was reinforced by a fragmented financing system, which ignored the interrelatedness of the interactions between physicians and hospitals in the treatment of the patient by paying physicians on a fee-for-service basis and hospitals on the basis of costs incurred.[1]

Because physicians controlled admissions to hospitals, they tended to be viewed as the buyer of hospital

***Charles Harris,*** *Ph.D., is President of Union Hospital in Elkton, Maryland. He has seven years' experience as a hospital chief executive officer and has held positions in academic programs and regulatory agencies.*

***Lanis L. Hicks,*** *Ph.D., is Associate Professor with Health Services Management in the School of Medicine at the University of Missouri—Columbia and is a medical economist.*

***Bruce J. Kelly,*** *C.M.C., is President of Kelly and Associates, a consulting firm that specializes in planning and implementing physician networks, preparing medical staff development plans, and conducting strategic planning and recruiting.*

services. Thus, the hospital focused on activities to encourage physicians to select its facility. In general, these activities were designed to increase demand for the hospital's services by decreasing the cost to the physician of using the services of the facility, without regard to the overall effect on hospital efficiency and costs.

The role of the physician as buyer, however, deviated from the conventional buyer–seller market. In most transactions, the buyer assumes responsibility for the product once the purchase occurs. In selling hospital services, however, the hospital retained much of the responsibility for the product purchased (patient care) after the sale was made.[2] This joint responsibility increased the autonomy of the physician by providing increased free time and resources the physician could use to pursue other activities. Hospitals assumed this role to facilitate the physician–patient relationship and increase the sale of their services because the costs incurred in such activities could be fully recovered.[3,4]

To facilitate the transactions between buyers (physicians) and sellers (hospitals), physicians organized into medical staffs. The medical staff entity served not only to establish clinical policies and procedures for the organization, but also to increase negotiating power and decrease physicians' costs associated with the transactions. The medical staffs provided a mechanism for minimizing the costs of performing the activities required by hospitals (quality assurance, utilization review, credentialing) for the privilege of being on staff and for maximizing the benefits of acquiring hospital privileges (increased referrals, access to expensive technologies, peer review, consultations, quality assurance). As long as the medical staff represented relatively homogeneous physicians and hospitals faced a single buyer, such a cooperative arrangement could be effective.[5] The current environment, however, places unprecedented stress on this physician–hospital relationship.

### Changing environmental pressures

Although physicians still control admissions to hospitals, they possess far less autonomy in the decision than previously. In the current buyer–seller market, physicians are no longer perceived as the single buyer of hospital services. Hospitals must now satisfy the demands of employer groups, organized health plans, third party payors, and the government. These competing demands must also be met under conditions of restrained resources, further altering the relationship between physicians and hospitals. Under prospective

payment, hospitals are no longer able to use unlimited resources to meet the desires of physicians, but now are asking physicians to justify their requests for hospital resources and increasingly monitoring physicians' decisions in providing patient care because the hospital has assumed the financial risk of these decisions.[6–9] This reduction in physician independence and autonomy is placing increasing stress on the physician–hospital relationship.

In addition to the internal demands being placed on a hospital's medical staff, hospitals are engaging in more and more activities that compete directly with physicians for patients. In turn, physicians are providing more and more services that were once reserved for hospital inpatient services. One of the major contributors to this movement from inpatient care to outpatient care has been the introduction of technologies decreasing the invasiveness of the procedures performed, allowing treatment to be performed safely on an outpatient basis.[10] As hospitals have watched their inpatient base erode, they have increasingly shifted their activities to organized outpatient departments, clinics, and satellite offices to maintain their financial viability. Such actions broadening the scope of services provided by hospitals, however, have placed them in direct competition with their own medical staff for patients.[11,12] This increasing competition for patients has placed considerable stress on traditional physician–hospital relationships.

Another factor intensifying the potential conflict between hospitals and physicians is the increasing specialization of medicine. As scientific knowledge grows and medical technologies proliferate, physicians increasingly specialize in a narrower area to master available knowledge. This specialization requires larger and larger population bases to generate sufficient cases for the provider, decreasing the ability of rural hospitals to provide the service. Also, each specialty has its own technology, which further increases the complexity of interactions and relationships and decreases the ability of rural hospitals to generate sufficient revenue to finance the specialized technology. In large organizations, specialization, therefore, decreases the homogeneity of the needs and desires of the medical staff, decreasing the ability of the organization to fulfill its traditional responsibilities to its members.[2] This internal conflict increases the costs (time, energy, emotions) to the physician and decreases the potential benefits (referrals, equipment, personnel) available to meet the desires of an individual physician or specialty group. The physicians must now compete with each other for the limited resources available in the hospital. This internal conflict again erodes the historical physician–hospital relationship.

Also affecting the independence and autonomy of physicians and hospitals has been the growth of organized health plans—health maintenance organizations, preferred provider organizations, and large multispecialty groups.[13] These organized health plans are placing increasing pressures on hospitals to be cost efficient through selective contracting with specific institutions for the services required by all their members. A dominant criterion for the selection of a given hospital is the total price of services offered by the institution. To be competitive, hospitals are being forced to control the use of their resources by physicians. Physicians are no longer insulated from the cost consequences of their clinical decisions, and the historical separation of administrative and clinical decision making and control is being eliminated.[14,15] With increasing frequency, the clinical decisions of the medical staff are being scrutinized as to their impact on the operating efficiency and cost effectiveness of the hospital as hospitals increasingly assume the financial responsibility and burden of the decisions. To maintain a flow of patients to their institutions, hospitals must increasingly demonstrate beneficial and cost-effective services to a number of different buyers. Given all these potentially disruptive factors, it is increasingly important that hospitals and physicians develop mutually beneficial relationships.

## CONCEPT OF PHYSICIAN–HOSPITAL NETWORKS

In the current turbulent environment, an increasing number of hospitals seem to be creating new types of physician–hospital structures, alongside their traditional medical staff organization, to provide vehicles for business planning and development. One of the more recent vehicles designed to maintain and increase a flow of patients to a hospital is the physician–

*An increasing number of hospitals seem to be creating new types of physician–hospital structures, alongside their traditional medical staff organization, to provide vehicles for business planning and development.*

hospital network. Networks are formed and function on the basis of mutual interests and responsiveness to change.

The concept of a physician–hospital network is one of linking patient entry points to the health delivery system to form an integrated continuum of services for the patient. The entry points to the wide spectrum of health services now available are undergoing vast change as a result of reimbursement changes, new technology, competition, and consumer education. As these entry points change, so do physician referral patterns to access the various services. It is this change in referral patterns that affects the flow of patients to the hospital. Therefore, these referral patterns must be managed to ensure an individual hospital's ability to survive. The purpose of an effective network is to manage these referral patterns on the basis of community need, institutional capability, and a sound understanding of the interests of physicians.

Networks are a direct outgrowth of recent experiences with the more formal joint venture responses to the sweeping changes occurring in the health care environment. Examples of joint venture activities can be found in such structures as the MeSH model[1] and PHOs.[13,16] Joint ventures are formal, legal entities created to meet the mutual needs of hospitals and physicians. During the past few years, many authors[17–21] have carefully outlined the business and legal considerations for hospital administrators and physicians to consider in forming joint ventures. Consequently, these facets will not be presented in detail in this article, although it must be emphasized that numerous business and legal problems may arise that must be addressed in implementing collaborative arrangements. Networks, on the other hand, may or may not lead to a formal joint venture. The benefits of using a prudent business approach and reviewing legal constraints, however, will provide valuable input into operating within a network.

Conceptually, networks do not differ significantly from the MeSH or PHO mode of creating organizations for the mutual benefit of physicians and hospitals. Groups may choose to use one of these formal structures to carry out their plans. A distinction of networks, however, is that they allow hospitals and physicians more flexibility because they involve less formal and less legally binding structures for accomplishing these mutual benefits. Basically, networks may be thought of as distribution systems that focus on managing patient entry points to the health care delivery system and physician referrals of patients within the system. If it is in the mutual interest of physicians and a hospital in a network to own real assets or equipment jointly, an appropriate form of joint venture might be used. It is not necessary, however, to establish a separate formal entity to start and operate a successful network.

The real function of a network is to create mutually beneficial linkages between hospitals and physicians on the basis of referral patterns. The fundamental activity of hospitals and physicians is serving and treating patients. Networks keep this basic fact in mind as they evaluate how competition, reimbursement, and other factors influence the access of patients and their referral to and through the system. Although the establishment of joint ventures without focusing on patient referrals and entry points to the system may entail legitimate business objectives, such as spreading risk or increasing access to capital, by using access and referral patterns as the basis for analyzing and planning the activities of the network, hospitals can ensure a unique understanding of the real interests of their medical staff.

---

**Network Formation Steps**

*Stage setting*
- Trust built
- Common vision created
- Values clarified
- Specific interests identified

*Incentives*
- Interdependence established
- Economic effects of interdependence demonstrated

*Data analysis*
- Market assessment
  —medical staff profile
  —patient origin
  —market research into consumer preferences
  —competitor profiles
  —analysis of entry points
- Organizational assessment

*Network structuring*
- Hub sites selected
- Core groups identified
- Hospital support and plans coordinated

*Network management*
- Tracking techniques
- Communication and problem solving
- Management support to hubs and core groups
- Information systems

---

## STEP-BY-STEP MODEL FOR IMPLEMENTING A NETWORK

There are five basic steps to undertake in establishing a network (see the box entitled "Network Formation Steps"):

1. setting the stage for network development
2. creating appropriate incentives
3. analyzing data and reporting relevant information
4. developing the network structure
5. managing the network.

Each of these steps will be developed in the following discussion.

For simplicity, the discussion that follows focuses on a single-hospital network, albeit with several ambulatory hubs. The same principles apply when multiple institutions are involved, although networking becomes more complex with multiple medical staffs involved.

### Setting the stage for network development

Good communication is at the heart of all successful relationships. Hospitals need to get past the current environment of mistrust, confusion, and disintegration, which has been provoked by several years of intense change in the health care environment. This requires that hospitals begin the process of establishing a network with an analysis of the effectiveness of their communications and decision-making processes with their medical staff. Decision making is, perhaps, one of the biggest areas of complaints among physicians.[6,15,22–24] Physicians feel manipulated when decisions come as a surprise and frustrated when actions are not taken in accordance with agreements. Successful networks must be built on good communications and open, straightforward decision-making processes.

Whatever steps must be taken by the hospital to ensure that these basic requirements of a good working relationship are met should be undertaken before engaging in any serious network development plans. Network development will involve conflict, and this conflict must be resolved through tolerant and enduring problem solving conducted in an atmosphere of fair play and mutual trust.

The main steps in any decision include analysis and input, recommendation, evaluation, and, finally, decision making. One way to engender trust is to be very clear about what role each major group or individual will have in making decisions affecting the welfare of the participants. Is the role of physician groups and leaders to be one of providing input or making recommendations, or do they have decision-making responsibility? Much confusion, distrust, and conflict can be prevented by the simple process of initially clarifying roles and setting routine mechanisms for providing feedback on the status of projects and their implementation. Physicians, like everyone else, understand legitimate delays, but they become suspicious when information is not routinely provided about matters that affect them.

Thus, the first phase in network formation is a candid assessment of current trust levels and the effectiveness of communications among the potential participants. This assessment should be followed by whatever actions are identified during the assessment to establish an environment of openness and fair play. Patience is an important part of achieving such an environment. Organizational trust can be restored in a relatively short time, however, if administrators will demonstrate a nonjudgmental, nondefensive attitude while acting to remove barriers to good communications.[25]

Once there is a reasonably good environment in which to work, the most difficult activity must be undertaken: the act of shaping a vision and clarifying values. This act of creating a common vision is very difficult because of ambiguities, conflicting values, and even a built-in clash of styles between physicians and administrators.[2] Unfortunately, there is neither a shortcut nor a firm method for framing a clear vision and gaining agreement about values. Various works on strategic planning, however, do provide useful information about such a process.[26–36] The selection of participants in discussions about the organization's vision and values is critical. Clearly, key board leaders, top administrators, and formal medical staff leaders should be involved. In addition, some thought should be given to emerging physician leaders and key physicians from the services that the hospital believes are important to its future.

The importance of having a vision explicitly stated and then gaining consensus about the vision is twofold. First, the very act of arriving at an agreement about the vision creates a powerful bond that can sustain a group through the conflicts inherent in the health care industry today. Second, a vision provides a direction, albeit general, that can guide groups through the incredible ambiguity of today's marketplace.

One of the important byproducts of discussions leading to a vision statement is the rather revealing lessons in self-interests. Administrators will learn much about what is most important to the medical staff and, likewise, should use this opportunity with physicians to be clear about the hospital's interests. The interests of physicians and the hospital, once understood and acknowledged, are a crucial piece of data for developing a network. In fact, the biggest challenge to successful network formation is to recognize where shared interests converge and provide opportunity for joint action. This knowledge can also be invaluable for gaining insight into areas of potential conflicts; perfect collaboration and uniformly easy agreement should not be expected. Namely, hospitals and physicians must learn that sometimes they may compete[2]: some specialists may not be able to secure sufficient referrals within one network to satisfy their professional and financial objectives and, therefore, participate in more than one network. Some physicians may find that their optimal self-interest involves performing certain diagnostic procedures in their own offices rather than supporting network resources. Small hospitals may find it more advantageous to develop certain specialty services rather than refer to network specialists. The foundation of trust, built by carefully shaping a vision and articulating interests, will allow parties to disagree without being disagreeable.

### Creating appropriate incentives

Conflicting incentives between physicians and hospitals have long been a tremendous obstacle to effective collaboration. Physicians' economic goals have depended, of course, on a fee-for-service payment system. In contrast, hospitals depend increasingly on fixed payments. Networks represent a very real opportunity to reduce the implications of this obstacle by focusing physicians' and hospitals' attention on their common interest in maintaining or increasing patient volume in a collaborative way. In the current constrained resource environment, it is in the physician's best interest to assist the hospital to operate efficiently because an inefficient hospital will be unable to continue to support product line improvements or grow in capacity and technologic capability. In turn, hospitals will not have as great a fear when unbundling services if they know network physicians will offset losses through increased volumes. In a managed care environment, in which both hospitals and physicians face discounting and other resource restrictions, networks can be a very effective means for both bargaining with third parties and seeking direct contracts with

*Before engaging in problem identification, however, it is important to provide education for physicians about key factors influencing their costs, volumes, payor mix, and relationships within particular referral patterns.*

employers. The ability to remove obstacles and further mutual interests begins when trust levels have arrived at the point where physicians and hospitals can engage in detailed discussions about the individual physician's style of practice and its impact on the hospital, as well as what impact the hospital's operating procedures have on the individual physician. In developing the network, the mutual benefits of such an endeavor must be emphasized to generate interest in participation. The type of network advocated here can enable both hospital and physician to capture more mutual market share.

### Analyzing data and reporting relevant information

The third phase of network development is fairly straightforward problem and opportunity identification. Before engaging in problem identification, however, it is important to provide education for physicians about key factors influencing their costs, volumes, payor mix, and relationships within particular referral patterns. Physicians usually welcome these kinds of data if they are summarized and presented carefully, because their training is in the area of specific information concerning cause and effect. For example, it is much more effective to show real data on serious losses from the indiscriminate use of ancillary services within a particular diagnosis related group than to exhort the staff to make prudent use of ancillary services. Along the same line, it is usually a stronger message to show a surgeon who is not providing referring physicians prompt information the difference in referral volumes from what one would normally expect in a surgical practice.

The point here is to summarize good information that illustrates what efficient, effective behavior on the part of both physicians and hospitals means to success, as well as to show clearly how there is an inextricable relationship with success on the part of both groups. The information necessary to design a net-

work can be divided into three main areas: market, medical staff profile, and organizational assessment.

The market data required for network planning are not markedly different from the kind of information most hospitals have been collecting and analyzing in recent years. They include the hospital's market share by major service or product line; results of patient origin studies and community attitude surveys; profiles of competitors; demographic trends; and other relevant data that yield as complete an understanding of the market and its makeup as possible.

The one unique analysis in this market category is an analysis of entry points. The hospital should attempt to show where and how patients enter the system in the primary and secondary service area. For example, in many areas, there are distinctive patient self-referral patterns for certain services (e.g., mammograms). In addition, there may be settings in which internal medicine groups act as much like primary physicians as do family practitioners. These unique patterns of patient entry points into the health care service delivery system must be well understood before undertaking the development of a network.

Medical staff profiles should provide information on the age and specialty of the staff as well as include estimates of productivity on the basis of admitting and procedure volumes. Hospitals should meet with their subspecialists to explore referral sources and factors influencing specialty referrals. Some comparison should be made of the overall medical staff's number and mix relative to the market demand. One result of this comparison should be an initial estimate of the need for additional physicians. Finally, a map showing the location of all physicians' offices should be prepared.

Organizational assessment is necessary to measure the effectiveness of the communications mentioned earlier and gain insight into the hospital's capacity to manage change and be responsive to the network partners. This assessment is especially critical because change is difficult for complex organizations like hospitals. If the organization does not have a history of planning and executing change and has, instead, actively sought stability in its operations and functioning, the focus should be placed on acquiring these transitional skills. The rationale is that effective networks can have dramatic effects on volume and medical staff makeup, and they may present opportunities that require prompt and organized responses.

Perhaps it is obvious, but the issue of who is selected from among the medical staff to participate in the review of the data and in the actual network development is not only sensitive, but also crucial. Although there are no hard and fast principles to be applied in making this choice, certain things may prove helpful.

First, it is wise to present to the entire medical staff the hospital's strategic direction and convey to them that one of the hospital's major goals is to take a systematic approach, conducted in collaboration with the medical staff, to maintaining and increasing patient volumes for both the hospital and its medical staff. Second, the initial group of physicians selected to participate in the planning activities should be from the recognized, formal leadership of the medical staff, as was mentioned earlier. The group, however, must be small in number and should also include those physicians who (1) are particularly heavy users of the institution, (2) have longstanding ties with the institution, (3) tend to think organizationally, and (4) have demonstrated a willingness to engage in cooperative activities. It is much easier to add physicians to the initial group as plans become clearer than to remove participants or work around them through ad hoc groups.

The real work of network design begins by drawing a picture, as it were, of the existing distribution system and identifying its effectiveness in bringing patients to the hospital and its core physician staff. From this work will come an understanding of where the primary care hub should be located and how much must be done to develop specialty capabilities to maximize referrals.

### Developing the network structure

The network structure is founded on an understanding, as well as serving the interests, of primary care physicians and other providers involved in key entry points to the health care delivery system. One of the basic building blocks of a network, therefore, is the hub, where *hubs* are concentrations of primary care physicians located in strategically important locations throughout a service area. In service areas encompassing a large geographic area, hubs may, in turn, operate satellites in sites not warranting the placement of full-time physicians.

Hubs may be owned and operated by their physician-owners, owned by a partnership of a sponsoring hospital and physicians, or owned by the hospital itself. The ownership of the hub is based on the answer to the question of what arrangement will ensure the most efficient operation of the network (see Figure 1).

In the case of already existing practices, the network needs to be able to show how its existence will benefit the primary care physicians. In general, there are two basic areas of benefit a network can bring to a primary care practice. First, one of the major concerns for primary care physicians is referring a patient to a specialist and not getting feedback or information helpful to managing the case. Even worse are those instances in which the patient is "stolen" by the specialist.[37-43] A basic benefit, therefore, is that the network can provide a structure for no-risk referrals. Because the network operates to benefit all parties, it can establish strict ground rules for receiving and handling referrals. These rules can include protocols for timely feedback and prompt return of the patient to the referring physician.

The second benefit offered by a network to a hub is practice support. The menu of support service can be as extensive as the hospital is capable of providing. At a minimum, the network can provide the physician support in the areas of insurance billing, personnel management, marketing, general management, and continuing medical education.

The other basic building block of the network structure is the core physicians. These core physicians are specialists who typically depend heavily on the services of a hospital to carry out their work. The composition of the core group or groups should reflect the area of clinical strength in the hospital.

Besides establishing trust as a result of respecting referring physicians' interests, core physicians should be assisted in analyzing each referral source to determine the practice styles of referring physicians. In short, specialists must come to know referring physicians and act on this information to serve the referring physicians better. This should, in turn, positively affect the practice of the specialists. One way of achieving this hub–core interaction is to establish a schedule of periodic visits by the specialists to the hub physicians. Another way is for the specialists to be involved in teaching the referring physicians new procedures or helping them acquire other necessary skills.

Core physicians can realize benefits from this approach in immediate ways. This kind of coordinated interaction guarantees a stronger referral base and creates a strong bond among primary care physicians, specialists, and the sponsoring hospital.

### Managing the network

As a result of clarifying values, selecting product lines or specialty services, and identifying potential hubs and referring physicians' interests, the basic features of the network should become clear to those de-

**FIGURE 1**

THE NETWORK CONCEPT ILLUSTRATED

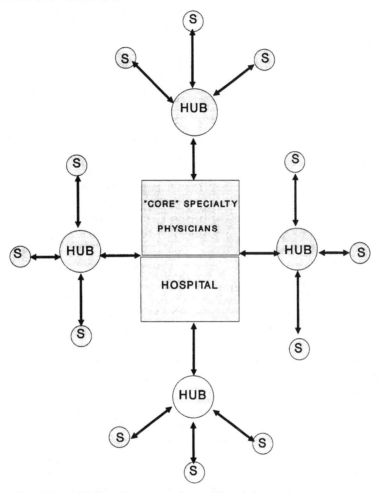

S = Satellite    HUB = Primary Care Physicians

signing it. Actually, creating the network and implementing it should be relatively straightforward. Appropriate legal structures can be selected if the network requires them for joint ownership of assets or for ongoing governance.

In addition to setting out specific implementation activities, there are the tasks associated with ongoing network management. Managing an emerging network is a full-time job. Ideal managers for the network include individuals with medical practice management backgrounds because these individuals already have a good working knowledge of priority concerns of physicians.

The daily flow of information across the network and periodic monitoring of patient flow are, perhaps, the most important ongoing responsibilities of the network manager. The network manager must also place strong emphasis on effective communications. Basically, there are five areas that require management attention as a network is established and operated.

First, management support must be provided to each hub to ensure that the new relationships, which have been created by the network, are functioning in the best interests of all parties. This means familiarizing office personnel with tracking techniques and or-

---

**Management Support Services**

*Recruitment services*
*Financial planning for office practices*
*Personnel support*
- Salary surveys
- Personnel policies and practices
- Contract office staff
- Education for office staff

*Marketing services*
*Administrative services*
- Coding
- Billing systems
- Negotiating for legal and accounting services
- Business planning
- Information systems

*Support services*
- Janitorial and maintenance
- Billing

---

dering patterns and ensuring that there is routine personal contact between hub staff and core staff.

Second, gathering information and acting as a liaison between hubs and the hospital and its core staff will ensure that the hospital takes a genuine service orientation to each hub. This may involve the network in ordering supplies, arranging for equipment, or scheduling hub patients. The continuous feedback across the network will ensure that sustainable working relations are formed.

Third, to the extent that hubs or core specialty practices require management support, the network should provide it. (See the box entitled, "Management Support Services.") In addition, the network should conduct practice management assessments to ensure that sound management is a uniform feature within the network.

Fourth, information systems need to be installed throughout the network to capture information that allows the tracking of individual patients throughout

---

*Typically, networks produce significantly improved problem-solving abilities between hospitals and physicians, provide for program enhancement and new services development, and facilitate physician recruitment and increased referrals.*

---

the entire health care delivery system. This system needs to have the capability of providing feedback to all participants in a timely manner.

Finally, as the network is formed medical staff development will quickly become a priority. So, management attention to the potential for rapid growth of the medical staff is necessary. Referrals should be analyzed for the number of cases generated for each core specialty, and projections should be made for new physician specialists. It is helpful to have a development plan for at least three years into the future. This will prevent crisis recruitment. Instead, recruitment is best done within an agreed on plan that incorporates new physicians with specific attributes into the network. Agreement by all parties to this plan will add strength to relationships between both hub physicians and core specialists.

Personal contact is the only way to really develop sound linkages. Careful scheduling of visits to hubs and the core hospital, for both business and educational purposes, is a key management function.

## RESULTS

Typically, networks produce significantly improved problem-solving abilities between hospitals and physicians, provide for program enhancement and new services development, and facilitate physician recruitment and increased referrals. Taken together, these results mean improved hospital performance.

The following is an illustration of one case in which a network was developed that improved the problem-solving performance of the entities involved. In this instance, a hospital's strategic plan called for improving and adding to its cardiac care capability. Yet, after three years of effort by administration, the hospital had not progressed and was, in fact, losing market share in that area. The administration had not been able to coordinate the necessary cooperation among the independent physicians in the area. To achieve this objective, a network was formed that linked the primary care physicians, the specialists, and the hospital into a mutually beneficial entity. The potential benefits of such a program were identified and communicated to all potential participants. Protocols were established to ensure appropriate follow-ups and referrals back to the originating primary care physicians. Within two years of network formation, the hospital had established a full-service heart center, including open-heart surgery, angioplasty, cardiac catheterization, and cardiac rehabilitation. The first full year of the surgery program led to 205 open-heart cases with lower than national mortality rates. The overall impact for the hospital was approximately $9 million in new revenues. Additional revenue was also generated for both the specialists involved and the referring physicians through increased activity and better follow-up and referrals back to the originating physicians.

In another example, a network plan identified a serious need to add physician capability to meet the network's goals. Through collaborative efforts, a medical staff development plan was activated by the board, including clear policies about mutual responsibility for recruitment with the medical staff. Although the recruitment of physicians into a community can be achieved without a network, the philosophy inherent in a network increases the probability of success because of cooperation, coordination, and mutual support. In a two-year period, 22 physicians in six specialties were added to the staff, and these new physicians enjoyed the support of the existing physician community. In this case, the network was able to demonstrate the potential benefits to the existing physicians of greater referrals, increased local retention of patients, and greater collegial interactions and to potential recruits of a supportive, viable medical community.

The total effect of networking can be dramatic. Because of new service capability and related volumes, one network hospital experienced a $1,500 per day average charge net of price increases. In another situation, a hospital increased overall revenues by 50 percent in a three-year period. Of course, not all network plans have results of this magnitude. In every case in which networks have been successfully established, however, communities, through their hospital board and physicians, have worked together more effectively and have gained greater control over the forces of change.

The outcome of successfully bringing together the interests of primary care physicians, specialists, and the hospital is a coordinated system of access points and referral practices. How the network is used depends on local demands and circumstances. How the network performs is a matter of earning trust on a daily basis through open communications, fair play, and a respect for each party's interests. Networks are an important means for bringing hospitals, physicians, and communities together to take greater control of the significant changes occurring in health care.

## ILLUSTRATION OF A WORK PLAN

The following proposed work plan illustrates the specific steps that must be incorporated into the development and implementation of a network. These steps are designed to incorporate the input of hospital management, the medical staff, and other appropriate parties into a compatible plan.

1. Develop available patient origin and physician referral pattern data to show utilization of existing products and services on an inpatient and outpatient basis, as well as by physician, payor, ZIP code, and so forth.

2. Develop information on the present drawing areas, including trends within various identifiable sectors by type of patient, form of insurance coverage, referring physician, and geographic area.

3. Develop the role of current marketing efforts to determine function, influence on referral patterns, and types of services consumed and provided, as well as the perceived consumers' response to these efforts.

4. Develop demographic information for the hospital's immediate service area and surrounding areas, including
   - analysis of population trends and projections as well as statistics on income, employment, age, and households
   - analysis and projection of the working population in the area
   - analysis of residential construction activities in the area
   - review of the activities of other health care institutions and organizations in the area as related to marketing strategy and outreach programs, outreach clinics, networking, and so forth
   - identification of patient needs with an evaluation of their intensity and likelihood of being met by current plans
   - accumulation of information about specific opportunities, physician resources currently available in the area, and targeted outlying acute care facilities

5. Develop demographic information on the area physicians and their affiliations through the determination of geographic location, age, specialties, referral patterns to the hospital, etc., and compare those data with the demographic and patient origin data.

6. Develop a profile of area physicians by payor mix, productivity, and loyalty to hospital.

7. Identify areas that are either lacking in primary care coverage or do not have adequate primary care coverage, and determine the physician re-

cruiting requirements to staff those sites. Target physicians currently in practice who could be approached to join the network, both in the local area and the surrounding areas, with input from the hospital's representatives.

8. Determine the role of the hospital and the functioning of the current marketing efforts. Detail the manner in which products and services are to be provided in cooperation with the targeted network physicians. Vertical and horizontal integration should be defined at this time.

9. Determine those products and services that can be realistically provided through the network. Detail those services and programs that show the greatest potential for immediate return, and develop a strategy for their use. Also develop a long-term strategy to link more closely the hospital, targeted primary care physicians, specialists, and the appropriate health care providers into a more synergistic relationship.

10. Project the potential consumers' response to the products and services available and the manner in which such services should be initiated, marketed, and so forth.

11. Develop a list of the products and services that will be provided on the basis of present marketability as well as future marketability to physicians, patients, community consumers of preventive and educational programs and services, and other identified groups.

12. Develop a sequential strategic marketing plan that delineates strategic considerations, assesses basic financial considerations, defines the network, identifies potential facilities for on-site specialty care, and specifies evaluation criteria. This marketing plan should include a
    - general listing of multispecialty ambulatory care centers, hub physicians, and primary care site locations;
    - projection of the products and services to be provided in each of the locations identified in the above listing;
    - projection of the physician requirements to provide the above products and services;
    - listing of physicians currently practicing in the targeted area;
    - listing of the differences between existing physicians and physician needs;
    - profiling of staff physicians by payor mix and productivity;
    - network map delineating the flow of patients through the network;
    - plan for marketing the hospital to the existing aligned and nonaligned physicians;
    - plan for marketing the hospital to new and nonaligned physicians; and
    - plan for marketing the hospital's network physicians to the people and employers in the area.

One of the most intriguing and yet dominant factors in the successful development of a network is the *absolute* necessity of matching the physician, both socio-economically and sociodemographically, with that population the network is targeted to serve. For example, a careful analysis of network results reveals that there is a median household income breakpoint of approximately $30,000 (±$5,000) as to whether the targeted population will access a family practitioner for routine care or for episodic care only. Above the $30,000 median household income breakpoint, one of us (B.J.K.) has found that the consumer is more inclined to select an internist, an obstetrician-gynecologist, and a pediatrician rather than a family practitioner for routine care. This targeted population is also much more likely to self-refer to orthopedists, otorhinolaryngologists, and related specialists. In developing a successful network, it is imperative to keep these points in mind.

## REFERENCES

1. Anderson, J.G. "The MeSH Model for Hospital–Physician Joint Ventures." *Health Matrix* 3, no. 1 (1985): 32–37.
2. Shortell, S.M. *Effective Hospital–Physician Relationships.* Ann Arbor, Mich.: Health Administrative Press Perspectives, 1991.
3. Bloomfield, R.D. "Hospital–Physician Relationships: A Changing Dynamic." *New York State Journal of Medicine* 88, no. 1 (1988): 5–6.
4. Goldsmith, J.C. "The Health Care Market: Can Hospitals Survive?" *Harvard Business Review* 58, no. 5 (1980): 100–12.
5. Burns, L.R., Andersen, R.M., and Shortell, S.M. "The Impact of Corporate Structures on Physician Inclusion and Participation." *Medical Care* 27, no. 10 (1989): 967–82.
6. Angell, M. "Cost Containment and the Physician." *Journal of the American Medical Association* 254, no. 9 (1985): 1203–7.
7. Kralewski, J.E., et al. "The Physician Rebellion." *New England Journal of Medicine* 316, no. 6 (1987): 339–42.

8. Shortell, S.M. "The Medical Staff of the Future: Replanting the Garden." *Frontiers of Health Services Management* 1, no. 3 (1985): 3–48.

9. Spivey, B.E. "The Relation between Hospital Management and Medical Staff under a Prospective-Payment System." *New England Journal of Medicine* 310, no. 15 (1984): 984–86.

10. Burchell, R.C., et al. "Physicians and the Organizational Evolution of Medicine." *Journal of the American Medical Association* 260, no. 6 (1988): 826–31.

11. Georgopoulos, B.S., D'Aunno, T.A., and Saavedra, R. "Hospital–Physician Relations under Hospital Prepayment." *Medical Care* 25, no. 8 (1987): 781–95.

12. Hughes, R.G., et al. "Hospitals and Physicians: An Organizational Model for a Changing Healthcare Environment." *Hospital and Health Services Administration* 29, no. 6 (1984): 7–20.

13. Kove, M., and Perry, B. "PHO's: Latest Product in the Health Care Supermarket." *Group Practice Journal* 37, no. 5 (1988): 26–32, 86–87.

14. Alexander, J.A., and Morrisey, M.A. "Hospital–Physician Integration and Hospital Costs." *Inquiry* 25, no. 3 (1988): 388–401.

15. Glandon, G.L., and Morrisey, M.A. "Redefining the Hospital–Physician Relationship under Prospective Payment." *Inquiry* 23, no. 2 (1986): 166–75.

16. Mick, S.S., and Conrad, D.A. "The Decision to Integrate Vertically in Health Care Organizations." *Journal of Hospital and Health Services Administration* 33 (1988): 354–60.

17. Bettner, M., and Collins, F. "Physicians and Administrators: Inducing Collaboration." *Hospital and Health Services Administration* 32, no. 2 (1987): 151–60.

18. Glusman, D.H., and Kepner, J.C.S. "Strategic Issues in Joint Ventures." *Medical Group Management* 35, no. 5 (1988): 18–25.

19. McDermott, S. "The New Hospital Challenge: Organizing and Managing Physician Organizations." *Health Care Management Review* 13, no. 1 (1988): 57–61.

20. Peters, G.R., and Carpenter, R.B. "Where to Venture Next?" *Healthcare Forum Journal* 32, no. 5 (1989): 32–35.

21. Wheeler, J.R.C., Wickizer, T.M., and Shortell, S.M. "Hospital–Physician Vertical Integration." *Hospital and Health Services Administration* 31, no. 2 (1986): 67–80.

22. Greifinger, R.B., and Bluestone, M.S. "Building Physician Alliances for Cost Containment." *Health Care Management Review* 11, no. 4 (1986): 63–72.

23. Smith, H.L., Reid, R.A., and Piland, N.F. "Managing Hospital–Physician Relations: A Strategy Scorecard." *Health Care Management Review* 15, no. 4 (1990): 23–33.

24. Zismer, D.K. "Hospital–Physician Alliances in an Evolving Marketplace." *Minnesota Medicine* 72 (1989): 661–63.

25. Fisher, R., and Ury, W. *Getting to Yes.* Boston, Mass.: Houghton Mifflin, 1981.

26. Drucker, P.F. *Managing for Results.* New York, N.Y.: Harper & Row, 1964.

27. Gronroos, C. "Service Quality Model and Its Marketing Implications." *European Journal of Marketing* 18, no. 4 (1984): 36–44.

28. Hayes, R.H. "Strategic Planning: Forward in Reverse?" *Harvard Business Review* 62, no. 6 (1985): 111–19.

29. Humble, J.W. *Management by Objectives in Action.* New York, N.Y.: McGraw-Hill, 1970.

30. Leemhuis, J.P. "Using Scenarios to Develop Strategies." *Long Range Planning Review* 18, no. 2 (1985): 30–37.

31. Linneman, R.E., and Klein, H.E. "Using Scenarios in Strategic Decisionmaking." *Business Horizons* 28, no. 1 (1985): 64–74.

32. MacStravic, R.S. "Hospital–Physician Relations: A Marketing Approach." *Health Care Management Review* 11, no. 3 (1986): 69–79.

33. McConkey, D.D. *Management by Objectives for Staff Managers.* New York, N.Y.: Vantage Press, 1973.

34. McConkey, D.D. *MBO for Nonprofit Organizations.* New York, N.Y.: AMACOM, 1975.

35. Muller, A. "Consumer Research and Strategic Planning for Hospitals." *Hospital and Health Services Administration* 28, no. 4 (1984): 21–29.

36. Thompson, G.B., and Pyhrr, P.A. "Zero-Based Budgeting: New Skill for Financial Managers." *Hospital Financial Management* 9, no. 3 (1979): 27–33.

37. Glenn, J.K., et al. "Continuity of Care in the Referral Process: Analysis of Family Practice." *Journal of Family Practice* 15, no. 4 (1983): 651–56.

38. Glenn, J.K., et al. "Physician Referrals in a Competitive Environment." *Journal of the American Medical Association* 258 (1987): 1920–23.

39. Hansen, J.P., et al. "Factors Related to Effective Referral and Consultation." *Journal of Family Practice* 15, no. 4 (1982): 651–56.

40. Harris, E.D., and Lieberman, J. "Art of Consultation and Referral." *Resident and Staff Physician* 30, no. 8 (1984): 55–60.

41. Henley, E.S. "Analysis of Referrals and Referral Rates." *Hospital and Health Services Administration* 30, no. 5 (1985): 120–129.

42. Hines, R.M., and Curry, D.J. "Consulting Process and Physician Satisfaction." *Canadian Medical Association Journal* 48 (1978): 1065–73.

43. Weiss, B.D., and Gardner, C.L. "Consultant Utilization by Family Physicians." *Journal of Family Practice* 24, no. 3 (1987): 283–85.

# Managing partnerships: The perspective of a rural hospital cooperative

Tim Size

*While a dairy cooperative provided the bylaws, managing a cooperative of rural hospitals has been a learn-as-you-go experience. This article presents the management principles that have been learned over the last 13 years. Its experience suggests that developing and managing partnerships requires behaviors different from those typically associated with the management of individual organizations.*

Cooperatives, alliances, coalitions, consortia, networks—there are a variety of names for health care providers seeking collaborative approaches to common challenges, developing partnerships. While cooperatives of health care providers by any name are becoming more common, not much is known about how they are most effectively managed. This article presents the experience of one rural hospital cooperative over the last 13 years.

While it is unlikely that something as complex as the development of even one multiorganizational partnership can be reduced to a single set of principles, the author believes that this article is a reasonable summary of what has worked for management of this cooperative. While not the focus of this article, the author's experience with developing partnerships between the cooperative and other associations, a university, and a state government leads him to believe that these principles do have a broader applicability. It is left to the readers to judge how applicable these ideas are to their work.

## THE RURAL WISCONSIN HOSPITAL COOPERATIVE

The purpose of the Rural Wisconsin Hospital Cooperative (RWHC) was and is to act as a catalyst for regional collaboration. Since its incorporation in 1979, it has tried to be an aggressive and creative force on behalf of rural health care. It has become nationally recognized as one of the country's earliest and more successful models for networking among rural hospitals. By actively sharing RWHC's experience and ideas, it has contributed to the implementation of similar efforts around the country. RWHC employs or contracts for the services of approximately 150 people (full- and part-time) and has an annual budget of close to $4 million, exclusive of affiliated corporations.

RWHC developed and provided the early administration of HMO of Wisconsin, one of the first rural-based health maintenance organizations (HMOs) in the country, currently with over 40,000 members and operating on a consistently profitable basis. It devel-

*Tim Size, B.S.E., M.B.A., has been the Executive Director of the Rural Wisconsin Hospital Cooperative since it was founded in 1979.*

Special thanks to Rural Wisconsin Hospital Cooperative hospitals and staff who continue after 13 years to teach the author about cooperative leadership and to the Robert Wood Johnson and W.K. Kellogg Foundations who have made significant investments in the development of the Rural Wisconsin Hospital Cooperative.

*Health Care Manage Rev*, 1993, 18(1), 31–41

oped and administered a trust for indemnity health and dental insurance, which saved members over $360,000 in its first year alone and continued until recently as a dual choice option for RWHC hospitals. With private investors and operators, the cooperative implemented a mobile computed tomography (CT) scanner and nuclear medicine services to rural hospitals, reducing cost and improving access to this service for RWHC members and other area hospitals. It has established a pilot loan guarantee program for RWHC hospitals in cooperation with the Robert Wood Johnson Foundation and the Wisconsin Health and Education Facilities Authority.

RWHC staff provides some services directly in areas such as advocacy, audiology, multihospital benchmarking (related to hospital-specific total quality improvement initiatives), grantsmanship, occupational therapy, physical therapy, physician credentialing and privileging, respiratory therapy, speech pathology, and ongoing rural-specific continuing education opportunities.

RWHC has negotiated special group contract arrangements for members to obtain high-quality consultant services in areas such as computer software services, legal services, personnel services, market research, patient discharge studies, and consultant pathologist services. A hybrid between the two approaches of hiring staff or contracting for services is the cooperative's regional program managed by RWHC staff to recruit and schedule physicians as independent contractors for the majority of RWHC hospital emergency departments.

A particularly productive and popular RWHC activity has been Professional Roundtables, which regularly bring together RWHC hospital staff of the same discipline for mutual sharing and problem solving, continuing education, and advising the RWHC board and staff on program and policy development. This has been recognized as one of the primary benefits of RWHC—learning from each other. The number of these roundtable groups that are active has significantly increased and now includes 22 professional or managerial groups (e.g., laboratory, pharmacy, radiology).

The cooperative began as the result of informal discussions among several hospital administrators in southern Wisconsin. The model of the dairy cooperative was chosen because it respected the autonomy of the sponsors and was a type of organization familiar to the community boards that would have to approve individual hospital participation. RWHC has been repeatedly studied as a national model for networking among rural providers, including several federal agencies: the Federal Office of Technology Assessment, the General Accounting Office, and the Secretary of Health and Human Services.

RWHC is governed by a board of directors consisting of one representative (usually the hospital administrator) from each RWHC hospital. Each RWHC hospital has one vote on the board of directors. While a consensus is usually sought, it is not required or always possible. The board meets monthly, except in relatively unusual situations in which the agenda is too light to justify a meeting. An executive committee is empowered to act on behalf of the board between regular meetings and performs the functions of planning and personnel committees. A finance committee is responsible for setting and evaluating financial goals and performance. Ad hoc committees are created as needed for specific time-limited functions. RWHC is now connected to the HMO of Wisconsin through an interlocking board of directors and informal staff liaisons.

RWHC hospitals have two distinct roles in decision making related to cooperative activities. As a director of RWHC, decisions are (usually) made from the perspective of what is best for the cooperative. As a hospital administrator, decisions about participation in a RWHC program are made from the hospital's individual perspective that includes the judgment of the hospital board, medical staff, and other local parties. Services provided to RWHC hospitals are based on written contracts between each participating hospital and RWHC. Apart from limitations within some of these contracts, RWHC hospitals are not required to buy services solely through RWHC.

## FRAMEWORK FOR DESCRIBING THE RWHC MANAGEMENT EXPERIENCE

This article makes the following assumptions:
- Significant management practices necessary for successful cooperatives are not commonly seen in traditional vertically organized institutions and systems.
- Most administrators have had little experience and even less training regarding leadership within the context of collaborative models.
- The "natural" administrative response will frequently come out of traditions that may be inconsistent with the actions needed to support networking.
- Cooperative development can look deceptively easy, but collaborative processes sometimes re-

quire more time up front than that needed in authoritarian models.

- Enlightened self-interest is necessary for organizations to work together.

The question of why consortia form was addressed by Zuckerman and D'Aunno[1] in a 1990 article on hospital alliances: "Organizations often cannot generate internally all of the necessary resources or functions; therefore, they enter into exchange relationships with other elements in the environment."[1(p.xix)] Providers, however, can choose among a number of alternatives, why networking? Zuckerman and D'Aunno[1] believe that the ability to maintain local autonomy while increasing their power as part of a group is a major attraction of consortia. While some work has been begun on developing a taxonomy for multihospital arrangements and collecting descriptive data about existing consortia, more work is needed in both these areas. Beyond that, those who work trying to develop and administer consortia are just beginning to learn what approaches are most effective.

James M. Carman, Director of the Graduate Program in Health Services Management at the University of California, Berkeley, has written a yet to be published paper on strategic alliances among rural hospitals and other providers that in part begins to address the issue of alliance management and governance. It is hoped that more of academe will begin to investigate and describe the administrative and leadership principles that are most consistent with the successful development of consortia.

Eisler[2] describes two basic models used throughout history for organizing human relationships: a dominator model emphasizing the vertical ranking of individuals and organizations and a partnership model emphasizing horizontal linkages. While both are ancient alternatives, the current development of practical partnership models in health care is still seen as innovative.

Cooperatives are abstractions, paper entities that are made up of other abstract corporate entities that are lifeless without the work of many people. The productivity of both local organizations and cooperatives are in large measure dependent upon meeting the needs of these individuals. Models of collaborative intraor-

ganizational relationships are a good source of models for interorganizational relationships as in both cases the outcome depends on the effective motivation of individuals.

DePree[3] offers a model for employer-to-employee relationships based on his experience that productivity is maximized by designing work to meet basic employee needs. His vision of the art of corporate leadership is bringing employees into the heart and soul of the organization. DePree's[3] experience is primarily within the world of the Fortune 500, but he provides a useful framework for nonprofit and public sectors. He describes eight fundamental interdependent conditions that workers need to have met within a company if the company is to be effective.[3] They are used here to organize the principles found or "invented" over the author's 13-year experience managing a rural hospital network.

Even though DePree is acknowledged as a strong and successful businessman, a cynical "real worlder" may dismiss him as a "dreamer," notwithstanding DePree's business success. Greenleaf[4] presents a pragmatic suggestion that may be helpful in thinking through the tension that DePree's principles can inspire. "For optimal performance, a large institution needs administration for order and consistency, and leadership so as to mitigate the effects of administration on initiative and creativity and to build team effort to give these qualities extraordinary encouragement."[4(p.60)] Kanter offers a similar vision of the future for corporate America: "The years ahead will be best of all for those who learn to balance dreams and discipline. The future will belong to those who embrace the potential of wider opportunities but recognize the realities of more constrained resources—and find new solutions that permit doing more with less."[5(p.18)]

## EIGHT FUNDAMENTAL PRINCIPLES FOR AN EFFECTIVE PARTNERSHIP

### Principle 1: There is mutual trust

Develop a relationship based primarily on mutual trust so that the cooperative is not limited to the minimum performance inherent in written agreements.

While responding to a rapidly changing market in 1984, the implementation in six months, "from scratch," of a rural-based HMO in Wisconsin was only possible due to the prior existence of a basic level of trust among the key actors. RWHC has been able to recruit and retain top talent in a relatively small non-

---

*Cooperatives are abstractions, paper entities that are made up of other abstract corporate entities that are lifeless without the work of many people.*

profit organization in large part by making the development of mutual trust a key part of its corporate culture. RWHC board and staff discussions are occasionally quite vigorous, but staff has a reputation that they can be trusted to implement the board's final decision.

RWHC's emergency department physician staffing program has worked well for a number of reasons that relate directly to the cooperative's commitment to developing mutual trust. The development of a network of physicians willing to work in this program and the development of an efficient central credentialing process are key components of the success of this program. Physicians, even resident physicians, know that they will be well treated by RWHC staff whether it be negotiating last minute schedule changes or recognizing birthdays. Hospitals have had faith in the ability of staff to develop a good system, cooperating with the need for more uniform credentialing forms and processes.

Contracts define minimum performance and penalties for failure; they are limited by yesterday's knowledge and vision. In contrast, mutual trust assumes the potential of limitless performance and visions not yet fully formed. These relationships fill deep needs, enable work to have meaning and to be fulfilling. True mutual trust, however, is risky because it requires individuals to depend on others, to be vulnerable to their performance.

Kanter characterizes in-house competition as usually counterproductive: "The minute people need anything at all from the efforts of others or share a future fate, cooperation has all the advantages."[5(pp.75–78)] However, she is quick to add that while cooperation inside a group is the path to greater productivity, competition leads to higher performance when it is among unrelated organizations. The understanding of who shares a common future or dependency clearly becomes a critical issue when trying to develop cooperative relationships.

Participants within a successful cooperative, sharing a common future, can develop a higher than average trust for each other, because a tradition of successfully working together has developed. Even in an era of uncertainty, participants trust that they can continue to be successful, together again overcoming barriers in a way that is mutually advantageous, accomplishing more together than they can separately. When it can be developed, mutual trust provides a security well beyond contracts and the limitations of numerous but necessarily finite contractual provisions.

Trust among multiple health care providers and other organizations is absolutely necessary to the timely implementation of significant new RWHC ventures. It is a fragile element between organizations, constantly in need of regeneration as key individuals and circumstances change. Initiatives that require the cooperation of many actors, whether individual or corporate, bog down if they require proof and underwriting every step along the way. Development of systems of any complexity requires collaboration, and collaboration requires trust.

Beyond legal contracts, there is a need to develop relationships based on a reasonable degree of trust that cooperative participants can do what is right if afforded the opportunity to do so. Relationships among multiple organizations are certainly equivalent in complexity to that found within any family; while many families rely on prior agreements regarding individual responsibilities and dispute resolution, this is not what makes a family work. It is the commitment to each other and shared goals that transcends rules held by a magnet to the refrigerator door.

These cooperative behaviors should be encouraged:

- Cooperative leaders and staff need to earn the trust of participants and then protect that reputation as the critical asset it is, both from real or perceived breaches.
- Work actively to build trust of the cooperative participants with each other.
- Recognize that earning trust takes time and has natural limits to how quickly it can be developed.
- Recognize that relationships within a cooperative do entail calculated risks and are more amorphous or messy than relationships built on control of one party over another.
- Be responsive to changing conditions and return whenever possible to the spirit rather than the letter of prior agreements.
- Periodically remind participants that the cooperative is not there to police or be responsible for their local, internal actions.
- When staff does not agree, or in the rare instance they cannot as a matter of professional judgment implement a cooperative direction, they need to say so.
- Without fanfare, admit all significant mistakes as soon as they are discovered.
- Implement with expediency all cooperative decisions or ask for timely reconsideration if new information surfaces.
- In general, treat all participant specific information as confidential unless already in the public domain.

These behaviors should be discouraged:

- Never undermine or appear to undermine local participant employer-employee relationships, however "right" you feel you are.
- Never launder participant or cooperative dirty linen in public or private.
- Never breach or permit the breach of confidentiality of any information given in confidence.
- Do not be quick to enforce your rights in a contract.

### Principle 2: Commitment makes sense

Participants may join a cooperative to explore its potential; they remain only if they perceive that they are receiving a good return on their investment of time and money.

RWHC started with a shared service mission to which advocacy was quickly added. The cooperative offers a broad array of shared services from which hospitals pick and choose according to their individual needs; on the other hand, support for the cooperative's rural advocacy role is relatively more consistent. Commitments have been made and continue to be made to the cooperative because they have been structured in a way that attempts to maximize the "fit" for each individual participant.

As health care reform gains momentum, the cooperative as a whole has been forming partnerships with other organizations and networks. A notable example is the development of an alternative regulatory model for its member hospitals. Through prior political initiatives, a consensus had developed in Wisconsin that an alternative provider type called Rural Medical Centers should be available for diversified rural hospitals. However, such reform demands significant state staff time to implement, and a state budget deficit had become an implementation barrier. In response, the state hospital association and RWHC developed an alternative funding strategy. A consortium application was developed for a Federal Rural Transition Grant with two thirds of the grant allocated for hospital-specific diversification projects and one third allocated as a subcontract to the state in order to help finance the necessary rule redrafting. The state hospital association and RWHC receive no money from the grant but receive assistance with one of their major policy initiatives. Each member of the consortium became committed to the collaboration because attention was paid to constructing a win-win scenario for each participant.

While it is not a new idea that most people want to do well and want to make a contribution, the recognition is less common that organizations can or should promote an environment where these commitments are willingly made. A fundamental choice for every cooperative is whether to try to build a network on subtle (or not so subtle) coercion or with participants given the opportunity to discover and develop their individual commitment. As this country's systems have become more complex, decisions are seen as more impersonal and less rational. Individuals and even individual communities have become in too many cases too small a portion of the larger picture for that larger picture to be seen by them as a coherent whole. Most people do not work for an abstraction, but for themselves and other people; the benefit must be made concrete.

Networks of rural hospitals that are on a scale that can be identified, known, and "touched" allow for individual participants to understand how their commitment can make sense. In an analogous manner, cities once made sense to their inhabitants when they were networks of neighborhoods or communities; cities do not makes sense and consequently do not work when they try or pretend to be a single community. It is the rare large, well-financed health care system that can match the supportive cooperative environment potentially available in the more modest scale of local cooperative with strong leadership.

These cooperative behaviors should be encouraged:

- Recognize that commitment to the cooperative will vary among participants, over time and across issues.
- Focus on the visionaries and that large middle group of participants that will go along with a good idea once its utility is reasonably shown.
- Structure a variety of opportunities for participants to discover and develop the particular set of commitments that makes the most sense for their unique situation.

These behaviors should be discouraged:

- Do not depend on past accomplishments to support future commitment; it must continuously be earned.
- Do not let the cooperative become impersonal as it grows; commitments are best understood face to face and tend to fail in the abstract.
- Listen to, but do not be preoccupied by the naysayers; they will always be with us.

### Principle 3: Participants needed

Each organization must know that it is needed for the success of the cooperative.

RWHC has benefited from a good deal of recognition within the "industry" but has tended to take a low profile with respect to local public relations. When RWHC staff or emergency department physicians work at a rural hospital they are providing patient services on behalf of the hospital, not on behalf of the cooperative; the success of RWHC is ultimately determined by the success of the participating hospitals. Staff intends to present every new program and each annual budget with the same energy and focus as if it was the first potential sale to a new client. It is considered by staff as a major mistake to ever take for granted the participation or commitment of any hospital. The RWHC communication budget is ample testimony to the RWHC belief in the importance of early and frequent communication and consultation. RWHC hospitals are involved in all stages of grantsmanship by staff beginning with idea generation and throughout the application and project implementation process.

---

*For health care providers in a network to be effective they must be given an unambiguous message that they are needed even while they are being asked to undertake significant change.*

---

Much of the need for hospital participation is obvious and reflects the ongoing challenge to have group participation large enough to justify joint action. RWHC is developing a Wisconsin franchise for the Iowa-based Patient Care Expert System (a computer-based resource for clinical nursing information and individualized planning of care). By individual hospitals making the effort to move forward together, multiple benefits are obtained: a group discount, local training sites, focused input into subsequent software modifications, and franchise revenue from sales to non-RWHC hospitals. Even more to the point, this major innovation is not currently available to individual rural hospitals. This type of scenario is not unusual and regularly makes clear why each hospital's participation is necessary for the good of the whole.

RWHC hospitals need to *know* that their work and the work of their organization is critical to the success of the cooperative; the cooperative must develop a culture that continually communicates that the maximum potential contribution from every participant is critical to the organization's success. RWHC hospitals and related organizations must know they are needed by the network as a whole. This contrasts sharply with the mixed messages frequently heard by RWHC communities, many of which have significant economic and social challenges. These mixed messages, "we are here to help but you need to do it our way," can leave them and their organizations feeling confused and belittled. For example, some regional medical centers talk about not working to take over rural health care, while proceeding to aggressively expand their market share at the expense of local access and services.

For health care providers in a network to be effective they must be given an unambiguous message that they are needed even while they are being asked to undertake significant change. All health care providers are a meaningful part of the nation's health care agenda and are a valuable resource, both individually and collectively, for the innovation of more cost-effective and accessible health care. They need to know it.

These cooperative behaviors should be encouraged:
- Develop a corporate culture in which the participants *are* the cooperative.
- Make it clear that the success of the cooperative is meaningless without the individual success of its participants.
- Serve the cooperative through the accomplishment of mutually agreed to goals and objectives.
- Make sure that all users of cooperative services know that as the "customers" they come first.
- Recognize and promote the use of the significant pool of knowledge and experience already available within the cooperative.

These behaviors should be discouraged:
- Never assume you know what participants need or think.
- Do not ask for the cooperative's guidance and then do what *you* want.
- Never use anyone's "expert" status to try to force a cooperative decision.
- Minimize depersonalizing references to participants in the third-person plural: "they," "them," or "those people."
- Discourage cooperative meetings becoming dominated by particular individuals.
- Discourage competition between cooperative programs and individual participant's programs.

### Principle 4: All involved in planning

The planning is interactive, with the plan for the cooperative being the result of, and feeding into, the plans of the individual participants.

One theatrical but powerful example of ignoring the need for local input and preferences involved the cooperative within months of its incorporation in 1979. Two regional health planners, with the very best of intentions, were practically driven from the bare wood stage of Wisconsin's historic Al Ringling Theater after their presentation of a *unilaterally* developed plan for local consolidations and closures. The plan was not implemented and did not contribute to further discussion of how rural health care in southern Wisconsin could be improved. Since then, local Wisconsin communities, understanding the scarce resources they face, have restructured more hospital activity than were ever dreamed of by central health planners during their zenith.

While the staff of RWHC are respected as well informed and creative professionals, the cooperative's planning process focuses on determining the preferences and needs of the participating hospitals. Both the annual work plan and budget are driven by how the hospitals perceive they can make the best use of the cooperative as a regional resource to assist their own local ability to survive and prosper. The state of Wisconsin's support for the Rural Medical Center as an alternative model for rural hospitals in 1992 flows directly, if not at some length, from a single RWHC administrator's input into the annual RWHC planning process in 1988.

With funding from the Robert Wood Johnson Foundation, RWHC implemented cooperative benchmarking: the continuous comparison of the functions and processes of similar hospital and nonhospital departments in order to identify and implement best practices. This project started from the request by a RWHC administrator for relevant comparative standards among RWHC hospitals but became more process oriented as an RWHC staff member became aware early of the potential application of total quality improvement methodology to health care. More recently, hospital feedback has led to the shortening of the time for completing an individual benchmarking cycle as well as increasing the involvement of other affected departments within each participating hospital. RWHC programs are not the result of central office direction nor of a single local hospital—they are the result of both, an interactive process among RWHC hospitals and staff.

Ackoff[6] promotes the idea that by meaningfully including all parts of the organization in the planning process, by making the planning process interactive, all those who can affect the organization's outcome develop a vested interest in its overall success.

Opposition to central private or public initiatives is frequently belittled as irresponsible local preferences for service regardless of cost. However, if for a moment the proposition could be entertained that people are not automatically "backward or ignorant" when they fight against centralizing initiatives, some local preferences might be discovered to be rational. From the perspective of a local provider, it is rational to oppose initiatives that certainly lose local services and employment while gaining only a trivial portion of the larger system's uncertain savings.

While desperate or weak organizations may have no option but to accept patronizing assistance within larger networks or submit to more explicit and bold direct takeovers, healthier communities with greater productive potential respond more favorably to an approach based on mutual respect and responsibility with an appropriate sharing of risk and benefit. Communities and health care organizations must have genuine involvement in the planning and implementation of decisions that affect them. Dr. Susan Jenkins (personal communication, 1990) from the University of Georgia's Cooperative Extension Service puts it all very succinctly when she says, "If you come out of a (traditional) central office but still have that corporate mind set, you're not networking."

These cooperative behaviors should be encouraged:

- Cooperative leaders and staff need to balance their personal vision with their responsibility to discover and implement the vision of the cooperative as a whole.
- Identify common opportunities and threats as threads to support united efforts.
- Work to facilitate cooperative programs consistent with local programs and vice versa; be aware of the variety of local situations facing individual cooperative participants.
- If you are based within a traditional organization, remember you need to "switch over" to a more interactive planning style when you are working with the cooperative.
- Consult regularly with the cooperative for ongoing "midcourse" corrections; every cooperative meeting is both a board meeting and a focus group of customers.
- Make sure that each time the cooperative meets it is doing so to make one or more significant decisions.
- Treat cooperative meetings as the important corporate meetings that they are.

These behaviors should be discouraged:

- Do not get "hung up" on administrative "rights" as the board of a cooperative is also its primary or only group of customers.

- Do not take a "vertical or authoritarian" mentality into your "horizontal or collaborative" relationships.
- Never say "yes" when you mean "no."
- Do not proceed until you have the critical mass of participants on board and do not judge your success by whether or not you had 100 percent of those in the cooperative agree to participate.
- Do not forget to check for "false-positive" approvals regarding new cooperative programs; they are a particular risk of "cooperative group think."

### Principle 5: Big picture understood

Participants need to know where the network is headed and where they are going within the network.

RWHC has a motto of saying it early and saying it often—we are not particularly concerned about "overcommunicating." A number of RWHC's more significant initiatives such as the development of a loan guarantee program, various quality improvement projects, and advocacy for major education reform within the University of Wisconsin's health professional schools are multiyear efforts. Such projects require the ongoing reminder of their significance to individual RWHC hospitals, notwithstanding their earlier participation in the planning processes that led to these projects.

Just as RWHC has begun to network more at the state level, it has been actively promoting the establishment of partnerships between rural hospitals and public health departments within each county. RWHC has taken the position that the nation's emerging health care reform movement will require rural hospitals to look beyond the individual patient to see the whole community as a "new patient." Simultaneously, it will require them to recognize and respect existing initiatives by a variety of important public health organizations. Typically, many individuals in the acute care sector have limited their definition of health care to patient care and that generally means visiting with a specific individual, forming a diagnosis, prescribing treatment, and providing or referring for treatment and follow up as appropriate. Successful outreach to a community requires similar activities in an expanded context of the community as "patient" with a more complex array of partners.

The experience that RWHC hospitals have had in developing partnerships with each other is now beginning to be expanded into other spheres. Two RWHC hospitals have been invited along with hospitals in New York City, Philadelphia, and Phoenix to develop proposals for a national demonstration project to develop community partnerships in order to better serve people with low income; three other RWHC hospitals have begun to work with their county public health department without any external funding. Wisconsin's Rural Health Development Council has accepted the suggestion of RWHC to make collaborative community decision making a priority for the technical assistance it is willing to provide rural hospitals and communities.

While not a new metaphor, participants need to see the larger picture printed on the puzzle box, a vision of how the puzzle fits together, how they fit in. What is the cooperative's mission and strategy, and how are they a part of it? Where is the cooperative headed and where are they headed within the organization? Each participant needs an opportunity to create a personal vision of its own future with respect to the cooperative.

Participants need to understand the "strategy and direction" of the network or government policy or of any other corporate power that can substantively affect their future; if a local organization's leadership does not have a reasonable understanding of its environment, its employees will be similarly in the dark. Without that understanding everyone's work will be substantially impaired.

These cooperative behaviors should be encouraged:
- Networking is in large measure information and communication—make sure this is an unequivocal strength for cooperative leaders and staff.
- Cooperative goals and objectives, once determined, need to be continually communicated: "Say it early and say it often."
- Recognize and without judgment account for the various levels of knowledge among the participants; develop efficient communication devices to allow for significant variation in the degree of prior knowledge or experience.
- Work to get all stakeholders, not just the participants' formal representative, the opportunity to understand the cooperative's plan.
- Give participants enough information to know when and how to ask for more information—a middle ground between keeping participants in the dark or hiding the forest in the trees of a million pieces of paper.

These behaviors should be discouraged:
- Do not assume that individual participants are too busy to be interested in a particular issue; this may often be the case (but let participants do the screening).
- Do not surprise the cooperative with unexpected news, good or bad.

## Principle 6: Participants affect their own future

The desire for local autonomy needs to be made to work for the cooperative through the promotion of collaborative solutions that enhance self-interest.

When RWHC began operations many observers were highly skeptical about whether or not it would last, let alone make any real contribution—that rural hospitals' traditional need for autonomy would prevent any meaningful joint activity. Certain initiatives such as the development of the capability for RWHC to manage some of its own hospitals have been seen as precluded in large part due to this issue of autonomy. Some shared services have been undersubscribed as hospitals have chosen local options when, at least from the perspective of RWHC staff, a cooperative approach offered a better service at a lower cost. These problems notwithstanding, the history of RWHC has been one of steady movement forward as collaborative approaches have been designed that respect the autonomy of each hospital.

RWHC staff attempts to look at the "half of the glass that is full"; they do not see it as their job to manipulate RWHC hospitals to do what staff perceives as the right thing; they see their job as developing and maintaining significant alternatives that will be accepted and sustained by the RWHC hospitals. The desire is not to make the hospitals dependent upon the cooperative but demanding of it through the strength that they gain, in part from the cooperative.

It is particularly destructive to the human spirit and body to hold an individual or group responsible for an outcome in a stressful environment but deprive them of the authority and resources to act. Karasek and Theorell have found that the right to have control over one's work affects more than personal dignity, that it is a significant risk factor for coronary heart disease: "The primary work-related risk factor appears to be a lack of control over how one meets the job's demands and how one uses one's skills."[7(p.9)] Unilateral externally imposed policies by a regional HMO or threatened cutbacks in the availability of visiting medical specialists are routine occurrences for rural providers, chipping away at their sense of being able to affect their own future.

---

*It is destructive to the human spirit and body to hold an individual or group responsible for an outcome in a stressful environment but deprive them of the authority or resources to act.*

---

Dr. Helen Grace, a senior staff member of the W.K. Kellogg Foundation, speaks to this issue when she says that the foundation ". . . assists communities in solving the problems which they define, according to solutions they propose. To make the best use of the available resources, staff members of the Kellogg Foundation seek to understand the problems facing communities around the world, and to work with these communities to clarify and prioritize their concerns and to identify first steps toward reaching doable answers."[8(p.20–22)]

The importance of individualism in this culture is one of the great American myths—not that it is not true but that it is so true that Americans fail to pay it much notice, encompassing their lives like water does a fish. While it is unlikely that such a powerful, culturally driven self-image can be hung on a hook outside the workplace door, many organizations seem to adopt that premise.

These cooperative behaviors should be encouraged:

- The role of the staff is to facilitate rather than control cooperative board decisions.
- The cooperative board decides what are its decisions to make.
- Make it clear nothing happens to participants unless they want it to happen.
- Use a decision-making process based on consensus for decisions that directly affect all participants.
- Avoid framing any issue that directly affects individual participants in terms of a search for a cooperative-wide right or wrong answer; facilitate each participant determining what is the right or wrong answer for its situation.
- Remember that a vote on the cooperative board for the cooperative to proceed with a project is not the same as that participant agreeing to be part of that particular project.
- Emphasize that the success of many projects is largely dependent upon the participant assuming full responsibility for implementation of the participant's piece of the cooperative-wide program.

These behaviors should be discouraged:

- Do not set up situations where the cooperative judges or uses judgmental language about a participant.
- Do not take on the responsibility of being a missionary to "save" each participant from the consequence of its own decisions.
- Do not ever take a participant's participation for granted either as a customer or as part of the governance process.

- Do not set up situations in which the cooperative or an individual participant feels pressure to move forward but has not had the opportunity to make an informed decision.

## Principle 7: Accountability up front

Participants in the cooperative, including cooperative staff, must always know up front what the rules are and what is expected of them.

The Rural Wisconsin Hospital Cooperative has been fortunate to have been a very stable group of hospitals; excluding an unsuccessful experiment with affiliate members and one merger, only one member has withdrawn over a 13-year period. Discussions at RWHC board meetings are frequently comparable to user focus groups and equally valuable—staff and hospital participants know what is and what is not expected of them. The one member that withdrew, a rural referral center, did so as its *undeclared* interest in using RWHC as a vehicle to market its own services had not been satisfied. Participation in all cooperative-shared services requires a signed contract, not so much as to permit legal enforcement but to ensure that all parties in the partnership have thought through up front the expectations of all the participants.

RWHC has been equally fortunate in being able to attract high-caliber personnel with minimum turnover, individuals who do more for less than they would in many less challenging jobs. In part this is because there is a tradition that even in a relatively unstable field, evaluation of individual performance is based on those elements of the job that the individual could personally affect and that individual contributions are recognized and rewarded to the degree possible.

The University of Wisconsin (UW) is one of the country's great land grant universities, and as such it has a greater, not less, responsibility to work to meet Wisconsin's need for generalist physicians, nurses, and physical therapists in underserved communities. The cooperative has been asking that the university assume co-ownership with it and others to more effectively address the state's need for additional providers in both its rural and intercity communities, that it works with us as a full partner. To that end and as a beginning point in the partnership, RWHC has advocated that the UW system should commit up front to saying how it will and to what extent it will adjust its production of health professionals in response to the state's need for providers in underserved communities while maintaining program quality.

The importance of accountability within a cooperative is based on the observation that individuals and cooperating organizations work best when they receive timely feedback and that this feedback is based on mutually agreed to expectations. To do otherwise is to generate hostility or withdrawal.

If instructions or rules that a RWHC hospital needs to follow are changed retroactively, there is the potential of a ripple effect within each hospital. A retroactive change to the hospital frequently translates into a retroactive change for individual hospital employees. While employee-oriented organizations can frequently buffer employees from external capriciousness, there are limits. At a minimum, they cannot diminish the damage done to an individual who has worked hard in one direction to find out that the results of his or her labor are now unimportant and unneeded. If that happens too often, RWHC hospitals and employees with options will begin to exercise them.

Picture the image of people working together within a network or organization when mutual expectations are understood up front and respected, compared with the ambiguous and faceless environment of most public or private bureaucracies. The fundamental variable in most networks or organizations may not be the participants but the environment; most people have experienced the power of their work to either inspire or to suffocate.

These cooperative behaviors should be encouraged:

- Clearly define roles: Who is responsible for what, who decides, who develops criteria, and who gets to see cooperative data?
- Record all agreements and expectations.
- Like all corporations, develop and utilize appropriate planning and budget documentation.
- Make the cooperative's verbal commitment its bond, particularly around "political" negotiations that have not or will not be reduced to writing.

These behaviors should be discouraged:

- Do not ever speak for or obligate the cooperative or individual participants without their prior consent.
- Do not let familiarity and a collaborative agenda create sloppy business habits when it comes to spelling out an agreement about who is responsible for what.

## Principle 8: Decisions can be appealed

A clear nonthreatening appeal mechanism is needed to ensure individual rights against arbitrary actions.

The use of the cooperative strength of RWHC hospitals has been used to force an appeals process when faced with a potential breach of contract by a single large urban-based HMO; individually, few could have justified the necessary prolonged legal challenge to enforce the contract but through concerted joint inquiry into the legal options available, further legal action became unnecessary. A particularly attractive feature of a multihospital insurance program, the RWHC Trust, was the ability of the participating hospitals to have appeals about disputed claims judged by their peers familiar with their work setting rather than a distant bureaucracy limited to only its written rules.

A need for relief from arbitrary action can also happen even before a relationship is developed. Rural health care providers, however financially sound, are frequently "red-lined" or excluded from increasingly national and international capital markets—an arbitrary action from the point of view of a well-run rural hospital. "Bond market looks askance at rural and small urban facilities that need cash; meanwhile, high powered institutions benefit from fat ratings, cheap rates."[9(p.59)] As an initial response, RWHC has established a pilot loan guarantee program for RWHC hospitals in cooperation with the Robert Wood Johnson Foundation and the Wisconsin Health and Education Facilities Authority. Use of the pool is based on objective rural-sensitive loan criteria applied by RWHC colleagues with a final determination by the state hospital bond authority. The pilot is initially financed by a $500,000 low-interest loan from the Robert Wood Johnson Foundation. The foundation's support for this private sector pilot was used as an incentive for the state of Wisconsin to invest $500,000 for the same purpose. Lenders to those hospitals who are accepted by both programs will have 50 percent of loans with a principal up to $500,000 guaranteed in case of default: 10 percent through a hospital reserve fund, 20 percent by the state, and 20 percent by RWHC.

These cooperative behaviors should be encouraged:

- Make it easy for participants to express a reservation, concern, or complaint.
- In the case of a dispute that is not being resolved to both parties' satisfaction, the participant should always be informed how best to make an appeal to the cooperative as a whole.
- Remember that the participant's right to appeal to a peer is one of the distinctive and appealing characteristics of a cooperative.

These behaviors should be discouraged:

- Do not enforce your "rights" unilaterally or quickly against any participants however clear you believe your case to be.

• • •

Most major reform alternatives to the single-payer Canadian approach require that private and public purchasers of health insurance or plans organize themselves cooperatively under a few regional brokers or sponsors to negotiate with newly organized regional networks of providers. As both sectors are more attuned to competition than the cooperation that will be required by such proposals, the experience of the Rural Wisconsin Hospital Cooperative and other networks is perhaps more timely than ever. There is a need for innovative interorganizational relationships that, in DePree's words, encourage participants "to do what is required of them in the most effective and humane way possible."[3(p.1)] Success in health care requires new private and public cooperative attitudes, processes, and structures built fundamentally upon an understanding and respect for real people working in local community-based organizations.

## REFERENCES

1. Zuckerman, H.S., and D'Aunno, T.A. "Hospital Alliances: Cooperative Strategy in a Competitive Environment." *Health Care Management Review* 15, no. 2 (1990): 21–30.
2. Eisler, R. *The Chalice and the Blade, Our History, Our Future.* San Francisco, Calif.: Harper, 1988.
3. DePree, M. *Leadership Is an Art.* New York, N.Y.: Doubleday, 1989.
4. Greenleaf, R.K. *Servant Leadership.* New York, N.Y.: Paulist Press, 1977.
5. Kanter, R.M. *When Giants Learn to Dance.* New York, N.Y.: Simon & Schuster, 1990.
6. Ackoff, R.L. *A Guide to Controlling Your Corporation's Future.* New York, N.Y.: Wiley, 1984.
7. Karasek, R., and Theorell, T. *Healthy Work, Stress, Productivity, and the Reconstruction of Working Life.* New York, N.Y.: Basic Books, 1990.
8. Grace, H.K. "Building Community: A Conceptual Perspective." *International Journal of the W.K. Kellogg Foundation* 1, no. 1 (1990): 20–22.
9. Nemes, J. "Hospital Borrowers Finding It Tougher to Scale the Wall on Wall Street." *Modern Healthcare* 22, no. 25 (1992): 59.

# Urban–rural hospital affiliations: Assessing control, fit, and stakeholder issues strategically

Grant T. Savage,
John D. Blair,
Michael J. Benson,
and
Byron Hale

*Urban–rural hospital affiliations are an outgrowth of both the external pressures on rural hospitals to survive and the need for urban hospitals to maintain or increase their share of the tertiary referral market. This article discusses the significant role of stakeholders in these affiliations, develops a fourfold typology of urban–rural hospital affiliations based on the notions of organizational control and fit, suggests four generic strategies for forming affiliations, and analyzes four actual cases of affiliation.*

*Health Care Manage Rev*, 1992, 17(1), 35–49
© 1992 Aspen Publishers, Inc.

**The future of** rural health care is at risk. Attributes of the rural environment include an aging population, high unemployment, and a high incidence of chronic disease.[1,2] These characteristics have placed immense strains on rural health care systems. Moreover, the confluence of changes in technology, reimbursement, and regulation have resulted in the closure of more than 200 rural hospitals from 1980 to 1989.[3]

In addition to challenges presented by declining populations and payment reductions by the Medicare program, rural hospitals must contend with shortages of health care personnel, such as nurses and laboratory, radiology, or respiratory therapy technicians. Many hospitals also have an aging staff and difficulty recruiting new physicians. These problems, coupled with the increasing complexity of state and federal regulations affecting hospitals, have sent many rural hospitals looking for external help.

Congress has responded by creating the National Rural Health Care Act of 1988. The Health Care Financing Administration has sponsored grants for rural hospitals that are financially unstable and in need of physicians, major causes of rural hospital closures.[4] Administratively, rural hospitals have begun to involve physicians in the governance and management functions of the hospital in the hopes of binding the physician to the hospital and improving policy decisions.[5] Rural hospitals have attempted to downsize operations and increase marketing. However, increasing marketing efforts is costly, and downsizing, in the long run, only serves to exacerbate the problem of attracting primary care providers.

Increasingly, rural hospitals are forming alliances,[6,7] forging affiliations,[8] or seeking some other means of collective action in an effort to survive.[9] Over one-third of all rural hospitals are owned, leased, or contract managed by multihospital systems.[10] For the rural facility, the benefits are usually the injection of much-needed capital, an operational evaluation, and the development of a more formalized financial struc-

*Grant T. Savage*, Ph.D., is Associate Professor of Management and Health Organization Management at Texas Tech University, Lubbock, Texas.

*John D. Blair*, Ph.D., is Professor of Management and Health Organization Management at Texas Tech University, Lubbock, Texas.

*Michael J. Benson*, M.B.A., is a Health Organization Management Fellow at Methodist Hospital, Lubbock, Texas.

*Byron Hale*, B.S., C.P.A., is Vice President and Chief Financial Officer at Methodist Hospital, Lubbock, Texas.

ture and controls. From the urban perspective, the affiliation serves as a protective marketing mechanism and a source of true referrals. While both facilities ultimately seek substantive and relationship benefits, their initial objectives are disparate in nature.

Affiliation agreements vary among hospitals. They may provide for total management responsibility by the urban facility or looser ties that may include access to clinical and technical expertise, participation in group purchasing contracts, or use of shared services. Traditionally, a number of national and regional hospital management firms have provided comprehensive management services to rural hospitals. Although these firms still represent a viable option, many rural facilities can no longer afford to pay for their services and/or desire to retain a greater degree of local autonomy and control. Urban hospitals have begun providing these services at reduced or minimal costs to the rural facilities. The urban hospitals view the opportunity to increase tertiary referrals as an adequate return for their investments in a rural affiliation network.

In this article, we examine additional issues that need to be considered in implementing such a collaborative business strategy. We then (1) discuss the significant role of stakeholders in urban–rural hospital affiliations, (2) develop a fourfold typology of urban–rural hospital affiliations based on the notions of organizational control and fit, (3) suggest four generic strategies for forming affiliations, (4) highlight how key stakeholder contingencies affect generic affiliation strategies, (5) analyze four actual cases of affiliation, (6) illustrate how modifications of the generic affiliation strategies make them sensitive to key stakeholders, and (7) discuss the implications for health care managers and researchers.

## STEP 1: CONSIDER THE FIT BETWEEN URBAN–RURAL HOSPITAL AFFILIATIONS AND BUSINESS STRATEGY ISSUES

Senior management teams at large urban hospitals across the country are facing empty beds because of pressures from Medicare's prospective payment system, health maintenance organizations (HMOs), preferred provider organizations (PPOs), and competing hospitals. Whatever the particular set of causes, these managers see capturing (or retaining) a large share of the tertiary care referral market as crucial to their hospitals' survival. Their thinking reflects the generic business strategy of *market penetration*. That is, they plan to grow through expanding the hospital's share of an existing market (tertiary care referrals) using the

same products (beds and services to provide tertiary care). Further, they have identified the key stakeholders of the urban hospital who are impacted by that strategy—and essential to its success—to include the rural hospitals and rural, primary care physicians in the hospital's secondary market area. Both of these stakeholders are what have been called "mixed-blessing" stakeholders because they are high on both the potential for threat and the potential for cooperation.[11,12] Stakeholder researchers suggest that the most appropriate management strategy for this type of stakeholder is *collaboration*.[13,14] Creating a formal relationship through an affiliation agreement between the hospitals would be a specific example of such collaboration.

## STEP 2: EVALUATE POTENTIAL STAKEHOLDER MANAGEMENT ISSUES IN URBAN–RURAL HOSPITAL AFFILIATIONS

Although the rural hospital is an important stakeholder for the urban hospital, it is just one of many key stakeholders for the rural hospital. Other stakeholders, whether primary or secondary, may enter the scene and exert influence upon an affiliation accord.[15] Primary stakeholders are those with formal, official, or contractual relationships who have a direct and necessary economic impact upon the hospital; secondary stakeholders are quite diverse and include those who are not directly engaged in the hospital's economic activities but are able to exert influence or are affected by the organization.[16,17] However, whether the stakeholders are primary or secondary, we refer to them as *key* stakeholders if the issue is salient to them.

In other words, the stakeholder management approach[13,18] accounts for those organizations, groups, and individuals whose stake in the affiliation agreement is large and who are free to influence the nature of the relationship between the urban and rural hospitals. Typical key stakeholders of a rural hospital are shown in Figure 1.

However, as noted previously, an affiliation agreement should further the urban hospital's business strategy. To ensure that patient referrals will follow as a result of the affiliation, urban hospital managers would be well advised to consider first the issues of organizational fit and control.

## STEP 3: ASSESS ORGANIZATIONAL FIT AND CONTROL ISSUES

The issue of organizational fit concerns the likelihood of a good match between the financial, human, and ma-

**FIGURE 1**

KEY STAKEHOLDERS IN A SMALL FREE-STANDING RURAL HOSPITAL NEGOTIATING AN AFFILIATION AGREEMENT WITH AN URBAN HOSPITAL

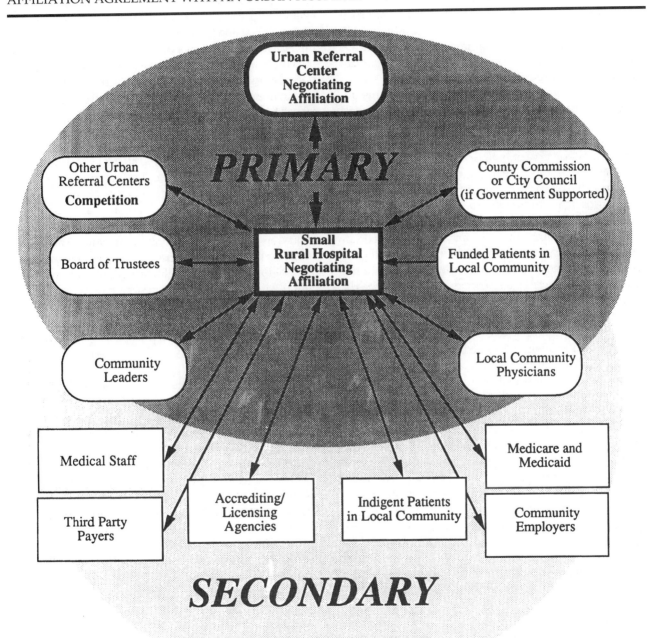

terial resources needed by the rural hospital and those offered by the urban hospital. Perhaps most significantly, the urban hospital may have the resources needed by the rural hospital, but the urban hospital may not have sufficient capacity—organizational slack—to deliver the resources in an effective manner. If the urban hospital has established an external division to coordinate affiliations with sufficient budget and staff, it has recognized the importance of providing the organizational slack to make collaboration successful.

The issue of organizational control centers on the potential for conflict between the urban and rural hospitals over strategic, operational, or financial control of the rural hospital. Note that the potential for conflict may be high under two very different sets of conditions: (1) the rural hospital desires to retain complete control, but the urban hospital foresees the need to provide strategic, operational, or financial direction; and (2) the rural hospital wishes to relinquish either strategic, operational, or financial control, but the urban hospital is unwilling or incapable of providing firm direction in one or another of these areas. Such factors as the following influence the potential for conflict: the degree of dependence of the rural hospital upon the urban hospital;[19,20] the existence of alternatives such as a cooperative network of rural hospitals;[6,7,21] the hospitals' access to financial institutions;[8,22] and the board–management–medical staff relationships within each hospital.[23,24]

To the extent that the likely resource fit is high and that the potential for conflict is low, the potential for a successful affiliation is increased. Alternatively, to the extent that either the fit is low or the conflict potential is high, the affiliation relationship is at risk. These issues can be captured in a simple model, as depicted in Figure 2, that characterizes each of the four basic types of situations potentially facing managers of urban hospitals.

When the proposed relationship between the two organizations is not problematic, then pursuing an affiliation agreement can become a priority. In other words, the *Dual-Benefit Affiliation* (Type 1) is one with a low potential for conflict over control and a high likely match between what a rural hospital needs and what

*The issue of organizational fit concerns the likelihood of a good match between the financial, human, and material resources needed by the rural hospital and those offered by the urban hospital.*

the urban hospital has to offer. If the situation is not as highly conducive, then managers should focus on the problematic issue (Types 2 and 3). On one hand, the *Potential-Conflict Affiliation* (Type 2) is one with a high potential for conflict over control of the rural hospital, even though there is a good resource match between the rural hospital and the urban hospital. On the other hand, the *Poor-Fit Affiliation* (Type 3) is one with low potential for conflict over control of the rural hospital and low potential for matching the particular rural hospital's resource needs with those resources that the urban hospital has to offer. Alternatively, if both the resource fit and the conflict potential are likely to be problematic, then managers should question the value of this particular relationship. The *Dual-Risk Affiliation* (Type 4) is a most unattractive one. The worst of both worlds is obtained: there is a high potential for conflict over control of the rural hospital, and there does not appear to be a very likely match between what the rural hospital needs and what the urban hospital has to offer. These situational types will be illustrated in a later section. Four cases of urban–rural hospital affiliation will exemplify not only the issues affecting assessment, but also those influencing strategy formation and modification.

## STEP 4: SELECT A GENERIC AFFILIATION STRATEGY

Assessing the favorableness of a potential affiliation relationship enables urban hospital managers to select an initial affiliation strategy. Figure 3 illustrates four strategies that correspond to the four types of affiliations previously discussed.

The *Nurturing Strategy* (N1) entails not only providing the necessary resources to the rural hospital, but also seeking to facilitate its growth through increased interdependence with the urban hospital. Although the urban hospital may offer an initial "quick fix" for the rural hospital's financial or operational problems, its long-term solution is to develop the capabilities of the rural facility. Rather than simply making the rural hospital dependent on the resources from the urban hospital, this strategy involves developing the organizational efficiency and effectiveness of the rural facility. In other words, the urban hospital invests in enhancing the managerial skills of the rural hospital's management, its board, and its medical staff.

The *Clarifying Roles Strategy* (C1) facilitates the urban and the rural hospitals' resolving the issue of control before entering into an affiliation. Because a high potential for conflict exists, efforts undertaken prior to the affilia-

**FIGURE 2**

ASSESSING ORGANIZATIONAL CONTROL AND FIT ISSUES IN URBAN–RURAL HOSPITAL AFFILIATIONS

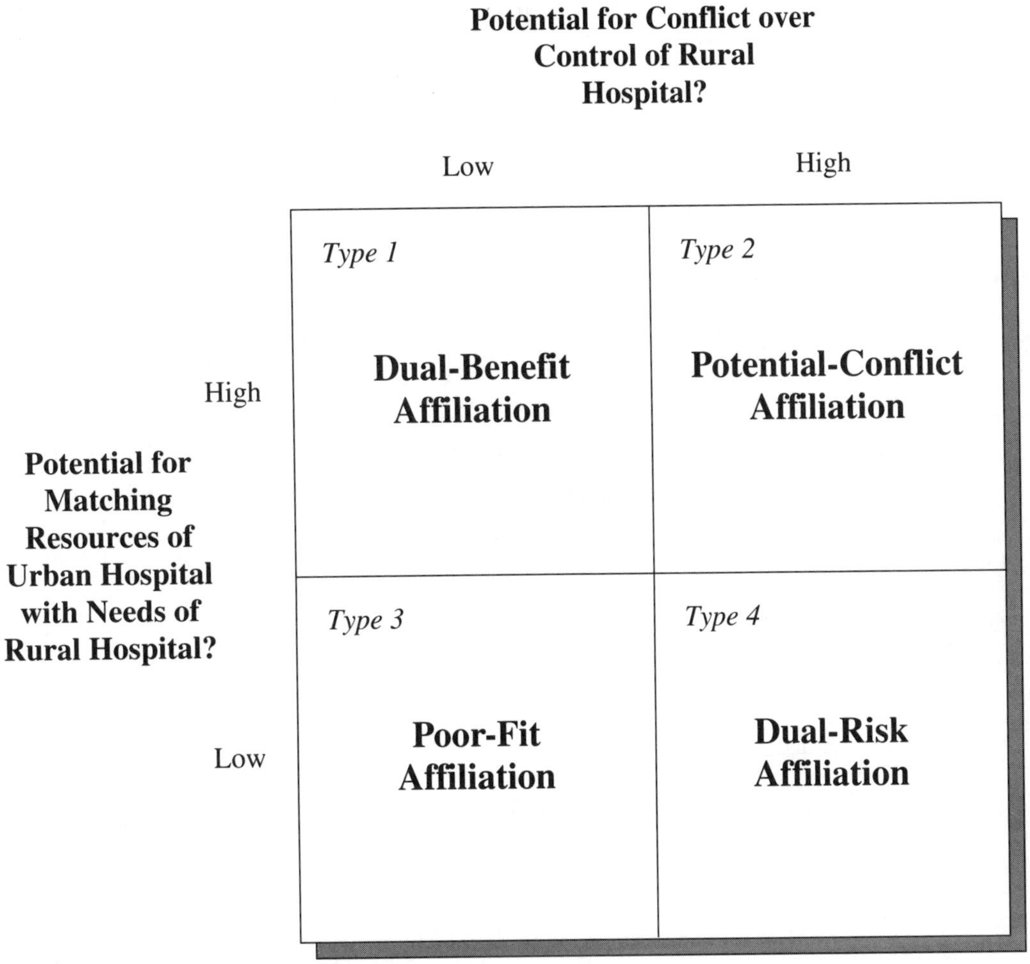

**Potential for Conflict over
Control of Rural
Hospital?**

|  | Low | High |
|---|---|---|
| **High** | *Type 1*<br><br>**Dual-Benefit
Affiliation** | *Type 2*<br><br>**Potential-Conflict
Affiliation** |
| **Low** | *Type 3*<br><br>**Poor-Fit
Affiliation** | *Type 4*<br><br>**Dual-Risk
Affiliation** |

**Potential for
Matching
Resources of
Urban Hospital
with Needs of
Rural Hospital?**

tion and directed toward clarifying the roles of the urban and rural hospital should help diffuse tensions and avoid misunderstandings. If financial control is an issue, then information about the different types of financial assistance that the urban hospital can offer will lessen apprehension. If managerial or operational control is a potential problem, discussion of the role of the urban hospital's management team will address the often unspoken concerns of the rural hospital's board of trustees.

The *Subordination Strategy* (S1) is more than simply "rolling over and playing dead" or "giving away the store." Rather, this strategy seeks to strengthen the long-term relationship with the rural hospital, even though it requires the urban hospital to endure short-term financial losses. In other words, to enact this strategy, the urban hospital must take a long-term perspective and be willing to provide the rural hospital with needed financial, material, or human resources. The payback—sufficient patient referrals to make the affiliation break even or profitable—is then more likely to occur. However, because of the risk involved, this strategy is probably more attractive as a way to *protect* patient referrals within a tertiary market rather than as a way to *expand* within that market.

The *Avoidance Strategy* (A) permits both the urban hospital and the rural hospital to seek more profitable

**FIGURE 3**

GENERIC STRATEGIES FOR DIFFERENT TYPES OF URBAN–RURAL HOSPITAL AFFILIATIONS

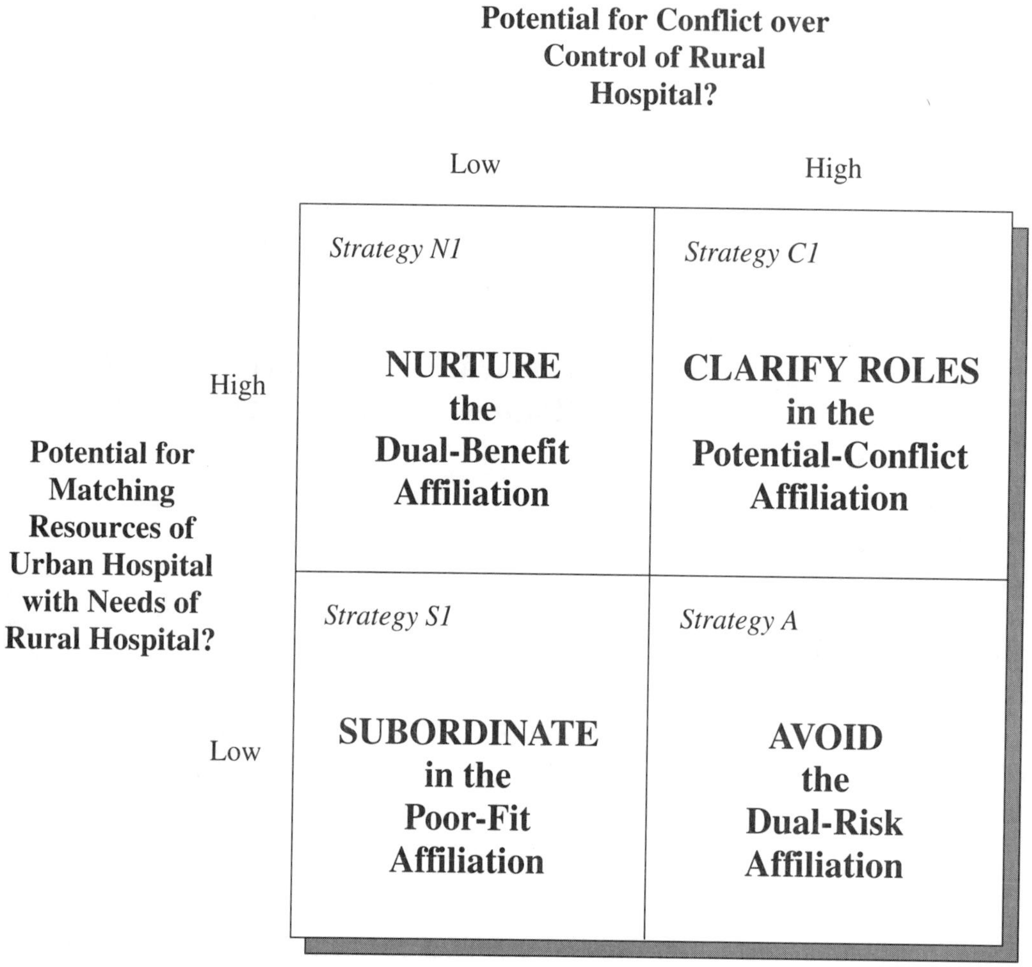

**Potential for Conflict over Control of Rural Hospital?**

|  | Low | High |
|---|---|---|
| **High** | *Strategy N1*<br><br>**NURTURE the Dual-Benefit Affiliation** | *Strategy C1*<br><br>**CLARIFY ROLES in the Potential-Conflict Affiliation** |
| **Low** | *Strategy S1*<br><br>**SUBORDINATE in the Poor-Fit Affiliation** | *Strategy A*<br><br>**AVOID the Dual-Risk Affiliation** |

**Potential for Matching Resources of Urban Hospital with Needs of Rural Hospital?**

alternatives. Rather than pursuing an affiliation that will strain the resources of the urban hospital and create conflicts with the rural hospital, both hospitals will probably be better off avoiding the dual-risk affiliation.

**STEP 5: CONSIDER KEY STAKEHOLDER CONTINGENCIES**

Although Figure 3 provides a useful framework for approaching affiliations, many times stakeholder issues need to be resolved before—or while—implementing a generic strategy. To diagnose the situation further, urban hospital managers may ask two key

questions: (1) Can the urban hospital influence the rural physician stakeholders effectively? and (2) Can the urban hospital influence other key stakeholders of the rural hospital effectively? Figure 4 displays the results of considering these two stakeholder contingencies and their impact on the generic affiliation strategy.

On one hand, the most favorable situation occurs when both sets of stakeholders are open to the urban hospital's influence. In this situation, the urban managers may either intensify their efforts to implement the generic affiliation strategy previously chosen or reconsider their initial affiliation strategy because of the support from key stakeholders.

**FIGURE 4**

THE EFFECT OF KEY STAKEHOLDER CONTINGENCIES ON GENERIC AFFILIATION STRATEGIES

**Potential to Influence
Other Key
Stakeholders?**

|  | High | Low |
|---|---|---|
| **High** Potential to Influence Key Physician Stakeholders? | **INTENSIFY** (Use Direct Influence) **or RECONSIDER** Affiliation Strategy | **POLITICIZE** Affiliation Strategy (Use Indirect Influence) |
| **Low** | **POLITICIZE** Affiliation Strategy (Use Indirect Influence) | **REASSESS** Affiliation Strategy |

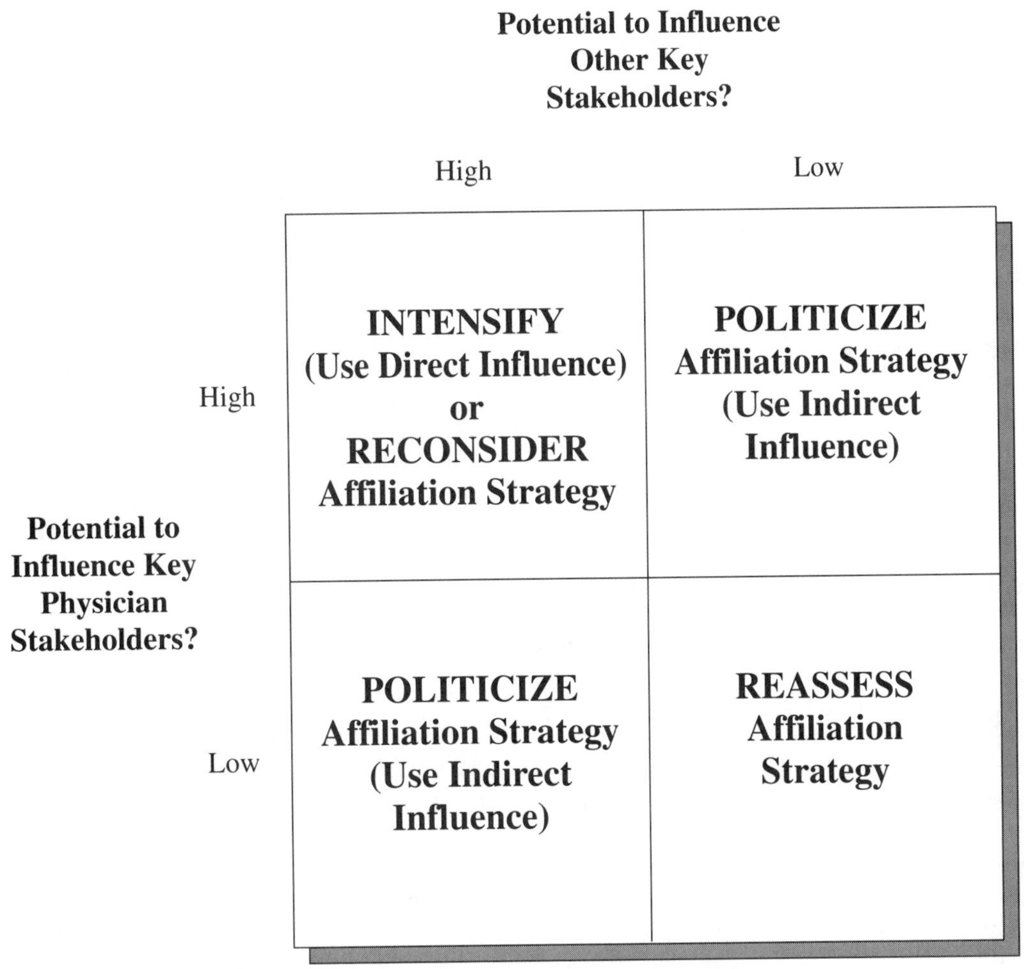

On the other hand, if both sets of stakeholders are opposed to the urban hospital's intervention, then the urban managers should carefully reassess the situation and the generic affiliation strategy they have chosen. Similarly, when one set of stakeholders supports but the other set opposes the urban hospital, then the urban team faces a politically risky situation. In these cases, the urban hospital may be able to implement its generic affiliation strategy by indirectly influencing the recalcitrant stakeholder or stakeholder coalition. Such indirect influence would include persuasive efforts from the other, supportive stakeholder group or from the rural hospital's managers.

We have referred to such use of indirect influence as "politicizing" the affiliation strategy. In so doing, we are simply recognizing explicitly that successful management of such key stakeholders will require considerable political skill and finesse, including building coalitions with supportive stakeholders.[25] See Blair and Fottler[13] for a systematic treatment of how to manage health care stakeholders successfully.

In the following section, we describe four actual affiliation situations. Through our discussion of each situation, we illustrate the generic strategies for affiliation, key stakeholder contingencies, and modifications to the generic affiliation strategies. (These research cases are drawn from actual affiliation agreements entered into by various urban and rural hospitals in the Southwest and Southeast. To maintain confidentiality, the hospitals and the principals involved in the affiliations have not been identified by name.)

### Case 1: Nurturing the dual-benefit affiliation

An urban hospital receiving over 50 percent of its admissions from the rural community recognized the importance of the preservation of rural health care. Having considerable managerial experience and capital, the urban hospital actively sought out rural facilities that could benefit from its resources. A rural facility with an urgent cash flow problem contacted the urban hospital because it had successfully assisted a neighboring rural hospital.

*Affiliation assessment*

During preliminary negotiations, the urban hospital assessed the rural hospital's resources and found that the cash flow problem was not because of low admissions; in fact, census was well above the break-even point. Instead, the urban hospital's management team discovered that the rural hospital's business manager was unable to bill and collect patient accounts in a timely fashion. During the last few years, various third-party payors had increased their clinical data requirements for submitting bills. As a result, the business office personnel had become less and less proficient at billing and collecting patient revenue. Additionally, the hospital's computer system was outdated and provided very little assistance to resolve this problem. In fear of losing his job, and with no one else in the rural community qualified to assist him, the business manager did not attempt to resolve the problem, but rather let the situation develop until it created a cash shortfall crisis.

Because a physician served on the rural hospital's board, the rural physician community was also aware of the cash problems facing the rural hospital. When the board decided that it would be in the best interests of the hospital to enter into an affiliation agreement with the urban facility, the community physicians readily supported this action. Moreover, the rural facility clearly signaled that it wanted to maintain operational control, but it was willing to open its books and accept the financial guidance of the urban hospital.

*Strategy implementation*

The urban hospital now formally agreed to affiliate, and it assigned an experienced financial manager to work with the business manager to resolve the problem. The manager determined that the problem was not so much the incompetence of the business manager, but the inadequacy of the billing system that the hospital used. Having only worked for this rural facility, the business manager did not know that something better existed.

Based upon this information, the urban hospital assisted the rural hospital in the purchase of an appropriate data processing system. The urban personnel supervised its installation and provided the necessary training to the rural business personnel. Claims were subsequently submitted more quickly, billing rejections were reduced, and cash flow was significantly improved. Both the board and the administrator were relieved to learn that the hospital's current cash flow problems were not the result of mismanagement of resources or because of blatant incompetence. The rural physicians were soon made aware of the actions initiated by the urban facility. They were pleased to find out that the problem was not the result of an incompetent administration, but rather the result of an outdated billing and collections system. The urban hospital also realized the benefits of its affiliation; the rural hospital's physician community soon began referring patients to the urban facility.

*Key stakeholder considerations*

The physician community and the board members of the rural facility were key stakeholders. The cooperation from these two stakeholder groups facilitated the urban hospital's nurturing of the rural hospital, enabling it to gain control of its cash flow through improved billing and collections. On one hand, there was a high potential for the urban hospital to match its resources with the rural hospital's needs. On the other hand, there was a low potential for conflict over control because the rural facility had clearly conveyed its desire to oversee its own operations following the urban hospital's intervention. However, the urban hospital was able to overcome what might have been a politically risky situation by focusing on ways to rectify the situation and nurture the rural facility, rather than assessing blame.

---

*The urban hospital was able to overcome what might have been a politically risky situation by focusing on ways to rectify the situation and nurture the rural facility.*

## Case 2: Clarifying roles in the potential-conflict affiliation

A rural hospital that had been successful began to experience eroding profit margins and problems with cash flow. The administrator had been at the hospital for over 10 years and was recognized by his peers as a capable manager. The rural hospital's financial problems, as the urban hospital's managers discovered during early negotiations, were symptomatic of a shrinking medical staff and declining census. Its board members believed an affiliation with the urban hospital would provide the resources necessary to turn the facility's operations around, and the rural community's physicians backed the board. However, the administrator was not in favor of the affiliation agreement because he felt his job would be in jeopardy and his authority would be diminished. Nonetheless, because the urban hospital had a well-established and successful physician recruiting function, the rural hospital's board decided to enter into the affiliation agreement.

### Affiliation assessment

The medical staff of the rural hospital was genuinely interested in maintaining the facility and augmenting the current physician complement. These physicians and many of the community leaders looked forward to the support the affiliation agreement would bring, and they were ready to follow the leadership provided by the urban hospital's management team. However, several community leaders had been associated with the hospital for many years and resented outside involvement. Some of these dissenting community leaders were on the board, while others were prominent business and civic leaders.

Several months prior to the formal affiliation, the rural hospital had lost a popular physician due to quality-related sanctions from a peer review organization. At an initial board meeting, the urban hospital representatives became aware that some of the rural board members had a strong desire to accept the sanctioned physician back once the period of suspension had expired. Unfortunately, the urban hospital could not support this position because of the physician's serious quality deficiencies. Indeed, if this physician were allowed back on the medical staff, the urban hospital would face great difficulty recruiting new physicians to that rural community. In short, the urban management team was concerned initially with its ability to influence a key stakeholder coalition within the community.

### Strategy implementation

To resolve the situation, the urban hospital's management team invited legal counsel to describe the liability implications to the board; it also arranged for an independent and highly qualified physician to describe the medical deficiencies specified in the peer review report. At no time did the urban management team issue an ultimatum or directly debate the merits of providing admission privileges to the sanctioned physician. This nonconfrontational, clarification strategy was successful, and the rural hospital board decided that the sanctioned physician could not be reinstated on the medical staff.

### Key stakeholder considerations

In this case, the potential to influence key stakeholders was limited. Although the physician stakeholders could be influenced directly, the other key stakeholders could not. The urban hospital was able to maintain a successful affiliation during the negotiations on the specific problem by clarifying the board's role and responsibility when deciding whether to reinstate the sanctioned physician. However, a certain amount of political risk was inherent due to the urban hospital's low ability to influence directly one key stakeholder coalition—the dissenting board members and civic leaders supporting the sanctioned physician. In this case, the use of a respected expert provided the type of indirect influence needed to sway the supporters of the sanctioned physician.

## Case 3: Subordinating in the poor-fit affiliation

An urban hospital aiming to be the premier tertiary facility in its region dedicated itself to the preservation of rural health care in its region. To achieve this mission, it engaged in numerous co-operative alignments with rural facilities. In most instances, there was a good pairing of the urban hospital's resources with the rural hospital's needs. However, in this case, the urban hospital, through a referral from a board member, became aware of a possible affiliation opportunity with a rural facility that was not a good fit.

### Affiliation assessment

Because the urban hospital had such a good reputation in the region, the rural facility was extremely receptive to a visit from the urban representatives. Fiscally and operationally, the rural facility was performing satisfactorily. Its need, as discovered by the urban hospital's management team, was for nurses. The rural hospital was increasingly experiencing severe staffing problems. Occasionally, admissions were diverted to other hospitals because of the inadequate staffing. Unfortunately, the urban hospital also had trouble recruiting nurses in adequate numbers.

### Strategy implementation

The urban facility, enthusiastic about a possible affiliation, decided to subordinate to the needs of the rural hospital: the urban hospital agreed during preliminary negotiations to assist the rural facility in locating the desperately needed nurses. During these early discussions, the rural hospital declared its intention to attract nurses with extremely high relocation incentives, thus overcoming objections they might have about living in a rural area. The urban hospital's managers persuaded the rural hospital's board that this would not only increase costs, but also cause dissension among the existing staff. In short, they argued that this was not a long-term solution to the problem. Having successfully prevented a potentially injurious situation for the rural hospital and having cultivated a trusting relationship with the board, the urban management team formalized the affiliation.

Just after signing the formal agreement, the rural hospital began pressing the urban facility to address the nursing situation. The medical staff at the rural hospital advocated borrowing some of the urban hospital's nurses to meet spot staffing shortages. When approached with this plan, the urban representatives quickly dismissed it as unreasonable and impractical for two reasons: (1) the urban managers could not influence nurses employed at their hospital to agree to such a plan; and (2) the cost, including transportation and lodging, would be prohibitive. (Additionally, the urban hospital faced its own highly competitive nurse recruiting market.) The urban representatives were quite emphatic about their position: they insisted that the urban hospital had never agreed *to supply* nurses; rather, it had agreed *to assist* the rural facility in its recruiting.

With no desire to wait for the urban hospitals' longer term solutions to be realized, the rural hospital soon lost faith. The relationship between the two hospitals deteriorated quickly. The rural facility felt abandoned by the urban hospital and eventually exercised its option for early termination of the agreement. Throughout the region, the failure was perceived to be caused by the urban hospital's unresponsiveness, tainting its image and efforts to assist other rural health providers.

### Key stakeholder considerations

Although the urban hospital faced low potential for conflict over control, it also encountered low potential for matching its resources with the rural hospital's needs. Initially, the urban hospital acknowledged the situation by taking a more subordinative posture with the rural hospital. However, it attempted only to point out the deficiencies of the rural hospital's original plan. Arguably, this affiliation was not successful because the urban hospital did not continue to employ a subordinating strategy. Because of the demeanor the urban facility had assumed with other rural facilities, the rural hospital was under the impression that the urban hospital was there to solve its problems.

Had the urban hospital reassessed the situation and embarked on an aggressive campaign of recruiting nurses for the rural facility, the affiliation might have been successful. In other words, rather than rejecting the second proposal, the urban management team should have realized its ability to influence the rural hospital board and its physician stakeholders. At the very least, the urban managers should have tried to persuade the hospital, its physicians, and community leaders to support a long-term recruiting solution.

## Case 4: Avoiding the dual-risk affiliation

An urban hospital had developed a substantial affiliation network to enhance its tertiary referrals. For several years, the hospital had committed considerable resources to provide management and technical personnel and to fund physician recruiting for rural affiliates. As expected, the indirect benefit of increased market share exceeded the direct costs of operating the rural affiliate management division. Knowing the success of this division, an urban hospital board member suggested the division pursue an affiliation agreement with a hospital in his hometown that was suffering financially and operationally.

### Affiliation assessment

Although the urban division was willing to offer assistance, the rural administrator realized that the urban facility was one of the causes of his problems. Not only had it pulled many of his former patients away, but because of a higher wage scale, many of his clinical personnel had gone to work for the urban facility. This knowledge translated into a disguised resentment for the urban facility and its management division. The urban hospital was aggressive in pursuing affiliations and expanding its secondary market. However, in this particular situation it was already getting the majority of the tertiary referrals. There was little for the urban hospital to gain by entering into the affiliation agreement.

### Strategy implementation

Within the rural community, a feeling existed that something must be done; however, neither the physicians nor other community leaders agreed on a course of action. A certain amount of division existed on nearly every issue associated with the hospital. Nonetheless, over the vocal objections of certain physicians and businessmen, the urban and rural hospitals entered into an affiliation agreement.

The urban hospital provided adequate support, including recruitment of an additional physician to the community. However, after a period of time, the urban hospital's management team realized it could not support the rural hospital unless the hospital could enlarge its market or the community could increase its population base. These were needs that could not be met by the urban hospital.

The urban management team recommended that the community's scarce health care resources would be better utilized and provide more benefit if the hospital were converted into an outpatient/emergency care/clinic operation. However, the rural community was extremely opposed to this idea. Although some physicians agreed that this was perhaps the right step to take, other key stakeholders would not accept the idea of anything less than the current level of services.

This conflict eventually resulted in an unpleasant termination of the affiliation agreement. As foreseen, the rural hospital eventually did have to phase out its acute services; however, many people within the community believed this conversion was caused by the urban hospital not supporting the affiliation agreement. Overall, the image of the urban hospital was tarnished within the community, and this affiliation was considered the least successful by the urban hospital.

### Key stakeholder considerations

In this case, the potential for conflict over control between the two hospitals was high. Additionally, in retrospect, there was a low potential for matching of resources and needs. Furthermore, several physicians and other key stakeholders were so committed to providing the full array of health care services that the urban hospital had a low potential for influencing them. In short, the urban hospital should have considered avoiding the affiliation. However, if the urban hospital perceived the need to protect its tertiary referral market, the generic strategy of subordinating possibly would have been successful.

## STEP 6: REFINE AFFILIATION STRATEGIES TO BE STAKEHOLDER-SENSITIVE

Figure 5 helps to summarize our discussion to this point. This figure models what we term "stakeholder-sensitive" strategies. It shows how an urban hospital manager's affiliation strategies are contingent on *both* fit and control issues *and* key stakeholder contingencies. The left-hand part of the tree diagram depicts the 4 situational types and associated strategies as suggested in Figures 2 and 3. This part of the figure simply reiterates our earlier discussion in a different format.

---

*An urban hospital manager's affiliation strategies are contingent on both fit and control issues and key stakeholder contingencies.*

---

The right-hand side of the tree diagram includes the stakeholder contingencies suggested in Figure 4 and links them to "stakeholder-sensitive" strategies. In other words, the earlier set of 4 basic strategic situations—reflecting quite different types of potential affiliations—are extended to 16, as the initial 4 are modified by the answers to the two diagnostic questions about stakeholder influence (see Figure 4). This part of Figure 5 shows how affiliation strategies may be refined based on these two stakeholder management issues.

Note that for some strategic situations two strategies are listed (see Situations 4, 6, 7, 10, 11, 13–15). For Situations 14 and 15, the first (left-hand) strategy is to avoid the affiliation. However, if that is not possible, then we suggest a strategy of *Politically Risky Subordination* (or S3), a stakeholder-sensitive strategy that we explain later. In the remaining situations, the first (left-hand) strategy is to *Reassess the Potential Relationship* (or R) with the rural hospital; the second (right-hand) strategy is the one to follow if the situation is unchanged by the reassessment.

### Stakeholder-sensitive strategies

As a result of considering key stakeholders, each of the three basic generic strategies—nurturing, subordinating, and clarifying roles—is modified in one of two

**FIGURE 5**

STAKEHOLDER-SENSITIVE STRATEGIES FOR URBAN HOSPITALS WHEN CONSIDERING AFFILIATION AGREEMENTS WITH RURAL HOSPITALS

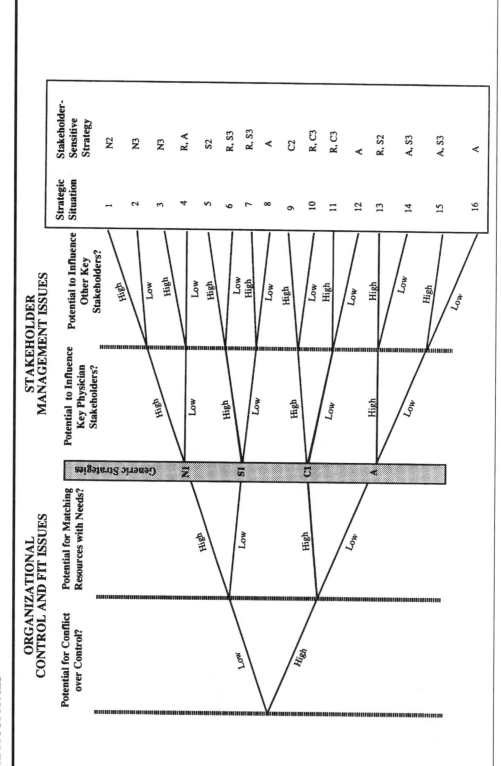

Suggested Affiliation Strategies: N1 = Nurture; S1 = Subordinate; C1 = Clarify Roles; A = Avoid; R = Reassess Potential Relationship; N2 = Intensive Nurturing; S2 = Intensive Subordinating; C2 = Intensive Subordinating; N3 = Politically Nurturing; S3 = Politically Nurturing; C3 = Politically Risky Subordinating; C3 = Politically Risky Clarification.

ways. Either the strategy becomes more intensive or it becomes politically risky.

For example, *Intensive Nurturing* (N2), *Intensive Role Clarification* (C2), and *Intensive Subordinating* (S2) differ from the generic strategies only in terms of degree. There strategies are suggested only when the key stakeholders—physicians and other leaders within the rural community—may be highly influenced by the urban hospital. Because of the key stakeholders' openness to influence from the urban hospital, we suggest that these *intensive* strategies be implemented both rapidly and persuasively. On the one hand, use of persuasive appeals to both groups of key stakeholders is particularly important if the strategy of *Intensive Role Clarification* (C2) is to have maximum impact. On the other hand, rapid enactment of the *Intensive Nurturing* strategy (N2) will enhance the already good relationship with key stakeholders and, equally significantly, preclude other urban hospitals from establishing an affiliation. For instance, the urban facility in Case 1 could probably solidify its relationship with the rural hospital by reviewing and helping to improve other managerial functions such as planning and staffing. Also, as negatively highlighted in Case 3, quickly and convincingly implementing the *Intensive Subordinating* strategy (S2) with a rural hospital should speed up the turnaround time for needed changes and produce greater commitment and referrals from the rural hospital's medical staff.

In contrast, the *Politically Risky Nurturing* (N3), *Politically Risky Role Clarification* (C3), and *Politically Risky Subordinating* (S3) strategies differ from their corresponding generic strategies by focusing and relying on the influence of only one key stakeholder group. For instance, to enact a politically risky strategy of nurturing, the urban hospital must convince the key stakeholders open to its influence (i.e., physicians in Strategic Situation 2, and other stakeholders in Strategic Situation 3) not only to support the affiliation, but also to persuade other key stakeholders to endorse the affiliation. Although this additional burden may not be too troublesome in such highly favorable situations, in less favorable situations it may put the urban hospital at considerable risk.

Recall that the *Politically Risky Clarification* (C3) and *Politically Risky Subordinating* (S3) strategies are listed as choices only after reassessing the affiliation situation (see Figure 5). Part of the reason for suggesting reassessment is that, when only key physicians or other key stakeholders are open to influence, the potential for conflict over control should increase. For

example, as illustrated in Case 2, the C3 strategy calls for the urban hospital to exert influence upon one stakeholder group and convince it to persuade the other stakeholder group of the appropriateness of the urban hospital's role in the proposed affiliation. Understandably, the added burden of convincing one stakeholder group to persuade another stakeholder group of the urban hospital's role makes the C3 strategy quite risky. Similarly, the S3 strategy relies on convincing one stakeholder group that the resources supplied by the urban hospital are sufficient to enhance the rural hospital's survival and to justify referring patients to the urban hospital. Moreover, the targeted stakeholder group must be persuaded to enlist the support of the other stakeholder group, again a risky strategy. In Case 4, for example, where only one of the stakeholder groups had a high potential for being influenced, a politically risky subordinative strategy would have been a viable choice.

### Reassessment and modification of strategies

The diagnostic process involved in choosing a stakeholder-sensitive affiliation strategy is a continuing one. Accordingly, affiliation strategies should change as circumstances change. To determine if a stakeholder-sensitive strategy should be changed, hospital managers must monitor the actions and responses of key stakeholders. These stakeholder reactions will help the management team determine whether strategically relevant elements are undergoing unanticipated changes. If they are, and the situation changes radically, the management team should be ready to modify its affiliation strategy.

## SUMMARY AND IMPLICATIONS

### Summary

Our discussion has shown that urban–rural hospital affiliations are both an outgrowth of the external pressures on rural hospitals to survive and the need for urban hospitals to maintain or increase their share of tertiary referrals. This business strategy perspective led to both an acknowledgment of the significant role of stakeholders in affiliations and a typology of affiliation situations. That typology relied upon the notions of organizational control and fit between the urban and rural hospitals. As indicated in Figure 2, the most favorable situation for an affiliation is one where the urban hospital can readily meet the resource needs of the rural hospital, and both hospitals are satisfied with the proposed control of material, operational, and human resources. Based on that and the other situations, we then suggested four generic strategies for forming affiliations (see Figure 3): nurturing, clarifying roles, subordinating, and avoiding. However, the four cases of affiliation presented and analyzed in this article highlighted the need to account for key stakeholders before entering an affiliation. Thus, the last section illustrated how modifications of the generic affiliation strategies (see Figure 5) would make them sensitive to key stakeholders such as physicians and other leaders of rural communities.

## Managerial implications

Health care executives who are experienced with urban–rural hospital affiliations agree that they are complex relationships, with varying degrees of success. When asked to explain a particular affiliation, they may point to a successful physician recruitment program or improvement in the business office function. Unsuccessful affiliations are often attributed to tactical mistakes or lack of enough time to allow programs to be effective. Rarely, if ever, are stakeholder management issues mentioned.

As we have seen, recognition of stakeholder types should begin at the onset of discussions regarding a potential affiliation relationship. If properly defined, an appropriate affiliation strategy may be taken that optimizes the opportunity for a successful relationship. Additionally, it will identify those situations where the inability to influence key stakeholders and poor organizational control and fit issues are present. Further analysis of this latter situation may lead the hospital to avoid the affiliation relationship, thereby saving resources and preserving a favorable image and reputation.

During the preaffiliation proposal process, business strategy concerns on both sides of the affiliation may deemphasize stakeholder management issues. The rural facility is interested in acquiring specific resources, such as physician recruiting or financial expertise, in a "what-can-you-do-for-me" frame of mind. To some degree, the urban hospital has a complementary agenda, analyzing the opportunity for tertiary referrals and potential new patient admissions.

This singular focus on services and tactics is necessary to justify the affiliation and to win acceptance by the rural hospital's Board of Directors. However, a change of focus should be made immediately after the affiliation aggreement is signed. Rather than building their strategy around applying resources to identified needs, urban personnel should first evaluate the ability to influence key stakeholders. This evaluation will allow the urban hospital to select an appropriate strategy and provide the opportunity to build a mutually beneficial hospital-to-hospital affiliation.

## Research implications

The cases of urban–rural hospital affiliation are direct results of qualitative research and led us to develop the theoretical models presented in this article. The organizational and stakeholder contingencies summarized in Figure 5 present health care management researchers with a set of research questions that can be further refined and tested through more rigorous empirical studies. For example, the line of reasoning developed in this article would suggest that successful and unsuccessful affiliations may be differentiated in terms of both organizational control and fit and stakeholder management. However, because this article assumes the perspective of the urban hospital in the affiliation strategy formation, we also encourage researchers to examine urban–rural affiliations from the rural hospital's perspective. Additionally, a fuller understanding of other types of hospital affiliations is promised by researchers following a stakeholder management perspective.

## REFERENCES

1. Unger, M., and Walker, W.R. "Rural and Urban Hospital Differences." *Health Progress* (1988 Summer): 59–64.
2. DeFriese, G., and Ricketts, T. "Primary Health Care in Rural Areas: An Agenda for Research." *Health Services Research* 23, no. 6 (1989): 932–63.
3. Hart, G., Amundson, B., and Rosenblatt, R. "Is There a Role for the Small Rural Hospital?" *Journal of Rural Health* 6, no. 2 (1990): 101–18.
4. Ermann, D. "Rural Health Care: The Future of the Hospital." *Medical Care Review* 47, no. 1 (1990): 33–73.
5. Morrisey, M., Alexander, J., and Ohsfeldt, R. "Physician Integration Strategies and Hospital Output." *Medical Care* 28, no. 7 (1990): 586–603.
6. Wirthlim, D. "Intermountain Health Care: A System Committed to Rural Health Care." *Hospital and Health Services Administration* 35, no. 2 (1990): 289–301.
7. Lutz, S. "Regional Alliances: Systems Are Coming to the Aid of Endangered Rural Hospitals." *Modern Healthcare* 18, no. 30 (1988, July 22): 48–50.
8. Budd, G., and Ross, D. "Affiliation: When Is It the Right Decision?" *Topics Health Care Finance* 15, no. 1 (1988): 73–81.
9. Mullner, R., and McNeil, D. "Rural and Urban Hospital Closures: A Comparison." *Health Affairs* 5, no. 3 (1986): 131–141.

10. Christianson, J., Moscovice, I., Johnson, J., Kralewski, J., and Grogan, C. "Evaluating Rural Hospital Consortia." *Health Affairs* 10, no. 1 (1990): 136–47.

11. Blair, J.D., and Whitehead, C.J. "Too Many on the Seesaw: Stakeholder Diagnosis and Management for Hospitals." *Hospital and Health Services Administration* 33, no. 2 (1988): 153–66.

12. Savage, G.T., Nix, T.W., Whitehead, C.J., and Blair, J.D. "Strategies for Assessing and Managing Stakeholders." *Academy of Management Executives*, no. 2 (1991): 61–75.

13. Blair, J.D., and Fottler, M.D. *Challenges in Health Care Management: Strategic Perspectives for Managing Key Stakeholders.* San Francisco, Calif.: Jossey-Bass, 1990.

14. Blair, J.D., Savage, G.T., and Whitehead, C.J. "Negotiating with Hospital Stakeholders." *Health Care Management Review* 14, no. 1 (1989): 13–24.

15. Ansoff, I. *Corporate Strategy.* New York, N.Y.: McGraw-Hill, 1965.

16. Carroll, A.B. *Business & Society: Ethics & Stakeholder Management.* Cincinnati, Ohio: South-Western Publishing Co., 1989.

17. Wood, D.J. *Business and Society.* Glenview, Ill.: Scott, Foresman/Little, Brown Higher Education, 1990.

18. Freeman, R. *Strategic Management: A Stakeholder Approach.* Marshfield, Mass.: Pitman Publishing, 1984.

19 Kotter, J.P. "Managing External Dependence." *Academy of Management Review,* 4, no. 1 (1979): 87–92.

20. Pfeffer, J., and Salancik, G. *The External Control of Organizations: A Resource Dependence Perspective.* New York, N.Y.: Harper and Row, 1978.

21. Porter, M.E. *Competitive Advantage: Creating and Sustaining Superior Performance.* New York, N.Y.: Free Press, 1985.

22. Mintzberg, H. *Power In and Around Organizations.* Englewood Cliffs, N.J.: Prentice-Hall, 1983.

23. Carper, W.B., and Litschert, R.J. "Strategic Power Relationships in Contemporary Profit and Nonprofit Hospitals." *Academy of Management Journal* 26, no. 2 (1983): 311–20.

24. Bacharach, S., and Lawler, E. *Power and Politics in Organizations: The Social Psychology of Conflict, Coalitions, and Bargaining.* San Francisco, Calif.: Jossey-Bass, 1980.

25. MacMillan, I.C., and Jones, P.C. *Strategy Formulation: Power and Politics.* 2nd ed. St. Paul, Minn.: West, 1986.

# Hospital markets and competition: Implications for antitrust policy

Nguyen Xuan Nguyen
and
Frederick W. Derrick

*Antitrust and competitive issues are intertwined with efforts to control health care costs. Whether hospital competition holds down costs is an issue of much controversy and is the topic of this article. The findings are consistent with the hypothesis that hospitals compete primarily on a nonprice basis. This suggests that a more flexible application of antitrust policy to hospital mergers will reduce cost increases and will improve efficiency. A step in this direction may be necessary if the managed care plans discussed by the Clinton administration create highly concentrated provider networks.*

*Health Care Manage Rev*, 1994, 19(1), 34–43
© 1994 Aspen Publishers, Inc.

**Applications of** federal antitrust laws toward hospital mergers are receiving attention at an accelerated pace. In June 1992, the Joint Economic Committee convened hearings to consider the market structure of the hospital industry. Six separate legislative proposals were introduced in Congress that would grant at least partial antitrust immunity. In early 1993, the American Hospital Association (AHA) released its proposed national health care reform plan, whose implementation would entail clarifications or modifications of current antitrust enforcement (the AHA plan calls for providers to enter into collaborative arrangements to create community care networks to deliver care). In the March 15, 1993 hearing by the Senate Judiciary Antitrust Subcommittee, drug manufacturers, physicians, and hospitals unsuccessfully made their case for weaker antitrust laws. The pace will probably pick up speed as the Clinton administration's health reform proposal, containing features of managed competition, is released. Under managed competition, providers will be encouraged to form networks to compete for the business of health care purchasing cooperatives or alliances. Would these networks and alliances be compatible with antitrust laws? Judiciary Committee ranking Republican Orrin Hatch (R-Utah), a free market proponent, argues that there is need for some reevaluation of the antitrust laws if the administration proposes managed competition as part of the health system reform.[1]

Hospital antitrust and competitive issues are intertwined with efforts to control health care costs. Health care accounted for 13.6 percent of the Gross Domestic Product (GDP) in 1992 and at the historical rate of 10 percent annual increase will account for 18 percent of the GDP in the year 2000. Hospital care has been a target of cost-containment efforts because it accounts for 43.7 percent of total health care spending.[2] Both private and public payers began to exercise restraint on their reimbursement rates and to encourage competition to control cost in the 1980s. Medicare imple-

*Nguyen Xuan Nguyen, Ph.D., is an economist at the International Bank for Reconstruction and Development/The World Bank, Washington, D.C.*

*Frederick W. Derrick, Ph.D., is Professor of Economics at Loyola College in Baltimore, Maryland.*

This article originated when the authors were at the Office of the Assistant Secretary for Planning and Evaluation of the U.S. Department of Health and Human Services. The views expressed herein are those of the authors. No official endorsement by the institutions with which the authors were or are affiliated is intended or should be inferred. The authors wish to express their gratitude for the helpful comments of M. Eugene Moyer, Stuart Schmid, Steve Walters, and Paul Gayer.

mented in 1984 the prospective payment system (PPS), which reimburses hospitals on a predetermined rate for each discharge. By the end of the 1980s, Medicare rates were about 90 percent of costs, whereas Medicaid rates were less than 80 percent of costs.[3]

The competitive approach included antitrust implementation as a means to preserve competitive markets. Whether the resulting hospital competition holds down costs is an issue of much controversy and the topic of this article. The medical arms race, spurred by competition among hospitals and a reimbursement system that encourages the rapid adoption of technology, was the main cause of hospital cost inflation in the 1980s, as reported by the General Accounting Office in March 1993.

The U.S. Department of Justice (DOJ) and the Federal Trade Commission (FTC) have shown commensurate interest in hospital mergers. They jointly released the revised horizontal merger guidelines on April 2, 1992. This revision poses continuing and new challenges for hospital mergers because federal agencies challenge nearly 3 percent of hospital merger attempts while investigating approximately 10 percent of hospital mergers. Moreover, the threat of a challenge may scare off a potential merger because the expenses of fighting a challenge may have a chilling effect on merger considerations. Hospitals in Roanoke, Virginia spent $1.5 million in legal fees and another $1 million in consulting fees over the three years of their case.[4] The nonprofit 43-bed Ukiah Valley Medical Center in Ukiah, California has spent $1.7 million fighting the FTC action against its merger with the 51-bed Ukiah General. Both facilities were financially failing and located in a rural area, where most of the patients were on Medicare and Medicaid.[5] States are also increasing their antitrust activities. Results from the multistate task force of the National Association of Attorney Generals indicate that states have filed or investigated more than 70 antitrust cases in the health care industry since 1985.[6]

Hospital mergers are important to the hospital industry. Mergers have taken place in many, if not most, urban areas.[7] More than half of 500 hospital administrators surveyed in 1988 expected their hospitals to merge in the next 5 years.[8] Of 1,700 hospital executives surveyed in 1990, 43 percent felt that their institutions

could fail financially within 5 years. Merger was considered the primary means of safeguarding their continued operation.[9]

With the strong industry and judicial interest in hospital antitrust, there is a critical need for an understanding of the updated criteria used to evaluate hospital mergers and the implications of hospital mergers on their services and costs. This article describes the joint DOJ and FTC merger guidelines and examines their application to hospital mergers. Special emphasis is given to the thorny issue of defining the product market and delimiting the geographic market of hospital services. The article then addresses the question of the effects of hospital antitrust (e.g., hospital competition) on prices, margins, and costs.

The literature survey suggests that increased hospital competition is associated with higher costs, lower occupancy rates, reduced efficiency, and more service offerings. These findings are consistent with the hypothesis that hospitals compete primarily on a nonprice basis, such as by competing for physicians or striving for a higher level of status, prestige, or amenities. This suggests that a more flexible application of the guidelines to hospital mergers will reduce cost increases and improve efficiency. The current literature, however, relies mainly on data from before or during the early implementation of PPS. This data constraint should be kept in mind when extending the conclusion drawn from the literature into the post-PPS era because PPS payments currently account for approximately 40 percent of hospital revenue.

## MERGER GUIDELINES

Mergers between competing firms may increase market power (i.e., the ability and likelihood of market manipulation by restricting output and therefore raising prices) and also may increase efficiency through economies of scale, economies of scope, or reductions in the duplication of services, facilities, and administrative overhead. Any efficiencies due to a merger must be weighed against any increase in market power to determine whether the merger may be substantially to lessen competition or will tend to create a monopoly, as defined in Section 7 of the Clayton Act.

The primary antitrust statutes are Section 7 of the Clayton Act and Section 1 of the Sherman Act. The acts are principally founded on the structure-conduct-performance paradigm of industrial economics, which maintains that high market concentration allows firms to set prices (and, hence, to earn high profit margins)

*A merger review follows the approach presented in the 1992 joint Department of Justice and Federal Trade Commission merger guidelines.*

at the expense of the consumers.[10] According to this theory, antitrust enforcement is necessary because mergers that substantially raise concentration will impede competition, reduce social welfare, and hurt consumers by reducing output and inflating prices.

It is unclear whether Section 7 of the Clayton Act is applicable to mergers of nonprofit hospitals as a result of contradictory court rulings in 1989. A federal district court decision in Roanoke, Virginia held that it cannot, whereas a decision in Rockport, Illinois held the opposite [*United States v. Carilion Health System et al.*, No. 88-0249-R (W.D. VA., filed May 27, 1988); *United States v. Rockport Memorial Corporation et al.*, No. 88-C-20186 (N.D. IL., filed June 1, 1988)]. Section 1 of the Sherman Act clearly applies to nonprofit hospitals as well as to proprietary ones. It prohibits all contracts, combinations, and conspiracies in restraint of trade.

A merger review follows the approach presented in the 1992 joint DOJ and FTC merger guidelines. The 1992 guidelines revise the DOJ's 1984 merger guidelines and the FTC's 1982 statement concerning horizontal merger guidelines. They are firmly based on the mainstream of industrial organization, notably the standard oligopoly theory and the advancement of game theory, which proposes that the easier it is for a group of firms to coordinate and monitor their policies, the more likely they will result in a monopoly outcome.[10–12] The guidelines establish a five-step protocol for evaluating the potential impact of a horizontal merger on the competitive environment of an industry. First, a relevant market is determined as the smallest group of firms spread across product and geographic space that could concertedly raise prices from their current levels by 5 percent (in most cases) and sustain them profitably for a year. Definition of the market is important because the measure of market concentration varies according to how the market area is defined.

In defining the product market, courts have usually resorted to the standard of reasonable interchangeability of use.[13] The standard of reasonable interchangeability of use in hospital mergers might dictate the creation of multiple, distinct, subproduct markets at, for instance, the level of diagnosis-related groups or similar groupings of diagnoses or procedures.[14–16] These approaches take into account the substitution in demand for different services but fail to incorporate the substitution in supply by hospitals.

Thus the relevant product market for hospitals is the cluster of services provided by the hospitals and not individual services or procedures. Landes and Posner argue that when there is relative ease of substitutability of supply by fringe firms the output of these firms may be included in the relevant product market.[17] The product market has been defined as consisting of general acute care hospital services excluding outpatient substitutes for the individual services in the cluster, short-term acute care hospital services, inpatient psychiatric care by private psychiatric hospitals and nongovernment general acute care hospitals, acute inpatient care, and inpatient hospital services including outpatient substitutes for those services. Inpatient admissions or days have generally been used to define the product of a hospital.

Geographic market delineation in the extant hospital merger opinions have been based primarily on geopolitical boundaries or patient flow statistics. The patient flow approach is based on commitment and relevance ratios. The patient flow approach was advanced in the early 1970s by Griffith and was modified by Zwanziger and Melnick.[14,18] It can be viewed as the hospital version of the LIFO-LOFI test of shipments into or out of the proposed market. According to this test, an appropriately defined market area is such that shipments can be described as a little in from outside (LIFO) and a little out from inside (LOFI).[19] Commitment is the share of hospital usage (measured by discharges) by residents in the market area that is provided by the local hospitals. Relevance is the share of hospital output going to local residents. An appropriately defined market will have commitment and relevance measures close to unity. The use of actual patient data underestimates the market size if an anticompetitive price increase would make patients willing to travel larger distances. On the other hand, if some firms in the defined market area are operating at full capacity, they could not increase output in response to an anticompetitive price increase of some other firms in the same market area. Yet some firms outside the market boundaries may find it profitable to respond. This implies that the commitment ratio using actual discharge data may underestimate the size of the geographic market.

The geopolitical boundaries in most cases are highly localized. The two most frequently used regions have been counties and standard metropolitan statistical areas (SMSAs).[20–23] Other market boundaries used include health facilities planning areas, health services areas, and 5- or 15-mile radii around a hospital.[24–28] Morrisey, Sloan, and Valvona suggest that hospital markets may be larger than believed in both urban and rural areas.[29] Their study shows that neither urban nor rural hospital markets are likely to be highly concentrated and implies that in most cases hospital mergers will not impede competition.

After the product and geographic markets are defined, market concentration is computed using the Herfindahl-Hirschman Index (HHI) to determine whether the merger would induce potentially adverse competition. HHI is defined as the sum of squared market shares of the firms in the market, where market shares are treated as whole numbers. It ranges from 0, depicting a competitive market, to 10,000, portraying a monopoly. If the postmerger HHI is less than 1,000, the market is considered unconcentrated, and the merger would not be challenged. If the postmerger HHI is between 1,000 and 1,800, the market is moderately concentrated, and the merger would not be challenged unless it would increase the HHI by more than 100 points. If the postmerger HHI is greater than 1,800, the market is highly concentrated. Usually, the DOJ and FTC would not pursue a detailed analysis of a proposed merger in that market unless it results in an increase in the HHI of at least 50 points. If the proposed merger passes the concentration test (i.e., the postmerger HHI is less than 1,000, between 1,000 and 1,800 and the resulting HHI increase is less than 100, or greater than 1,800 but the resulting HHI increase is less than 50), it would be allowed to be completed in most cases. Otherwise, additional steps will follow.

The third step assesses whether entry would be timely, likely, and sufficient either to deter or to counterbalance the potential adverse competitive effects. A perfectly contestable market is an example of perfect ease of entry and is often characterized by the absence of sunk costs.[30] In addition, it is a market where potential producers have access to the same technical and productive attributes. High supply substitutability is also a property of easy entry. Easy entry could justify a merger resulting in a potential monopoly because economic theory predicts that monopoly behavior could not be sustained in this market.

In addition to the criterion of ease of entry, other factors will be considered to verify that the merger will not harm consumer welfare. These factors represent potential efficiencies and imminent financial failure. The fourth step assesses whether efficiency gains claimed by the parties cannot be reasonably achieved through other means. The efficiency criterion is based on the potential trade-off between enhanced market power and efficiencies resulting from a merger.[31] Compared with the earlier guidelines, the 1992 version is apparently more receptive to the efficiency

gains argument by the proposed merger. The fifth step analyzes whether either party would fail but for the merger. The financial failure factor requires three conditions: (1) The firm is failing or will fail in the immediate future, (2) the firm has a limited chance of reorganizing itself successfully under Chapter 11 of the Bankruptcy Act, and (3) there are no alternative buyers or acquirees who would be less anticompetitive.

## THE EFFECTS OF HOSPITAL COMPETITION

Application of the guidelines to hospital mergers is based on the premise that competition leads to increased efficiency and reduced costs and encourages the development of managed care. This section evaluates the empirical support for the application of antitrust policy to hospital mergers. The studies in the literature took two approaches to assess the effects of hospital competition on their performance. One approach considers each merger an event and compares the performance of the merging hospitals before and after the event relative to comparable hospitals. If the event study shows that merging hospitals (even in a concentrated market) do not necessarily raise prices, then a stern antitrust enforcement toward hospital mergers might not always be necessary. Moreover, if mergers eventually lead to lower costs, then efficiency consideration may be given a heavier weight in hospital merger analysis and review. The second approach examines the relationship between market concentration and performance. Most studies in the literature rely on the latter approach.

### Service intensity, availability, and costs

In one of the earliest studies on hospital competition, Salkever found that hospitals in areas with a large number of rivals experienced higher average costs.[32] This finding was supported in a number of later studies based on pre-PPS data.[22,23,26,33] More recent studies raise the question of the balance between potential reductions in price competition and improvements in efficiency resulting from hospital mergers.[34,35]

Joskow, using 1976 data on 346 private, nonprofit hospitals, found that hospitals in areas with low concentration (i.e., competitive areas) maintain a high reserve supply of beds.[21] This result is based on a queuing model characterizing the bed supply decision as dependent on demand uncertainty, industry organization, nonprice competition, and regulation. The variables that characterize competition include the HHI, the number of physicians per hospital (describing nonprice competition or quality/intensity of care competition), and the percentage of insured patients enrolled in health maintenance organizations (HMOs) in the area (depicting competition for physicians). The market area is defined to be the SMSA. Joskow concluded that policies to encourage hospital competitive behavior may induce hospitals to expand quality and quantity beyond the efficient level. The conclusion that empty beds are inefficient may exaggerate the true long-run social cost because Friedman and Pauly estimated that the cost of empty beds was about 8 percent of the cost of a full bed.[36] Nevertheless, given a national hospital occupancy rate of 60 percent, policies that might exacerbate this waste would not be the most desirable ones.

Hersch found that increased competition (decreased concentration) entices more intense nonprice competition as measured by expenditures, registered nurses, and licensed practical nurses per day of care.[22] The study also showed more ardent competition for physicians through better staff support and longer average hospitalization associated with lower concentration. Nonprice competition was concluded to lead to higher service intensity, divergence of resources away from patient care and toward attracting physicians, and therefore higher costs.

Providing further supporting evidence, Luft et al. found evidence of duplication of 29 specialized clinical services in competitive market areas.[33] Their survey contained information about 5,900 short-term general hospitals extracted from the 1972 *Survey of Specialized Clinical Services*, the AHA's annual survey, and the *Area Resource File*. They defined the geographic market area of a hospital as that region within a 5- or 15-mile radius around that hospital.

Robinson and Luft investigated the impact of hospital market structure on inpatient admissions, inpatient cost per diem, and inpatient cost per case using the same market definition and 1972 data.[26] Hospitals in competitive areas experienced relatively lower patient volume and higher costs both per diem and per case. Hospitals with 2 to 4 competitors incurred costs 9 percent higher than hospitals with 1 competitor. Those with 5 to 10 competitors reported costs 16 to 17 percent higher, and those with more than 10 rivals incurred costs 20 to 21 percent higher. Later, Robinson and Luft updated their study to test whether hospital performance changed from 1972 to 1982 as a result of market structure.[27] They again found that hospitals with more rivals incurred higher average costs per admission. In a later update from 1982 to 1986, however,

Robinson and Luft found that hospitals in highly competitive areas experienced lower adjusted cost inflation than those in more concentrated markets.[37] This conclusion is not robust given that "in both years hospitals in more competitive local markets experienced significantly higher costs than did hospitals in less competitive markets." Thus the rate of cost increase in the more competitive markets may be smaller even though the absolute dollar increase may have been larger.

Farley examined the effect of market structure on various performance variables using data on 400 short-term, general, nonfederal U.S. hospitals from 1970 to 1977.[20] Based on the HHI using county as the market area, hospitals were classified into one of three groups: monopolistic, intermediate, or competitive. After controlling for urban/rural location, ownership, geographic region, and other factors, Farley did not find statistically significant differences in profit margins associated with market structure. Operating expenses per case, a proxy for intensity of care, were 19 percent higher in competitive than in monopolistic markets, and lengths of stay were longer in competitive than in monopolistic markets. Farley concluded that hospitals in competitive markets produce more expensive care by employing more capital and labor resources, offering more services, performing more procedures, and keeping patients longer.

Noether, in an FTC study using 1977 and 1978 data, defined the market as the SMSA (or county for rural areas) and used the HHI to measure market concentration.[23] Other variables were used to describe hospital market structure, including concentration ratios, share of beds owned by public hospitals, voluntary and for-profit hospitals, HMO market penetration, system affiliation of hospitals, and physicians per capita. Although unable to establish any significant relationship between concentration and price, the study found that hospital costs per admission increased significantly more in competitive markets. This can be attributed to differences in nonprice competition. The study also found that certificate of need laws led to higher prices and costs; that HMO membership affected neither prices nor costs significantly, although the study speculated that this relationship would probably change in the future; and that more physicians per capita or per bed drove up costs. The study also found some indication that hospitals are beginning to compete more on price than previously.

Nguyen examined the relationship of market concentration and production efficiency to the financial performance of U.S. short-term general hospitals using post-PPS data from 1987 to 1988.[38] The study derived a market competition indicator for an industry composed of nonprofit firms that maximize a utility function in both quality and quantity of output. The study again found that hospitals in less concentrated markets incur higher average total costs (controlling for urban/rural location, case mix, teaching status, etc.). Moreover, the significant negative impact of concentration on profit margins suggests that hospitals in concentrated markets, albeit experiencing lower costs, may not be able to exercise their market power to restrict output and raise price. (This inability may be attributable to the impact of PPS, which severely restricts the capability of hospitals to set prices on at least 40 percent of their revenues.) The study concluded that the significant negative correlation between concentration and profit margins suggests that enforcement of Section 7 of the Clayton Act could tolerate more flexibility.

Although the preceding studies define market areas based on geopolitical boundaries or geographic radii, a RAND study by Zwanziger and Melnick broke away from this tradition.[14] The HHI in that study was calculated in three steps: (1) Define service-specific market areas for each short-term general hospital; (2) for each service, identify each hospital's competitors and calculate its service-specific HHI; and (3) obtain the overall measure of competition faced by each hospital by service case weight averaging its service-specific HHIs. The service-specific market area is based on the ZIP codes of patients' origins, an approach parallel to Griffith's.[18] The study examined the impact on the rate of increase of total hospital expenses due to market structure, selective contracting, and PPS using the California Office of Statewide Health Planning and Development data from 1980 to the third quarter of 1985. The study found that since the implementation of California's procompetition legislation in January 1983 the structure of California's hospital competition changed from nonprice competition to price competition. Specifically, hospitals in less concentrated markets experienced less cost inflation than

---

*Since the implementation of California's procompetition legislation in January 1983 the structure of California's hospital competition changed from nonprice competition to price competition.*

---

those in more concentrated markets. Fuchs, however, noted that hospitals in highly competitive markets had almost 50 percent higher expenses per case in 1983 to begin with.[39] Hence their rate of cost increase would be smaller even with similar or greater absolute dollar increases.

In a more recent study focusing on California, Melnick et al. again confirmed that greater hospital competition leads to lower prices.[40] Specifically, using 1987 data on 190 hospitals in the Blue Cross of California preferred provider organization (PPO) network, the investigators found that Blue Cross pays higher prices to hospitals located in less competitive markets. This conclusion should be qualified given that the investigators found that higher prices are associated with more costly hospitals that provide a more expensive mix of services. The study also showed that the use of county to define market areas leads to an underestimate of the price-increasing effects resulting from hospital mergers. The investigators, however, recognized that the study was highly specific and suggested that before findings were generalized they should be replicated for different payers in different areas under different time periods.

An event study using stock prices was used by Wooley to study 29 mergers of for-profit hospitals in the period from 1969 to 1985.[34] The use of stock prices instead of traditional accounting profit margins has two advantages. First, stock prices better reflect expected future revenues after the merger, and second, they are less prone to measurement errors as a result of the variety of accounting approaches used in calculating profit margins. The mergers resulted in increased stock prices for both merging and nonmerging hospitals in the market. Wooley maintains that, if the merger reduces competition, then the stock prices of all hospitals within the market area (merging and competitors) will rise. On the other hand, if the merger is due to efficiency, then the stock prices of the merging hospitals will rise while those of the competing ones will fall. Wooley's results suggest that mergers of for-profit hospitals result in less competition and higher revenue. The higher revenue may be driven by the reduction of duplication of services or enhanced occupancy due to the drop in the number of hospitals in the area. Wooley notes that mergers may reduce competition but may also serve to increase efficiency by reducing overconsumption of both the quantity and quality of health care.

An event study of 36 mergers during the post-PPS era from 1985 to 1987 showed that the merged hospitals did not behave as monopolists. In the period from 2 years before merging to 2 years after merging, the hospital average total profit shrank. During this time, the average operating expenses per adjusted admission decreased, albeit after an initial surge after the event, and the average net patient revenue declined.[35]

A more current report by the Inspector General for the U.S. Department of Health and Human Services compared 11 hospital mergers in 1987 to a control group of hospitals that were geographically similar to the 11 hospitals.[41] The report found that merged hospitals reduce the cost of doing business but otherwise are not different from those that have not participated in a merger.

In summary, the literature supports the hypothesis that hospitals compete primarily on a nonprice basis. Increased hospital competition is associated with higher costs, lower occupancy rates, reduced efficiency, and more service offerings. The recent literature is less consistent on this point and may imply that some features of price competition may be applicable in the future.

### Managed care

Antitrust issues will also become more prevalent as medical care moves toward managed care as a means of limiting cost increases. Managed care is generally defined as a system that integrates the financing and delivery of appropriate medical care. The most common types of managed care organizations are HMOs, PPOs, and independent practice associations (IPAs). These structures offer a greater concentration of purchasers of hospital services while providing greater concentration of physician services. The evidence regarding whether managed care plans save money is mixed.[42]

Early research conducted in the 1970s and 1980s found that managed care failed to live up to the expected cost reductions. For example, Kralewski et al. found that HMOs that gave large discounts did not have lower per case costs.[43] Moreover, these discounts did not appear to make the hospitals more efficient in the long run.[44,45] Johnson and Aquilina showed that discounts merely shifted higher prices to other payers without producing any overall cost reduction.[46] Langwell and Hadley found in their evaluation of the Medicare HMO demonstrations that almost all HMOs studied had experienced favorable selection.[47] Their evaluation suggests that the Health Care Financing Administration paid between 15 and 33 percent more for beneficiaries enrolled under risk contracts than

would have been paid for those individuals in the fee-for-service sector.

Newer evidence, however, suggests that managed care can contain cost. Feldman et al. found evidence to suggest that HMOs lead to the use of more price-competitive hospitals (i.e., lower-price hospitals).[48] Robinson strengthens this conclusion by finding that competition between insurers and HMOs had a significant impact on reducing cost inflation.[49] The study argues that the earlier findings were a result of legal and institutional constraints. A recent survey of nearly 2,000 employers by A. Foster Higgins & Co. also suggests that managed care can limit costs.[50] According to the survey, companies spent on average $2,683 in 1990 for each employee enrolled in an HMO compared with $3,214 for an indemnity plan. The cost increase of HMO coverage in 1990 of 15.7 percent was substantially lower than the 21.6 percent rise in the cost of indemnity plan coverage. The survey did not address the questions of cost shifting and favorable selection.

A Congressional Budget Office report summarizes the picture:

> The available evidence suggests that group and staff model HMOs can have a significant impact on use and costs of services for their enrollees, although these effects may not lower systemwide costs. Research on IPAs and PPOs is more limited, particularly when considering only well designed studies with data to control for selection effects. The limited evidence suggests that these forms of managed care may reduce use and costs, but there is much less certainty about this conclusion.[51]

Regardless of the cost impact, antitrust issues will be of concern because of the increased level of concentration in managed care providers, especially if managed competition is a part of system reform by the Clinton administration. An originator of the managed competition concept estimated that a market with a population of 1.2 million could only support three fully independent plans. A population of 180,000 could support three plans but would have to share many inpatient services. The study found that 71 percent of the U.S. population lives in health markets with populations greater than 180,000. The rest live in even less densely populated areas. One implication of this finding is that with managed competition the health plan market will be concentrated.[52]

### IMPLICATIONS FOR ANTITRUST POLICY

A policy of active enforcement of antitrust laws to maintain and further competition in the hospital industry could increase health care spending. Competition is advocated as a remedy for controlling hospital costs on the grounds that it would increase efficiency, thereby reducing prices. Antitrust enforcement is designed along this logic. The crucial question is whether the nature of hospital competition is price or nonprice. In most other markets, price competition is the norm. In the health care market, consumers tend to be poorly informed about both price and quality of care. In addition, consumers are largely insensitive to price because of insurance and government entitlements. These factors limit the price-reducing market pressures and induce hospitals to compete on a nonprice basis. Moreover, the risk-averse and defensive nature of medical care encourages perceived quality competition. Consequently, it has been the case that the higher the competition, the higher the costs. The recent trend toward competitive reform in health care, such as higher consumer copayments and deductibles and deeper market penetration of HMOs, PPOs, for-profit hospitals, and hospital chains, may lead to greater price competition in the hospital industry.

The literature review supports the conclusion that increased hospital competition is associated with higher costs, lower occupancy rates, reduced efficiency, and more service offerings. The maintenance of lower market concentration through antitrust enforcement runs the risk of encouraging nonprice competition and, in turn, increasing total hospital expenditures.

An active enforcement of antitrust laws is not always supported by recent developments in economic theory. Farrell and Shapiro show that mergers can be welfare enhancing.[53] Daugherty demonstrates that leader-generating mergers can be socially desirable.[54] Additional findings in this literature include the following: Mergers that simply lower the number of competitors without increasing the number of leaders reduce welfare; breaking up a leader firm into two followers reduces welfare, although the number of competitors increases; and under some conditions leader-generating mergers within markets with fewer than 28 competitors are not only welfare enhancing but also profit increasing. This third point may explain Wooley's results, discussed above.[34] Levin shows that, if a group of firms with less than 50 percent of market share considers a horizontal merge, then any contraction of output by the merged group will cut profits below the level obtained by only reallocating its premerger output, and any profitable merger will raise welfare.[55] These new developments in economic theory show mergers can increase social welfare even if profit margins also increase.

Application of Telser's 1978 work to hospitals would argue that cooperation among hospitals is not only desirable but imperative under specific conditions.[56] If the hospitals in the market face declining average total costs over the range of total patients in the market, the marginal costs will lie below the average costs. In this instance, competition for patients will prevent hospitals from breaking even through price competition. In such an instance, it could be potentially advantageous from society's view and from the hospital's view that hospitals cooperate rather than engage in detrimental price competition. Application of Bittlingmayer's work would argue that antitrust action could be counterproductive because it would encourage mergers that may be less competitive and less efficient.[57]

The surveyed literature on hospital competition and the recent developments in economic theory suggest that active antitrust enforcement to ensure strong competition among hospitals may not always be beneficial. It may be costly because of the cost of nonprice competition and the cost of antitrust enforcement. The cost–benefit analysis of antitrust implementation, as implied in the efficiency criteria of the guidelines, would suggest a more flexible enforcement. The 1992 merger guidelines make a noticeable step in the direction of more flexible application because the issues of entry, efficiencies, and the failing firm are given greater emphasis than in earlier guidelines. It remains to be seen, however, whether antitrust enforcement of hospitals will reflect this direction. A step in this direction may be necessary if the managed care plans discussed by the Clinton administration create highly concentrated provider networks.

## REFERENCES

1. "Managed Competition: Antitrust-Buster?" *Medicine & Health* 47 (1993).
2. Committee on Ways and Means, U.S. House of Representatives. *Health Care Resource Book.* Washington, D.C.: Government Printing Office, 1993.
3. Prospective Payment Assessment Commission. *Medicaid Hospital Payment.* Washington, D.C.: PPAC, 1991.
4. *Healthweek* (5 November 1990): 36.
5. *Medicine & Health* 47, no. 10 (1993).
6. *Modern Healthcare* (17 December 1990): 4–7.
7. Muller, R.M., and Andersen, R.M. "A Descriptive and Financial Ratio Analysis of Merged and Consolidated Hospitals: United States, 1980–1985." *Advances in Health Economics and Health Services Research* 41 (1987).
8. "Antitrust Barriers Threaten Hospital Mergers." *Medicine & Health* (16 October 1989).

9. "Hospital Execs See Mergers, Closures Coming in 1990s." *Health Care Competition Week* 7, no. 27 (July 2, 1990).

10. Stigler, G. "A Theory of Oligopoly." *Journal of Political Economy* 72 (1964): 44–61.

11. Chamberlain, E.H. *The Theory of Monopolistic Competition*. Cambridge, Mass.: Harvard University Press, 1933.

12. Fellner, W. *Competition Among the Few*. New York, N.Y.: Knopf, 1949.

13. U.S. Department of Justice. "Merger Guidelines." *Federal Register* 49 (1984):26, 824.

14. Zwanziger, J., and Melnick, G.A. "The Effects of Hospital Competition and the Medicare PPS Program on Hospital Cost Behavior in California." *Journal of Health Economics* 7, no. 4 (1988): 301–20.

15. Jacobs, P. "Antitrust Consideration for Hospital Mergers: Market Definition and Market Concentration." Unpublished paper presented to the Conference on Mergers in Health Care, 10–11 April 1986.

16. Wilder, R.P., and Jacobs, P. "Antitrust Considerations for Hospital Mergers." *Advances in Health Economics and Health Services Research* (1987).

17. Landes, W.M., and Posner, R.A. "Market Power in Antitrust Cases." *Harvard Law Review* 94 (1981): 937–96.

18. Griffith, J.R. *Determining Population Service Areas and Calculating Use Rates, Quantitative Techniques for Hospital Planning and Control*. Lexington, Mass.: Lexington Books, 1972.

19. Elzinga, K.G., and Hogarty, T.F. "The Problem of Geographic Market Delineation in Antimerger Suits." *Antitrust Bulletin* XVIII (1973): 45–81.

20. Farley, D.E. *Competition among Hospitals: Market Structure and Its Relation to Utilization, Costs and Financial Position*, 1985.

21. Joskow, P.L. "The Effects of Competition and Regulation on Hospital Bed Supply and the Reservation Quality of the Hospital." *Bell Journal of Economics* 11 (Autumn 1990): 421–47.

22. Hersch, P.L. "Competition and the Performance of Hospital Markets." *Review of Industrial Organization* 1, no. 4 (1984).

23. Noether, M. "Competition Among Hospitals." *Journal of Health Economics* 7 (1988): 259–84.

24. Schramm, C.J., and Renn, S.C. "Hospital Mergers, Market Concentration and the Herfindahl-Hirschman Index." *Emory Law Review* 33, no. 4 (1984).

25. Erickson, G.M., and Finkler, S.A. "Determinants of Market Share for a Hospital's Services." *Medical Care* 23 (1985).

26. Robinson, J.C., and Luft, H.S. "The Impact of Hospital Market Structure on Patient Volume, Average Length of Stay, and the Cost of Care." *Journal of Health Economics* 4, no. 2 (1985): 333–56.

27. Robinson, J.C., and Luft, H.S. "Competition and the Cost of Hospital Care, 1972 to 1982." *Journal of the American Medical Association* 257, no. 23 (1987): 3, 241–5.

28. Garnick, D.W., et al. "Appropriate Measures of Hospital Market Areas." *Health Services Research* 22 (1987).

29. Morrisey, M.A., Sloan, F.A., and Valvona, J. "Defining Geographic Markets for Hospitals and the Extent of Market Concentration." *Law and Contemporary Problems* 51, no. 2 (1989): 165–94.

30. Baumol, W.J. "Contestable Markets: An Uprising in the Theory of Industry Structure." *American Economic Review* 72 (1982): 1–15.

31. Williamson, O.E. "Economies as an Antitrust Defense: The Welfare Tradeoffs." *American Economic Review* 58 (1968): 18–36.

32. Salkever, D.S. *Hospital Sector Inflation*. Lexington, Mass.: Lexington Books, 1979.

33. Luft, H.S., et al. "Competition among Hospitals: The Role of Specialized Clinical Services." *Inquiry* 23 (1986).

34. Wooley, M.J. "The Competitive Effects of Horizontal Mergers in the Hospital Industry." *Journal of Health Economics* 8 (1989): 271–92.

35. *Modern Healthcare* (19 March 1990): 24–36.

36. Friedman, P.J., and Pauly, M.V. "Cost Functions for Service Firms with Variable Quality and Stochastic Demand: The Case of Hospitals." *Review of Economics and Statistics* 63 (1981): 620–5.

37. Robinson, J.C., and Luft, H.S. "Competition, Regulation, and Hospital Costs, 1982 to 1986." *Journal of the American Medical Association* 260, no. 18 (1988): 2, 676–81.

38. Nguyen, N.X. "Industrial Economics of the Hospital Industry: The Relationship of Market Structure and Market Share to Hospital Performance." Ph.D. diss. George Mason University, Fairfax, Va., 1990.

39. Fuchs, V.R. "The 'Competition Revolution' in Health Care." *Health Affairs* 7, no. 3 (1988).

40. Melnick, G.A., et al. "The Effects of Market Structure and Bargaining Position on Hospital Prices." *Journal of Health Economics* 11 (1992): 217–33.

41. Inspector General, U.S. Department of Health and Human Services. *Effects of Hospital Mergers on Costs, Revenues, and Patient Volume*. Washington, D.C.: HHS, 1992.

42. Iglehart, J. "Health Policy Report, the American Health Care System: Managed Care." *New England Journal of Medicine* 10, no. 327 (1992): 742–7.

43. Kralewski, J.E., Countryman, D., and Shatin, D. "Patterns of Interorganizational Relationships between Hospitals and HMOs." *Inquiry* 19 (1982): 357–62.

44. Luft, H.S., Maerki, S.C., and Trauner, J.B. "The Competitive Effects of Health Maintenance Organizations: Another Look at the Evidence from Hawaii, Rochester, and Minneapolis/St. Paul." *Journal of Health Politics, Policy and Law* 10 (1986): 625–58.

45. McLaughlin, C.G. "The Effects of HMOs on Overall Hospital Expenses: Is Anything Left after Correcting for Simultaneity and Selectivity." *Health Services Research* 23 (1988): 421–41.

46. Johnson, A.N., Aquilina, D. "The Impact of Health Maintenance Organizations and Competition on Hospitals in Minneapolis/St. Paul." *Journal of Health Politics, Policy and Law* 10 (1986): 659–74.

47. Langwell, K.M., and Hadley, J.P. "Insights from the Medicare HMO Demonstrations." *Health Affairs* (Spring 1990): 75–84.

48. Feldman, R., Chan, H.-C., and Kralewski, J. "Effects of HMOs on the Creation of Competitive Markets for Hospital Services." *Journal of Health Economics* 9 (1990): 207–22.

49. Robinson, J.C. "HMO Market Penetration and Hospital Cost Inflation in California." *Journal of the American Medical Association* 266 (1991): 2,719–23.

50. *Wall Street Journal* (August 12, 1991).

51. Langwell, K. *The Effects of Managed Care on Use and Costs of Health Services* Washington, D.C.: Congressional Budget Office, 1992.

52. Kronick, R., et al. "The Market Place in Health Care Reform: The Demographic Limitations of Managed Competition." *New England Journal of Medicine* 328 (1993): 148–52.

53. Farrell, J., and Shapiro, C. "Horizontal Mergers: An Equilibrium Analysis." *American Economic Review* 80 (1990): 107–26.

54. Daughety, A.F. "Beneficial Concentration." *American Economic Review* 80 (1990): 1,231–7.

55. Levin, D. "Horizontal Mergers: The 50-Percent Benchmark." *American Economic Review* 80 (December 1990): 1,238–45.

56. Telser, L. *Economic Theory and the Core.* Chicago, Ill.: University of Chicago Press, 1978.

57. Bittlingmayer, G. "Did Antitrust Policy Cause the Great Merger Wave?" *Journal of Law and Economics* 28 (1985): 77–118.

# Integrating health care with information technology: Knitting patient information through networking

Joseph K.H. Tan
and
John Hanna

*This article discusses the importance of integrating health care with information technology to improve the efficiency, effectiveness, and innovation of health care institutions. It is argued that in addition to networking and the selection of a distributed client/server architecture that conforms to open systems protocols, the adoption of standards and the establishment of a management technology infrastructure would provide the necessary steps and mechanisms to allow for a smoother transition to greater sophistication in the development of total systems integration.*

*Health Care Manage Rev*, 1994, 19(2), 72–80
© 1994 Aspen Publishers, Inc.

**In today's environment** of spiraling health care costs, those responsible for managing the delivery of health care are increasingly charged with the task of providing more for less. A recent report by the British Columbia (BC) Economic and Statistical Review[1] unveils that expenditures on health programs in BC totaled $5,618 million, or 32 percent of the total provincial government programs for the year. A variety of solutions have been proposed to reduce the cost of health care, for example, a capping of physicians' salaries, the instituting of user fees, or the prioritizing and rationing of health care services. Alternatively, strategies involving the use of information technology (IT) to increase productivity, improve quality of care, provide better performance measures of services, and assist strategic planning are increasingly being explored as innovative, viable, and cost-effective solutions. As the price of IT continues to drop and the power of these technologies continues to increase, it appears inevitable that IT will play a leading role in health care management.

It has been observed that there is no lack of computerized or automated applications in modern health care.[2] In fact, IT found in health care facilities in the form of computers, hardware and software, and distributed or autonomous systems, are being improved faster than the cost benefits are being realized.[3] Hammer and Champy[4] asserted that it is time to critically reexamine Adam Smith's concept of the specialization of labor and to shift IT focus away from unchecked automation toward reengineering the business process. They noted that "automation simply provides more efficient ways of doing the wrong kinds of things."[4(p.48)] Information systems were implemented in the health care setting to reduce costs of health care services; instead, however, costs steadily rose in many instances since the introduction of computerized solutions. Several possible explanations for this disappointing outcome include:

Key words: *information technology, telematics, networking, standards, management technology infrastructure*

***Joseph K.H. Tan***, *Ph.D., is Associate Professor, Division of Health Policy and Management, Department of Health Care and Epidemiology, Faculty of Medicine, The University of British Columbia, Vancouver, British Columbia, Canada.*

***John Hanna***, *B.Sc., M.B.A., is Managing Partner, Strategic Intent Management Consulting, Vancouver, British Columbia, Canada.*

This work is partially funded through a research grant to Dr. J. Tan from the Social Sciences and Humanities Research Council (SSHRC) of Canada.

- the lack of futuristic approach to IT planning among health care provider organizations;
- the lack of both physical and system integration among existing information systems used in hospitals and other health agencies;
- the lack of agreeable standards in the health information system software industry; and
- the lack of a theoretic framework for understanding the role that IT actually plays in managing the IT growth process in the health services industry.

Thus, although automation should be an effective means of cost containment, there now needs to be a follow-up analysis on how innovative planning, reassessing of the rapid changes in available technologies, and better managing of technology can attain fuller benefits. The purpose of this article is to describe the need to integrate health care with IT to facilitate the evolution of the hospital of the future and to discuss how health care organizations can begin to plan for such a vision.

## THE TREND TOWARD TOTAL SYSTEMS INTEGRATION

Partly contributing to shortfalls in IT planning may be its past emphasis on transaction processing and management control.[5] During most of the previous two decades, IT was mainly thought of as "islands" of computerized data processing applications such as accounting, payroll, drug inventory, computerized medical records, computer-assisted clinical decision making, computer-assisted medical instrumentation, and laboratory systems. In this sense, the narrow confinement of IT to specific operational as well as specialized clinical tasks has precluded the use of IT in organization-wide data sharing and strategic decision-making applications—applications that would capitalize on advances in teleprocessing and office automation technologies to enhance the quality of patient care beyond the limited benefits that are known and can be derived from existing systems. From such a confined view and without any visionary recognition of IT potential, it is not surprising to see IT either stagnates in the hands of dissatisfied users who were unmotivated in its use or grows in an unmanageable and undirected fashion.

Stories about the short-sightedness of IT solutions abound in almost every health organization. One example is a case involving a 448-bed, acute care hospital in Ontario that serves a community of 250,000 citizens.[6] In this hospital, approximately 198 personal computers (PCs) and 114 terminals in the hospital-wide information system were found to operate basically on a "stand-alone" basis; instances of data sharing occurred infrequently and when they did, it was only among a few users who were connected to each other. Although senior management recognized the importance of systems integration in the long term, the problem perpetuated. There was no policy in the adoption of software standards among various departmental end-users; specifically, there were four versions of Lotus being used, three different versions of WordPerfect, two versions of DBase, and a range of similar but noncompatible specialty software such as desktop publishing, form generators, and schedulers. Another case involved a local (i.e., BC) health care facility where an assortment of computer equipment had been acquired over the years, but was now mostly obsolete. Thus, despite the availability of computers, the internal tracking of patients in this facility was done entirely on paper to avoid the costly maintenance of these obsolete machines and the expertise required for handling them. As a further consequence, vital patient information could only be in one place at a time, and attempts to integrate this paper-based tracking system into a larger network became either a frustrating or impossible endeavor. The lack of an initial clear vision with regards to changing technology and the planning of an integrated hospital information system have resulted in obstacles that are detrimental to the efficient and effective functioning of the organization.

Information technology is a tool and its value depends on how we plan for it and how we use it. Properly employed, IT can play a strategic role in supporting staff and can provide the difference between mediocre and excellent service.[7] Walton,[8] in his book *Up and Running: Integrating Information Technology and the Organization*, suggested that IT strategy must be compatible with both organizational strategy and business strategy. That is to say, executives can no longer segregate the management of IT from the management of their hospitals.

A key question for health information systems analysis and hospital executives therefore is: "What is

*The importance of connectivity among hardware devices is of significance in the trend to move away from mainframe systems toward decentralized, integrated systems.*

the most prevailing trend to which hospital information systems planning should be geared?" In a recent survey of hospital information systems (HIS) executives, Zinn indicated a trend toward the integration of HIS: "Facing increased competition, regulation, and a strong need to tie costs of care to measurable outcomes or quality improvement, these hospitals are relying on connectivity and greater information systems' influence to strengthen them in the '90s."[9(p.32)]

Shortliffe and Perreault[10] described in some detail the evolution of three waves of HIS during the last few decades: (1) the centralized model of HIS in the early 1950s and 1960s; (2) the modular HIS of the 1970s; and (3) the distributed systems of the late 1980s. The importance of connectivity among hardware devices is of significance in the trend to move away from mainframe systems toward decentralized, integrated systems. The decline in the cost of microcomputers has enabled individual departments to operate independently and yet share data to reduce redundancy of information. Recently, a fourth wave of technology has arrived—the communication software (telematics) and networking infrastructure.[11] The move toward networking departmental and organizational data will have widespread implications in making health care services more accessible by eliminating various existing forms of communication barriers such as functional, geographical, and technological barriers.

Hale[12] predicted that automation of health care systems in the future will have to be both standards-based and distributed. Being distributed means that the different systems, often on different platforms, will have to be able to communicate with each other. Over the past years, health care institutions have simply ignored the need to share data and eliminate data redundancies by implementing systems that focus only on the needs of departmental users. Cavanaugh[13] comments that although these systems were beneficial to their users, many "islands of automation" resulted. Figure 1 depicts the traditional structure of piecemeal

**FIGURE 1**

ISLANDS OF AUTOMATION

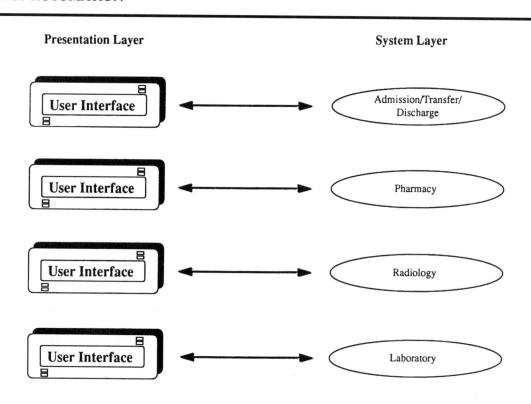

**FIGURE 2**

KEY ELEMENTS OF SYSTEMS INTEGRATION

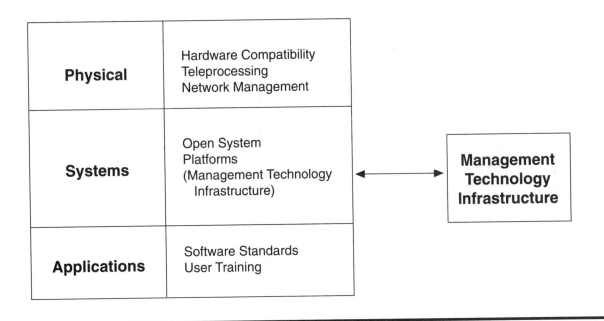

| | |
|---|---|
| **Physical** | Hardware Compatibility Teleprocessing Network Management |
| **Systems** | Open System Platforms (Management Technology Infrastructure) |
| **Applications** | Software Standards User Training |

**Management Technology Infrastructure**

IS development, which often resulted in systems fragmentation and duplication.

Our foregoing analysis based on our experience with health organizations suggests the following four steps as being necessary to integrate health care systems and to achieve an effective information sharing environment:

1. the physical networking of existing systems,
2. the evolution to an "open system" platform,
3. the adoption of software standards, and
4. the establishment of a management technology infrastructure (MTI).

In the following sections, we discuss in some detail what health care executives, planners, and managers should know about the development toward achieving total systems integration. In this era of rapid technological diffusion, the myth of total systems integration[14] is becoming a reality.

## NETWORKING EXISTING SYSTEMS

Networking is a term referring to the connections between computer systems and their attached communications devices, such as terminals and multi-

plexes.[15] Donovan[16] sees the acquisition and deployment of telecommunications capabilities as a starting point to network among existing IS and argues for a three-tier implementation of connectivity standards throughout the organization—physical, systems, and applications (see Figure 2).

Figure 2 shows that physical connectivity is achieved by first ensuring hardware compatibility, then applying teleprocessing technology to link the hardware, thus enabling the sharing of common information processing capabilities, and, finally, maintaining the linkage through routine network management. The trend in telecommunications technology is for more people to be able to communicate more information, over greater distances, at a faster rate. Rapid communication reduces the amount of time individuals have to wait to get information they need to make business decisions. Numerous types of telecommunications with a variety of costs and reliability are available today. Reductions in telecommunication costs and the use of private branch exchanges (PBX) have made local area networks (LAN) and wide area networks (WAN) a reality. Demand for high bandwidth applications that are capable of exchanging images, video, and large amounts of data is considered to be growing rapidly.

In light of these rapid changes, new technological and organizational ground rules must be made. For example, the need for enterprise-wide distributed processing is becoming more important to support the flow of information horizontally, vertically, and between organizations. Horizontal (interdepartmental) flow of information in real time is a prerequisite to providing quality care and is a basis for the measurement of that care. Conflicts in procedure scheduling and drug-to-drug interactions are two examples that affect the quality of care due to poor or inadequate interdepartmental communications. In addition, vertical flow of information is critical to satisfying institutional goals and providing timely, relevant information for decision making. For example, administrators require information from the admissions-discharge-transfer (ADT) system in order to analyze utilization rates for strategic planning and resource allocation decision making. From a competitive advantage standpoint, information is being shared between organizations in the customer-supplier relationship in order to reduce costs. A classic example of this interorganizational information sharing is the on-line order-entry system developed by American Hospital Supply.[17] Such electronic data interchange (EDI) capabilities are beginning to appeal to the health services industry because of their ability to ensure the timeliness and integrity of information that is captured within the system.

The recent development of a broadband technology, known as an integrated services digital network (ISDN), has promised to lead to standardized digital communications.[18,19] ISDN can combine different forms of communications (voice, data, and images) in one architecture. Whereas standard analog telephone lines require a modulator-demodulator (modem) to convert data from digital to analog and vice versa, ISDN provides common carrier lines that are digital, and therefore conversion devices are not required. In addition, data can be transferred at significantly higher speeds. The main reasons for merging voice and data are cost and management control. However, while maintenance costs may eventually be reduced, the initial costs of integrating voice and data are high. In addition, equipment incompatibilities, high costs, and poor marketing by the carriers has curtailed the potency of ISDN's adoption.[20,21]

Parallel investment in the development and standardization of other high bandwidth switching technologies has also begun. Fiber distributed data interface (FDDI) is a shared connection LAN with a variable packet size. FDDI can transfer data at rates up to 100 million bits per second (mbps) compared to 56,000 bps for a standard business phone line. Asynchronous transfer mode (ATM) is the newest and fastest technology. ATM breaks data down into packets of uniform size (53 groups of 8 bits) that can be sent asynchronously (i.e., out of sequence); the packets are then reassembled in the proper sequence at the other end. This uniform cell size enables different platforms to talk. An ATM network can handle from 50 to 155 mbps. There is no definitive answer as to which technology is the best. Currently, two advantages that FDDI has over ATM are (1) lower prices and (2) tested interoperability.[22] However, many FDDI users are intrigued by ATM's potential and plan to switch to ATM in the future.[23]

The Medical Colleges of Georgia and Bell South are using broadband videoconferencing technology to enable specialists at the teaching hospital in Augusta, Georgia, to examine patients 130 miles away. Through sophisticated telemetry (e.g., electronic stethoscope, digitized X-rays, microscopy, and EKG) and interactive video equipment, physicians at the Medical Colleges of Georgia have actually heard heartbeats, studied radiographs and laboratory results, and peered down the throats of patients at rural hospitals without having actual physical contacts with the patients. In its limited application to date, these video consultations have resulted in an 88 percent reduction of patient transfers from the rural hospital to the Medical Colleges.[24]

The telecommunications industry has invested heavily in digital switches and fiber-optic transmission technology. Now that fiber-optic transmission is becoming cost competitive with copper wire transmission, it is being rushed into service. In 1992, the Science Council of Canada[25] reported that 85 percent of Bell Canada's long distance toll trunks and 35 percent of its local lines are using digital technology right to the handset terminal. Although many businesses already have a need for the bandwidth offered by ISDN, few residential subscribers would be willing to pay for such a service today. However, the future of ISDN depends on the fact that optical fiber not only allows present operations to be carried out faster, but it also provides the opportunity for entirely new applications. These applications must be developed to take advantage of the power of high-speed networks for fulfilling business needs.

Paul Thiel, marketing manager at MPR Teltech, foresees the transfer of radiologic images as an initial step in developing broadband applications for the health sector (discussion with Paul Thiel at MPR

Teltech Ltd. on March 10, 1993). He notes that the administration of radiologic images is largely inefficient; for example, hospitals in the United States report that as many as 5 percent of radiographs must be retaken as a result of being lost. Massachusetts General Hospital (MGH) has joined with New York New England Exchange Corporation (NYNEX) to offer a fiber-optic network that transmits high-resolution patient images quickly (e.g., up to 45 mbps) for its main hospital in Boston and its various satellite centers. The savings have been considerable since MGH produces as many as 1,200 images a day.[24]

## OPEN SYSTEMS ARCHITECTURE

Organizations are sometimes locked into the technologies of the past. They retain systems that are poorly integrated, costly, difficult to maintain, and hard to change. They want to lever these investments to take advantage of both existing systems and new technologies. While an open systems solution may be difficult to obtain, it is critical that organizations understand the architecture and plans needed to advance to such a platform.

There are two basic approaches for adopting open systems: (1) revolution or (2) evolution. Not many organizations can afford to pull the plug on proprietary systems and build open systems from scratch. Often, there exists a large installed base of equipment that needs solutions varying from point-to-point connections to networking on an enterprise-wide level.[26] Evolution appears to be the only logical and practical approach for existing systems in health care, especially for those that have invested heavily in their current systems. However, for new systems, revolution—the selection of a distributed client/server architecture that conforms to open systems protocols—would provide the best flexibility.

An example of the benefits of an open system has been demonstrated in Dallas, Texas. The Zale Lipshy University Hospital, a 160-bed private teaching hospital, chose a standards-based distributed architecture anchored by a fiber-optic Ethernet backbone that interconnects a variety of multivendor departmental systems. The distributed architecture allows care providers and administrators, using one of 150 workstations, network access to data on radiology, pharmacy, and patient records systems. Based on Health Level 7 (HL7), the distributed architecture gives the hospital departments the flexibility to implement IS that meet their needs and allows employees to access any type of information. The fiber Ethernet backbone supports five Hewlett Packard (HP) file servers running 3+Open LAN Manager and a clinical management application from Quantitative Medicine, Inc. (QMI). The QMI software compiles clinical data, as well as data from other departmental systems, and presents it in a standard format to users working at HP Vectra workstations. The open systems architecture project took less than a year to complete and cost $3 million.[27] George Horne, a consultant with George Horne Associates, noted that the success of this project can be attributed to the commitment of the CEO, who had a vision of an electronic medical record.

Keen[28] notes that there are *open systems purists* and *corporate realists* when it comes to the standards on which technical architecture is based. The purists would argue that the open systems interconnection (OSI) model is essential for creating a platform that would fully utilize existing IT capabilities. However, the realists point out that OSI is a long way off and that IBM's Systems Network Architecture (SNA) is already here. These purists focus on the integration of information rather than just the extension of connectivity. In addition, Keen points out that: "This means the path to open systems in practice is via IBM architectures. That does not necessarily mean IBM products; a firm can implement its IBM architecture by adopting, say, Amdahl host computers, Northern Telecom communications switches, and Toshiba personal computers."[28(p.208)]

## SOFTWARE STANDARDS

Keen[28] notes that incompatibility is the bane of integration. Eventually, when widespread standards are established, the ultimate "open system" will allow access to any data, on any computer, from any database. Obviously, this would facilitate the flow of more complete information with much less effort and expense necessary to provide the integration of networks that will work together. The result of such a system would be the availability of information through a common interface, thereby making all the heterogeneous systems appear as one homogeneous system to the end-user.[29]

Figure 3 illustrates the structure of an integrated HIS that uses an open systems architecture. The con-

---

*Software standards facilitate the integration of resources and ensure compatibility.*

**FIGURE 3**

AN INTEGRATED HOSPITAL INFORMATION SYSTEM

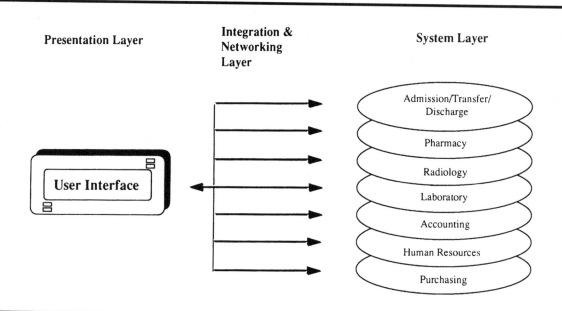

nectivity of the different platforms implies a need for using organization-wide standard software.

Without standards, the path to any integrated approach to IS has proven to be a costly venture. Indeed, the absence of standards has slowed down the adoption of IT in the health care sector.[30]

Most health care technology environments are made up of heterogeneous applications and platforms. Multi–health care organizations face unique challenges in providing information services for all of their entities. For example, they must consider corporate philosophy, geography, computing configurations, and whether their IS approach capitalizes on centralized economies of scale or on regional flexibility and control.

Software standards facilitate the integration of resources and ensure compatibility. These standards promote communications and the sharing of data, thereby reducing data redundancy. Software standards have to be set for operating systems, database management systems, and user applications. In addition, standards must encompass programming issues such as the languages used, the structure of codes, the naming of variables, documentation, and the verification of data. With the proliferation of easy-to-use fourth generation programming languages, it has become easier for end-users to

develop personal programs, but the lack of documentation and transferability make the real benefits of these programs questionable.

In the short term, a good strategy for adopting software standards is to reduce the different brands of application software that are being run, and then to ensure that the versions of those programs are consistent throughout the organization. By eliminating the variety of software, standards also reduce end-user training requirements.

## MANAGEMENT TECHNOLOGY INFRASTRUCTURE

The challenge in selecting a MTI is in forming an overall plan to interconnect and reconcile the ever evolving perspectives of general management, the IS department, and user groups. Halloran notes that "This technical infrastructure design process for an organization is one of the most important activities IS departments can undertake in providing the enterprise with an enabling infrastructure."[31(p.9)]

IT can provide opportunities for, and impose constraints on, infrastructure design. Opportunities exist in using technology in ways new to the organization.

Constraints are those aspects of existing technology infrastructure that limit the possibilities for innovation, and that cannot be changed in the relevant time frame. For example, the British Columbia Heart Health Demonstration Project (BCHHDP)[5,32] advocates the use of IT for community heart health promotion through the diffusion of expert systems technology and through the transfer of technology from one community group to another. A major constraint, of course, would be the computing expertise and technical assistance that each community group has access to during and after the BCHHDP funding period.

It is no longer acceptable to take a laissez-faire attitude to establishing an organization's MTI. Organizational culture and the strategic role of IT should be explicitly considered. To prepare the organization for growth and maturation in IT investment for the future, management must clearly provide three primary functions: (1) direction, (2) support, and (3) control.[33]

1. Direction focuses on discovering and evaluating leading-edge technology to improve organizational competitiveness or service excellence.
2. Support focuses on providing the necessary technical assistance to end-users to interconnect the various user groups with common technology and on empowering them with accessible information and knowledge.
3. Control provides a means of standardization and integration toward universal compatibility and provides a means of control on wasteful replication of end-user programming efforts.

It is the user and the operational unit that ultimately decide on the need and appropriateness of IT. Thus, innovation lies not only in the domain of the IT staff, but also in the domain of users. Conflicts often arise when users strive to fulfill short-term needs at the expense of orderly long-term IT development.[34] In an environment characterized by local systems development, there is often a poor technology transfer between similar users, which leads to a lack of unity within the organization resulting in a loss of competitive leverage.

•   •   •

Without top management initiatives, islands of automation will continue to exist. Three general benefits of IT are worth noting. First is increased productivity and faster user response. Productivity will be significantly improved because programmers, analysts, and staff will have portable skills. Integrated, open systems architecture means that new application development and user-requested changes will be handled more quickly. The second benefit is better control of the IT environment. Advantages provided under the open systems environment will include smoother investment streams in IT and an inherently flexible IT structure that can adjust to corresponding changes in needs and objectives. Finally, cost control will be improved. Software development and maintenance costs are lower because the same software can run on multiple platforms without modification. Software costs are also lower due to the growing availability of purchased software packages. Training costs are reduced through consistency in software regardless of the underlying platform. Hardware costs are reduced through increased industry competition resulting in an improved price/performance ratio.

Keen[28] notes that we will need more empirical research to measure the impact of telecommunications on organizational effectiveness. We do not yet know how to measure the value of a telecommunications infrastructure. As in other industries, the movement in health care toward adopting unified standards is progressing by taking the best of what exists and merging them into a unified whole. Fortunately, major progress in enabling the interconnection of heterogeneous computer systems and applications is being made.

## REFERENCES

1. *British Columbia Economic And Statistical Review.* Province of B.C.: Ministry of Finance & Corporate Relations, 1992: 22–25.
2. Tan, J. "Graduate Education in Health Information Systems (HIS): It's Like Having All Your Eggs in One Basket." *Journal of Health Administration Education* 11, no. 1 (1993): 27–55.
3. Pugh, G., and Tan, J. "Computerized Databases for Emergency Care: What Impacts on Patient Care?" *Proceedings of the ITCH Conference*, Victoria, British Columbia, Canada, 1992.
4. Hammer, M., and Champy, J. *Reengineering the Corporation: A Manifesto for Business Revolution.* New York, N.Y.: Harper Collins, 1993.
5. Tan, J., and Green, L. "The Application of Artificial Intelligence and Expert System Technology to Heart Health Program Planning and Evaluation." *Canadian Journal of Public Health.* In press.
6. Tan, J., and Omoruyi, O. "A Case Study on the Design of a Management Technological Infrastructure (MTI) for a Hospital." WP No. 93-MIS-012. Vancouver, B.C.: Department of HealthCare & Epidemiology, 1993.

7. Kropf, R. *Service Excellence in Health Care Through the Use of Computers*. Ann Arbor, Mich.: Health Administration Press, 1990.

8. Walton, R. *Up and Running: Integrating Information Technology and the Organization*. Boston, Mass.: Harvard Business School Press, 1989.

9. Zinn, T.K. "Healthcare I/S Executives Look Toward the Next Decade." *Computers in Healthcare* (February 1992): 32–39.

10. Shortliffe, E., and Perreault, P., eds. *Medical Informatics: Computer Applications in Health Care*. Don Mills, Ont.: Addison-Wesley, 1990.

11. Morrell, J., and Smith, D. "International Data Corporation White Paper: Open Systems from an End-user Perspective." *Computerworld* (April 1992): 27.

12. Hale, P. "Tactical Considerations for HIS Strategy." *Computers in Healthcare* (October 1989): 39–40.

13. Cavanaugh, F. "Information Architecture: Bridging the Islands." *Computers in Healthcare* (November 1991): 41–42.

14. Dearden, J. "MIS is a Mirage." *Harvard Business Review* 50 no. 1 (1972): 90–99.

15. Stamper, D. *Business Data Communications*. Redwood City, Calif.: Benjamin/Cummings, 1991.

16. Donovan, J. "Beyond Chief Information Officer to Network Manager." *Harvard Business Review* (September–October 1988): 134–40.

17. Moriarty, D. "Strategic Information Systems Planning for Health Service Providers." *Health Care Management Review* 17, no. 1: 85–90.

18. Burn, J., and Caldwell, E. *Management of Information Systems Technology*. Orchard, Oxfordshire: Alfred Waller, 1990.

19. Denzel, W. "High-speed ATM Switching." *IEEE Communications*, (February 1993): 26.

20. Cross, T. "ISDN: Under Construction." *Infoworld* (13 January, 1992): 64–66.

21. Lai, V., Guynes, J., and Bordoloi, B. "ISDN: Adoption and Diffusion Issues." *Information Systems Management* (Fall 1993): 46–52.

22. Hurwicz, M. "FDDI: Not Fastest But Still Fit." *Datamation* 1 (1993): 31–36.

23. Kerr, S. "ATM: Ultimate Network, Or Ultimate Hype?" *Datamation* 1 (1993): 30–34.

24. Doremus, C. "Can Telecommunications Help Solve America's Health Care Problems?" In *Arthur D. Little, Inc. Corporate Communications Report*. Cambridge, Mass., 1992.

25. Science Council of Canada, Ottawa. "Sectoral Technology Strategy Series: The Canadian Telecommunications Sector." DSS cat. no. S525-1, 1992: 2–17.

26. Dunbar, C. "The Networking Standards Evolution: Toward a Real Electronic Medical Record." *Computers in Healthcare* (February 1990): 18–21.

27. Eckerson, W. "Hospital Hopes HL7-Based Net Will Ensure Versatility." *Network World* 20 (1990): 19–20.

28. Keen, P. *Shaping The Future: Business Design through Information Technology*. Boston, Mass.: Harvard Business School Press, 1991.

29. Wu, G., Ahlfeldt, H., and Wigertz, O. "Multilink—an Intermediary System for Multi-Database Access." *Methods of Information in Medicine* 32, no. 1 (1993): 82–87.

30. Mougayar, W. "Information Technology: Communications Standards in Healthcare." *Healthcare Computing & Communications* (April 1992): 38–42.

31. Halloran, J. "Achieving World-Class End-User Computing." *Information Systems Management* (Fall 1993): 7–12.

32. Tan, J., Green L., and Hall, N. "The Role of Information Technology in Community Heart Health Promotion." WP No. 93-MIS-010. Vancouver, B.C.: Department of HealthCare & Epidemiology, 1993.

33. Alavi, M., Nelson, R., and Weiss, I. "Managing End-User Computing as a Value-added Resource. *Journal of Information Systems Management* (1988): 26–35.

34. Cash, I., MacFarlan, F., and Applegate L. *Corporate Information Systems Management: Text and Cases*. 2nd ed. Homewood, Ill.: Irwin, 1992.

# PART IV

# GOVERNANCE IN TRANSITION

# The role of governing boards in multihospital systems

Robert E. Toomey
and
Richard K. Toomey

*Governance is a complicated, sensitive, and complex element of management. When exercised by individuals not thoroughly conversant with the intricacies of the health care business, it can lead to a variety of organizational and operational tragedies. Appropriate understanding and implementation of strategic governance and operational governance will greatly strengthen and enhance the governance function in hospitals and hospital systems.*

**Governance exists today** as it always has, as an essential and required part of the voluntary hospital field. Although the hospital field has undergone dramatic changes, governance is essentially unchanged. There have been occasions of major and historic importance leading to paradigm shifts in the structure, process, provision, and results of hospital services and care. However, governance has not changed as the major shifts have occurred.

The 1950s witnessed the first of the major changes with the development of graduate programs in hospital administration by many major universities in the country. The passage and implementation of the Hill-Burton Act was the second change with a major impact on the hospital field during the 1950s. Under the Hill-Burton legislation, the bricks-and-mortar facet of health care dramatically changed. During a period of over two decades (1946 to 1969) the Hill-Burton Act was responsible for approximately 10,240 projects providing nearly 447,000 inpatient beds in hospitals and nursing homes. Through the matching of state and local funds with $3 billion of Hill-Burton funds, some $11.5 billion was made available for construction costs.[1] By 1974 the Hill-Burton Act had provided $4.6 billion in grants and approximately $2 billion in loans.[2]

The 1960s witnessed the discussion and eventual passage of Medicare and Medicaid by the U.S. Congress. The passage of the Medicare and Medicaid programs in 1965, many historians believe, marked the turning point in American health care. With the seemingly unlimited capital resources the Medicare program provided, the provision of health care moved from a cottage industry focus to a corporate business.[3]

As the health care industry changed and grew, so did the health care expenditures as a percent of the gross national product (GNP). In 1950, health care expenditures represented 4.5 percent of the GNP. This amount increased to 11.1 percent in 1987.[4] The U.S. Commerce Department estimates that health care will represent 14 percent of the GNP in 1992.[5]

The 1970s and 1980s have seen two paradigm shifts. The first of these has been the changes in the structure of the field. These changes are to be seen in the development of hospital and health care systems and hospital alliances. At the end of the 1970s, approximately 31

*Robert E. Toomey, LL.D., is President of Toomey Consulting Service in Greenville, South Carolina.*

*Richard K. Toomey, M.H.A., is Executive Vice President/CEO of Nash General Hospital, Inc. in Rocky Mount, North Carolina.*

*Health Care Manage Rev*, 1993, 18(1), 21–30
© 1993 Aspen Publishers, Inc.

percent of community hospitals were members of a health care system. By 1987 this number had increased to 46 percent. American Hospital Association (AHA) data indicated there were 303 systems in 1987. Of these systems approximately 47 percent or 142 were unaffiliated, 32 percent or 97 were church related with the majority of the church-related systems (80) being Catholic, and 21 percent (64) were investor-owned systems. Investor-owned systems accounted for 47 percent of the hospitals and 34 percent of the beds within a system.[6]

Data provided by AHA in 1990 indicated there were 302 nonfederal systems with 2,562 hospitals and 433,290 acute care beds. These numbers represent 46 percent of the nation's community hospitals and acute care beds.[7]

The second change had a major and still continuing impact. This was the initiation and continuing development of health maintenance organizations (HMOs) and preferred provider organizations (PPOs). Both these relate to the mechanisms for the provision of and the financing of care. Both affect price and costs for hospital and medical care. By 1989, there were 614 HMOs with an enrollment of approximately 32.6 million individuals.[8] This article is committed to looking at governance. It will do so with particular concern for its role with multihospital systems, both the vertically integrated systems and the horizontally integrated systems.

Left for the future will be a concern for governance of stand-alone hospitals and the structure thereof, its operational mechanisms, and its concern with outcomes related to the institutions for which they have a responsibility.

## TYPES OF SYSTEMS

### Vertically integrated hospital system

The most advanced vertically integrated system is one in which clinical services are developed to provide a continuum of care. The continuum begins with the prevention of disease and promotion of health. It starts with a concern for the quality of life and the health and well-being of the individual. The continuum then moves to primary care service for the treatment of an illness. The next step is to specialized care services for those with an acute illness or condition. Specialized care may be in specialized clinical service facilities (e.g., children's hospital, women's hospital, orthopedic hospital, cancer treatment institution, psychiatric hospital). On the other hand, it may be in an acute care general hospital with all these specialty services. The fourth step in the continuum is rehabilitative or restor-

*Vertically integrated systems emphasize the integration of clinical services under a single management entity and a medical staff that is committed to the system.*

ative care. This latter may be provided in a nursing home or in a home care program. Next comes custodial or assisted living care in a retirement village. Finally comes care in a hospice.

The continuum is not initiated by an illness or a disease as previously noted. It is initially represented by a concern and a commitment to health and a healthful quality of life.

Vertically integrated systems emphasize and are identified by the integration of clinical services under a single management entity and a medical staff that is committed to the system. In this type of system the provision of services may be defined as a system in which services to patients move forward or backward in the production or distribution of care being rendered to patients using the services of the system.

When these services are integrated with one owner and each service is provided in a separate institutional facility, it may be categorized as a vertically integrated *macro* health care system. The system would be centrally administered even though the facilities of a macrosystem might be geographically decentralized throughout a region or a locale.

On the other hand a vertically integrated *micro*system can best be visualized when applied to a particular condition, for example, a heart disease.

At the first level (prevention and health promotion) a variety of programs is possible. At the next level, primary care is probably most available in ambulatory care programs. Subsequently, specialized services may be both ambulatory outpatient care as well as specialized inpatient care. Subsequent rehabilitation programs may be developed as part of the hospital ancillary services. Finally, chronic care may be offered in an affiliated nursing home. Home care and hospice care will be part of the free-standing hospital's program.

For this continuum no separate facilities are necessary. And yet a continuum can be adequately and well provided.

This kind of integration can be offered from a single free-standing hospital or an institution that is part of a horizontal system or a large institution in a vertically integrated system.

## Horizontally integrated hospital system

A horizontally integrated hospital system is one in which a number of institutions (two or more) providing similar services operate under a single management. The institutions may comprise, for example, a number of acute care general hospitals, rehabilitation hospitals, psychiatric hospitals, or nursing homes. They may be and usually are geographically dispersed within a large region, a state, several states, or the entire country. However, they do not and cannot integrate their clinical services into a local geographically identified continuum of care. The system they represent is a group of services of an administrative nature. However, many of these horizontally integrated systems are struggling to find a process that will allow transition into vertically integrated clinical services providing for continuity of care.

As an administrative system, these institutions have central office capabilities that are made available or committed to the administrative enhancement of all the hospitals they own or manage. Each entity or unit is clinically capable of providing only the services for which it is designed. The units are not clinically differentiated. They are not as a rule integrated to provide a continuity of clinical services into a continuum of care as are vertically integrated systems.

In all instances in which systems are found, governance is at two levels. At the corporate level governance is or should be strategic in nature. At the institutional level in both vertically and horizontally integrated multiunit systems, governance is or should be at the operational level and advisory to institutional management both central and local in nature.

## TYPES OF GOVERNANCE

Governance of a health care system relates to the exercise of authority by a group of individuals who are responsible and accountable for the direction and control of the system as an organizational entity. The usual term in the nonprofit health care field for this group of individuals is "board of trustees." The board of trustees holds power in "trust" for the owners. The owners are usually a group, individuals, or organizations who have created the organizational entity as a mechanism to serve others. In the health care field the services relate to the health of the individuals being served.

In a corporation created to serve individuals in a community or region, the board of trustees seeks to select and appoint an individual with education, training, background, and experience in operating one or more hospitals or health care institutions as the corporation's leader to provide full-time direction and management of the system.

The first step in governance of an institution—however large, however diversified, and however geographically centralized or decentralized—is to consider the organizational structure.

A vertically integrated organization devoted to a continuum of care will of necessity be structured in such a way that the system is comprised of institutions or programs of care offering a variety of levels of care of a specific clinical nature. A horizontally integrated system of whatever nature—comprising similar, replicative, or duplicative facilities and whether local, regional, state, multistate, or national—will of necessity be systematized in administrative services. The administrative services will most likely be financial, human resources, materiel, marketing and planning, and public relations. There may be some centralization of pharmacy management and nursing service management. However, these management activities will be concerned with services in institutions that are providing similar levels of care.

These administrative services will be of an advisory consultative nature available equally to all units of the system. Because there will be a corporate board in both types of systems the role of this board will be unique. It cannot in any sense take on operational concerns for geographically dispersed, clinically differentiated institutions in a vertically integrated system. Nor can the corporate board take on operational concerns in a horizontally integrated system spread over a geographic area.

Thus, there is created a situation in which direction and guidance are of a different nature for the corporate board in contrast to the direction and guidance for the operations of a geographically decentralized entity board.

At the corporate level for both types of systems, the concerns are of a strategic, short- and long-term nature. At the local institution entity level the concerns are of a short-term operational nature. Because the perspectives of the boards are different, the governance or managerial imperatives will be different.

At the corporate level, the authors have categorized the system board as exemplifying "strategic governance." At the institutional level, the authors have categorized the board as exemplifying "operational governance."

## STRATEGIC GOVERNANCE IN ACTION

The board then, with the active cooperation and assistance of the president or chief executive officer

(CEO) of the system identifies the imperatives that must be defined in order for the corporation and all its elements to operate effectively.

Specifically, these imperatives are
- humanistic and organizational philosophy,
- purpose, usually from the charter or act of incorporation,
- mission,
- social vision,
- strategies for attainment, and
- values or ethics.

The corporate board must be assured that the aforementioned imperatives are developed and approved. It is through the system president or CEO who must be responsible for ensuring that these imperatives be incorporated into the "culture" of the system including all the units that comprise the system. The system must create criteria for which the culture may be monitored and evaluated.

These imperatives are concepts that must be created and adopted as part of the psyche of the system. They will not be seen on an operational statement. Rather they represent a level and a kind of governance that is strategic in nature.

At the strategic or corporate level, board members should be outstanding business and professional leaders who are accustomed to development of long-range strategies. They should be capable of developing both social and economic visions and goals. Ideally they should number from 7 to no more than 15 members.

### Humanistic and organizational philosophy

Humanistic philosophy should be represented by emphasizing a commitment to a code of conduct and to values and ethics relating to life, actions, and activities within the institution. Similarly they must also relate to society, the environment, the community being served, and finally to the stakeholders of the institution. Stakeholders include physicians, patients, population being served, volunteers, suppliers, and, of particular concern and emphasis, the employees. In addition, consideration of policies, actions, and activities must include payors of services (i.e., insurance companies, government at all levels in the public sector, business and industry in the private sector, and others who may be involved in the ongoing concerns of the institution).

Organizational philosophy means the principles underlying the conduct and mechanics of management of the affairs of the organization. These principles may be looked at as management style. The most clearly differentiated are the principles and mechanics related to centralization of authority, responsibility, and power. Its opposite philosophy is decentralization of power, responsibility, and authority but with coordination of organizational entities and elements.

The selection of the specifics of managerial philosophy must be acknowledged for the remainder of the imperatives to be acted on with wisdom and intelligence.

### The purpose for which the institution exists

The purpose is usually to be found in papers relating to the origin or incorporation of the institution. Statements of purpose to be found therein reveal the intent of the founders. Evolutionary changes may have occurred. If so a new statement should be formed.

With a purpose established, the remaining imperatives can be developed. At Johns Hopkins Hospital in Baltimore the purpose as originally conceived was to serve the people of Baltimore. The Duke Hospital, functioning as part of the Duke Medical School, focused on research and education as well as patient care. The purpose of the M.D. Anderson Hospital in Houston, Texas, was to do research into the cause and cure of cancer. In Greenville, South Carolina the statement of purpose was to care for the poor.

Hospitals and hospital systems can be founded and established for a number of different purposes:
- Some are created for economic gain for stockholders or individual owners.
- Some are created to support an educational effort on the part of a university.
- Some are established for research purposes. New knowledge must be developed because new information is available.
- Some are developed as political rewards or political fulfillment of promises to a community. Politically it may be seen as an opportunity for government to fill an unmet need.
- Some are established for sociological or religious purposes:
  — Sociologically they are created to meet the health care needs of the community.
  — Religious groups establish a hospital for special reasons, for instance a Jewish hospital to

---

*Organizational philosophy means the principles underlying the conduct and mechanics of management of the affairs of the organization.*

accommodate the special concerns of Jewish population in a community. There are also Baptist-sponsored, Presbyterian-sponsored, and Catholic-sponsored hospitals. All of these were created to accommodate to merging social and religious needs and desires of a community or parts of a community.

In each of the above purposes the entire organizational structure, the management and governance process, and the desired strategic and operational results will likely be different. Each must be approached with the expectation that achievement of purpose will carry the organization down different roads and will involve a variety of organizational structures. The specific structure will be determined by the purpose for which the hospital system was created and how it has evolved over time.

### The mission statement

Once the purpose, or *raison d'être*, has been determined it is then possible to move on to a mission statement. In strategic governance the mission may change or evolve from year to year. Ownership may have changed. Managerial leadership may have changed. The community may be larger or smaller. Clinical emphasis may have evolved, and new services and programs may have been adopted. Any or all of these may have created the need for an updated mission statement. Presumably the mission will identify what major services will be provided and to whom these services will be rendered. For instance, the authors see the mission of the Greenville Hospital System as follows: To provide a comprehensive system of specialized services and facilities embracing a continuum of care from promotion of health to hospice care. In the continuum will be found in-patient and out-patient services; acute and chronic and long-term care; educational services for undergraduate medical students; clinical and other research programs; and a full spectrum of professional and technical health education.

### The vision statement

The vision statement is manifested in the values of the institution—the suitability and appropriateness, compassion, responsiveness and dedication to excellence that are identified in its long-range plan. In some organizations there also may be included an economic dimension.

One example of a vision from President George Bush is a "kinder and gentler America." An Episcopal prayer seeks "comfort and succor to all those who in this transitory life are in trouble, sorrow, need, sickness or any other adversity."

The vision looks to the future. Johns Hopkins Hospital may want to serve Maryland. Duke Medical School may envision a decentralized medical school with four or five satellites in four or five community hospitals in North or South Carolina. Greenville may envision a fully developed regional operation with a network of medical care groups and a network of hospitals, both large and small and provided in a supercontinuum of care.

### Strategies

At the corporate level governance must be seen, accomplished, and evaluated by the development of appropriate strategies. The appropriateness refers back to and must apply to the specifics of the mission imperatives.

These strategies are in the areas of

* market position;
* development and use of financial resources (capital, operational, gifts, and contributions);
* facilities and services;
* quality care levels;
* physician resources and medical care;
* community needs;
* education and size; and
* human resources.

As a subsection to strategies are goals and objectives. These represent the plans to accomplish the strategic direction and provide action toward the fulfillment of the mission.

The mission of the hospital system is usually stated in terms of services that will be provided by the system. The strategies are the plans developed by the system's leaders, which are or will be the means by which the mission will be accomplished. There are at least eight major areas for which plans must be enunciated and developed if the mission is to be accomplished. These are discussed below.

#### Market position

There is the market position currently held by each of the service entities of the system. A hospital system is in reality a multiproduct enterprise. For each product or service line, studies and evaluations must be analyzed and appropriate goals established by the governing body and management relative to actions to be taken to maintain or enhance the present situation. The variables are or may be age, sex, degree of illness, or need for a changed health status; geography, that is locus or place of residence from which patient-consumers may be sought; the economic aspects of the market and from which economic base the system plans to recruit as recipients of services.

### Financial resources

The variables that exist here are many. Each must be considered and plans developed for desirable outcomes. Included are the following: Should capital formation come from fund-raising philanthropy, profits from operation, or bond issues? If from bond issues, should these be taxable or tax exempt? Should these be paid back by hospital revenues or if possible by government?

How should Wall Street be involved? What agencies should be involved? Without a strategy for raising capital and reimbursing the lender the potential for growth may be inhibited.

A five-year plan and a one-year plan should be established for operational finances. The strategy here is basic. What degree of profit can be planned? What level of deficit can be sustained and for how long? Each product or service line should have its operational plans approved by the system's corporate board.

### Facilities and services

If the mission statement represents a continuation of what is currently being done, then the strategy here is simply to make sure that the facilities and equipment are sufficient to carry on. If not there may be the need to plan for new facilities and services.

This as part of strategic planning relates back to the mission statement and desires that are noted therein.

### Quality care levels

This strategy is becoming increasingly important. As more managed care contracts are signed and as more direct contracting by hospital systems with business and industry is accomplished, two factors will be increasingly scrutinized: quality and cost. Quality is not only a hospital concern but also a physician concern. HMOs and PPOs must become more and more aware that the future well-being of each will be affected by quality matters. Assessing quality will be a major area for strategic governance.

### Physician resources and medical care

The two major strategies here relate to the most desired and desirable mix of primary care and special-

> *Now physicians are looking for a stronger voice in day-to-day operational concerns and in both strategic and operational governance.*

ized care physicians for the system and the record of each and all relative to quality outcomes.

Other areas for strategic direction relate to credentialing. Physicians were once seen as the hospital's customers. Now they must be looked at as consumers of hospital resources in their care protocols and procedures.

Coming to the fore because of product-line management and centers of excellence are potential uses of physicians in management. The idea of a physician in the corporate office as a symbol of concern for the medical staff's feelings is disappearing. Now physicians are looking for a stronger voice in day-to-day operational concerns and in both strategic and operational governance.

### Community needs

Communities change: They grow, they lose population, neighborhoods change, they want more, they need less. A hospital system market is a vibrant, living, changing organism. To maintain a careful oversight on a region is a full-time and frequently exciting task. But corporate-level strategic governance must do this or managers may lose control of that element of community health care that they must treasure.

Commercialism of medical, hospital, and health care services is not a facet of community health care in which governing boards can take pride. Some elements of increasing cost are due to increasing commercialism of health and due to increasing unhealthy medical and hospital staff competition that is akin to cannibalism. Medical and hospital commerce is eating up the very resources that were once a saving grace in a community.

### Education and size of program

If the mission of the system involves medical education, strategies relative to its size, faculty, and clinics, use of patients for teaching purposes must be developed. The question of continuing education for employees and medical staff must be handled.

### Human resources

People are the backbone of the system. If the board is to be assured of the perpetuation of the institution, it must arrange for a continued source of well-trained personnel. The strategic course is recruitment. Of even greater importance is the identification of young people (junior high and high school) who can be brought into training programs to replace older workers or to staff new or expanded programs.

A strategic concern has to be a salary and fringe benefit program suitable to the board and the region.

### Values or ethics

Finally, adoption of a set of ethical, moral, and *spiritual* values should be included as an imperative. These would be applied to policies that will or may impact the stakeholders for whom the hospital has a responsibility. These would include employees, patients, physicians, volunteers, visitors, vendors, and others with whom and for whom the institution does business.

Some examples of the values are as follows:

- *Dignity of each person serving and being served:* It is important to recognize the worthiness of an individual and to honor him or her with kindness and concern whether that individual is an employee, patient, or visitor.

- *Compassionate and competent care:* It is also important to care for an individual with total dedication to excellence. One must perform services to patients with a concern for the feelings of that patient and with a feeling that those things being done are important. Care should be provided with a dedication to superior outcomes.

- *Effective and efficient management:* Special emphasis must be placed here because success or failure in achieving the mission and implementing the strategies is directly the result of appropriate managerial efforts. Special efforts by corporate-level governance must be directed at this value entity. If this aspect of the board's responsibility is not carried out with great thoughtfulness all else might come to naught. There are indicators that may be monitored and studied. Results may be bottom-line oriented, but looking closely at the strategies chosen and establishing criteria in advance of implementation will allow the board an opportunity to measure and evaluate both the efficiency and effectiveness with which management pursues its work.    Selection of appropriate and pertinent criteria for each of the strategies and goals selected and implemented is a tremendously critical and challenging task and should be studied closely by the board. Approval of the

criteria is a necessity. The authors cannot emphasize too much the critical nature of criteria selection and measurement. This is a major key to any successful endeavor subject to the board's oversight and evaluation.

- *Responsiveness to unmet needs in the community:* Change in every facet of society brings with it opportunities to move into areas that the organization or institution has never previously operated. As well as needs emanating from all the changes, new and better ways of measuring needs are coming from more sophisticated demographic and epidemiological methods of measuring "where we are now, and where we should be going." As the needs come into perspective, consideration and decisions at the board and management level should be taken to determine appropriate responsibility for action.

- *Willingness to take risks:* Creativity, progress, and leadership are not the hallmarks of the tired and cautious. One must not look at the services provided by the hospital as something sacred and sacrosanct. The present must be seen as the base for action, which has no guarantee of success. If change is successful it may give the hospital the opportunity to provide a superior product. Faint heart will not pave the way into the future. It will not meet the demands of creativity and entrepreneurship. Boards must be willing to listen to managerial change agents.

- *Care for the poor:* This element in values and ethics is the basis for the tax-free situation for nonprofit hospitals. If public tax funds were appropriately applied to a governmental hospital, voluntary nonprofit hospitals might not be necessary.

  As well as being a mark of a humanistic philosophy this ethic has a more practical aspect. For hospitals with a religious and sociological purpose it eases into an educational purpose. Under the guidance of attending staff (full- or part-time) this ethic makes medical education and other educational activities feasible within a community hospital. It accomplishes this by extending the scope of private practitioners' time and energy.

- *Participation with others with the same or similar interests:* Competition between hospitals increases costs. Cooperation, collaboration, and sharing have the possibility of reducing costs. The public does not purchase institutional care based on costs nor on traditional economic factors. Choice of a hospital is based on quality of care, reputation for kindness and concern for patients, recommendation by personnel and physicians, and many factors of a nature not involved in the economics of care.

In the future there will be a return to pre-1980 culture when institutions devoted to patient services and care shared facilities, equipment, and people in order to meet community needs. These concepts are returning. The governing boards can hasten that transition to a nobler situation and time. Investor-owned institutions and proprietary organizations establishing privately owned medical care services to compete with voluntary hospitals is a travesty on the religious basis and the altruistic past of medicine and hospitals.

Community-based voluntary services committed to the well-being of the citizens must cooperate and work together in order to maximize the value and use of community resources. Such commitment may lead to leveling off of the costs of care.

- *Fairness:* Today much is heard about "level playing fields" and about fairness in all aspects of life. This implies justness, honesty, freedom from prejudice, and freedom from discrimination against those of different race, beliefs, religion, and ethnic background.
- *Concern for fellow workers:* The traditional hospital culture emphasizes teamwork. With a relative multitude of specialists caring for the variety of needs inherent in acute illness, each worker must be cognizant of the emotional, psychological, and personal needs of fellow workers. Without mutual support hospital workers would be "burned out" in a relatively short period of time.
- *Adequate reward and recognition:* The corporate board in its policy-making responsibilities must recognize that altruism is a motivation to bring workers to the hospital. However, the work efforts must be adequately rewarded. This is so at this time when cost of living has become a grave matter for all workers. It is generally recognized that unlike earlier generations it may require two salaries to achieve a reasonable standard of living. As well as financial rewards, concern for individual workers and their families' well-being must be exhibited. The contributions of each person who is a part of the hospital family must be recognized. The recognition is not always required to be financial. Other methods to recognize the contributions of those involved in pur-

*As well as financial rewards, concern for individual workers and their families' well-being must be exhibited.*

suit of a successful patient care operation should be investigated and adopted.

These ten values and ethics of the corporation must become a major element or concern for those in governance. Without these, the footings, the base from which the corporate board operates can become as quicksand into which one may be drawn into a struggle for relief. But as in contending with quicksand a sustaining safety mechanism like appropriate values and ethics is necessary.

One additional note concerning ethics: Two major areas for ethical behavior must be recognized. One relates to medical matters. This is literally a massive concern for ethicists. Life and death are the participants.

The second is called "organizational ethics." In this aspect of management there must be articulated an ethical framework for decision making. At the board level the major and continuing decisions are in the form of policies.

Policies must be developed to enhance the well-being of the institution. The policies must relate to the interests of the institution. They must be created and established to further, unselfishly, the interests of the institution and its organization and purpose, mission, strategies, and values.

These policies must accommodate the many responsibilities the institution possesses. These are to the community being served, the employees, physicians, patients, visitors, auxiliaries, and suppliers. As policies are developed they must be considered in light of the best interests of the institution and in light of the many and varied responsibilities the institution has, including responsibility to the many groups of people who are or will be affected by policies and procedures.

A third area of board concern in organizational ethics relates to the vision of the future in both social and economic terms. Without a vision it is almost impossible to plan for the future. One must establish a vision in order to develop a plan leading to a desired future.

## OPERATIONAL OR ADVISORY GOVERNANCE

The work and accomplishments of the system's individual institutions are partially dependent on operational governance. While the corporate CEO manages managers, local institutional managers manage the work. Frequently, many boards assume they are not only responsible for the work performed, but have a desire for personal participation in work being done.

The HCA, as one of the largest and most successful health care corporations, effectively differentiates strategic governance from operational governance. At the strategic corporate level it has outstanding business and professional leaders involved in long-range strategies for both social and economic visions and goals.

At the operational governance level HCA has an advisory board for each institution in its hospital system. This operational board comprises the local administrator as chairperson, local physicians, and local business and professional persons and key hospital managers. Inasmuch as each local organizational entity must relate closely to the employees and to the citizens being served in the local community the composition of the local operational or advisory board should be reflective of the local citizens being served.

There should be no question that the local board is advisory only. Major problems exist when there is ambivalence about the power of the corporate board and responsibility of the local entity operational or advisory board. In a sense the local operational or advisory board is a strategy established to give local citizens a voice but no vote.

It is the authors' contention that hospital systems should recognize there are, or should be, two levels of governance. One would be for organizational strategies and the other for local operations. If this is done effectively, governance will become an area of strength for the hospital or health care system. If not done effectively governance and boards will be burdens to be carried by the organization.

Operational governance should be advisory to the institutional manager. The operational board must be assured that local institutional needs and concerns receive appropriate and adequate attention. This might not be the case if governance is accomplished with only one board at the corporate level. The operational governance the authors have conceptualized and recommend as a guide for nonprofit hospitals and healthcare systems should be carried out through a management-by-objectives program. Additionally, participative management and anticipative management consideration activities should be developed.

This approach at the institutional level represents results-oriented operations that can be monitored and evaluated institutionally by the operational or advisory board. The quantitative and qualitative measurement of the results of operational objectives gives every promise of a rational approach to governance.

## Modus operandi for the operational or advisory board

To effectuate the local voice the following should be accomplished:

- review of operational objectives that have been developed by management (What should be accomplished?);
- approval or modification of the operational objectives;
- review of the rationale that must be developed by management for each objective (Why was the objective chosen?);
- review of the modus operandi for achievement of each objective (How will the objective be accomplished?);
- review of time frame for achievement of each objective (When will it be accomplished?);
- acceptance of the criteria for accomplishment and the results of each objective (measurement of the results); and
- assignment of responsibility, authority, and accountability for the person or persons related to each objective.

## Evaluating effectiveness

The following methods should be used by governing bodies to appraise the results of the operational or advisory board and the strategic or corporate board.

- Each year all the plans (financial, personnel, production, marketing, quality, and other strategies, goals and objectives) should be reviewed.
- The plans should be accepted, rejected, or returned for modification.
- The plan should be initiated.
- The progress toward accomplishment should be monitored, and the results appraised and evaluated.
- The boards should be willing to participate as a first step in any appeals process from patients, employees, physicians, or others.
- The boards should act as an advocate for the corporation or for the unit which they have been asked to represent.

## Governance in action

In this dissertation on governance the authors have differentiated between strategic governance and operational governance. In a hospital or health care system the differences are relatively easy to follow, particularly if the system is geographically dispersed. This mechanism makes it relatively easy to move a board of trustees into a role that matches the level at which the holding company or corporate board and operational board perform. It also allows for the determination of who they are, what they are, and for what they legitimately should be held responsible.

### Vertically integrated microsystem

A vertically integrated microsystem will provide for a clinically oriented continuum within the medical specialty. However, the various aspects of a continuum will not be provided through the medium of separate institutions and facilities. Rather they can be provided by programs created by and administered within the context of a single freestanding hospital. Those with product-line management or separately administered centers of excellence may choose to develop a continuum of care out of the single facility or program.

A further differentiation is the possibility of a continuum of care as a microsystem developed around a single program such as heart disease, cancer, pediatrics, and women and children's, or ambulatory care programs.

Again, governance can be at two levels. Corporate trusteeship will oversee and develop governance imperatives for the organization as a single entity but with subordinate parts, each part of which should have an operational or advisory board. These subordinate parts can be product lines or a segment of the continuum of care. Regardless, the operational or advisory board will work with the product line managers or the manager of the clinical aspects of the continuum.

• • •

Governance is important. It establishes the future direction for the system. It is in a constant state of monitoring the present. It creates a culture based on values, ethics, and an organizational philosophy.

Despite these major responsibilities it utilizes people who are not educated for these tasks in a sociologically oriented institution. This lack of preparation for these responsibilities requires a major commitment of time and intellectual effort to ensure competence and excellence in the performance of their governance duties.

Health care is a complicated facet of societal existence. Powerful forces are involved. Coping with the conflicts, desires, needs, and aspirations of the communities, patients, physicians, and employees creates many frustrations. But when all is meshed, the achievements and accomplishments are quite magnificent.

## REFERENCES

1. *Hill-Burton State Plan Data, A National Summary as of January 1, 1968*. Washington, D.C.: U.S. Department of Health, Education and Welfare, Public Health Service, 1969.
2. Dowell, M.A. "Hill-Burton: The Unfulfilled Promise." *Journal of Health Politics Policy and Law* 12, no. 1 (1987): 156.
3. Micling, T.M. "Market Overview." *Topics in Health Care Financing* 15, no. 4 (1989): 1–2.
4. Schneider, E.L., and Guralnik, J.M. "The Aging of America, Impact on Health Care Costs." *Journal of the American Medical Association* 263, no. 17 (1990): 2,335.
5. "U.S. Health Spending Soars." *Modern Healthcare* 22, no. 1 (1992): 3.
6. "System Membership Up; For Profits Consolidate Hospitals." *Hospitals* 62, no. 21 (1988): 112.
7. Greene, J., and Nemes, J. "Earnings Escalate at Hospital Systems." *Modern Healthcare* (1991): 29.
8. Gold, M., and Hodges, D. "Health Maintenance Organizations in 1988." *Health Affairs* Winter (1989): 125.

# Introduction to governance papers

Montague Brown
Editor
*Health Care Management Review*

**It is always** a delight when an opportunity presents itself to have an in-depth treatment of a subject available for commentary by others whose views of what is happening and what is important differ . . . or at least take off in different directions regarding what is important.

Alexander, Zuckerman, and Pointer draw from a small number of case vignettes to illustrate, elaborate upon, and analyze issues and questions of governance by organizations, most of which aspire to become integrated health systems. An integrated system definition adopted from Shortell and colleagues calls for "a network of organizations that provides or arranges to provide a coordinated continuum of services to a defined population and is willing to be held clinically and fiscally accountable for the outcomes and health status of the population served." No one meets such lofty requirements to date, so the examples used are operating with less than a full complement of activities and risk for the health status of a population, however defined. Thus Alexander et al. take off with a futuristic definition of systems and follow it with examples of concern from a few system aspirants.

The commentators elaborate on what they perceive to be a current environment shaping system aspirants and then proceed to suggest the kinds of issues system governance faces and how they would suggest that systems approach the issues. McCool comes at the issues from a perspective of an organizational design expert who has served on two multistate religious system boards. Johnson has worked with thousands of hospitals over the past 45 plus years. Robert Toomey built one of the nation's more effective regional hospital systems and often writes on issues of governance.

Needless to add, this mix of consultant, practitioner, and current-problem-focused group of commentators adds spice to a lively examination of a very important subject. We thank them one and all.

*Health Care Manage Rev,* 1995, 20(4), 68

# The challenges of governing integrated health care systems

Jeffrey A. Alexander,
Howard S. Zuckerman,
and
Dennis D. Pointer

*As health care delivery organizations develop into integrated health care systems, new and significant challenges arise with respect to how such systems should be governed. This article explores several key governance issues that organizations are likely to encounter as they attempt to effect the transition from hospital or multihospital system governance arrangements to those appropriate for integrated systems.*

*Health Care Manage Rev*, 1995, 20(4), 69–81
© 1995 Aspen Publishers, Inc.

**Integrated health care systems** (IHCS) are receiving a great deal of attention as organizational models for health care delivery.[1-4] While many aspects of such systems are being focused upon, one area clearly deserving more attention is governance. The distinctive governance issues and challenges that must be faced by such systems often are neither fully recognized nor addressed. Yet, governance can serve as a critical facilitator of, or a barrier to, achieving integration. As integrated systems assume greater responsibility for the health status of a defined community, it will be governance that will carry much of the burden of transcending the needs and interests of both community and system.[5,6] Furthermore, as interorganizational relationships are expanded, governing across traditional boundaries will represent a major new dimension of the system organization.[7,8]

This article focuses on a number of key issues and challenges related to system governance. Each issue will be summarized, the challenges explicated, and the responses of several organizations used for illustration. The concluding section will outline several preliminary guidelines for governance development based on experiences of IHCS to date.

## KEY ATTRIBUTES OF INTEGRATED HEALTH CARE SYSTEMS

Shortell and colleagues define an integrated system as: "... a network of organizations that provides or arranges to provide a coordinated continuum of services to a defined population and is willing to be held clinically and fiscally accountable for the outcomes and the health status of the population served."[3(p.447)]

*Accountability* may well be the most fundamental distinguishing feature of integrated systems. Systems are seen as being accountable for the health status of a

Key words: *accountability, board composition, governance, physician integration*

*Jeffrey A. Alexander, Ph.D., is Richard Carl Jelinek Professor of Health Services Management and Policy, Department of Health Management and Policy, School of Public Health, The University of Michigan, Ann Arbor, Michigan.*

*Howard S. Zuckerman, Ph.D., is Professor, School of Health Administration and Policy, Arizona State University, College of Business, and Director, Center for Health Management Research, Tempe, Arizona.*

*Dennis D. Pointer, Ph.D., is John Hanlen Professor, Health Services Administration, School of Public Health, San Diego State University, San Diego, California.*

defined population, enhancing health, not only reducing illness. Thus, these systems move beyond provision of medical care into the arenas of prevention and wellness. Integrated systems offer a continuum of care, a comprehensive array of programs and services, available through a "seamless" network with multiple points of access and easy entry into and flow through the system. Emphasizing primary care, individuals are moved to the most appropriate locus of care, both clinically and economically.

These systems are characterized by *multidimensional integration*—vertical as well as horizontal; clinical as well as administrative; and financial as well as delivery. Such attributes are designed to achieve the "systemness"[1] unattained by earlier multihospital systems. *Physician relationships* are central to integrated systems, reflecting the notion that physician–organization destinies are interdependent and inextricably intertwined.[9] Within integrated systems, physicians and organizations share risk, enter the marketplace jointly, and operate under aligned incentives. It is presumed that, over time, integrated systems will experience capitation as the predominant *method of payment*, with a fixed, predetermined pool of funds available to provide a comprehensive package of services to a defined population. In order to meet its broadly based responsibilities and accountabilities, integrated systems will move to *new forms of partnering*, forging strategic alliances with a variety of providers, physicians, purchasers, insurers, employers,

and other community health, educational, social, and welfare agencies. Transcending models of ownership and control, such alliances will be based on trust, commitment to shared goals, and interdependence as participants seek to take advantage of their respective strengths and capabilities, avoid unnecessary duplication, and do together what none could do alone.[10]

While these attributes are not necessarily unique to integrated health care systems, they constitute their key building blocks. These distinctive qualities pose a set of important challenges and questions for governance in these organizations. In the following section we will focus upon governance functions, authority and power, coordination, accountability, membership, physicians, and development/change.

## GOVERNANCE RESPONSIBILITIES AND AUTHORITY

As illustrated by the hypothetical organization in Figure 1, integrated health care systems typically incorporate multiple operating entities and levels of administrative hierarchy. Governance systems in IHCS often parallel this complexity in being comprised of multiple boards responsible for these various units. Each of the governance elements may be accountable for similar, but often different, aspects of performance. Furthermore, because the units within an IHCS often are very different (e.g., hospitals, clinics, nursing homes, health maintenance organizations

**FIGURE 1**

TOTAL HEALTH CARE SYSTEM

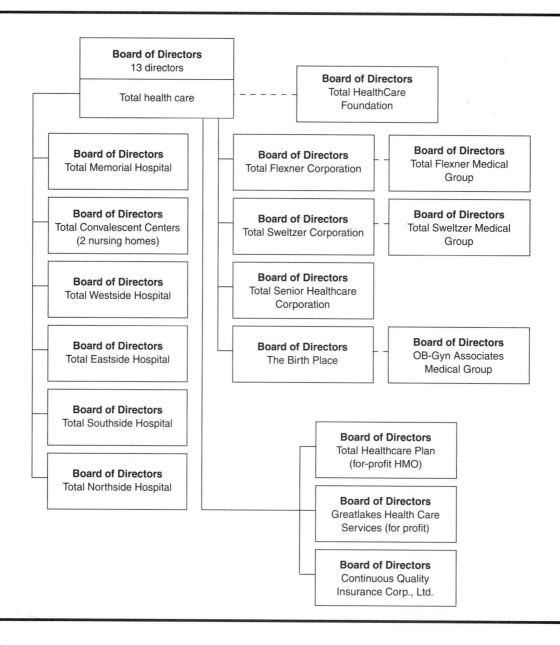

[HMOs]), a potentially confusing array of governance functions may result. (We employ the term "functions" to denote what boards do: fulfill responsibilities and execute roles. Boards are responsible for specifying organizational ends [vision, mission, and goals], ensuring the quality of care, and ensuring the effectiveness and efficiency of governance. Boards'

roles include formulating policy, making decisions, and maintaining oversight.) Overlaid on this mix are the overarching goals of the system itself that should, in principle, shape those of the operating entities and their governing bodies.

In any organization, a clear definition of roles, responsibilities, and authority is needed to ensure unity of purpose, efficient and effective operation, and avoidance of conflict and duplication. This is particularly true of governance systems in IHCS. Given the potential array of multiple, heterogeneous governance arrangements in IHCS, a major challenge is to subdivide functions among boards to achieve system goals, facilitate formulation of policy, provide a coherent framework for decision making, and enable oversight. Clear delineation of governance functions also is essential for fostering the sense that operating entities are not connected loosely, but are integral components of a system.

A related governance issue is how effectively to empower governing entities within the system in a manner consistent with the risks they assume. Agency theory tells us that if the transfer of risk to agents is not accompanied by effective control over outcomes on the part of the agent, dysfunctional behavior will result.[11] Once board functions have been defined and allocated within a system, it is imperative to provide as much authority to these boards as necessary for them to perform their functions effectively. While this principle holds in most agency relationships, putting it into practice is quite another matter.

---

*Another related issue with respect to the allocation of responsibility and authority is the tradeoff between timely and flexible responses to change on the one hand, and the maintenance of system goals and strategies on the other.*

---

Several key challenges arise within the context of the responsibility and authority of these complex entities. One such challenge is how mechanisms can be established by which systems can encourage independent action and decision making on the part of governing bodies without compromising overarching system goals and integration. That is, there is a balance that must be struck between allocating sufficient authority to subordinate boards to effectively carry out their roles and functions without providing so much authority that the well-being of the operational unit assumes precedence over the larger system. For example, if the board of a nursing home belonging to a system is given responsibility for its financial performance, board decision-making authority should be commensurate with that level of responsibility. How-

ever, if the nursing home board renders decisions that financially benefit the home, but are inconsistent with overall system goals, then a question may be raised with regard to either the amount of authority given to the nursing home board or to its specific responsibility for the financial performance of the home. Similar issues arise with regard to individual hospitals that are part of the same larger system, but seek to build integrated networks in their respective markets.

A solution to this dilemma might be to recommend that all decision-making authority reside with a corporate/system board. While such a solution makes considerable sense in theory, in practice it is often more difficult. One reason is that system-level (corporate) governing boards have a finite capacity to process information, particularly when the decisions concern the operation of multiple entities that are removed from the observation, expertise, or experience of system board members. The sheer volume of decisions and information related to them may very well produce information overload, with adverse consequences for both the quality and timing of decisions.

HealthTrust, an investor-owned system based in Nashville, Tennessee has defined a clear strategic role for its system board, concluding that there is but one ultimate governing body to provide oversight and protect the shareholders' interests, namely the corporate or system board. In exercising its fiduciary responsibility, the system board will evaluate and approve a corporate strategy and capital budget and must approve any material asset purchase or sale as well as any material risks the company might assume, such as accepting underwriting risks. However, no one board could provide strategic direction on a market by market basis. Thus, the development of integrated relationships and arrangements within local markets is made on the basis of the system's overall assessment of service to the community in the long term. It is then local management's responsibility to establish and implement individual market plans.

Another related issue with respect to the allocation of responsibility and authority is the tradeoff between timely and flexible responses to change on the one hand, and maintenance of system goals and strategies on the other. The challenge is to balance the pattern of authority to involve subordinate governing entities in responding to conditions in local markets without subverting overall system objectives. Local board could be authorized to make operational and strategic adjustments without having to defer such decisions to a higher governance authority, a decision-making pattern that may result in avoidance of responsibility for such adaptive responses. In today's competitive environment, change and adaptiveness are the watch words of health care delivery. The question for systems is whether or not such decisions can be made effectively at the system governance level, where a comprehensive perspective on all component elements of the organization should be present, or at the local operating level, where information is frequently more accessible and specific to the entity being affected.

This discussion leads to yet another critical issue concerning functions and allocation of authority and responsibility. What are the appropriate distributions of authority among system, regional and local boards? What functions should be retained, delegated, and/or shared among these governance levels? As yet, no governance design has emerged as dominant among integrated systems. One straightforward approach, noted earlier, is to establish a single, system board responsible for performing all governance functions. Geisinger Foundation of Pennsylvania, for example, instituted such a structure. All system components are structured as separate corporate entities for legal purposes, but neither independent boards nor management structures identify them as such. Rather, Geisinger has corporate and regional managers for the system's east, west, and central regions.

Another possible design is to divide the many functions that constitute organizational governance between a system board and local boards of individual system entities. Unihealth America, for example, employs a multitiered governance structure wherein strategic and control functions are shared between the parent boards and the boards of participating medical centers. Still a third possibility is to divide the functions of governance between a system-level board and two or more regional boards. Clearly there are many other possible designs/forms for governance in integrated systems. A central consideration in the choice of alternative governance design is acknowledgment that there is a trade-off involved in governing integrated systems through different authority distributions. Retaining authority at the corporate governance level is particularly advantageous to strategic decision making and internal control. However, this approach is at odds with the advantages of adaptability at the local level, risk–authority balance and the longstanding emphasis placed on constituent representation in health care governance.

Some integrated systems resolve tension between these competing approaches by dividing governance functions among multiple governing boards. For example, the parent board performs strategic and control functions of governance by acting as final authority to approve or disapprove clinical services, strategic plans, budgets, and the appointment and termination of local board members. Local boards in these systems perform a service function by acting as advisory bodies to the parent board and system management. Local boards, for example, might assist systems to better understand the local community by (1) representing local interest groups, (2) conducting a community needs assessment, (3) recommending programs, services, and strategies to fit market needs, and (4) enhancing system representation in the public eye. In some cases, local boards also have a say in strategic control issues such as asset transfer decisions and chief executive officer (CEO) performance and evaluation.

Such an allocation is illustrated by the Legacy Health System, a single market system in Portland, Oregon. Facing rising costs and loss of market share, Legacy redefined governance responsibilities as part of its strategic adaptation. Responsibility of the system board for all corporations within the organization was reaffirmed. Local community boards continued in place, albeit absent fiduciary responsibilities, retaining such key roles as medical staff credentialing, providing advice and counsel to the system, and enhancing community support. To streamline decision making, the size of the system board was reduced from 23 to 16, the criterion calling for selection of system board members from among local boards was dropped, and term limits were introduced.

## PHYSICIANS IN GOVERNANCE

Physicians have long been acknowledged for their ability to bring valuable clinical knowledge and expertise to the governance process. Because systems emphasize integration of clinical services and functions as well as patient-driven strategies, physician participation in governance is not only desirable but essential. Indeed, many of the recent changes in governance structure of integrated systems reflect an increasingly central role for physicians. Physician participation in governance may serve to reduce potential conflict between the goals of the system and those of the medical groups and may align the interests of the organization and affiliated physicians. Indeed, integrated systems are expected to take on significant financial risk by providing care for a defined population for a fixed amount of funding. To do this successfully requires that systems bind physicians to the organization by providing them with a meaningful voice in governance and management of the system (among other means of involvement).

Despite the widely acknowledged importance of physician participation and integration in the governance of IHCS, several notable challenges present themselves. First, boards will have to confront and conquer the fear and mistrust that often separate physicians and management. These may be less of an issue where there are close, historical ties between the physician group and hospitals. For many emerging systems, however, this may be a very difficult issue. Boards will have to confront the single most divisive issue for management and physicians—who will control the actual practice of medicine? Boards and their physician members must assess the appropriate degree of clinical independence to be retained by physicians, given the financial risk they bear under capitated reimbursement. Boards must also consider how physician financial incentives should be structured to encourage them to provide neither too much nor too little care.

Physician board members face the challenge of adopting a broader, more systemic perspective in strategic decision making and financial planning. For example, physicians often operate with a shorter-term framework for strategic and financial decision making. Shifting this orientation to a longer term will be imperative if the goals of the IHCS are to be achieved. In a similar vein, physicians have been trained to think of health care in terms of treating individual, rather than groups of, patients. Expanding this orientation is imperative if the population-based care provided by integrated systems is to be successful.

A number of related challenges present themselves in terms of physicians in system governance. How should physicians be selected for roles in governance and by whom? Should physician board members be selected from particular medical constituencies, or chosen for their overall leadership abilities and clinical expertise? How should the governing bodies of physician organizations (e.g., PHOs, MSOs, physician group practices) relate to the governance of the system itself? What is the role of physician advisory groups as a vehicle for providing clinical input into governance matters in parallel with physician participation on boards themselves?

## COORDINATION OF GOVERNING BODIES

A critical responsibility of IHCS governance is the integration of diverse operating entities, activities, and strategies under the umbrella of the system. In parallel, coordination of governance activity across levels and types of organization becomes a fundamental challenge. What mechanisms are best suited for sharing information, ensuring adherence to system strategies, and instilling common decision-making premises among constituent boards in the system?

Several approaches suggest themselves, including interlocking board membership, common education and board member orientation, governance information systems, and the development of a common governance culture. What is less clear is the efficacy of these strategies in ensuring consistency of purpose, goals, and vision across constituent boards.

Overlapping board membership potentially can smooth the flow of governance-related information and ensure that system-level priorities are communicated clearly. "Spinning up" system board membership from constituent organizations is one such strategy. This approach potentially tightens the linkages among boards and unites governance and management in strategic decision making and financial planning. A potential drawback is that board members selected from operating entities may act on their behalf, rather than the system as a whole. Interlocking board membership can also be used in a "spin-down" fashion to place system board members/management representatives on the boards of operating units, thus bringing to such boards a system perspective. A common complaint associated with overlapping board membership, however, is the time spent attending meetings of the various boards.

Cross membership on boards also can be used to coordinate governance activities both horizontally and vertically. This might be coupled with rotating board membership to improve understanding among board members of how the activities of each organization within the system contributes to the system as a whole. Membership might be rotated among the parent board and entity boards, among entity boards, or both. Many questions remain, however, about how these structural coordinating mechanisms should be employed in IHCS. How much overlap in board membership should there be? Who should be selected to serve on multiple boards? How often should board membership be rotated? Answers to these and related questions are likely to vary by the particular circumstances under which the IHCS operates.

A second challenge in coordinating governance activities is to obtain and effectively use the governance information necessary to monitor and evaluate both the performance of organizational units and of the system as a whole. Specifically, what types of information are needed to govern effectively and how can such information be collected, reduced, and presented so as to make better governance decisions?

Boards of integrated systems will have different information needs than the boards of free-standing, acute care hospitals or even multihospital systems. For example, boards of IHCS probably will require a different set of performance indicators. Given the mission of covering lives rather than simply treating patients, boards of IHCS necessarily will give less emphasis to traditional performance measures such as occupancy rate, admissions per bed, or even financial ratios. Instead they will give greater weight to health care outcome measures, epidemiological indicators of community health status and community surveys on access and unmet health care needs. In addition, IHCS boards will need new forms of information to evaluate the extent and progress of system integration. To gauge the degree to which health care is delivered in a smooth, seamless fashion, boards will need to supplement information about departmental and organizational performance with data about the performance and process capability of functional, cross-functional and systemwide work processes. They will also require information that documents progress and problems in achieving strategic, financial, and clinical integration.

In some instances, structural change may be needed to achieve effective governance of integrated systems. For example, the Sisters of Providence Health System is a multiple market system serving communities in Washington, Oregon, California, and Alaska. Prior to 1991, the Provincial Council served as the system board, while individual facilities had local boards serving in an advisory capacity to management. A new system board was formed to include lay members as well as religious sisters. Furthermore, because integrated system development occurs primarily at the service area level, governance structure was shifted accordingly. For example, in the Greater Portland service area, the three hospital advisory bodies have been consolidated into a service area board, in keeping with changes in the management structure. The hospital advisory bodies each had 18 members;

the new service area board will have 22 members, including 7 physicians and representation from the system's health plan. Furthermore, the system board has delegated certain decisions to the regional service area board. Thus, the system recognizes important governance transformations at several levels: (1) formulating relationships between the system board and the regional boards, and (2) creating a single governing board at the regional level, designed to emphasize the needs of the emerging integrated systems, thus moving beyond the individual institutional focus.

## ACCOUNTABILITY

Traditionally, accountability in health delivery organizations and, by extension, their governing boards, has been very loosely tied to the community served. This notion has been reinforced by a long tradition of voluntarism in the nonprofit health care sector and by the widely held notion of health care as a public good. In integrated health systems, however, the accountability issue is complicated by the fact that multiple governance entities may operate within the system and by the broader orientation to populations and "covered lives." In the past, trustees have been able to confine activities to those of direct concern to the hospital and its patients. Governance of integrated systems, however, calls for a broader perspective on community needs. These needs are likely to require organized systems that address not only clinical needs but other social concerns including poverty, unemployment, housing, and nutrition. Thus, accountability for community health status might involve governance in a much broader range of issues. For example, boards might find themselves working with other community agencies to secure more federal prenatal care dollars to lower the infant mortality rate. This, in turn, would reduce the use of and cost for perinatal critical health services.

Broadened accountability presents several challenges for governance in integrated systems. First, boards need a different mix of skills and expertise to fulfill a broader community service mission. Thus, in

---

*Traditionally, accountability in health delivery organizations and, by extension, their governing boards, has been very loosely tied to the community served.*

addition to recruiting members based on their knowledge of health care, boards might also recruit new members based on their political influence in the community or their ability to link the system to key constituencies.

A second challenge is that a community-focused system of external accountability may conflict with the goal of the system to structure governance capable of developing, coordinating, and controlling integrated health care systems internally (control and coordination). The skills needed to perform the two sets of functions may be very different. Thus, IHCS may be faced with the dilemma of how to simultaneously address both community accountability and coordination/integration of system components. A number of potential solutions present themselves. One is to assign the strategic function of governance to the parent board and the service function of governance to local boards. Another is to form a board-level or executive-level community relations committee to act as a liaison and perform community needs assessments. Boards also may create community advisory groups to represent local health care providers and community groups. These committees could be charged with interviewing representatives of local governments, public health agencies, schools, police and fire departments, and churches to identify unmet health care needs. They also could be given responsibility for coordinating a community needs assessment for particular services. Fundamentally, however, the challenge for governance will be to strike a balance between internal and external accountabilities and devise a mechanism to deal with both in an effective fashion.

A third challenge of accountability concerns establishing criteria by which the governance function itself should be evaluated. Historically, evaluation of governing bodies has been an underdeveloped area, even in free-standing delivery organizations. Just as governance of IHCS assumes responsibility for ensuring that the component structures and processes of integrated systems are functioning in a manner to maximize the goals and objectives of the system, governance should not be exempt from the same type of scrutiny and evaluation. Governance accountability will need to address issues such as: What value does governance add to the organizations and to the community served?

Another challenge is to establish accountability relationships among constituent boards of the IHCS. What mechanisms can be introduced, for example, to allow a parent board to assess the performance of a regional or operating unit board? What balance should be sought in assessing governance effectiveness related to the operating performance of system members and their contributions to the overall performance of the system? Alternatively, how can governance accountability in systems be tied to the respective roles of member organizations within the system? To the extent that such roles will differ, it seems logical that boards should be held accountable for different criteria and standards.

Successfully meeting growing demands for accountability probably will rest on establishing a mission that is consistent with the economic incentives of capitated reimbursement and the philosophical priorities of health care reform. A cornerstone of this mission will be covering lives rather than simply treating patients. Governing boards and board members accountable for a new set of priorities will not be effective unless the system of governance is structured such that both individual boards and individual board members have fully embraced this new mission. To accept this new mission at anything more than formal level, providers will have to change the way they think about and the way in which health care is delivered. Encouraging providers to make the transition from a hospital mindset to a health care system mindset will not be easy since this involves breaking decades-old cognitive and behavioral patterns. Little research or advice has emerged on how to institutionalize this new focus and the new set of values and priorities that it demands.

A related difficulty that governance will face in embracing a new set of rules and a new organizational mission is getting hospitals in the system to accept a more restricted role in health delivery. Under capitated reimbursement, systems will face strong economic incentives to keep patients outside of hospitals by emphasizing outpatient and preventive care. Given these economic incentives, board members and executives will have to fundamentally change how they view different system components. For example, hospital boards will have to understand the ramifications of hospitals as cost centers, rather than as the revenue generators they once were.

In a related vein, another challenge that governance of integrated systems faces is to maintain a clear, consistent focus on system goals in group deliberations. To obtain true integration, boards and health care executives must develop and sustain a system-level perspective in strategic decision making. Unfortunately system leaders often interpret strategy from the standpoint of their individual institutions. Both management and governance of IHCS may lack experience or familiarity with multidivisional forms of organizations. For example, members of system governing boards run the risk of overfocusing on the individual hospital, not because the hospital is the only or even the most important component of the system, but because that is what they know. This very much impedes broader strategic agendas and system development. Such concerns raise issues as to whether accountability can best be maintained through careful selection of governing board members whose orientations are consistent with the strategic purposes of integrated systems, whether a formal set of sanctions or evaluation procedures can influence the behavior of governing bodies, or whether a process of education and orientation might best redirect the cognitive and strategic focus of boards to system thinking.

## GOVERNANCE DEVELOPMENT AND CHANGE

IHCS are truly dynamic organizational forms, seemingly in constant states of development and flux. Their initial configuration may begin with a loose combination of entities, often centered around an acute care hospital or group of hospitals. As the system develops and moves toward greater integration, this simple structure is replaced with successively more mature configurations characterized by greater risk sharing, managed-care-driven incentives, and physician/clinical integration. Simply put, IHCS will probably experience continuing change as they continually reinvent themselves with maturity and growth. Governance of the IHCS might also be viewed as a system component that undergoes a series of changes as the system itself evolves. A pressing challenge for governance in IHCS is to both lead the system through its growth and maturation toward full integration and, at the same time, be prepared to transform itself as the needs of the system warrant. This combination of leadership and adaptability must be achieved by striking a balance between retaining the core features of the governance system while constantly reviewing, redesigning, and even replacing those features of governance that are suited to one stage of system development but that may be dysfunctional in another. Systems need to provide for transitional stages in governance that parallel the system's movement towards full integration. In par-

ticular, systems must be cognizant of barriers and resistance to change in governance as the system goes through these transitional stages and must work out mechanisms to overcome such resistance.

A key task in the transitional/developmental approach to governance in IHCS is distinguishing between those "traditional" elements of governance that should be retained, representing a potential strength of integrated systems, and those that are not as well suited to integrated systems. For example: Is it desirable to retain locally autonomous boards in the context of integrated systems or should such boards either be converted to advisory groups or eliminated altogether in favor of one central system board? Both alternatives have, in fact, been implemented by various systems. Similarly: How should decisions to retain or not retain specific board members be made?

The Samaritan Health System in Phoenix, Arizona is moving toward becoming an integrated system in a regional market, and is illustrative of these developmental issues. With some 40 corporations, each with its own board, system management recognized the need for consolidation and simplification of governance. The number of boards was reduced to 6 and a single system board established, eliminating local institutional boards in the process. The system board is composed of 21 members, including 7 physicians, the CEO and chief operating officer (COO), and community members. Assisted by several key board members and selected community leaders, the process of implementing a new governance structure and identifying new members required about a year. Through formation of the Samaritan Resource Group, the system has reached out broadly to involve many individuals from the community and former board members in an array of board committees and task forces to address issues of importance to the system. Thus, Samaritan has focused governance responsibility in a single board while maintaining community involvement through mechanisms other than institutional boards.

If the identification of appropriate governance structures at different stages of development of the IHCS is a key priority of IHCS, a related challenge is how to overcome barriers/resistance to change in order to effect a variety of arrangements once they have been identified. Barriers to change can emanate from both external and internal sources. For example, a common complaint among system executives is the inconsistency between changing market and organizational realities and external, inertial forces that preclude change. Although market forces may be driving organizations toward integrated systems, accreditation standards, payment systems, and regulatory requirements continue to impose constraints that render the organization, including governance, slower to adapt to these changing forces. In some cases, these external forces demand governance structures, composition, and activities that are better suited for less complex organizations operating in fee-for-service/noncompetitive environments. The challenge for systems is to work around these constraints or to change them to develop governance mechanisms that are consistent with new organizational demands.

A second set of inertial forces is internal. These are often based on a lack of readiness for change. This is especially true when constituent units of a system are "doing well" in terms of traditional operational indicators of success, and are thus not likely to perceive the need for governance restructuring or reorientation.

These internal barriers to change include (but are not limited to) the following:

- overcommitment to individual operating entities
- fear of change/comfort with status quo
- desire to preserve autonomy
- organizational history and tradition
- lack of system perspective
- aversion to economic and social risk
- lack of understanding of environment, governance roles, and responsibilities
- lack of trust among key constituencies of the system.

## BOARD MEMBERSHIP AND MEMBER SELECTION

We earlier argued that just as different entities within an IHCS should have clearly defined function vis-à-vis the system, so too should governing bodies take on functions that promote the goals of the system as a whole and, at the same time, reduce duplication and conflict among the multiple governing bodies of the system. While specific functions may be assigned to the various governing bodies in an IHCS, a related challenge is to staff these boards with members who are qualified and available to carry out assigned governance roles. What individual and collective qualities are most needed at different levels and in different components of the system? For example, at the level of the system board, a decision must be made as

*We argued earlier that just as different entities within an IHCS should have clearly defined function vis-à-vis the system, so too should governing bodies take on functions that promote the goals of the system as a whole.*

to whether to staff the board with ex officio representatives from operational units or to seek board members who have no ties to these units. Representation from subordinate units on the board may provide valuable information on the operational and strategic situations of system operations, but it may also render the system board into a "legislative" body where constituent politics and priorities are played out. Staffing the system board with detached, nonaffiliated members may lend more objectivity to the board's decision making and perhaps promote a stronger system orientation in such a decision making. However, the risk of such an approach is one of potentially alienating constituent organizations and shutting off a valuable source of policy and strategic information.

The issue of membership becomes even more complex with the integration of delivery organizations and managed care companies, as evidenced, for example, by the merger of HealthSpan, a not-for-profit health care system, and Medica, a managed care organization, to form Allina in Minnesota.

Given the complexity and continual development of most IHCS, board membership takes on added responsibility for active decision making and strategic development, relative to other forms of health care delivery. These may place severe time demands and dedicated effort on the part of board members. With these increased responsibilities, several controversial changes may be required in the operating rules or bylaws of the board as they pertain to board membership. For example, should term limits be established for board members to allow the introduction of new perspectives as IHCS develop into more fully integrated forms? The same set of increased responsibilities and accountability also may suggest that a full-time, paid board chair and board staff be introduced as common practice in system governance. Such practices may ensure continuity and dedicated leadership by system-level governance. The Sisters of Providence system, for example, has appointed a full-time board chair. Working for the board and reporting to the religious sponsors of the system, this individual represents the board externally, conducts evaluations, prepares board agendas and background information, works closely with the CEO, and supports board committees. Currently, the chair is a Sister of Providence, appointed for a 4-year term, renewable once, and for whose services the congregation is compensated. It is hoped that a full-time chair will provide stability and continuity in governance leadership. Among the potential issues associated with such an arrangement are possible overlap of activity with the CEO and perceived inequity in having the chair paid while other board members serve on a voluntary basis.

Yet another membership issue is whether management should play a more active role in the governance of IHCS. Some systems are looking to the corporate sector for examples of how to govern their organizations. In that sector, it is common to have the CEO not only serve as a board member, but often as the board's chair. Because of the presence of multiple organizational entities (hierarchical and nested) and the parallel governance structures these relationships engender, the difficulty increases of drawing a distinction between the roles of management and that of governance. A more central role of management in system governance is a potentially effective mechanism to further integrate the strategic, policy-making, and operational systems in IHCS. At the same time, however, not clearly specifying a separation of management and governance in IHCS may undermine the agency relationship between board and management (and, consequently, imperil accountability). This dilemma is further compounded because the issue of management involvement in system governance may have different solutions depending on the level of governance in the system. For example, it may be advisable to have active management participation on lower-level boards where discontinuities and conflict among boards may be likely, but to have a more limited role for management in governance at the system level.

Membership questions also may arise with respect to strategic partners that are not owned by the system, but whose affiliation is vital to the functioning and development of the IHCS (group practices, insurers). Should such partners have a role in IHCS governance? Membership on the board of the IHCS can serve an important linkage function (analogous to interlocks found in the corporate sector) but systems run the risk of having their policies and agendas coopted by outsiders if not controlled carefully.

Finally, it should be noted that many of the membership issues and board policy questions raised above can be very threatening to board members (and managers) who have been used to the traditional, philanthropic style of governance that places great emphasis on voluntarism, separation of management and board, and a self-perpetuating membership of community influential. Lessening the resistance of this group in order to introduce major governance changes may be the most fundamental challenge facing governance in IHCS.

## MANAGING THE TRANSITION IN GOVERNANCE

The transition from hospitals to multihospital systems to integrated delivery systems to community care networks will require profound changes in governance. Governance structures and processes suited to one type of organization probably will not work equally well in others.

It is evident from the discussion that the issues and challenges involved in governing integrated health care systems are complex and demanding. There is a good deal of experimentation in the approaches being employed by systems as they seek to address these issues and challenges. As yet, no definitive models have yet emerged to clearly suggest what structures and processes are likely to work best under differing conditions. Nevertheless, indications from the available literature, from discussions with governance and management leaders, and from the experience of the authors suggest that there may be several guidelines for managing the transition.

### Recognize the paradigm shift

The changes associated with moving from an institutional to a system perspective, accompanied by significantly expanded governance accountabilities and functions suggest abandoning a business-as-usual orientation. For example, those assuming roles in governance will be obliged to make resource allocation decisions in the context of such a shift, taking into account the needs of the overall system and not suboptimizing by considering only the situation of an individual institution. This shift will require substantial time, effort, and patience to initiate and sustain among governing board members at all levels of the system.

## Ongoing education is essential

In order to keep pace with a rapidly changing environment and emerging organizational strategies, both formal and informal education will be needed for those responsible for governance. It will be critical for trustees/directors to remain abreast of social, legal, regulatory, political, and economic developments and to be well informed about and involved in strategic adaptations by the organization.

## Structure mechanisms for shared learning

To facilitate continuing implementation of the integrated system, it is important to share learning from the early stages of development and transition. Thus, key constituents within the system should have forums for and mechanisms by which to examine what has been experienced from earlier stages of the evolution of the system. Furthermore, it should be recognized that many integrating organizations are undergoing similar transformations in their governance systems. It would be wise to seek out other such systems, sharing information and experiences and enhancing mutual learning.

## Communicate often, openly, and candidly

Within the integrated system, communication is essential not only substantively but also as a means to build requisite trust among key constituencies—trustees/directors, manager, clinicians, and other health professionals. Communication is especially important given the complexity and sensitivities involved in the transition. It will also be essential to provide opportunities for communication and exchange of information across components of the system and among levels of governance.

## Clarify vision and expectations

The vision for the integrated system must be clearly articulated and well understood. It is from such a vision that responsibilities, expectations, and accountabilities of governance derive. In turn, what is expected of governance must be clear. It is often the lack of such clarity that leads to misunderstandings and conflicts among levels of governance and between governance and management.

## Change incentives

In order to change professional and managerial behavior within the integrated system, incentive struc-

tures must be changed. Such changes must reflect concern for performance of the system, not simply the individual components, and must reflect the goals, objectives, and new accountabilities of the system. It is within this context that governance meets its responsibilities for oversight and performance oversight.

## Expand community involvement

New governance accountabilities can offer opportunities to expand community involvement in the system. Such opportunities go well beyond membership on boards. Key stakeholders and constituents can have meaningful participation through task forces, advisory councils, and committees, providing needed advice on such matters as the health needs of a given community, the gaps between health needs and services available, and community assessments on the progress of the system in closing such gaps.

## Begin to keep score

To reflect and monitor the new accountabilities of integrated systems, it will be necessary to develop broadly based "balanced scorecards." Such scorecards can serve to help trustees/directors evaluate the extent to which the system, in fact, demonstrates anticipated advantages and adds value. These scorecards can also contribute to assessment of the effectiveness of system governance.

•   •   •

For many organizations, the journey leading to the development of an integrated system is just beginning. There will be profound and continuing challenges along the way. Governance must evolve in ways that are aligned with and that facilitate this complex and difficult transformation. Those in governance have an opportunity to lead in this transformation, reaffirming a commitment to community service and community health, responding to broadened accountabilities, and strengthening the bonds between systems and their communities.

## REFERENCES

1. Shortell, S.M. "The Evolution of Hospital Systems: Unfulfilled Promises and Self-Fulfilling Prophecies." *Medical Care* 45, no. 2 (1988): 177–214.

2.  Burns, L.R., and Wholey, D.R. "Factors Affecting Physician Loyalty and Exit: A Longitudinal Analysis of Physician–Hospital Relations." *Health Care Management Review* 18, no. 4 (1993): 7–20.

3.  Shortell, S.M., et al. "Creating Organized Delivery Systems: The Facilitators and Barriers." *Hospital and Health Services Administration* 38, no. 4 (1993): 447–65.

4.  Gregory, D. "Strategic Alliances between Physicians and Hospitals in Multihospital Systems." *Hospital and Health Services Administration* 37, no. 2 (1992): 247–58.

5.  Coddington, D.C., and Bendrick, B.J. *Integrated Health Care: Case Studies.* Englewood, Colo.: Center for Research in Health Care Administration, 1994.

6.  Pointer, D., Alexander, J., and Zuckerman, H. "Loosening the Gordon Knot of Governance in Integrated Health Care Systems." *Frontiers of Health Services Management* 11, no. 3 (1995): 3–37.

7.  Walter, W.P. "Neither Market nor Hierarchy: Network Forms of Organization." In B. Staw and L. Cummings (eds.), *Research in Organization Behavior* (vol. 12). Greenwich, Conn.: JAI Press, 1990.

8.  Griffith, J.R. *The Well-Managed Community Hospital.* Ann Arbor, Mich.: AUPHA Press–Health Administration Press, 1992.

9.  Burns, L.R., and Thorpe, D.P. "Trends and Models in Physician–Hospital Organization." *Health Care Management Review* 18, no. 4 (1993): 7–20.

10. Zuckerman, H.S., and Kaluzny, A.D. "Strategic Alliances in Health Care: The Challenge of Cooperation." *Frontiers of Health Services Management* 7, no. 3 (1991): 3–23.

11. Fama, E.F. "Agency Problems and the Theory of the Firm." *Journal of Political Economy* 88, no. 21 (1980): 288–307.

# Commentary on "The challenges of governing integrated health care systems"

Richard L. Johnson

## THE ISSUES

Two basic organizational structures are under development as hospitals transform themselves from free-standing institutions into integrated health care delivery systems as a result of what is happening in the marketplace. The rapid development of managed care has led physicians and hospitals to conclude the best strategy for both of them is to become larger so they are able to negotiate on an even playing field with managed care organizations. For-profit hospitals have become for-profit health delivery systems and nonprofit hospitals are becoming alliances. Or, stated in other terms, the for-profits have centralized controls while the alliances are voluntary organizations where only limited authority is ceded to the integrated health care systems (IHCS). The difference between a centrally controlled IHCS and an IHCS that has very restricted authority is substantial.

Both forms of organizational structures view competition in the same light but have different approaches to consolidation because their respective orientations are dissimilar. The dissimilarities are important to understand in terms of system development and include the following:

- a for-profit orientation versus a nonprofit orientation
- a vertically and horizontally organized IHCS that is solely on the provider side versus that same system but with a managed care component
- the role of governance versus the role of senior management in an IHCS
- the IHCS, as a provider of health care services only, versus an enlarged role that encompasses communitywide responsibilities for prevention and wellness
- the enforcement of the reserved rights of the parent corporation versus local autonomy
- the acceptance by physicians of a collective role with the IHCS versus individual autonomy
- the amount of executive time spent on governing board interrelationships versus the time required to manage a complex organization.

Each of these is an issue that stands alone but, in addition, often is interconnected in ways that lead to different outcomes.

*Richard L. Johnson*, B.S., M.B.A., is Chairman of the Board, Tribrook Group, Inc., Westmont, Illinois.

*Health Care Manage Rev*, 1995, 20(4), 82–87

## NONPROFIT VERSUS FOR-PROFIT

One of the most important considerations is whether the IHCS is for-profit or nonprofit. Leaving aside the fact that the for-profit is taxable and the nonprofit is not taxable, the organizational ramifications of the form of ownership are significant. If the IHCS is for-profit, then provision must be made for a return on the investment (ROI) to those holding shares of stock. For-profit governing boards believe the provision of an annual dividend or an increasing value per share of stock has precedence over community good, though both are desirable. Since the ROI is a closely watched indicator, a for-profit IHCS will carefully restrict the authority of subsidiary governing boards to make decisions by routinely enforcing the rights that have been reserved to the parent corporation. To ensure that the executives of the subsidiary organizations devote their time and energies to their managerial responsibilities, local boards are most likely to be advisory, with greatly expanded roles for management decision making. Concern about interlocking boards, cross-board relationships, rotation of board members among boards, and spinning up or spinning down as ways of coordinating governance are not matters of significance, since the executives are held accountable for making the organization successful. Controls are centralized since it is the parent corporation that must answer to the investors. To accomplish this end, the number of boards are reduced and limited to advisory roles.

This pattern of simplified board structures, and greater responsibilities and authorities for executives, is now being adopted by nonprofit IHCSs as they mature as systems. Geisinger, Samaritan, and Legacy systems are all moving in the direction of putting greater reliance on management and less on board structures, even though they are nonprofit.

As a free-standing, nonprofit hospital acquires other health-care-related activities and determines its future lies in becoming an IHCS, it faces two problems that force consideration of a for-profit status. The creation of a physician hospital organization (PHO) likely will be for-profit, since the physician component will seek to replace potential lost revenue from controls on practice payments by having an opportunity to receive dividends or share in the profits that may result from PHO activities. The desire for a for-profit organization is enhanced if a managed care plan (for-profit) is part of the IHCS. Combining a for-profit PHO and a for-profit managed care plan as major participants in an IHCS makes it inevitable that the IHCS becomes for-profit. In the event the IHCS determines it has to acquire additional health care organizations if it is to have a regional presence in a time frame that requires moving rapidly, the dependence on the "cash cow" hospital to acquire long-term debt may prove to be inadequate. To accomplish the desired end, equity funding may be the financial vehicle of choice. While the hospital may remain nonprofit, it often will be surrounded organizationally by a parent that is for-profit, a for-profit managed care plan, and for-profit PHO. Under such circumstances, the philosophy of the IHCS will be dominated by the for-profit frame of mind.

Even if the IHCS remains nonprofit, the parent corporation has the same problem as the for-profit IHCS when it comes to measuring the performances of the subsidiaries. Can separate and distinct criteria be applied, or does the parent governing board use a common denominator to reach conclusions about individual subsidiary performance? The common denominator in this type of organization, be it for-profit or nonprofit, is the financial results. Did the subsidiary make or lose money?

Profitability is the foremost criterion because governing boards have a continuing concern about the perpetuation of the corporation. As a result, the degree to which the IHCS engages in programs of community good means that this interest is always secondary to that of turning a profit.

When the IHCS is an alliance, no such common denominator is available. As a result, alliances are based on trust, commitment to shared goals, and interdependence. However, alliances are weak structures and cannot withstand the type of pressures that may be applied to them by aggressive managed care plans that seek to split apart alliances by offering to increase the volumes of patients to selected providers in the same alliance.

## PROVIDER IHCSs VERSUS IHCSs WITH MANAGED CARE

As an IHCS develops from a free-standing hospital into a vertically and horizontally organized provider system, a decision has to be made about developing its own managed care plan, becoming part owner of an existing one, or remaining only as a provider of health care services. This is a tough question to answer because it requires the executives of the IHCS making determinations about:

- If the IHCS starts its own managed care plan, will the other managed care plans in the area continue to contract for provider services offered by the IHCS?
- Are there any managed care plans in the area that will permit investment?
- If an IHCS remains only as a provider, will the managed care plans eventually purchase other providers in the local area and freeze others out?
- Can a provider-only IHCS remain sufficiently competitive to be able to underbid competitors?

If the opportunity exists to own a successful managed care plan as part of the IHCS, the hospital component becomes a cost center of the larger parent organization. This provides a built-in financial protection in the event utilizations decline and losses occur in the hospital, since this may well be offset by increasing profits in the managed care component. However, when the IHCS only encompasses providers, any losses sustained by the hospital due to declining utilization cannot be offset because it is a separate and independent revenue center. Hospitals are cost centers only when they are part of a larger organization but are revenue centers when they are unaligned with managed care plans.

## ROLE OF GOVERNANCE VERSUS MANAGEMENT

Coordination of the activities of a variety of subsidiaries is difficult to accomplish through interrelating governing board structures. Even though the transition of a free-standing hospital into an IHCS is a developmental process, through the acquisition of other providers there comes a point where increasing the number on a governing board or adding additional boards becomes a real burden to management. Rather than devoting their time and attention to operational matters that become increasingly complex, management personnel are forced to divert their efforts to the care and feeding of the board structures and members. Decisions are slowed as a result of having to conform to schedules of board meetings and, as a result, marketplace opportunities may be missed. Executives recognize that dealing with multiple boards is an unproductive use of their time and talents and will seek ways of shifting this decision making into administrative hands. As an IHCS matures, these problems will be faced and steps taken to simplify board structures.

On the other hand, if the IHCS is an alliance of health care providers composed of autonomous units who have banded together on a voluntary basis, the possibility of simplifying board structures may not be available. Joint planning may take place, but the implementation of projects remains in the hands of alliance members. The process is both slow in decision making and uncertain in the timing of implementation, as well as uncertain of results. Voluntary alliances do not consolidate balance sheets so that the financing of capital projects is dependent upon each member's ability to handle the obligations it agrees to on behalf of the alliance. This makes alliances weak structures that are likely to have increasing difficulties as competition intensifies in their marketplaces.

## COMMUNITY ROLES FOR IHCSs

The extent to which an IHCS should assume a broad community role is an open question. Many hospitals are supportive of the IHCS having a broad community service mission where the IHCS addresses the social concerns of poverty, unemployment, housing, and nutrition by working cooperatively with other community agencies. However, attacking these issues is no more of a responsibility of an IHCS than it is of other corporations in the local area. From the perspective of prevention and wellness, managed care plans should take the lead in having an active program in this regard, since they stand to reduce their own expenditures by keeping patients out of the hands of specialists and hospitals through these efforts. If the IHCS does not have a managed care subsidiary but is only a provider of health care services, then its role is simply to encourage that such programs be undertaken by managed care plans operating in the local community.

## RESERVED RIGHTS VERSUS LOCAL AUTONOMY

When IHCSs are formed, one of the first hurdles to be encountered is the extent to which local autonomy will be retained. By their very nature, alliances largely are unwilling to permit the organizing entity to have control over the decision making of the participating organizations. Since the decision to join is voluntary, the role of an alliance is restricted greatly and may be limited to securing managed care contracts that provide information and outcome results. In carrying out this role, the alliance may develop utilization guidelines for the participants so as to attract managed care contracts. However, the scope of its activities are much narrower than that of more highly integrated health care systems.

In the case of a nonprofit hospital consolidating with another nonprofit hospital, both institutions may retain their governing boards even though a parent corporation board may be formed. Where Catholic Orders have systems, they tend to leave local governing boards in place. In both situations, as well as when a single hospital creates a parent organization, reserved rights typically are written into the bylaws. Reserved rights often restrict the subsidiary organizations with regard to the appointment of board members, appointment of the chief executive, amendment of bylaws, approval of capital and operating budgets, sale of property, and dissolution or acquisition of debt but, because the formation of the IHCS occurs through voluntary agreements, the reserved rights are not enforced. Since the parent organization is a coordinating activity, it most often does not have its own sources of revenue but is dependent upon assessing the subsidiaries for funds to cover its operations. Because of this dependent relationship, the parent, in reality, becomes a subsidiary of the subsidiaries and is in no position to enforce the reserved rights. Where ownership of a subsidiary is bought and paid for, the parent organization feels free to enforce reserved rights.

## COLLEGIAL DISCIPLINE OF PHYSICIANS VERSUS INDIVIDUAL AUTONOMY

The most difficult challenge in the formation of a system is the integration of the physician component. However, the basic issue separating boards and management from physicians is not, in the author's judgment, the control of the actual practice of medicine. This is and will remain a prerogative of physicians. Rather, the difficulty faced is a cultural issue. Physicians are trained to make definitive decisions and to act independently in diagnosing and treating patients. This habit spills over in the management of a practice as well. In both patient care and practice management, they are willing to seek advice and refer patients to other physicians, but their frame of reference is to other physicians, not outsiders of the profession. As a result of this mind-set, physicians accustomed to making their own decisions have difficulty in accepting organizational rules that are inevitably part of a large organization. On the other hand, physicians who join large multispecialty group practices early in their professional careers do not develop the

same habits and are much more willing to acquiesce, since they are conditioned culturally to do so. For example, physicians joining the Kaiser-Permanente system or the Mayo system know that by doing so they have to play by the rules that are in place. Simply by joining they are acknowledging a willingness to do so.

Forming a PHO as part of an IHCS, where the physicians are unaccustomed to being part of a larger whole, leads to many unanticipated problems for the PHO and the IHCS. Bringing about a cultural change among physician members is a long-term process that may interfere with the rate at which the IHCS is developed. This will be particularly evident in the thoughts expressed by physician board members. One of the real advantages of having physicians on the governing board is that they think about health care in terms of individuals, an orientation that counterbalances those who think in general terms. The thought process of physicians is from the particular to the general; while the thought process of executives is just the reverse, from the general to the particular. Both approaches are necessary in an IHCS, since the aim of an IHCS should be to achieve an optimal balance between the provision of acceptable care and the costs of that care. Striking such a balance is an ongoing struggle that will never be solved to everyone's satisfaction. Instead, it should be recognized that dynamic tension always will be part and parcel of the decision-making process of an IHCS.

## BOARD ROLES VERSUS MANAGEMENT ROLES

Given the history of health systems having developed from free-standing hospitals whose roots were charitable institutions where board members served in a governance capacity because of their willingness and ability to annually cover any losses that might result at year's end, the concept of board involvement has been considerably different from that of corporate America. Because they were expected to contribute funds to either cover losses or to make major contributions to fund-raising activities, nonprofit hospital boards tended to view hospital managers as not being their equals as business persons. As a result of the financial responsibilities they accepted, board members saw themselves as community-minded citizens looking out for the welfare of the poor and the needy. Because of their commitment to charitable work, these boards decided who became board members, what buildings would be built, and what new programs would be undertaken. It was a simple world, uncomplicated by the complexities of today's health care environment.

While these developments were taking place, corporate America was also undergoing its own transition. Individual entrepreneurs started up companies that would eventually become the giants of industry, where governing boards became extensions of the chief executive. The role of the board was to provide insights, and to assist in bringing about the vision as determined by the chief executive. Economics, profits, and financial viability were the keys to growth. As complexity increased, management expanded and took on a wider and wider scope of activities. If other companies were bought, their governing boards simply disappeared as part of the transaction. Executives replaced governing boards. There would not be a question of whether or not to continue the board functioning of the acquired company, even with multiple functions and multiple locations. Even in health care where large systems have developed as for-profit enterprises, they remain tied to economic considerations. It is in the nonprofit systems where confusion as to roles looms large. At the board meeting what prevails—community good or investor well-being? How do community concerns and interests get expression if not through the involvement of local boards? Yet, what do they contribute to the economic well-being of an IHCS that has a billion dollars or more of annual revenue, employees numbering in the thousands and, if not properly managed, an ability to have a profound negative impact on the communities in which its activities are located? How is a proper balance to be obtained and sustained in a health care environment that is undergoing rapid changes? Or is it likely that as the IHCS grows, it takes on more of a life of its own, that the needs of the organization become so much larger and more important to those associated with the IHCS that the relationship to the numerous local communities that health care serves fades into the background?

Among nonprofit integrated health care systems, board seats and numbers of governing boards are often the medium of exchange, not dollars. The question, "Are all of these boards necessary?" is not addressed. If the answer is negative, the next question that arises is how to get rid of them—can they be eliminated or must they be continued? In for-profit health care systems, they are eliminated and replaced with advisory boards that lack organizational authority. But in nonprofit systems the typical structure retains governing boards. Why? The answer lies in the way in which IHCSs are built or established.

The question of retaining a governing board when one nonprofit entity joins with another nonprofit entity is never an issue. The only issue is whether to form a consolidated board or leave them separate. The basis of this type of decision is that the acquired entity has not been purchased as an economic activity. Had it been, the concern would have been over the purchase price, not the board seats. When an activity is purchased, an economic transaction occurs; one party acquires the assets and liabilities of the second party. The second party receives either cash, shares, or a debt instrument, which ultimately converts to cash. Value has been exchanged, dollars received in exchange for an operational entity.

But, when two nonprofits enter into an agreement, no exchange of economic value takes place. The first party acquires the decision-making authority over the second party, but the second party receives no economic value, even though it is now controlled. Since no exchange has taken place that is tangible, the only way of bringing it about is to provide for board seats in the successor organization. Whether or not an additional board is useful, or whether or not an expanded board size is necessary is not of concern at that point in time. To bring about the desired end result, all hands recognize the governance issue is the key, since money is not the medium of exchange. In order to join the two entities, the question about board size or numbers of boards is evaded, leaving that issue to be resolved at some distant time in the future. Management is left with the problem of struggling to cope with the governance structure.

In time, an aggressive IHCS will consist of many boards and even more board members, which can reach as high as 20 boards with 200 or more board members. At such a point, it becomes apparent to the key stakeholders that something needs to be done to alleviate the confusion that has built up in the process of creating the IHCS. Having avoided the purchase of entities and, instead, opted for alliances or consolidations, the route of disbanding governing boards cannot be used. Other measures have to be taken. Yet, at the same time, there will be a recognition that finances have to be centralized. When seeking long-term debt or equity funds, investors are likely to insist on involving all of the related organization's assets. Knowing this to be a standard requirement for investments, the key decision makers know that the coordinating body for the IHCS needs to establish several reserved rights in order to comply. To properly carry this out, the reserved rights include approval of budgets, capital expenditures beyond a given amount, sale or purchase of property, and changes in rate structure.

Left to the discretion of individual boards typically are fund-raising, credentialing of physicians, operational oversight, recommendations for new programs, and community development activities. Concurrence between the coordinating body and the individual entity usually is required for the employment of a new chief executive of an entity. When reserved rights are put in place and enforced, the role of the individual entity becomes one of looking out for the health care interests of the local community. In essence, it becomes the local health care watch dog. So long as local concerns are met, the coordinating body is free to expand, to undertake new activities, and to behave in a manner that satisfies that vision and objectives that it has determined meet the needs of the IHCS.

Since the enforcement of reserved rights is crucial to the success of the IHCS, the role of management expands to a considerable extent. Freed up from having to answer to the plethora of governing boards for more operational activities, the IHCS takes on more of the characteristics of a for-profit organization with the executives taking on more responsibilities, exercising greater authority, and being held accountable through the chain of command rather than to their respective governing boards.

In the process of developing these new relationships, the opportunities for misunderstandings to occur between the roles of the executives and the governing boards are increased considerably. Frequently, board members may believe that the chief executive officer and other executives have moved too far in front of governance and are undertaking tasks and projects before giving the board members sufficient time to review and approve what is going on. Slowing down the decision-making process to the speed with which the various governing boards can cope may not seem to be the appropriate thing for the executives to do as they assess what is going on in the marketplace. Under such circumstances, difficulties may arise between management and governance with the result that management may be replaced.

The transition from an alliance of affiliates to an integrated health care system is likely to be the most difficult challenge facing nonprofit organizations. Simply providing for a variety of ways of interlocking existing governing boards deals with symptoms, not underlying needs. If the desired end result is an integrated delivery system, the decision-making authority of multiple boards will be reduced significantly and the authorities of management increased. In time, local government boards that are part of an IHCS will come to appreciate that their role is to be the advocate of local health care interests and to make enough noise to the parent organization so that their local interests are not neglected.

# Commentary on "The challenges of governing integrated health care systems"

Barbara P. McCool

*Health Care Manage Rev*, 1995, 20(4), 88–90
© 1995 Aspen Publishers, Inc.

**The Alexander, Zuckerman, and Pointer** article, "The Challenges of Governing Integrated Health Care Systems," presents a framework for debating issues faced by board members of integrated health care systems (IHCS). Using the article as a back drop, my remarks focus on three issues that need to be discussed more fully and that reflect 8 years' experience as a board member on two large multistate health care systems. Three important concerns pertaining to integrated system development governance are the

- coordination of governance activities
- need for financial solvency, strategic direction, quality of service, and mission integrity
- need for mutual trust, support, and communication between governance and management.

## COORDINATION OF GOVERNANCE RESPONSIBILITIES AND AUTHORITY

I agree with the authors that in the presence of integrated health care systems, with their multiple corporations and boards, it is essential to have a clear definition of governance roles, responsibilities, and authority. In my experience, the integrated system board does not spend time sorting out differences among hospitals, nursing homes, and primary care centers since these vertical integration activities occur at the local health care system level. It is the responsibility for the macro system board to monitor the activities of each local system board and intersect with the governance of these activities through a systemwide strategic, financial, quality, and mission plan. It is the approval by the system board of these four major initiatives that gives direction to the entire system and to the variety of governance levels. Within each local market, the individual health care system makes all the decisions about serving the population in the area including credentialling personnel, using resources, and engaging in collaborative negotiations.

For unity of action, it is essential that the system board focus on developing action parameters through the strategic, financial, quality, and mission plans and monitor the performance of individual regional systems against these standards. When these essential parameters are operative, coordination of governance is easier and the local units have the freedom to move in the marketplace as they see fit.

*Barbara P. McCool*, B.S.N., M.H.A., Ph.D., M.T.P., is President, Strategic Management Services, Inc., Tucson, Arizona.

Governance coordination also is strengthened by a clear delineation of the reserve powers of system governance and the delegated powers of the local system governance. Furthermore, a delegation of responsibility for such things as selected capital expenditures, joint venture discussions, and local network formation gives the local system freedom to carry out strategies quickly.

The authors argue that system governance can have difficulty making decisions that affect all the units in a large system because of the information needed for these decisions. It is up to the system board to ask for reports that profile unit performance against predetermined financial, quality, mission, and strategic planning goals. When this information is in place and when there is a clear delegation of activities to the local governance and to management, a system board can make decisions quickly and information processing is not onerous.

## FINANCIAL SOLVENCY, STRATEGIC DIRECTION, QUALITY SERVICE, AND MISSION INTEGRITY

The authors suggest that because the integrated system board members have the new responsibility of improving the health status of a given population, they may not spend as much time analyzing financial ratios and other operating statistics of the provider units. I believe it's just the opposite. As an integrated system becomes more complex and engages in multiple collaborative relationships, it is imperative that the board focus more attention on all the dimensions of financial solvency, quality assurance, strategic direction, and mission effectiveness.

When local health care systems engage in managed care contracting, they must deliver quality service and be price competitive to be successful. When they succeed in securing managed care contracts, unit and system revenues are enhanced. If the units fail in managed care contracting, they are vulnerable in the local market and the system as a whole suffers. This is particularly true in statewide contracts where the system is negotiating for a broad-based service agreement. One or two weak local units can compromise these discussions or cause the other participants to suspend negotiations.

Because all the operating units are assuming risk agreements, the system board needs to closely monitor profitability, gross days in accounts receivable, cost per case, full-time equivalents (FTEs), outpatient visits, debt to equity, and days of net cash for each local delivery system and the system as a whole. Monitoring these financial indicators across the system units assists the board to know when a local entity is in trouble and when corrective steps should be taken.

As integrated systems become more involved in complex negotiations with insurance companies as well as other integrated systems and physician organizations, the board has to appreciate the trade-offs of forming new managed care structures even though the system has their own managed care programs in place. They need to be aware of the increased risk the system bears along with the new costs of capitalizing a primary care base or new information system for a developing provider network. The board will make these decisions against the reality of enhancing the system while having to minimize some of the system's services in the interest of collaboration.

Furthermore, with governmental and managed care reimbursement schemes becoming more restrictive, the board has to take an active role in supporting philanthropy to supplement the system revenue. When mergers among hospitals occur, the board has to factor the impact of these transactions on the already committed obligated bond group. They also must assess the amount of debt the system can handle realistically. It's my opinion that instead of worrying less about financial matters, boards will spend more time on complex financial decision making.

This is also true of quality service, strategic direction, and mission effectiveness. As systems engage in complex negotiations among new provider groups, it is the responsibility of the system board to ensure that the patients continue to receive quality service and that the direction of the system and its mission are not compromised. Negotiations between providers have to include agreements on standards of quality of practicing physicians and other clinicians who will be collaborating within the provider network. As the mega systems develop, it is easy to become so bogged down in the complexity of the negotiations that the importance of the core principles and values of the system is forgotten. It is the responsibility of governance to insist continually on financial solvency, quality service, and mission/strategy integrity.

Maintaining mission and direction integrity is tricky in collaborative arrangements among organizations with different philosophies and cultures. In local markets where religious hospitals are collaborating with for-profit and not-for-profit community providers, it is important that the religious principles guiding these institutions are not diluted to secure profitable structural arrangements. This issue is compounded at the total system level when deals are made among for-profit corporations, governmental bodies, and other health care providers. In the rush of events, there is a temptation to give on advocacy for care of the poor or meeting community needs when the pressure to align with successful providers and capture market share is strong. The values and philosophy of the system need to be guarded throughout the negotiation process.

For these reasons, it is incumbent on the board to decide ahead of time which partners will be compatible and which ones should not be considered. There is nothing more frustrating than to approach a memorandum of agreement only to find the parties are miles apart on core values.

## MANAGEMENT/GOVERNANCE RELATIONSHIPS

Organizations are only as effective as the relationships among the people in governance and management. In successful organizations, there is respect and trust among board members and executives; cooperation is evident; information on issues is concise, well organized, and sufficient for decision making; and, there is open, honest communication. Positive relationships between governance and management become critical in today's health environment as the managers of the integrated systems assume more responsibility for managing and often governing the collaborative arrangements.

Joint ventures and other collaborative agreements are now a reality among integrated systems and insurance companies, physician groups, and other integrated systems. Usually a new corporation is formed to reflect the network and its parties. In many cases, this new organization is managed by the executives, and in some cases the executives are also on the board. When these new corporations negotiate managed care contracts or share a common bottom line, they become more significant because they are revenue generators for the system. What also happens is that the most important decisions about market and profitability are made in these corporations, with the respective boards ratifying these decisions, not approving them.

Also, within these complex structural arrangements, board members have to understand the relationships between their system and other system players and the role system governance does or does not play. They have to be aware that the management role within integrated systems is an evolving discipline, and support is needed for ambiguity in executive responsibilities in these hybrid organizations.

The learning for governance is that the managed care corporate forms and these new corporations are now operative and very complex. Board members have to keep themselves informed about them and trust the executives to manage them for the benefit of the system.

Finally, in rapidly changing markets that are highly competitive, decisions about strategy and resource allocation have to be made quickly. In these situations, if management needs guidance, board members should give it quickly and in a straightforward manner, armed with the essential facts of the situation. There is no time to beat around the bush or ask for endless analysis. And after a decision is made, then the total board supports it and moves on. The markets today will not tolerate lengthy discussions about strategy, and the board cannot hold movement back.

• • •

I wish to commend *Health Care Management Review* for providing me an opportunity to comment on the Alexander, Zuckerman, and Pointer article. I am convinced that in today's chaotic health care environments, we don't have pat answers for the challenges we face. The only way we will attain some clarity on the complex issues of integrated system governance is through open and honest dialogue with each other. HCMR is providing this forum.

Governance of integrated systems needs much thoughtful discussion and experimentation. In this short response, I have tried to make three points:

- The levels of governance within an integrated health care system can be coordinated effectively through mission, quality, financial, and strategic parameters and through a clear delineation of reserved and delegated powers.
- As complex collaborative arrangements grow, system trustees need to pay close attention to their organization's financial solvency, mission effectiveness, strategic direction, and quality service in order to protect organizational integrity.
- Trustees will ensure their organization's vitality only by working closely with executives and insisting on mutual trust and respect, good information, quick decision making, and honest communication.

# Commentary on "The challenges of governing integrated health care systems"

Robert E. Toomey

## SOME THOUGHTS ON HEALTH CARE GOVERNANCE

During the past 50 years societal changes have been quite tremendous and even thrilling, yet frightening and threatening. As negatives, we now have the homeless, addicts, poor, and violent. We also have the rich, the well-to-do, and the millionaire professional athletes. We have seen major technical advances in medical care equipment, computers, telecommunications, telemedicine, and also have seen many new and wonderful changes in medicine. We also have experienced a large growth in the for-profit hospital segment of the health care industry.

One thing, however, has remained constant. Writers in hospital and health care journals still are writing about hospital governance as it has been for 50+ years. The entire world has and is changing but the question of how to govern multiinstitutional systems comprised of a number of decentralized facilities still absorbs some of the best minds in health care academia but nothing new is being proposed.

The latest example is the article by Alexander, Zuckerman, and Pointer entitled "The Challenges of Governing Integrated Health Care Systems."

Basically, the authors of this article say that integration (physicians becoming part of the hospital) in integrated health care systems (a multiplicity of institutions) must not be allowed to drastically affect the institutions in the systems because governance is governance and it must not change. Rather, the integrated systems must accommodate to the governance we have grown with over the last 50 years. The major concession to the present and the future is the organizational structure in which governance is carried out.

It is my opinion that the hospital's role today is different from what it was 50 years ago. Multiinstitutional systems, a new and major change since the 1970s, and integration, a major change of the 1980s, have created a new hospital culture and a need for a new kind of governance.

Physicians are leaving private practice and joining the move to managed care. As they move into some form of group activity broadly labeled managed care, they become part of the institution's infrastructure. I believe they will become the dominant force in the institutions. They will be the change agents for the generation ahead. They will be the decision makers. They

Health Care Manage Rev, 1995, 20(4), 91–92
© 1995 Aspen Publishers, Inc.

*Robert E. Toomey*, L.L.D., is President, Toomey Consulting Services, Inc., Greenville, South Carolina.

will make or break the institutions with which they are integrated.

A new culture, a new structure, a new power will create a new role for physicians, administrators, community leaders, government, business, and industry.

Care will be managed by physicians who will be organized to control care, hospitals, diagnostic and treatment centers, and all aspects of medical care for which they will be responsible. Medicine and hospitals will be integrated and thus fully accountable for all home care, nursing home care, wellness center care, etc. Where there are patients there will be accountable physicians. Governance will be that which will be established by the managed care organization. It will include all institutions in the system and will move physicians into the power positions.

Whether the structure be one institution or many, whether it is a horizontally or vertically integrated structure, the most important decisions will not be related to business and economics—they will be related to physicians, ancillary medical personnel, patient care, and medical care outcomes.

Managed care is medical care and medical care is the responsibility and accountability of physicians. The structure will be geared to this fact and governance as we have known it for generations will be transitioned to medical outcomes.

When such major changes take place, one must re-evaluate the purpose of the institution.

It now appears that the acute care hospital and its medical staff have changed and perhaps reversed their roles. The hospital is no longer the dominant partner in patient care. Now the physician has become dominant. When the physician was organizationally outside of the hospital structure and simply had the privilege of using the facilities for patients, questions of responsibility and accountability were subject to legal interpretation. In an integrated institution there is no question but that the physicians are responsible and accountable for the quality of care they offer in the institutions.

When the institutions are integrated and the medical care provider is the dominant party, the purpose of the organization changes. No longer is the hospital governed and managed to assist the physician in patient care. The purpose is now to render care to all members of the community who come to the institution in need of medical care.

If structure follows purpose and strategies, then the governance facet must reflect the dominance of medicine. And while many of the functions of governance will remain unchanged, the membership will change. In integrated health systems the board membership will be made up of a majority of physicians, a lesser number of professional management personnel and some community representatives. With this membership situation there will be a medical care bottom line and one which will resemble the past, that is to say, operating and financial results. In fact the pathologists' clinical–pathological conference looking at deaths, complications, infections, and interesting cases will be moved to the board room and will become the major bottom line. Individual physician evaluations—both clinical and economic—will be a board agenda item. The financial and administrative reports will be important but less so than the clinical report.

Change is attacking the hospital and health care industry. The leaders of the industry, both intellectual and operational, are reacting slowly. The response of the leaders seems to be what *was*, *is*, and *will be* in the future.

Not so. In the past, communities demanded a hard-headed business-type trustee. I believe managed care firms will demand trustees who know and understand the medical care being provided and who can take action to affect that care. Physicians will become the trustees in the years to come.

It will take time to see the change and even longer to see results but I believe that structure will follow purpose. I believe the purpose of health care institutions is and will be to provide a high quality of fully appropriate medical care and the governing boards will ensure such results.

# Authors' response to commentaries

Jeffrey A. Alexander,
Howard S. Zuckerman,
and
Dennis D. Pointer

**We are delighted** to read the thoughtful commentaries to our article prepared by Richard Johnson, Barbara McCool, and Robert Toomey. Their insights provide breadth and depth to the consideration of governance in integrated health care systems, a topic whose fundamental importance calls for continuing discussion and debate.

Perhaps where our article diverges most sharply from the commentaries is in its emphasis on describing the current, sometimes messy realities of governing organizations that aspire to become integrated health care systems (IHCS). The commentaries, by contrast, emphasize more ideal states of governance in IHCS and are necessarily more prescriptive. The two emphases are complementary rather than contradictory.

Substantively, much of the commentary relates to two overriding issues—the emergence of integrated health care systems in general and the attendant role of governance in particular. With regard to the latter, the commentators raise a series of important questions about levels of governance, governance–management relations, the role of physicians, governance and organizational performance, community responsibility, and evolving linkages between for-profit and not-for-profit entities. We would underscore McCool's point about governance responsibility for performance oversight. Indeed, performance of integrated systems must be viewed as a multidimensional construct, with greater complexity in definition, measurement, and understanding than has been the case heretofore. In light of growing external demands for performance, limited resources, and calls for broadened public accountability, governance will indeed be challenged to meet its responsibilities in this area.

McCool also notes the importance of coordination among levels of governance. In this context, it would seem we begin with a common premise—the not-for-profit health care system that has evolved from hospital roots, moving from hospital to hospital system to health care system, with multiple levels of governance and active community involvement. We recognize that integrated systems are evolving from other bases as well, some forming through the initiatives of managed care companies and insurers, others driven by physician groups. Indeed, Toomey sees governance as being driven by managed care organizations and dominated by physicians. Given the premise, however, it is not uncommon to find not-for-profit organizations wrestling with issues of multiple levels of accountability, coordination, interlocking boards, re-

*Health Care Manage Rev*, 1995, 20(4), 93–94
© 1995 Aspen Publishers, Inc.

lationships among governance levels, etc. Johnson suggests that such matters essentially are nonissues in the for-profit world, often characterized by a single governing board with clear responsibility and accountability and thus absent the issues discussed here. Putting aside the extensive literature describing the significant problems within corporate governance, there is a more profound issue involved. The continuing development of integrated systems brings closer together the delivery organizations, physician organizations, and managed care and insurance organizations, whether through common ownership or strategic alliances. In so doing, we are witnessing a "clash of cultures" in several domains, including that of the appropriate role of governance. We would not be as quick to say that the for-profit mentality will necessarily dominate; rather we see these potential partners struggling with mechanisms to accommodate different and sometimes conflicting views on how and by what means to govern these emerging integrated systems.

Perhaps the key point, however, is to take a step back and consider why we have governance. We would agree with John Carver, who, in describing the framework for his model of governance, identified several key elements:

- "A useful framework for governance must hold and support vision in the primary position . . ."
- "The governing board is a guardian of organizational values. The framework must ensure that the board focuses on values. Endless decisions about events cannot substitute for deliberations and explicit pronouncements on values."
- "All functions and decisions are to be made rigorously against the standard of purpose. A powerful model would have the board not only establish a mission in outcome terms, but procedurally enforce mission as the central organizing focus."[1(pp.19–20)]

Especially in light of the current environment, Carver's views offer significant challenges to governance of integrated systems.

A response to the commentaries would not be complete without reference to our definition of integrated systems, since it is from this definition that our comments about and expectations of governance flow. We have adopted the framework that envisions the provision of (or arranging for the provision of) a coordinated continuum of services to a defined population with accountability for both the clinical and financial outcomes achieved and the health status of the population served. We would argue that integrated systems, as defined, afford health care organizations the opportunity to "return to their roots" and reaffirm their commitment to community service and community health. It is within this context of social mission, accompanied by economic responsibility, that integrated systems can differentiate themselves from their organizational predecessors.

## REFERENCE

1. Carver, J. *Boards that Make a Difference*. San Francisco, Calif.: Jossey-Bass, 1990.

PART V

# SUMMARY

# Where in networking and vertical integration are we?

Montague Brown

**This volume contains** a variety of answers to this question. Close examination also brings new questions. One can only wonder how a Martian might view the events. There are major differences in views depending upon what each interest group thinks is important.

If one seeks an opportunity for physicians to play a meaningful role in managed care, then vertical integration might well be needed to put physicians at the apex of the triangle. People who operate managed care plans like to have physicians involved primarily in the micromanagement of patient care and financial incentives to tilt their behavior toward economic practice. Managed care firms go from contracts, to ownership, to spinoffs and more contracts with independent physician firms. Physicians who have owned managed care and sold it off seem to come back in other forms still wanting more control and more revenue than they had in earlier iterations of the arrangements.

Hospital administrators want physicians on their payroll or on a payroll of a foundation which isolates management from some of the hassle of allocating physician revenue. Unfortunately the hospitals often want this outcome so much that they overpay and then find it difficult to justify the cost. Money doesn't buy loyalty.

The world is uneasy in its approach to physician integration. Physicians naturally want control over their business and, when they lose that, they want control over their practice style. Managed care often intrudes here as well. So it should be no surprise that the world of physician integration with hospitals and managed care is churning.

Investors and entrepreneurs seek business opportunities which always emerge where all existing major parties are dissatisfied with the status quo. The industry is rife with this change today. Niches within niches seem to be constantly emerging. Some of these will succeed, others fail. Nothing at this point seems locked in and foreclosing further innovation.

The Blue Cross and Blue Shield plans seem to be undergoing the most complete transformation of all the more traditional health service organizations. The Blues are becoming public stock companies and are moving quickly away from their more traditional community role. In their wake will be a series of community foundations that might help make up for some of this loss of these essentially local institutions. It may be that the Blues themselves may awaken to the desirability of keeping an important local presence for their plans while perhaps centralizing the finance and back-room operations functions. Nothing today causes more consternation among providers than having to deal with a person on a remote 800 number, a situation that stresses the national aspects of this business and less the local aspect.

Employers see the interplay of managed care and provider systems as potentially beneficial to them because of the promise of having price competition among providers. But when they see price cuts that fatten the bottom lines of managed care firms but don't reach them they look for other ways to break through the system to get more affordable care.

Trustbusters worry about concentration in markets while some states are trying to put together local mergers that protect local providers from competition and thus price pressures from managed care. This problem will get worse before it gets better. Neither community institutions, church-sponsored organizations, nor Wall Street–financed corporations can be trusted to always perform in the consumer's best interest. "Let the buyer beware" is more of an apt motto today in health care than at any time in our recent history. This is not a gratuitous slam at these organizations. The industry is under great pressure for performance when many forces scream to stop the change, and so it takes no organizational genius to predict that power will be used and abused when it is available. The tension put on the industry by the antitrust laws is a necessary element in helping those with power to use it properly.

There are abundant research questions for those who seek research opportunities. There are also abundant opportunities for entrepreneurs to carve out new niches for their ideas. At the same time, there are few markets where concentration of power is such that new ideas cannot be tried. In five years a volume such as this will deal with some of the major failures of current approaches and the promise of still evolving strategies.

# Index

manpower considerations in, 39
nonowned vertical integration options, 78
organizational effects of, 75–76
physician-hospital organization, 166
and physician linkage to system, 38
and quality process management, 39
staff model, 166
and technology, 35
Veterans Administration, 57

Virginia Mason Medical Center, 90, 91
Vision statement, and hospital governance, 237
Voluntary consolidation, 24
Voluntary Hospitals of America, 6

## W

Wall St., and managed care, 51

# About the Editor

Montague Brown is Editor of *Health Care Management Review*, consultant on strategy, and author.

He holds an AB and an MBA from the University of Chicago, a Doctor of Public Health and a Juris Doctor from the University of North Carolina. He has held research and teaching positions at the University of Chicago, Northwestern University, and Duke University.

Dr. Brown's practice focuses on strategic issues and policies including integration of delivery systems, managed care, strategic alliances, delivery networks, and joint ventures.

Dr. Brown is currently working on a new book dealing with the widespread commercialization of health care. This writing builds on insights gained from 30 years of active teaching and consulting around issues of strategy, vision, vertical integration, and governance. In addition, he exults in the opportunity to hike frequently in the mountains and deserts around Tucson, Arizona, where he and Barbara McCool, wife and consultant partner, are taking a pause in their active careers.